Environmental Stewardship

Emily Sharman

Environmental Stewardship

Critical Perspectives – Past and Present

Edited by R.J. Berry

T & T CLARK INTERNATIONAL
A Continuum imprint
LONDON • NEW YORK

Published by T&T Clark
A Continuum imprint
The Tower Building, 11 York Road, London SE1 7NX
15 East 26th Street, Suite 1703, New York, NY 10010

www.tandtclark.com

British Library Cataloguing-in-Publication Data
A catalogue record for this book is available from the British Library

Library of Congress Cataloging-in-Publication Data
Environmental stewardship : critical perspectives, past and present / edited by R.J. Berry.– 1st ed.
   p. cm.
   Includes bibliographical references and index.
   ISBN 0-567-03017-2 (hardback – ISBN 0-567-03018-0 (pbk.)
  1. Human ecology–Religious aspects–Christianity. 2. Stewardship, Christian. I. Berry, R. J. (Robert James)
   BT695.5.E587 2006
   261.8'8–dc22

            2005020452

Typeset by YHT Ltd, London
Printed on acid-free paper in Great Britain by MPG Books Ltd, Cornwall

ISBN   0567030172 (hardback)
        0567030180 (paperback)

Contents

Contents

Contents

Foreword

Any book on stewardship of the environment is most welcome at this time when so much of nature – God's creation – is under threat. The loss of species, the growing threat from climate change, unsustainable population growth, the overexploitation of resources and many other factors are threatening the very existence of human life on earth. In spite of some twenty or more years of a growing environmental movement and good legislation relating to such areas as wetlands, climate change and biodiversity the overall situation is still deteriorating rapidly. In the week I write this, Brazil has confessed to the second largest amount ever of Amazonian rainforest deforestation in a single year. Politicians and legislators have been relatively ineffective in bringing about the radical changes that are needed to ameliorate the situation despite the sterling efforts of environmental organizations around the world. This shows that we are facing a moral, philosophical, religious and ethical crisis that needs more than political solutions and more than pressure from secular environmentalists. I therefore welcome a book that addresses many of the moral and ethical aspects of environmental stewardship and all the more so because it is mainly from a Christian point of view.

The more that I study the Bible the more I am convinced that it is not a textbook for environmental destruction, but rather a compelling work on the care and stewardship of creation. This theme is developed in different ways by many of the authors of this book. Creation brings pleasure to God (Psalm 104; Job chapters 38–41) and we have been appointed its caretakers. In spite of the command to take care of the earth (Genesis 2.15) and to enjoy the beauty of the trees (Genesis 2.9), many Christians have ignored this responsibility. This book is particularly pertinent at a time when the one remaining superpower is governed by Christians whose fundamentalist way of interpreting the Bible allows them to believe destruction is permitted on the grounds that we live near to a prophesied end time. This allows them to assume that they have a mandate to destroy rather than steward the earth. Here in these chapters we have a much more rational theology and ethic for taking care of our planet. Sam Berry has brought together a well-balanced series of chapters of new as well as previously published work; it should stimulate an increased effort for the stewardship of creation. It is to be hoped that this book will promote both thought and action, both within and beyond the Church.

Ghillean Prance

Professor Sir Ghillean Prance is Scientific Director of the Eden Project. He was Director of the Royal Botanic Gardens 1988–99. Prior to that he was Vice-President for Science and Director of the Institute of Economic Botany at the New York Botanical Garden. He is a Fellow of the Royal Society of London and a recipient of many honours, including the Victoria Medal of the Royal Horticultural Society. He has written widely on the ethics of conservation and the consequences of environmental mismanagement.

Editor's Preface

Four of the papers in this volume (those by Attfield, DeWitt, Lovelock and Rae) were originally prepared for a Consultation in September 2000 on 'Environmental Stewardship' organized by the John Ray Initiative and Canon Barry Thompson of St George's Chapel and held at St George's House, Windsor Castle. The authors have revised them and they are published here alongside some of the classical statements about stewardship, plus a number of contributions written specially for this collection. It is not comprehensive – the ramifications of the subject are too great for a normally sized volume (for example, there are no more than passing mentions here of the eschatological implications of creation care; and the text contains little about the environmental concerns of non-Christian religions – although the Islamic concept of *khalifa* shares many of the attributes of the biblical steward, while Buddhists have a strong ethic of care for the natural world with no doctrine of a Creator), but it is the most complete examination hitherto available of the nature, criticisms and applications of environmental stewardship.

My thanks are due to all who have allowed their work to be included in this book, not least for tolerating the shortening of their texts in the interest of reducing overlap and repetition, while producing as complete a collection as possible; and to Sir Ghillean Prance for contributing a Foreword. My particular thanks go to those who wrote papers especially for this collection. Besides the original 'Windsor authors' these are Elving Anderson and Bruce Reichenbach, Susan Bratton, Martin Holdgate, John Houghton, Michael Northcott, Derek Osborn and Chris Southgate. I am grateful to the other contributors for permission to include their work, particularly to Chris Patten and Crispin Tickell for allowing me to use previously unpublished lectures. Other papers are reproduced with the permission of their respective publishers: those by Richard Bauckham (Westminster John Knox Press), John Black (Edinburgh University Press), Anne Clifford (World Vision), René Dubos (Simon & Schuster), Clare Palmer (SPCK), Paul Santmire (*Christian Scholar's Review*), Lisa Sideris (Columbia University Press) and Larry Rasmussen (World Council of Churches and Orbis Books). Finally – but not least – I must record my gratitude for the courtesy and tolerance of Philip Law, Becca Vaughan-Williams and their colleagues at T&T Clark International, and to John Sargant for his meticulous removal of many solecisms.

I dedicate this work to the John Ray Initiative that exists 'to bring together scientific and Christian understandings of the environment in a way that can be widely communicated and lead to effective action'.

R.J. Berry
October 2005

Introduction

Stewardship: A Default Position?

R.J. Berry

R.J. (Sam) Berry is Professor Emeritus of Genetics at University College London. He is a former President of the British Ecological Society and of Christians in Science. His publications include The Care of Creation *(2000), a series of commentaries on the 'Evangelical Declaration on the Care of Creation' which was produced in 1994 as a reaction to the series of Consultations on the World Council of Churches Programme on 'Justice, Peace and the Integrity of Creation' which culminated at Seoul in March 1990 (Niles 1992; Thomas 1993). His Gifford Lectures given at Glasgow University in 1997–98 were published as* God's Book of Works *(2003).*

Stewardship is about caring, and the recognition that we care for what we value – clothes, car, house, family. Underlying our caring are relationships – with family, friends, community, environment, even ourselves and our own peace of mind. Put another way, relationship is at the root of stewardship.

While relationships generally indicate positive interactions, we may for a whole range of reasons forswear particular sorts of relationship – marriage, community living, dependence on alcohol or particular foods or air travel. Indeed, for some the idea of a 'steward' is wholly negative, conjuring up undesirable traits of subservience and hierarchy, absentee landlords and exploitation. This distaste is echoed in some of the essays in this book, while other contributors seek to avoid such negative associations by exploring alternatives: trustee, agent, companion, priest. And digging still further, the impotent (or even impertinent) constraints on stewardship described by Stephen Gould (1993 – see the essay by Bruce Reichenbach and Elving Anderson, p. 120) or Jim Lovelock (in the feedback loops of Gaia, p. 106) are still forms of relationship.

Paul Santmire (p. 254), Michael Northcott (p. 215), John Black (p. 95) and Susan Bratton (p. 211) make clear that 'steward' has come to have a very restricted meaning in public relations and much church usage. It may be used as a simple euphemism for resource use – or even resource depletion (as in 'wise use'). But most commonly, it is nothing more than an unconscious synonym for the unavoidable interactions between us as living beings and the physical, biological, social and cultural – and for believers, the divine – environment which surrounds us. It is a default word, not a considered concept.

Can we improve on this? Some of the authors in this volume (e.g. Calvin DeWitt, p. 146, and John Zizioulas, p. 273, writing from very different starting points) insist that a firm theology must underlie any ethic of stewardship; others concentrate simply on what may be called 'enlightened self-interest'. The latter was the emphasis of a series of Reith Lectures given by a group of world leaders (including Chris Patten, one of the authors in this book (p. 199); Gro Harlem Brundtland, who chaired the World Commission on Environment & Development and whose report *Our Common Future* ['the Brundtland Report'] popularized the concept of 'sustainable development'; and the Prince of Wales) and broadcast in 2000 by the British Broadcasting Corporation (Patten *et al.* 2000). It was somewhat ironical, since the subtitle of the series was 'Sustainable Development'. 'Self-interest' is intrinsically short-term and inward looking (e.g. Kasser 2002) while sustainability necessarily involves long-term survival. It has been defined as 'living today as if tomorrow will happen'. Chris Patten (p. 199) quotes Ruskin's definition, paraphrased by Margaret Thatcher (see *This Common Inheritance*, 1990) as 'acknowledging that we do not own this world, but only have a full repairing lease'.

At this point, we could be side-tracked into the range of apocalyptic enthusiasms which lead some to neglect or even despise environmental care since they are waiting for a 'New [as distinct from a "*Re*newed"] Earth' for which they expect the Messiah to return imminently and establish. A notorious holder of such an interpretation was US Secretary of the Interior in the early 1980s, James Watt. Northcott (2004: 59) comments, 'The premillennialist scorns all efforts to correct the ills of society for to inaugurate any programme of social betterment or to set the church as a whole upon an upward course would be to thwart the divine purpose and to delay the advent of Christ'. Tempting though a discussion of different forms of millennarianism would be, I have resisted it. The topic is dealt with from an environmental point of view by Boyer (1992), Fowler (1995) and Finger (1998).

To return to stewardship: John Black writes in this volume (p. 92),

A society which includes among its earliest and most tenaciously held beliefs a concept of its right to dominion over nature is faced with a paradox: the fullest exploitation of nature involves its eventual destruction ... The Hebrews achieved a reconciliation by evolving a concept of man's responsibility to God for the management of the earth ... Man could see himself as responsible and accountable to God for the management of the earth, over which he has in turn been given complete control. In other words, man saw himself as a steward. This concept of man as a steward of the earth, acting there on God's behalf, has a central place also in the Islamic faith.[1]

Chris Patten (p. 202) quotes Francis Bacon, often pilloried as begetting a ruthlessly instrumental approach to the natural world. Bacon wrote 'It is not possible to direct nature, except by obeying it'. Patten calls this an early definition of sustainable development. DeWitt (p. 158) speaks of 'stewardship dynamically shaping and reshaping human behaviour in the direction of maintaining individual, community and biospheric sustainability in accord with the way the biosphere works'. Anne Clifford (p. 248) and Martin Holdgate (p. 235) argue for the inseparability of ecology and economics if we are to have a sustainable world; in other words, we cannot divorce our treatment of our world from its long-term future.[2] The dangers of forcing them apart are highlighted by Jared Diamond in his book *Collapse* (2005), a remarkable survey of societies that survive or fail. Diamond identifies five recurring factors which interact in this process: the damage people inflict on their environment, usually inadvertently; climate change; hostile neighbours; support (or not) from friendly neighbours; and response to such problems, whatever their source.

Diamond's five factors are only loosely connected with 'stewardship' in the dictionary sense of 'manager' or 'superintendent', but they are really what this book is about: how we relate positively to our surroundings in the widest sense. A number of contributors contrast ways which confuse this in practice: anthropocentric versus biocentric, despotic or stewarding, co-creatorial or deep ecology, working to exercise control over or to work with nature.

But the debate is really about deeper questions. The Duke of Edinburgh, at the time President of the Worldwide Fund for Nature and fired by the 'Assisi Declarations' prepared by the world's major religions for the WWF's 25th Anniversary in 1986, challenged a series of Consultations at Windsor on the 'Christian Attitude to Nature' by asking *why* should we act? His view was that there are many skilled in knowing *how* to act, but little thought had been given to the *why* question (Duke of Edinburgh and Mann 1989). His son, the Prince of Wales, said in his Reith Lecture,

The idea that there is a sacred trust between mankind and our Creator, under which we accept a duty of stewardship for the earth, has been an important feature of most religious and spiritual thought throughout the ages. Even those whose beliefs have not included the existence of a Creator have, nevertheless, adopted a similar position on moral and ethical grounds. It is only recently that this guiding principle has become smothered by almost impenetrable layers of scientific rationalism. If we are to achieve genuinely sustainable development we will first have to rediscover, or re-acknowledge, a

3

sense of the sacred in our dealings with the natural world and with each other (Patten *et al.* 2000: 81).

Leaving aside the blame to scientific rationalism, this sounds fine, although it implies that one can be a steward without having someone to whom one is responsible. Arguing as a Christian, Attfield answers 'yes' to this (p. 87), while Tickell (p. 223) and Lovelock (p. 106) from an agnostic position imply 'probably', adopting a 'halfway house' which is effectively pantheism or panentheism; as heavyweight theologians, Zizioulas (p. 289) and Rae (p. 293) are definite that stewardship is a clear outcome (and necessity) of theistic belief. Is it possible to be less equivocal?

Whence Stewardship?

It is rare for discussions about religious attitudes to the natural world not to turn to Lynn White's paper 'The Historic Roots of our Ecologic Crisis', first published in *Science* in 1967 and reprinted many times since (e.g. in Berry 2000). White laid the blame for environmental damage squarely on the Genesis mandate for humans to 'have dominion' over the rest of living things, and the development of technology for making this possible. He notoriously wrote 'we [Christians] are superior to nature, contemptuous of it, willing to use it for our slightest whim' (1967: 1206). He argued that this was because Christianity has 'de-sacralized' nature, allowing it to be exploited without restraint. He quoted Ronald Reagan as saying, 'When you've seen one redwood tree, you've seen them all'.

White's thesis has been challenged on both historical and theological grounds (e.g. Sheldon 1989, 1992; Whitney 1993), but it retains considerable influence. For example, Francis Schaeffer (1970) included its text in his pioneering *Pollution and the Death of Man*, describing it as 'a brilliant article ... I believe he is completely right'. The agnostic Max Nicholson (1970: 264), one of the chief architects of global conservation, averred 'The first step [for responsible environmental care] must be plainly to reject and to scrub out the complacent image of Man the Conqueror of Nature and of Man Licensed by God to conduct himself as the earth's best pest'. In contrast, Max Oeschlaeger begins his book *Caring for Creation* (1994: 1) with a testimony of conversion:

> For most of my adult life I believed, as many environmentalists do, that religion was the primary cause of ecologic crisis ... I was a true believer [in environmental experts]: if only people would listen to the ecologists, economists, and others who made claims that they could 'manage planet Earth', we would all be saved. I lost that faith by bits and pieces, especially through the demystification of two ecological

4

problems – climate heating and extinction of species – by discovering the roots of my prejudice against religion. That bias had grown out of my reading of Lynn White's famous essay blaming Judeo-Christianity for the environmental crisis.

White (1973) tells how 'the roots of [his] personal theology of ecology' came during a visit to Ceylon [Sri Lanka], which is, of course, a deeply Buddhist culture with no doctrine of a Creator. He accepts that 'more and more of us are inclined to think we should have a decent respect for our living fellow-creatures, although the arguments are usually providential: if we damage the biotic system, won't it produce a backlash that will hurt us? We should ask whether a prudential ethic can rightly be called an ethic' (p. 63). And in fairness to him, he concluded his 1967 essay by asserting that 'since the roots of our [ecological] trouble are so largely religious, the remedy must also be essentially religious, whether we call it that or not' (1967: 1207).

There is no doubt that the biblical injunction to 'have dominion' has been a major element in determining environmental attitudes, encouraged by the incorporation of Greek philosophical ideas of the hierarchical nature of the world into the doctrines of the early Church (in particular through Philo and Origen). The world came to be seen in strongly utilitarian terms; all creatures were viewed as existing for the sake of humanity and inferior to it because only we were reasoning beings. Aquinas accepted the Greek interpretation of a hierarchical world: God rules over humanity; humanity rules over non-human nature. Notwithstanding, Bauckham (2002a: 138–41) has pointed out that the increasing dominance over the natural world through technology described by White did not overly influence theological understanding:

- Neither the theological nor the exegetical tradition was particularly interested in the human relationship with nature.
- Human dominion was interpreted in terms of the usual ways people used nature, not an achievable despotism.
- The world was seen as created and adapted for human use, not open to radical re-shaping.
- The anthropocentricity of dominion was part of a broader theocentricity; although non-human creatures exist for human benefit, nature reflects and exists for the glory of God.
- Anthropocentricity was qualified by subservience to the angels – at least until the Renaissance exaltation of humanity above the angels.
- Combining the last two points, since angels, humans and other creatures are all God's creatures, they exist to glorify God – a worship expressly seen in the Benedicite.

- Human dominion was checked by the responsibility to treat non-humans as God's creatures.

Putting all this together, the dominant – although never the sole – theological tradition before the modern period was a strongly anthropocentric view of human dominion arising from a Greek-derived understanding of nature imposed on the biblical text. The vertical relationship to creation suggested by 'dominion' was complemented by a horizontal relationship in which humans related to other creatures because all are creatures of one Creator. Dominion in the early Christian centuries was predominantly concerned with a mutual sharing of creation and not a legitimization of despotism.

This changed in mediaeval times. The change is conventionally linked to a 'de-sacralization' of the natural world, prompted by the incipient study of science promoted by Francis Bacon and leading to the 'Enlightenment' of the eighteenth century, especially John Locke's justification for private, unequal and unlimited property rights (Black 1970; Porter 2000). This desacralization was assumed by Lynn White. But the real situation was more complicated and instructive. At least three factors were operating:

- At a time when academic biology was submerged by the mythical representations of herbals and bestiaries, the carvings in new buildings for worship showed detailed observations of real animals and plants (Raven, 1947, 1953). In contrast, the Italian humanists during the same period were emphasizing the supreme dignity of humankind, exalting the vertical relationship with God at the expense of the horizontal one with other animals (Bauckham, in this volume, p. 34).
- Bacon's project was to provide the means for humanity to recover through scientific research its dominion over nature promised by Genesis 1, 'by divine bequest'. In other words, to restore humanity to the state that God had originally intended for it.[3]
- Harrison (1998b and in this volume) has shown how Bible understanding shifted at the Reformation from allegory to literalism, allowing the emergence of science through the study of reality.

The Reformation was not simply an assault on superstition; it was an engine of a new world-view. G.M. Trevelyan (1938: 53–54) described its radical impact:

> The idea of regular law guiding the universe was unfamiliar to the contemporaries of Francis Bacon. The fields around town and hamlet were filled, as soon as the day-labourers had left them, by goblins and will-o'-the wisps; and the woods as soon as the forester had closed the door of his hut, became the haunts of fairies; the ghosts could be

heard gibbering all night under the yew-tree of the churchyard; the witch, a well-known figure in the village, was in the pay of lovers whose mistresses were hard to win, and of gentlemen-farmers whose cattle had sickened. If a criminal was detected and punished, the astonishing event was set down as God's revenge against murder; if a dry summer threatened the harvest, the parson was expected to draw down rain by prayer ... The world was still a mystery, of which the wonder was not dispelled in foolish minds by a daily stream of facts and cheap explanations.

Nature was not so much de-sacralized as reified by the Renaissance and the Reformation; science became possible and stewardship a necessity, because our ancestors were dealing with physical processes rather than metaphysical abstractions. Change was the result of a shift in attitudes, not, as White suggested, through technological advance. The challenge now is not so much to re-sacralize nature, but to recover the awe and wonder of the natural world.

Whither Stewardship?

The Renaissance and the Reformation introduced the modern concept of a steward with a responsibility to care for Creation. We are not so much *vice-regents* for God (acting in his place) as *vice-gerents* (acting with delegated authority). But history has not helped us: the Enlightenment and sub-sequent Industrial and Darwinian revolutions blurred the simple connection of human beings responsible to a divine Creator. If we are but cogs in an enormous biophysical machine, we can do little more than maintain our own bit of the mechanism. This imports a new set of distinctions which have only surfaced in relatively modern times: we are 'above nature' in the sense of being able to manipulate and affect it (often negatively – as with soil erosion, watershed damage through deforestation, greenhouse gas emissions), but we are also part of it, dependent upon it for food and air, and energy – from both fossil and renewable resources.[4] Although for some (primarily technologists and economists such as Beckerman 1995; North 1995; Lomborg 2001), environmental setbacks are temporary and man-ageable, the majority of informed opinion acknowledges that the world is being damaged, perhaps irreparably, by human activity (e.g. Pimm 2001; Houghton 2004, 2005).

The latter opinion is set out clearly here by Tickell (p. 226), while Holdgate (p. 234) describes how international thought has come to recognize that environmental care is essentially a human activity. Several authors identify the only practical way forward as 'humans *with* nature', not *over* or *in* it. This converges on the considerable discussion about the relationship between science and religion in recent decades. God does not act merely in the places that science does not reach; by faith we see him working in and through natural processes (Jeeves and Berry 1998; Alexander 2001; Deane-Drummond 2004). As Aubrey Moore (1889: 100) wrote, 'Darwin under the disguise of a foe, did the work of a friend ... Either God is everywhere present in nature, or He is nowhere ... In nature everything must be His work or nothing'. Deism is not a credible option. Zizioulas (p. 281) emphatically agrees.

Hall (pp. 139–43) in particular emphasizes the importance of the preposition '*with*' throughout scripture. This brings us back to the idea of stewardship as relationship. For Santmire (p. 269) and Page (p. 104) the key expression is 'partnership'. Southgate (p. 192) extends the concept and sees 'priesthood' as a sensible intermediate concept between the unacceptable extremes of identifying too closely with God (as co-creators) or with the earth (in 'deep ecology'). Zizioulas (pp. 286–89), from his Orthodox position, treats us as operating within a 'liturgical dimension' with, in his words, 'the notion of priesthood freed from its pejorative connotations and seen as carrying the characteristic of 'offering' in the sense of opening up to the 'other', an idea corresponding to that of love in its deepest sense'. Rasmussen's concept (pp. 175–82) is similar – that we are the voice of God to creation and creation to God. Jones (2003) has pointed to the number of occasions that Jesus speaks of 'the Son of Man' (the only title he uses of himself) in connection with 'the Earth' (Mt. 9.2–8; Mt. 12.38–42; Mt. 24.27–30; Lk. 18.8; Lk. 21.35–36; Jn. 12.23–24; Jn. 12.32–34).

In contrast, the idea that we are 'priests' is firmly rejected by Bauckham (p. 49) on the grounds that 'it intrudes our inveterate sense of superiority exactly where the Bible will not allow it'. He cites Northcott (1996: 131–34) who points out that a number of modern authors (Paul Gregorios 1978, Pope John Paul II's 1989 encyclical *Sollicitudo Rei Socialis*, and Philip Sherrard 1992) all elevate humankind above nature and deny any intrinsic value to the latter. For Bauckham, the role of the non-human creation is to 'assist' our worship; he writes of 'human dominion in creation', 'humanity within the community of creation', but most importantly, the Bible's way of placing us among the creatures and not over them is 'the creation's worship of God portrayed in the Psalms and, with christological and eschatological character, in the New Testament ... The creation worships God just by being itself, as God made it, existing for God's glory. Only humans desist from worshipping God'.

This faces us squarely with anthropocentricity: in what sense are we central to the working of the world and to the outworking of God's plan in it? The Bible (and Qur'an) influence the debate at this point, because they distinguish between humans 'in God's image' and all other creatures who do not have God's image. We are *Homo divinus* as well as *Homo sapiens*

8

(Berry 2004). This places us in a privileged but responsible position. We cannot escape from a form of anthropocentricity. But we remain an animal as well as an 'imaged' being. Paul Santmire draws out three major themes from the Bible: the priestly story particularly associated with Genesis 1 and our 'vertical' relationship with the Creator; the Yahwist story of Genesis 2 and our 'horizontal relationship' with creation; and Job's recognition of the awesome sublimity of the Creator's work. Our 'vertical relationship' is emphasized throughout the Bible by the uniqueness of our being 'in God's image' and the emphases in both Testaments of our ability to accept or reject God's sovereignty. Bauckham speaks of 'human dominion in creation' coexisting with 'humanity within the community of creation', both conditioned by 'the praise of God by all creation'.

One consequence of our special status is the 'Fall'. Peter Harrison (p. 19) relates how 'science' was seen in early modern times as providing the way to recover from the problems introduced by the Fall. In fact, the primary effect of the Fall was separation of human beings from God rather than any specific effects of the 'curses'. This alienation led consequentially to the moral, social and political disorders described in the history of Israel, not to mention the catalogue of sins listed by almost all the Bible writers. Writing to New Testament Christians, Paul repeatedly reminds them that they had been *dead*, but now were in a new state of life ('new creations') through the redemption of Christ.

In the most direct New Testament reference to the Fall, Paul specifically links 'The created universe waiting for God's sons to be revealed' with the confidence that 'The universe itself is to be freed from the shackles of mortality and is to enter upon the glorious liberty of the children of God' (Rom. 8.19–22). Derek Kidner (1967: 73) commented on Genesis 3, 'Leaderless, the choir of creation can only grind on in discord. It seems from Romans 8: 19–23 and from what is known of the pre-human world that there was a state of travail from the first, which man was empowered to "subdue" until he relapsed into disorder himself.' Charles Cranfield (1974: 227) uses the same analogy with reference to the Romans passage, 'The praise of the whole creation [is] prevented from being fully that which it was created to be so long as man's part is missing, just as all the other players in a concerto would be frustrated of their purpose if the soloist were to fail to play his part' (see Southgate, p. 192).

It is ironical that commentators often downplay both 'the Fall' and 'stewardship' on the grounds that neither is repeatedly emphasized in the Bible. If the Fall is understood as a representation of the four-fold break in relationship of humankind with God, our fellow humanity, ourselves and with the rest of creation, then stewardship can be seen as a description of the proper outworking of those relationships: we are faced with a central theme of the Christian faith as revealed in the scriptures (Vischer 2004).

9

The Indispensable Imperative of Stewardship

Environmental understanding has increased enormously over the past few decades. Unfortunately, self-interest often induces a state of denial. Even those who acknowledge the reality of environmental damage may get no further than frustrated impotence or defensiveness. If, on the other hand, understanding is taken as requiring responsible care for our environment (or creation, depending on one's language), our response becomes virtually synonymous with stewardship. Unfortunately, many approaches are over-simplistic. Cost-benefit analyses are the most common procedures adopted by government and business, but notoriously exclude relevant factors, often because they cannot be expressed in monetary terms (Banner 1999). For example, measures to limit greenhouse gas emissions are rejected as ineffective or too expensive despite the virtually unanimous agreement about their growing and potential damage. But these are pragmatic, instrumental issues. We need to use every appropriate rational and ana-lytical faculty in dealing with them. The Precautionary and Polluter Pays principles need constant application. But at least as important, we must be properly humble before the power and majesty of creation: God spelt this out to Job; the tsunami of December 2004 and Hurricane Katrina in August 2005 reminded us of it all too brutally. Attfield writes of the importance for environmental sensitivity. Rae goes further (p. 309): 'Whatever language we use – be it dominion or priesthood or stewardship or anything else – that language will be filled with its proper content only in attentiveness to the action of God through Christ and the Holy Spirit.'

'Stewardship' is often used as little more than a formal response to environmental situations, without teeth or depth; Southgate (p. 185) refers to it as 'the default position' within ordinary Christian groups. It is often uncomfortably equated with asceticism and denial or, less stressfully, with diligent recycling. This misunderstands the concept; it is both different from and much more than these responses. The essays, which follow, give the lie to them (see also Paterson 2003, who helpfully classifies stewardship behaviours into 'domination' and 'earth-keeping' traditions; the latter are described in detail in *Earthkeeping*, edited by Loren Wilkinson 1991 [1980]). Those grouped in the 'Applications' section are concerned with the useful effectiveness of practical stewarding. But the contributors to this volume do not give a uniform message. Some of the contributors are devotees of stewardship; others are less convinced for a variety of reasons. But whether expressed or implied, there are a number of common themes. Perhaps most immediate is the recognition that stewardship is a key link between economy and ecology which produces sustainable development, a viable *oikos* – an essential element which extends over generations and cultures in a world in which we are seeking to make poverty history. As René Dubos has pointed out, it describes the 'dirty-hands, sleeves-rolled-up' behaviour associated with Benedict better than the contemplative attitude of Francis of Assisi. Following Black, Page and Bratton, stewardship may involve hard decisions about resource use or appropriate technology. Derek Osborn (p. 231) identifies 'four great giants to slay': they are the assumption that growth, efficiency, money or immediacy is supreme. Bill McKibben's (1994: 10) take on this is, 'We have raised "More" on a pedestal; it is every bit as unchallenged a heresy as the piety of Job's friends or the mechanical earth-centred universe of Ptolemy'.

But the implications of stewardship extend much further – into apologetics and soteriology.

In 1990, the Anglican Consultative Council added to the accepted four-fold definition of mission (to proclaim the good news of the Kingdom; to teach, baptize and nurture new believers; to respond to human need by loving service; to seek to transform the unjust structures of society), a fifth necessity: 'to strive to safeguard the integrity of creation and sustain and renew the life of the earth' (King 2002). This fifth Mark of Mission represented a coming together of the theological debates described by Hall and Rasmussen with the secular imperatives recognized by the World Conservation Strategies of 1980 and 1991, the Brundtland Report of 1987, and the Earth Summit of 1992, described by Tickell (p. 220) and Holdgate (p. 234). Practical stewardship is where the world and the Church meet. It gives people of faith important apologetic opportunities.

But creation care is more than pragmatic witness and evangelistic possibility; it is fundamental to our faith in the God who is Redeemer and Sustainer as well as Creator: He has commissioned us to be his agents, factors, stewards, trustees – the name does not matter. Good theology and good science are essential complements, not simply uneasy sparring partners. Their marriage is a long-delayed response to the old idea that we need to read God's Book of Works as well as his Book of Words (see the essay by DeWitt in this volume; also Berry 2003). We fail God in many ways. But what is far, far worse than overt sin is when we turn our back and ignore him, claiming that stewardship (or whatever we call it) is an option for the few but irrelevant to our calling as Christians. That is not disagreement about a few verses in Genesis; it is to misunderstand and endanger our whole purpose here on earth. It is Sin with a capital 'S'.

This brings us full circle. Through his reconciling work, Christ restored the links broken by the primal disobedience of humankind. Incomprehensibly, we are valuable to God. We need no longer act independently of God and his creation. We can value other people and other things in the context of our restored relationships. As in Blake's model (DeWitt in this volume, p. 147), we are enabled to work with creation and not over or against or subservient to it. The natural world is full of marvels and mysteries. Psalm 111.2 is sometimes called the research scientist's text: 'Great are the works of the Lord; studied by all who delight in them.' We are right to marvel at them. But we must beware lest we confuse our reverential awe with the apparent 'harmony' or 'balance' of nature beloved by Romantics and many eco-theologians; it has nothing to do with ecological fine-tuning, but everything to do with our acting as responsible stewards.

Notes

1. Like the Bible, the Qur'an teaches that we are stewards or trustees (*khalifa*) answerable to God. Writing as a Muslim, Serageldin (1991: 62) notes, 'God's grace is conditioned on the proper execution of stewardship', but 'the concept of 'stewardship of the earth' ... is curiously under-represented in the scholastic tradition of Islamic theology, although references are plentiful in the Qur'an'.
2. British Prime Minister, Tony Blair (1999): 'The last hundred years have seen a massive increase in the wealth of this country and the well-being of its people. But focusing solely on economic growth risks ignoring the impact – both good and bad – on people and the environment. Had we taken account of these links in our decision making, we might have reduced or avoided costs such as contaminated land or social exclusion ... In the past, governments have seemed to forget this. Success has been measured by economic growth – GDP – alone. We have failed to see how our economy, our environment and our society are all one.'
3. Donald Worster nicely satirizes 'the key American environmental idea, and at once the most destructive and most creative, the most complacent and the most radical, [as] the one that ironically has about it an aura of wonderful innocence. America, we have believed, is literally the Garden of Eden restored. It is the paradise once lost but now happily regained. In Judeo-Christian mythology the first humans, Adam and Eve, discovering evil after yielding to the Devil's temptation had to be kicked out of the Garden on their nearly naked bums. But *mirabile dictu*, Americans of the eighteenth century found a way to sneak back in to the garden. A band of their ancestors had made their way to the New World and there rediscovered it, with the gate standing wide open, undefended. What a blessed people. They brought along with them some Africans in chains to help enjoy the place, and by and by they let in a few others from Asia, but mainly it was a fortunate band of white Europeans that destiny allowed to re-enter and repossess the long-lost paradise. No other people in the world have ever believed, as Americans have, that they are actually living in Eden' (Worster 1993: 9). An extended critique of North American understandings of millennarianism is given by Northcott (2004).

4. A very crude estimate of the world's 'ecosystem services' (i.e. the value of natural input – through photosynthesis, climate regulation, water-flow control, reduction of pollution, etc.) is worth two to three times the gross national product of all the nations of the world combined (Costanza *et al.* 1997). A massive and well-documented international study, the Millennium Ecosystem Assessment (2005) concluded 'Any progress achieved in addressing the goals of poverty and hunger eradication, improved health and environmental protection is unlikely to be sustained if most of the ecosystem services on which humanity relies continue to be degraded.'

Part I
History of the Idea

Chapter 1

Having Dominion: Genesis and the Mastery of Nature

Peter Harrison

Peter Harrison is Professor of History and Philosophy at Bond University, Gold Coast, Queensland, Australia. He has worked on the interplay between scientific, philosophical and religious ideas from the sixteenth to the nineteenth centuries; his book The Bible, Protestantism and the Rise of Natural Science *(1998) was a major advance in recognizing the change in biblical understanding at the Reformation from allegory to literalism. This paper shows that the traditional idea of 'stewardship' changed significantly at this period; it was only at the Reformation that the modern notion of a despotic steward arose. This article is a revised version of Harrison (1999).*

Lynn White (1967) famously declared that the ideological source of the environmental problems of the modern West was 'the orthodox Christian arrogance toward nature' (p. 1207). In White's view, the Christian doctrine of creation posits a sharp division between human beings and nature, advocates control of the natural world, and teaches that the world exists to serve human ends. He concluded that Christianity 'bears a huge burden of guilt for environmental deterioration' (p. 1206).

Critics from various quarters have subjected White's thesis to searching criticism (e.g. Barbour 1973; Gowan and Schumaker 1980; Attfield 1983; Spring and Spring 1974; Mitcham and Grote 1984; Cohen 1989; Whitney 1993). Equally important, perhaps, has been the appearance of more nuanced historical accounts of the Western interactions with the natural world. John Passmore, to take an influential example, has argued that the exploitative attitudes of the West originate less in biblical sources than in Greek thought. In Passmore's view, moreover, the apparently chauvinistic elements of the former were ameliorated by the fact that the Bible seems also to preach a more positive view of human responsibilities towards nature. This ambivalence within Christianity led Passmore to speak of two countervailing traditions – 'despotism' and 'stewardship' (Passmore 1974; see also Black 1970: 44–57; Glacken 1967). Despite these wide-ranging discussions, however, the 'White thesis' has proven persuasive, and is frequently encountered in literature on the history of Western attitudes to nature. It is also significant that many within the Christian tradition itself have responded to the challenge of White's views not by attempting to refute them, but by calling for a revision of those aspects of the theological tradition thought to be culpable in the promotion of irresponsible attitudes towards nature.

My aim here is to explore the ways in which the Genesis narratives were understood in the mediaeval and early modern West with a view to identifying the kinds of attitudes and behaviours that these texts actually promoted. As will become apparent, it is fairly clear that the biblical imperative 'have dominion' did in fact play a significant role in promoting an active and manipulative engagement with the natural world, particularly during the seventeenth century. At this time, it provided legitimation for the new science and for the mastery of nature that this science promised. By the same token, the intention behind this energetic engagement with nature, then understood in the light of the Fall, was to restore the earth to its prelapsarian perfection. Control of the natural world was thus sought in order to perfect, rather than exploit, nature. What this means is that the two apparently conflicting characterizations 'despot' and 'steward' turn out to be twin aspects of the same role. As for the purported anthropocentric emphasis of the Judaeo-Christian tradition, this is probably far less significant than has often been imagined, for it was precisely during the period when large-scale attempts to master the natural world were under way that anthropocentric attitudes began to wane. In light of this, there is a need to revise commonly held views about the religious origins of Western attitudes towards nature, and to reassess the historical significance of the categories 'despot' and 'steward'.

Beasts Within

It is important to clarify the kind of argument that is to be proposed here. Neither White nor myself should be seen to be making normative claims about the true meaning of particular biblical narratives. This point seems to have been lost on a number of critics who have laboured to explain that biblical texts that speak of 'dominion' over animals or of 'subduing the earth' actually promote a much more congenial and ecologically sensitive view than would first appear (see Steffen 1992; Westerman 1974: 52, 82; Westerman 1984: 159; Bratton 1984; Coats 1975; Gowan and Schumaker 1980: 16f., 22; Hiers 1984). White, it is sometimes argued, has simply misunderstood the true import of these critical passages. However, these claims have no direct bearing on White's historical contentions, as has been pointed out by a range of commentators (Barr 1972; Whitney 1993; Nash 1988: 89). The White thesis is not concerned with the true meaning of the text, nor even its meaning for those who first compiled it, but rather with what the text was taken to mean in particular periods of history, and how it may have shaped attitudes and motivated particular activities.[1] In sum, White's contentions are impervious to the assaults of biblical criticism, for his thesis is historical rather than hermeneutical. It is the reception of the text – what it meant to the relevant actors in particular historical eras – that is the key issue.

In fact, we encounter little in the history of the interpretation of the Genesis text in the patristic and mediaeval periods that provides support for White's major contentions. This is owing in large measure to the fact that allegorical and 'moral' readings of biblical narratives were common-place during these periods. The Genesis injunction to exercise dominion over the beasts was commonly understood as a counsel of interior control. The 'beasts' that were to be mastered were nothing other than fractious human passions that had become wild and uncontrollable as a con-sequence of the Fall (Harrison 1998a). Adam's disobedience was widely understood as having precipitated a dramatic overturning of the natural hierarchies of an originally perfect creation, paralleled in the psychological realm by a revolt of the passions against reason. This interior insubordi-nation had its counterpart in the natural world: beasts that had been docile and domesticated became wild and intractable, and the earth, which once had yielded abundant provision for human needs, became barren and infertile. But while the rebellion of the animals and infertility of the earth served as constant reminders of the fallen condition of human beings, there remained the prospect of a partial recovery of a moral mastery of unruly human passions. Christian faith offered moral prescriptions specifically directed towards that end.

The exegetical writings of the Church Fathers bear abundant witness to these readings of the Genesis text. Origen (*c.* 185–*c.* 254), who played an important role in the promotion of the allegorical reading of scripture, pointed out that the human being was a 'little world' which contained, in a manner of speaking, 'herds of cattle', 'flocks of sheep and flocks of goats' and 'birds of the air'. The animals in the external world represented dis-positions and desires, the thoughts of the heart and the motions of the flesh. In this context, the directive to exercise dominion over the beasts was understood as an advocacy of self-control. Other patristic writers adopted a similar view. John Chrysostom (*c.* 347–407) wrote that our ideas 'resemble brute beasts' and that we are enjoined 'to control and tame them and submit them to the rule of reason'. In the West, Augustine (354–430) pointed out that the 'wild animals' and 'beasts' are allegorical repre-sentations of 'the affections of the soul'. In the Christian life, he writes, 'there will be beasts that have become good by the gentleness of their behaviour'. These inner beasts 'serve reason when they are restrained from their deathly ways' (Chrysostom, *Homilies on Genesis* VIII.14).

These exegetical traditions suggest that the literal force of the divine command 'have dominion' was for long understood to be more about the contemplative life and the ascetic disciplines that accompanied it than the manipulation of nature. In accordance with this view Chrysostom wrote that the practice of fasting was intended 'to curb the exuberance of the flesh and bring the beast under control' (Chrysostom, *Homilies on Genesis* VIII.14). All such ascetic exercises had as their aim the suppression of 'unworthy passions'. This is not to say that these practices were completely internalized, for it was also believed that a sign of self-mastery was the capacity to exercise control over wild beasts. This accounts for the numerous mediaeval associations of saints and wild animals. Most familiar, perhaps, is the image of Jerome and his lion. But there were a number of other traditions linking saintly individuals with beasts of various kinds: St. Simeon Stylites and the dragon, the Abbot Helenus and the crocodile, St. Marcarius and the hyena, Gerasimus and the lion, St. Columban and the beasts of the Vosges (Waddell 1949: 25–29; Bell 1992: 17; Salisbury 1994: 168f.). St. Francis of Assisi epitomizes this restoration of the happy pre-lapsarian relations between humans and animals. His biographer, the thirteenth-century Franciscan Bonaventure (*c.* 1217–74) pointed out that 'the piety of this blessed man ... had such remarkable power that it subdued ferocious beasts, tamed the wild, trained the tame and bent to his obedience the brute beasts that had rebelled against fallen mankind' (Bonaventure 1978: 261). In short, references to exercising command over nature were typically associated with inner control. The capacity to exercise dominion over the natural world was simply an external sign of far more important moral self-mastery.

These patristic readings of the Genesis narratives carried over into the mediaeval period and, to some extent, the Renaissance. Thomas Aquinas (*c.* 1225–74) wrote in his *Summa theologiae* that 'Man in a certain sense contains all things; and so according as he is master of what is within himself, in the same way he can have mastership over other things' (Aquinas [1964–76]: I, 96,2). Over 200 years later, the humanist scholar Juan Luis Vives (1492–1540) articulated a similar view of the corresponding hierarchies within the natural world and the human microcosm: 'This is the order of Nature, that Wisdom be the rule of the whole, that all creatures obey man; that in man, the body abides by the orders of the soul, and that the soul itself comply with the will of God'. In the pious man, Vives goes on to say, 'the lower passions should be controlled by reason' (quoted by Noreña 1970: 201f.). Yet, despite these survivals of the earlier view, it must be said that from the time of Aquinas onwards, there were significant new developments that added a further dimension to understandings of the human relation to nature. Most important was the reintroduction of Aristotelian texts into the West.

The twelfth century witnessed the beginning of the translation into Latin of the entire Aristotelian corpus (Dod 1982: 45–79). The significance of this here is that Aristotle's biological writings presented information about animals and plants in a way that was quite different from that found in the mediaeval bestiaries and the ancient work from which they originated, the *Physiologus*. These traditional works depicted animals and plants in terms of their symbolic meanings. For example, part of the description of the fox found in the *Physiologus*: is 'The fox is a figure of the devil. To those who live according to the flesh he pretends to be dead. Although he may hold sinners in his gullet, to spiritual men and those perfected in faith, however, he is dead and reduced to nothing'.[2] These kinds of descriptions were typical of mediaeval bestiaries. In Aristotle's natural history, however, animals and plants were described in a quite literal, matter-of-fact fashion, with no reference to their moral or symbolic significance. Such was their impact that the twelfth-century Aristotelian renaissance has been described as the discovery of nature (Chenu 1968). Indeed, the dissemination of Aristotle's biological writings sparked a new interest in a more literal knowledge of the natural world and prompted a new encyclopaedic movement that was oriented towards the accumulation of factual knowledge of the natural world (Boüard 1930: 258–304).

Yet, in spite of the this-worldly orientation of Aristotle and his mediaeval imitators, notions of the mastery of nature were still, for the most part, internalized. Understandings of the Fall remained important. One of the original perfections of Adam, it was thought, had been an encyclopaedic knowledge of nature. With the Fall, however, this knowledge had been lost. The accumulation of information of the natural world, practised by mediaeval encyclopaedists, was thus again an attempt to revisit the kind of mastery that Adam had enjoyed in Eden. Contemplation of the creatures rather than their material exploitation was a means of overcoming human alienation from God. According to Bonaventure, Adam 'possessed knowledge of created things and was raised through their representation to God and to his praise, reverence and love' (*Opera Omnia* V. 390). After the Fall, Adam and his progeny were alienated from God, and their once extensive knowledge was lost. Bonaventure thus reasoned that the regathering of these lost pieces of knowledge was a means by which creatures 'are led back to God' (quoted by McEvoy 1972–74: 330). To know natural things was thus to provide them with a new mental organization. Dominion over nature, in this scheme of things, was accomplished through the mental ordering of the creatures.

At this point it must be conceded that in addition to what I have referred to as an 'internalized' conception of dominion, we also encounter during the Middle Ages clear examples of more practical attempts to master nature. As a specific instance of this, White himself drew attention to the introduction of the heavy plough into northern Europe. As he points out, this made possible the cultivation of land on an unprecedented scale and for the first time Europe moved from subsistence farming to the production of agricultural surpluses. On White's analysis, such developments signalled the fact that whereas 'once man had been a part of nature; now he became her exploiter' (White 1964: 56). There is also little doubt that the Middle Ages witnessed significant technological developments, evidenced in the use of a remarkable variety of mechanical devices – waterwheels, windmills, flywheels, treadles, cranks, cogs and con-rods. Such applications, according to White, point to a desire to harness natural energies for human purposes (White 1964: 129; Glacken 1967: 318–51). Yet in none of this is any explicit reliance upon the kinds of ideological considerations that in White's view were significant motivating factors in the development of exploitative attitudes towards nature. Neither is it clear that the use of ploughs, windmills and water wheels requires ideological sanction. In order to account for these technological innovations we need look no further than the universal human need to secure the means of food production and, when that has been catered for, to secure additional creature comforts. In this respect it is not clear that the mediaeval West was different from any other culture (Moncrieff, 1970; Thomas 1983: 23f.).

One of the shortcomings of White's argument, then, is the failure to provide a convincing account of the link between those biblical texts thought to promote a despotic attitude towards the natural world and specific material practices. In light of the standard historical understandings of these biblical texts outlined above, this is hardly surprising. While biblical imperatives relating to dominion are consistently interpreted in moral and symbolic ways and the utility of nature is perceived to lie primarily in its provision of symbolic resources for the religious life, the thesis of biblically or theologically motivated exploitation of nature is difficult to sustain. In the most important study of the history of Genesis 1.28 ('be fruitful and multiply, and fill the earth, and subdue it; and have dominion ...') in the period under discussion, Jeremy Cohen concludes that the primary understanding of this passage in ancient and mediaeval times is 'an assurance of divine commitment and election, and a corresponding challenge to overcome the ostensive contradiction between the terrestrial and the heavenly inherent in every human being'. More specifically, Cohen observes that in the Middle Ages the Genesis text that refers to human dominion over nature 'touched only secondarily on conquering the natural order' (Cohen 1989: 313).

The time frame of Cohen's study is highly significant, however. In the early modern period a rather different pattern emerged. In the seventeenth century, and in England in particular, we encounter numerous instances of attempts to provide biblical sanctions for the material exploitation of nature. Apologists for the new sciences, advocates of more efficient agricultural practices, promoters of colonies – even humble gardeners – all appealed to the text of Genesis in an attempt to show that their activities were expressly authorized by scripture. In particular, the legitimation of the new science and the mastery of the world that it made possible were closely linked with new, literal readings of the Bible.

The Literal Turn

One of the striking features of the seventeenth-century treatment of the text 'Have Dominion', when compared with mediaeval and patristic commentaries, is the fact that the majority of exegetes now take this passage in its literal sense and consider it to be a directive concerning the natural world (Williams 1948; Duncan 1972: ch. 5). There are a number of related reasons for this interpretive shift: the demise of the ancient idea of microcosm-macrocosm; the collapse of the 'symbolist mentality' of the mediaeval period and a growing suspicion of sacramentalism; the rise of Protestantism with its this-worldly orientation and attendant work ethic; the elevation of the active over the contemplative life. Most important of all, perhaps, and related to each of these factors in some way, was the development of a new hermeneutic in which the literal or historical sense displaced most of the non-literal readings of scripture (on these transitions and their significance, see Harrison 1998b).

The literal approach to texts that typifies modern hermeneutics was strongly promoted by Renaissance humanists and Protestant reformers. Martin Luther maintained that the literal sense was 'the highest, best, strongest, in short the whole substance nature and foundation of the holy scripture' (Luther [1955–75]: 39, 177). Allegories, he declared, were for idle men with weak minds. Calvin agreed that the only permissible allegories were those specifically identified as such by scripture itself. Both reformers were sharply critical of Origen, whom they credited with having introduced this dubious practice into the Church (McGrath 1987: 186; Pelikan 1996). The significance of this hermeneutical revolution is difficult to overestimate, and it had far-reaching consequences for how the natural world was viewed. The assumption of allegorical interpretation was that the purpose of the material world was essentially symbolic – natural objects served to point to more fundamental theological and moral truths. As Irenaeus of Lyons (*c.* 130–*c.* 200) had expressed it, 'earthly things should be types of the celestial' (*Against Heresies* 4.19). Origen, likewise, had thought that 'this early scene contains patterns of things heavenly' (*Song of Songs*, p. 218). The collapse of allegory thus entailed a new conception of nature in which more practical uses were sought for a natural world that had previously been regarded primarily as a complex web of signs laden with transcendental meanings (Harrison 1998b: 107–20).

It is these transformations that account for the fact that the injunction to exercise dominion over nature was taken quite literally from the late sixteenth century onwards. The beasts of Genesis did not represent unbridled passions that needed to be brought under the dominion of reason, nor were the creatures to be ordered in a mental taxonomy that restored their original harmony and reconciled them to their estranged human masters. Rather, Adam was held to have once quite literally commanded all the creatures, and this was the kind of dominion that seventeenth-century readers of scripture thought should be re-established. Not surprisingly, such readings of Genesis played an important role in the legitimation of the new science, which sought not merely to understand nature, but to imitate it and manipulate it. There is no better illustration of this principle than Francis Bacon's (1561–1626) justifications for a new project to master the natural world:

> For man by the Fall fell at the same time from his state of innocency and from his dominion over creation. Both of these losses however can even in this life be in some part repaired; the former by religion and faith, the latter by arts and sciences. For creation was not by the curse made altogether and for ever a rebel, but ... is now by various labours ... at length and in some measure subdued to the supplying of man with bread; that is to the uses of human life (Bacon [1857–74], IV: 247f.).

Bacon, whose methodological prescriptions were to play an important part in the reconceptualization of the scientific enterprise, insisted that the purpose of science was to extend 'the narrow limits of man's dominion over the universe' to their 'promised bounds'. These notions became integral to the rhetoric of the Royal Society, established in 1660. In his apologetic *History of the Royal Society* (1667), Bishop Thomas Sprat announced that it was the aim of the group to re-establish 'dominion over *Things*'. Another clergyman and a leading figure in the Society, Joseph Glanvill, wrote in a similar vein that the new science provided 'ways of *captivating Nature*, and making her subserve our *purposes* and *designments*'. This, he suggested, would promote the theological goal of restoring 'the Empire of Man over Nature' (Glanvill 1665: sig. b3v, original emphasis). The natural world, according to Glanvill's vision, did not serve symbolic purposes but was rather to be 'master'd, managed, and used in the Services of Humane life' (Glanvill 1668: 87, 104). This rhetoric was matched by a variety of practical projects that entailed the clearing of land, draining of fens, increased efficiency of agricultural production, and the reform of mining and manufacturing (Webster 1975).

The movement towards this more active engagement with the natural world received further impetus from a new emphasis on the active life and critiques of the 'idleness' thought to characterize the monastic ideal. The mediaeval West inherited from classical antiquity a distinction between the active and contemplative lives, and Christian thinkers tended to concur with the consensus of ancient philosophers who valued contemplation over action (Mason 1961; Butler 1966). The Renaissance saw a reopening of this discussion, partly on account of republican movements that stressed the importance of citizens' participation in government. As a consequence, a number of humanist writers argued for the priority of the active life (Kristeller 1985: 133–52; Copenhaver and Schmidt 1992: 76–84; Skinner 1988: 418–30). The Protestant reformers also questioned the superiority of the contemplative life as part of their affirmation of the 'priesthood of all believers'; all Christians had a divine vocation. Luther insisted that rather than emulating the indolence of cloistered monks the true Christian will 'use' the world: 'to build, to buy, to have dealings and hold intercourse with his fellows, to join them in all temporal affairs' (Luther: Sermon for the Third Sunday after Easter). Calvin argued similarly that the life of the Christian in the present world should be directed towards 'utility', 'profit' and 'advantage', and that in this manner individuals contribute to the welfare of the commonwealth (Little 1970: 60). Even more than Luther, Calvin cherished the conviction that society could be transformed and restored if Christians were actively engaged in useful worldly affairs (Hart 1995). Sentiments such as these were echoed in Bacon's 'utilitarian' justifications for a new scientific programme.[3]

These developments were reflected in readings of the first chapters of Genesis. The Garden of Eden was now read as a literal garden, and not as a symbol of paradise or an allegory of the soul. The fruits of the garden were literal fruits (not fruits of the spirit) (Williams 1948: 110; Duncan 1972: 152–54). Adam's original assignment was now understood to be that of a gardener or a farmer. Luther thus reacted against the view according to which work was seen to be primarily a curse for Adam's sin (Gen. 3.17–19): 'Man was created not for leisure, but for work, even in the state of innocence'. Calvin made the same point, observing that because God had placed Adam in the Garden of Eden to 'tend it and keep it' (Gen. 2.15), it followed that 'men were created to employ themselves in some work, and not to lie down in inactivity and idleness' (Calvin, *Genesis*, p. 125). Seventeenth-century exegetes such as Lancelot Andrewes and Richard Neve followed suit, stressing the fact that labour was required if the dominion that Adam had enjoyed was to be reinstated. John White argued that when God issued the command to 'subdue the earth', he meant that human beings were 'by Culture and Husbandry, to Manure and make it fit to yield fruits and provision' (White 1656: bk 1: 113f.). The Genesis imperatives concerning dominion and subjection thus came to be understood as commands to render the earth fit for agriculture – as one commentator expressed it, 'subduing' the earth meant 'plowing, tilling, and making use of it' (Pettus 1674: 83). Labour was now understood not simply as an unfortunate consequence of the Fall, nor as a means to provide for the necessities of life, but as a divine vocation and an end in itself.

There is little doubt that in the works of both early modern exegetes and advocates of the new sciences we encounter new readings of the biblical imperatives relating to dominion over nature and subduing the earth. During this period the first chapters of Genesis play a central role in sanctioning both the investigation of nature and its material exploitation. Thus, while some of the specific practices of the Middle Ages may seem to evince an exploitative attitude toward the natural world, it is only with the advent of modernity that we encounter an explicit ideology of the subjection of nature. 'It is in the thought of this period that there begins a unique formulation in Western thought, marking itself off from the other great traditions, such as the Indian and the Chinese ... The religious idea that man has dominion over the earth, that he completes the creation, becomes sharper and more explicit by the seventeenth century' (Glacken 1967: 494f.). Lynn White, it may be said, was correct to identify in the Judaeo-Christian tradition an important ideological source of Western attitudes towards nature, but mistaken in focusing exclusively on the Middle Ages.

Despot or Steward?

The analysis to this point may still seem to support the general contention that biblical accounts of creation played a major role in the development of an exploitative attitude towards nature – the notion of the human being as despot over nature emerged somewhat later than Lynn White originally suggested, but it emerged nonetheless. However, close reading of the rhetoric of early modern advocates of dominion reveals some interesting nuances that call for a more significant revision of the standard view. Notions of dominion were almost invariably associated with the Fall. The common view was that dominion over the earth had been originally granted to Adam but was subsequently lost as a consequence of his sin. The goal of early modern projects to 'improve' nature thus in reality aimed at a restoration, or partial restoration, of the dominion once enjoyed by Adam. Equally important, loss of dominion was not the only tragic consequence of the Fall. It was generally believed that the natural world itself had fallen from its original perfection. As St. Paul expressed it, the whole creation 'groans in travail' (Rom. 8.22). This point is crucial for an understanding of the motivations of these early modern thinkers. The fallen world was, in an important sense, an unnatural world. The savagery of wild animals, the infertility of the ground, the existence of noxious weeds and insect pests – these features of the world stood as silent witnesses to the terrible consequences of Adam's disobedience. Even the irregularities of the surface of the earth, thought once to have been a perfect sphere, along with the vicissitudes of the seasons, were attributed to the effects of human sin (e.g. Walker 1641: 23–25; Senault 1650: 319–90; Franck 1687: 124–70). What follows from this is that early modern discussions of dominion are less to do with the exercise of a tyrannical authority over a hapless natural world than they are about attempting to undo the damage wrought by human sin in the first age of world.

There is ample evidence of this in the early modern literature. Thomas Traherne (1675: 103), one of the foremost metaphysical poets of the period, observed that the earth 'had been a Wilderness overgrown with Thorns, and Wild Beasts, and Serpents: Which now by the Labor of many hands, is reduced to the Beauty and Order of *Eden*'. John Pettus (1674: 83), who made explicit reference to 'subduing the earth' and 'conquering nature', insisted that his aim was 'the replenishment of the first creation'. Timothy Nourse (1700: 2) set out the view that agriculture 'heals' the land of 'the Original Curse of Thorns and Bryers'. Placing land under cultivation, he thought, would bring about 'the *Restauration of Nature*, which may be looked upon as a *New Creation of things*'. The common aim of these writers was encapsulated by John Donne. Our chief business, he wrote, is 'To rectifie nature to what she was'. This attempted restoration of nature was thus part of a more general redemptive process in which both the earth and its human inhabitants would be transformed into something more perfect. As John Flavell wrote in *Husbandry Spiritualized* (1669): 'A skilful and industrious improvement of the creatures' will lead to 'a fuller taste of Christ and Heaven'. Dominion, in this context, is really about redemption. The rhetoric of subjection that we encounter in this period does not arise out of an indifference to the fortunes of nature, nor does it promote the instrumental use of the natural world. Rather the concern is with the restoration of the earth to its original and 'natural' condition.

Another feature of the thought of this period is the widespread expression of doubts about the centrality of human beings in the cosmos. A number of historical accounts of Western attitudes towards nature have stressed the connection between anthropocentrism and environmental arrogance. White maintained, for example, that 'Christianity is the most anthropocentric religion the world has seen' (1967: 1205). Whether this is true or not, the active engagement with nature that characterizes the early modern period does not seem to have been motivated primarily by anthropocentric impulses. On the contrary, at this time the view that all things had been created solely for the human race first attracted serious challenges (Brooke 2000). A number of leading lights of the new sciences expressed major reservations about the centrality of human beings in the cosmos. Naturalist John Ray observed that it was 'vulgarly received' that 'all this visible world was created for Man', but added that 'Wise Men now think otherwise'. William Derham, who like Ray was given to enumerating evidences of design in the created order, spoke similarly of the 'vulgar

27

opinion, that all things were made for man' (Derham 1715: 39). Thomas Burnet, who famously attempted to show that the biblical narrative of the Deluge was consistent with contemporary science, thought it extremely unlikely that the earth and all the countless celestial bodies had been brought into being for the use of 'the meanest of all the Intelligent Creatures'. Archbishop William King also concluded that anthropocentrism was a view beset by 'inextricable difficulties'.

It is not difficult to identify at least some of the reasons for this shift in Western sentiment. The Copernican revolution had dethroned human beings from their place at the centre of the cosmos, and the Cartesian and Newtonian cosmologies postulated a universe of enormous proportions with countless numbers of stars. Not only did this make the earth relatively insignificant in the larger scheme of things, but it also encouraged speculation about the existence of other inhabited worlds. John Ray wrote in 1691 that it was now a 'received hypothesis' that every star is a sun with planets 'in all likelyhood furnished with as great a variety of corporeal Creatures animate and inanimate as the Earth is' (Harrison 1998b: 177–84). This was another reason, perhaps, that the ancient idea of the human being as a microcosm fell from favour. In addition, during the seventeenth century the legitimacy of physical explanations in terms of final causes attracted strong criticism, in particular from René Descartes. Although it is important to distinguish different senses of 'final cause' – not all such explanations are to be understood in terms of features of the natural world designed for human use – it remains true that aspects of the attempt to expel teleological explanation from the sphere of natural science were related to anti-anthropocentric tendencies (Harrison 2004: 132–34).

When combined with convictions about the fallen state of the world, doubts about the extent to which the cosmos had been specifically designed for human use alone sponsored new, more critical, approaches to the study of nature. If the world had not been specifically designed for us, why should we assume that it would be intelligible and amenable to scientific investigation? Moreover, if the world had fallen away from an original orderly perfection, would this not render its operations more obscure? (Harrison 2002). One of the chief assumptions of the Aristotelian science of the Middle Ages had been that the world as it appears to us is in fact the world as it really is. Seventeenth-century investigators resisted such sanguine assumptions about the ease with which the natural world could be known. Galileo wrote that nature does not care 'a whit whether her abstruse reasons and methods of operation are understandable to men'. Francis Bacon famously insisted that the natural world must be interrogated and subjected to 'trials and vexations of art' if it was to yield up its secrets. This resistance of the natural world to our attempts to investigate it was linked with the question of human uses of natural things. Robert Boyle concluded that it was false to assert that everything in the visible world had been specifically created for human use, yet insisted that systematic investigation of nature would yield hitherto unknown applications of many things that were apparently useless (Boyle 1688: 10, cf. 230f.).

In sum, while the seventeenth century witnessed an active engagement with the natural world and concerted attempts to transform it and render it useful, these were not motivated by arrogance or indifference to the plight of nature. Rather, they are better understood as well-meaning attempts to restore an original order that was thought to have been lost as a consequence of the Fall. The new experimental science, while it was clearly more invasive than the Aristotelian natural philosophy it replaced, was also informed by a modest conception of what human beings could know of nature. Furthermore, the relationship between anthropocentrism and the exploitation of nature is more complex than is commonly assumed. To a degree, it was doubts about the centrality of human beings in the cosmos that promoted the quest for knowledge and its practical applications.

Conclusion

What I hope to have shown in this brief survey is that some long-standing assumptions about the relationship between the Christian doctrine of creation and Western attitudes towards nature stand in need of revision. Lynn White was basically correct to identify particular biblical texts and aspects of Christian theology as important ideological sources of Western attitudes towards nature. However, he was mistaken in assuming that these played a significant role in the history of the West prior to the emergence of modern science in the seventeenth century. And while there were, undoubtedly, systematic efforts in the Middle Ages to harness the latent capacities of nature, it is not clear that these owe anything to specifically Judaeo-Christian ideas or to the creation narratives of Genesis. Only with the onset of modernity – characterized for our purposes by literal readings of scripture, an emphasis on action over contemplation, and a decline in microcosmic conceptions of human nature – do we encounter religious and biblical motivations for an active engagement with nature.

The distinction between 'stewardship' and 'despotism' that is firmly entrenched in the vocabulary of environmental philosophy now also appears somewhat problematic. While it is often thought that 'stewardship' represents a minor emphasis in the Christian tradition and one opposed to a more dominant 'despotism', seventeenth-century developments suggest that, for this period at least, no such distinction can be sustained. Early modern advocates of the large-scale transformation of nature saw themselves not as exploiters but as restorers. For them the world in its given state was a fallen world, and its wildness a consequence of Adam's disobedience. Virgin territory was thus a constant reminder of past human sin and present human idleness. Projects for the large-scale transformation of nature were aimed at redeeming it from the curse laid upon it following Adam's expulsion from Eden. It was during this period that, for the first time, the 'exploitation' of nature, if we may still call it that, became an end in itself – an end that went beyond provision for basic human needs. Seventeenth-century 'improvers' and many contemporary environmentalists thus share a common goal – the return of the earth to its primitive 'natural' condition.

It should also be apparent that the posited link between a strong anthropocentric programme and the ideology of exploitation is problematic. For Aristotle and his mediaeval successors the centrality of human beings in the cosmos was unquestioned. In the early modern period this assumption was subjected to increasing scrutiny. Arguably, moreover, it was precisely the demotion of human beings in the scale of things that promoted the corporate, long-term, experimentally oriented programme that has a significant place in the genealogy of modern science.

There are elements of this history that are directly relevant to contemporary theological discussions. Many advocates of an environmentally sensitive theology have concurred with White's judgement concerning the culpability of aspects of the Judaeo-Christian tradition. Accordingly, there have been suggestions that these aspects of the tradition need to be jettisoned, modified or downplayed. Thomas Berry, for example, believes that what is now needed is 'a new type of religious orientation' because our environmental plight is related to 'our identification of the divine as transcendent to the natural world' (T. Berry 1988: 113–15). Sallie McFague has expressed similar reservations about the traditional conception of a God who is 'distant from the world and relates only to the human world'. This image of divine sovereignty, she insists, 'supports attitudes of control and use toward the non-human world' (McFague 1987: 68). In an even more specific critique of the tradition, Matthew Fox blames 'Augustinian fall-redemption theology' for what he identifies as an openly antagonistic approach to the natural world (Fox 1983: 10f.). Without wishing to downplay the importance of attempts to make theology relevant to contemporary concerns, it might be said that suggestions such as these capitulate too readily to the agenda of White and his successors. The claim that certain religious ideas have given rise to particular attitudes towards nature is not one that can be settled simply by pointing to what appear to be plausible historical connexions. While the brief historical analysis provided in this article may not be the final word on the matter, it should at least give pause to those who wish to advocate a simple historical thesis about the impact of theological doctrines on Western attitudes towards nature. As for the apparently unfashionable Augustinian 'fall-redemption theology' and the early modern programme it inspired – that of redeeming a natural world which had fallen into a ruinous state on account of human transgressions – these do not seem entirely irrelevant to those who wish to advocate on nature's behalf in the twenty-first century.

Notes

1. Equally irrelevant are sociological data that show no positive correlation between external indicators of Christian commitment and lack of environmental concern. For examples see Wokomir *et al.* 1997; Eckberg and Blocker 1989.
2. Curley 1979: 27f. On the *Physiologus* see Cox (1983). For the story of the fox in twelfth- and thirteenth-century bestiaries, see Barber (1993:65); White (1954: 53f).
3. It should be noted that, contrary to the views of some commentators, Bacon preached a subtle and nuanced utilitarianism. See Vickers (1984: 281–314); Watanabe 1992; Harrison 2001.

Chapter 2

Modern Domination of Nature – Historical Origins and Biblical Critique

Richard Bauckham

Richard Bauckham is Professor of New Testament Studies at the University of St Andrews and a member of the Doctrine Commission of the Church of England. He has published widely in theology, including influential studies of Jürgen Moltmann's theology. This article is a shortened version of a chapter from his book God and the Crisis of Freedom *(2002); fuller notes and references are given in the original, together with a detailed critique of Lynn White's paper 'The historical roots of our ecologic crisis' predating but along similar lines to that given by Peter Harrison (pp. 17–31). Bauckham shows that until the early modern period 'dominion' was understood as a prescribed right for humans to make use of other creatures, but that this was balanced by the fundamental doctrine that we are creatures of God along with them. The technological domination of nature has its roots in Greek thought via Renaissance humanism and the influence of Francis Bacon; stewardship in the modern sense arose as an alternative to the excessively anthropocentric Baconian view. Bauckham argues that we must recover the biblical doctrine of the theocentric community of creation in order to balance the otherwise one-sided emphasis on stewardship.*

A crucial area of current discussion is human authority over the nonhuman creation on this planet, often described as the human dominion over creation, following the usual English translation of Genesis 1.28. I prefer to speak of human authority in creation rather than over creation, because it is vital for Christians today to recover a lively sense of human creatureliness. In Genesis 1 itself, it is clear that humans, while given a special status and responsibility for other creatures, are themselves creatures alongside their fellow creatures. Their dominion is within the created order, not, like God's, transcendent above it. Distinguished from other creatures in some respects, they are also like them in many respects. A crucial issue in assessing interpretations of the dominion is the extent to which this sense of a horizontal relationship has been retained along with the vertical relationship of dominion that sets them in some sense above other creatures.

Treating humans as gods in relation to the world was probably the most fateful development in Christian attitudes to the nonhuman creation. Only with this development did interpretation of Gen. 1.28 take its place in the ideology of aggressive domination of nature that has characterized the modern West.

Beliefs about the human relationship to the rest of creation, regarded for most of Christian history as the Christian view and associated with the Genesis text, are really Greek philosophical rather than biblical ideas. Before the modern period, the dominant theological tradition articulated a strongly anthropocentric view of the human dominion. However, this dominion was understood as a static fact, not a mandate for extension, and the world was understood as created ready and adapted to human use, not requiring large-scale technological modification. This is what sharply distinguishes the tradional view from the interpretation of the dominion that accompanied the rise of the modern project of technological domination of nature.[1] Moreover, the anthropocentricity of the dominant tradition was significantly qualified by other convictions about the relationship between God, humanity, and the rest of creation: that human beings are part of God's creation, which itself is theocentric, existing for the glory of God; that not humans, but angels, are the summit of creation; and that all creatures worship God and have the value of creatures created by God. This meant the vertical relationship in which the dominion over nature placed humanity to the rest of creation was complemented by a real awareness of the horizontal relationship in which humans relate to their fellow creatures as all creatures of the one Creator. As we shall see, all these qualifications fell away in the Renaissance interpretation of the human dominion that paved the way for the modern subjugation of nature. When any sense of the value of creation for God and of a common creatureliness in which humans share was lost, the idea of human dominion acquired quite new significance.

Creating the modern tradition: (1) Italian Renaissance humanists

A major development occurred in the Italian humanist writers of the Renaissance. It could hardly have taken place except on the basis of the dominant theological tradition of the patristic and mediaeval periods, but it was also a major step beyond that tradition. Wybrow (1991: 166–71) provides one of the few serious discussions of the subject. It is this step that can he said to have created the ethos within which the modern project of aggressive domination of nature has taken place.

The Renaissance humanists were preoccupied with the theme of the supreme dignity of humanity, which they not infrequently expounded as exegesis of Gen. 1.26 (see especially Trinkhaus 1970). Even where reference to the text is not explicit, it is frequently implicit. Moreover, the traditional understanding of the human dominion, which these writers knew not only from the theological tradition but also from the classical sources that had influenced that tradition, is taken entirely for granted. The rest of creation was made for humanity (it was, says Petrarch, 'dedicated to nothing but your uses, and created solely for the service of man' [quoted in Trinkhaus 1970: 180]). The unique superiority of human nature over the rest of creation equips human beings to rule the world. But these traditional themes are given unprecedented emphasis and at the same time developed in a novel direction.

A striking feature of the Renaissance humanist idea of humanity is that the vertical relationship of humanity to nature (human beings as rulers over the rest of creation) is emphasized to the virtual exclusion of the horizontal relationship of humanity to nature (human beings as creatures who share with other creatures a common creaturely relationship to the Creator). Humanity's place within creation is abolished in favour of humanity's exaltation above creation. While this takes to an extreme one aspect of the traditional hierarchical thinking, other aspects of the mediaeval hierarchical view of creation are left aside. Human beings are no longer regarded as occupying a metaphysical status below that of the angels, but are exalted above the angels, if not by virtue of their creation, then at least by virtue of their deification in Christ. With this is connected a rejection of the idea that humanity occupies a given, fixed place within the created order. Human beings are understood as uniquely free to make of themselves what they will and to transcend all limits. In effect, humanity becomes a kind of god in relation to the world. Human creatureliness is forgotten in the intoxication with human godlikeness. The Renaissance humanist vision of humanity is of a creative and sovereign god over the world.

For writers such as Giannozzo Manetti, Marsilio Ficino and Pico della Mirandola, the image of God in human nature is understood not simply as the rational or moral capacity that distinguishes humans from other creatures – as the dominant theological tradition had understood it – but as likeness to God in the divine activity of creating and mastering the world. The rather traditional theme, inherited from classical antiquity, of stress on humanity's ingenuity and inventiveness, is heightened and emphasized in the typical Renaissance adulation of the artistic and technological achievements of humanity. As Manetti commented:

After that first, new and rude creation of the world, everything seems to have been discovered, constructed and completed by us out of some singular and outstanding acuteness of the human mind ... The world and all its beauties seems [sic] to have been first invented and established by Almighty God for the use of man, and afterwards gratefully received by man and rendered much more beautiful, much more ornate and far more refined (quoted in Trinkhaus 1970: 247).

This new sense of the godlike creativity of humanity should be contrasted with the traditional concept that human beings can do neither the work of God nor that of nature, but can only imitate nature. According to Ficino, 'Human arts make by themselves whatever nature itself makes, so that we seem to be not servants of nature but competitors ... Man at last imitates all the works of divine nature and perfects, corrects and modifies the works of lower nature'. Human sovereignty over the world in knowing and creating is such that the human soul must be termed divine: 'The mind in comprehending conceives of as many things in itself as God in knowing makes in the world. By speaking it expresses as many in the air; with a reed it writes as many, on paper. By making it constructs as many in the material of the world. Therefore he would be proven mad who would deny that the soul, which in the arts and in governing competes with God, is divine' (quoted in Trinkhaus 1970: 484).

It is clear here that Ficino's aim is to envisage humanity in terms of the attributes traditionally restricted to God as creator and ruler of the world.[2] The human relationship to the world is described in terms that, for all the magnificence of the vision, are ludicrously hyperbolic. All creaturely limitations are deliberately suppressed, as in the following passage which is worth quoting at length:

In these industrial arts ... man everywhere utilises all the materials of the universe as though all were subject to man. He makes use of all the elements, the stones, metals, plants and animals, and he transforms them into many shapes and figures, which animals never do. Nor is he content with one element or few, as animals, but he uses all as though he were master of all. He tramps the earth, he sails the water, he ascends in the air by the highest towers ... He acts as the vicar of God, since he inhabits all the elements and cultivates all. Indeed he employs not only the elements but all the animals of the elements, terrestrial, aquatic, and flying, for food, comfort and pleasure, and the supernal and celestial ones for learning and the miracles of magic. He not only uses the animals but he rules them ... He does not only use the animals cruelly, but he also governs, fosters and teaches them. Universal providence is proper to God who is the universal cause. Therefore man who universally provides for all things living is a certain god. He is the god without doubt of the animals since he uses all of them, rules them, and teaches some of them. He is established also as god of the elements since he inhabits and cultivates them all (quoted in Trinkhaus 1970: 483–84).

If we understand Renaissance humanism as in some sense giving birth to the spirit of the modern project of unlimited domination of nature, then it is extremely instructive to see how explicit Ficino is in connecting a human aspiration to subjugate all things to human control with a human aspiration to divinity:

> [Man] will not be satisfied with the empire of this world, if, having conquered this one, he learns that there remains another world which he has not yet subjugated . . . Thus man wishes no superior and no equal and will not permit anything to be left out and excluded from his rule. This status belongs to God alone. Therefore he seeks a divine condition.

The gap between such a view and the traditional Christian view of the human dominion is vast. Anthropocentric as the latter was, it nevertheless understood the human dominion in static and very limited terms and qualified it by a consciousness of humanity's creatureliness in common with the rest of creation. In Ficino, on the other hand, human beings are godlike in their restless will to power. Human dominion over the world has become a limitless aspiration. The attitudes that have led to the contemporary ecological crisis can be traced back to this source, but no further.

The sixteenth-century Italian pantheist philosopher Giordano Bruno illustrates just how far the idea of humanity's divine creativity could be taken:

> The gods have given man intelligence and hands, and have made him in their image, endowing him with a capacity superior to other animals. This capacity consists not only in the power to work in accordance with nature and the usual course of things, but beyond that and outside her laws, to the end that by fashioning, or having the power to fashion, other natures, other courses, other orders by means of his intelligence, with that freedom without which his resemblance to the deity would not exist, he might in the end make himself god of the earth (quoted in Farrington 1964: 27).

This idea of humanity's capacity to refashion the world at will into whatever form of new creation we desire has provided the ethos of much of the modern project. It has been one of the myths by which modern Western civilization has lived. But, of course, the scientific and technological means by which modern society has attempted to put this myth into practice could not relate to nature in quite the way Bruno (inspired by Renaissance magic) envisaged. Science and technology cannot act outside nature's laws. Much as they might aspire to refashion nature, their ability to do so depends on their mastery of nature's laws. To find a version of the Renaissance humanist aspiration that recognized this and thereby provided more precisely the ideology of the modern scientific movement in its attempt to subjugate nature to human use, we must turn to Bruno's English contemporary Francis Bacon.

Creating the modern tradition: (2) Francis Bacon

The extraordinary achievement of Francis Bacon (1561–1626) was to set out a programme for the modern scientific enterprise that can still stand as a classic statement of the ideology which has inspired and governed scientific research and technological innovation from the seventeenth to the twentieth centuries. His contribution to the modern scientific method has been frequently discussed and debated, but his main contribution to modern science lay rather in his vision of a utopian goal to be realized through scientific innovation and progress. It was this dream that inspired the pioneering scientists of seventeenth- and eighteenth-century England. Central to Bacon's vision of scientific progress is his understanding of the goal of science as the implementation of the God-given human dominion over nature, which Bacon himself presents as the meaning of Gen. 1.28.

Taking entirely for granted the traditional view that the rest of creation exists for the sake of humanity, Bacon understands the human dominion as humanity's right and power to use nature for human benefit. This human dominion was severely impaired at the Fall, but can be recovered: 'Man by the Fall fell at the same time from his state of innocency and from his dominion over creation. Both of these losses can in this life be in some part repaired; the former by religion and faith, the latter by arts and sciences' (Spedding *et al.* 1857–58: IV, 247–48). The words of God to Adam after the Fall – that 'in the sweat of thy face shalt thou eat bread' (Gen. 3.19) – Bacon takes to mean that 'by various labours' the earth can be 'at length and in some measure subdued to the supplying of man with bread; that is, to the uses of human life' (Spedding *et al.* 1857–58: IV, 248). These labours are primarily the intellectual labours of scientific research that make possible the technological exploitation of nature for human benefit. The human task is to recover the dominion over the earth to its fullest extent. This is 'the real business and fortunes of the human race' (Spedding *et al.* 1857–58: IV, 32). It is also the central goal of Bacon's own work, which is devoted to 'my only earthly wish, namely to stretch the deplorably narrow limits of man's dominion over the universe to their promised bounds' (in Farrington 1964: 62). Hence the title of 'The Great Instauration' for Bacon's projected but never completed masterpiece. By this term he means precisely the restoration of the human dominion over nature that was promised in Genesis 1: 'that right over nature which belongs to [the human race] by divine bequest' (Spedding *et al.* 1857–58: IV, 21). This restoration of dominion is a vast enterprise, not to be accomplished quickly. It is to be the work of dedicated scientific labour over many generations.

Thus, for Bacon, much more clearly than in the Italian humanists, human dominion becomes a historical task to be progressively accomplished. Indeed, it is the great task of the human race. The restoration of human dominion is not, as sometimes it was conceived in mediaeval tradition, given by God to those who live according to his will and not, in that sense, a concern of religion, though Bacon does expect the exercise of dominion to be 'governed by sound reason and true religion'. He effectively drew a very firm distinction between the restoration of human innocence, which was the province of religion, and the restoration of human dominion, which would be accomplished by science and technology.

The task is very explicitly that of subjecting nature to human use. The language of domination comes readily to Bacon's pen: 'I am come in very truth leading you to Nature with all her children to bind her to your service and make her your slave.' In a revealing passage, Bacon refers to three sorts of ambition. Those who desire to increase their own power in their own country are not to be admired. The desire to increase one's own country's power over other nations is more admirable, but still culpable. By contrast, the endeavour 'to extend the power and dominion of the human race itself over the universe' is wholly admirable, 'a work truly divine'. This is because it is unselfishly directed to the benefit of all humanity. Bacon equates 'the instigator [i.e. restorer] of man's domination of the universe' with 'the champion of freedoms' and 'the conqueror of need'. Appearing probably for the first time, this is the modern vision of the scientific and technological enterprise: dedicated to the good of humanity by acquiring power over nature and using it to liberate humanity from all the ills of the human condition. It has a high ethical motivation and goal. But the ethical limit it places on human domination is solely that of the love of humanity. The scientific enterprise should be governed not by desire for personal gain or glory but by love of humanity. No limit is imposed by any sense that nature has intrinsic value for itself or for God. Because Bacon assumes that nature exists solely for human benefit, to exploit it for human benefit as far as possible is not only right but a prime human duty.

There is a practical limit to human power to dominate nature, imposed by the facts of nature. Nature has been constituted by its Creator in a certain way that human beings must understand if they are to be able to use nature to the fullest possible extent for human benefit. This is the point at which Bacon so significantly does what the Italian humanists had not been able to do: he connects the vision of human dominion with the empirical science he advocates and inspires. Nature's laws cannot be ignored or set aside or breached. They must be understood if humanity is to exercise realistic power over nature. This is Bacon's famous doctrine that 'knowledge is power':

> For man is but the servant and interpreter of nature: what he does and what he knows is only what he has observed of nature's order in fact or in thought ... For the chain of causes cannot by any force be loosed or broken, nor can nature be commanded except by being obeyed. And so those twin objects, human Knowledge and human Power, do really meet in one: and it is from ignorance of causes that operation fails (Spedding *et al.* 1857–58: IV, 32).

In this sense, Bacon advocates a kind of humility which sounds a different note from the rather more promethean vision of some of the Italian humanists. It is the humility of the believing scientist, who respects the way God has made nature, studies its laws, and thereby gains the power over it that God intends humanity to have. In this sense, 'nature cannot be conquered except by obeying her'. But the aim is certainly to conquer nature, and Bacon's vision of what it is possible for human power over nature to achieve is far from the limited mediaeval concept of imitating nature. He attacks the error 'of looking upon art [i.e. technology] as a kind of supplement to nature; which has power enough to finish what nature has begun or correct her when going aside, but no power to make radical changes, and shake her in the foundations'. This language of conquering nature is a metaphor that came to be used standardly and unreflectively until the quite recent development of ecological consciousness made it questionable. As a typical expression of the nineteenth-century view, the following quotation from Thomas Carlyle is plainly in direct descent from Bacon: 'We war with rude nature; and, by our resistless engines, come off always victorious, and loaded with spoils' (Blackwell and Seabrook 1993: 24).

Unlike the Italian humanists, it is significant that Bacon does not speak of human deification or of humanity as a kind of god over the world. According to Bacon, the traditional natural philosopher created the world as he would have liked it to be – thereby playing God – instead of humbly observing the world that God has actually made, as Bacon's empirical scientist does. In this sense, Bacon sets the tone for the early modern scientific enterprise. Bacon's scientist is not a god who can recreate the world in any way he will, but he can by mastering the laws of nature subject it to the purpose for which God created it, human benefit. Bacon's achievement is to transfer the Renaissance vision of unlimited dominion away from its association with magic and alchemy, harnessing it instead to the practical pursuit of scientific knowledge and technological innovation, and relating it to biblical and religious ideas in a way more congenial to Protestant England. But it is also significant that Bacon's formulation of the idea of human mastery of nature turned out to be easily secularized as the cultural impact of Christian belief steadily diminished in the following centuries. As Leiss (1972: 53) puts it, '[Bacon's] contention that science shared with religion the burden of restoring man's lost excellence helped create the climate in which earthly hopes flourished at the expense of heavenly ones.'

All this seems to show a total loss of any sense that human beings belong within creation alongside other creatures: Bacon's humanity simply stands above nature, mastering it by knowledge and power. As with the Italian humanists, the vertical relationship entirely replaces the horizontal. The value of nature has become purely utilitarian; the notion that all creatures exist for the glory of God and thereby assist humanity's contemplation of God has disappeared in favour of nature's usefulness for practical human needs. Despite the continued reference to God the Creator, this is the point at which Western attitudes to nature became exclusively anthropocentric rather than theocentric. It made little practical difference when atheistic scientists eventually took their place alongside believing scientists in the Baconian tradition.

The 'Judeo-Christian tradition' has been both praised and blamed for the so-called desacralization of nature in the Western tradition. It has been praised by those who think the achievements of modern science were thereby made possible, and blamed by those who think the modern exploitation of nature – the root of the ecological crisis – was thereby made possible. But we need to be clear about the meaning of desacralization. The Judeo-Christian tradition certainly dedivinized nature. Nature is not reverenced as divine in a pantheistic or animistic sense. But deeply rooted in the Judeo-Christian tradition is the sense that all creatures exist for the glory of God and reflect the glory of God. Human beings both praise God along with the rest of creation and praise God for the beauty and worth of the rest of creation in which they see the Creator's glory reflected. Only with the loss of this non-utilitarian sense of the value of creation for and in relation to God can we properly speak of a desacralization of nature. Significantly, it is in the seventeenth-century Christian scientist Robert Boyle that we find a call for the desacralization of nature, explicitly linked with a Baconian understanding of the human dominion: 'The veneration wherewith men are imbued for what they call nature has been a discouraging impediment to the empire of man over the inferior creatures of God: for many have not only looked upon it, as an impossible thing to compass, but as something of impious to attempt' (quoted in Passmore 1974: 11). Without the Baconian desacralization of nature, a scientific enterprise would have been possible, but not the actual scientific and technological enterprise of aggressive domination of nature that has been so significant a feature of modern Western history.

Reading Bacon is to experience frequent shocks as one finds all too familiar features of the modern scientific enterprise clearly stated. For example, he expressed the conviction so often voiced by contemporary scientists that scientific work itself is value-free so that only its use can be right or wrong (with the implication, in contemporary discourse, that scientists are absolved of any responsibility for the use made of their discoveries): 'light is in itself pure and innocent; it may be wrongly used, but cannot in its nature be defiled' (Farrington 1964: 92). Another instance has only recently become observable. In his utopia, the *New Atlantis* (Weinberger 1980: 73), Bacon anticipates scientific manipulation of animals such as has only now become possible through genetic engineering:

> By art, likewise, we make them greater or taller than their kind is; and contrariwise dwarf them, and stay their growth: we make them more fruitful and bearing than their kind is; and contrariwise barren and not generative. Also we make them differ in colour, shape, activity, many ways. We find means to make commixtures and copulations of different kinds, and them not barren, as the general opinion is ... Neither do we do this by chance, but we know beforehand of what matter and commixture what kind of those creatures will arise.

Bacon had no notion of the means by which these results would be achieved four centuries later, but he could anticipate the results because he coined the ideology that still inspires twenty-first-century biotechnologists. I am attaching huge importance regarding the historical transformation of ideas of human dominion to the work of this one man, but it seems that the scale and enduring impact of his influence really does justify this.

Domination of nature after Bacon

A history of the idea of mastery of nature after Bacon remains to be written.[3] It certainly passed through the Baconianism of seventeenth-century English scientists into general modern thinking about science, technology, and their place in the utopian idea of human progress that developed at the time of the European Enlightenment. It became *the* ideology of the modern West. Essentially Bacon's ideas prevailed: it was as though he had already expressed all that the modern age felt it necessary to be thought about this concept.

However, one very important 'variation on a Baconian theme' could only emerge much later than Bacon's own time, because it depends on the nineteenth- and twentieth-century idea of the evolution of life. It is the notion that scientists are becoming masters of the evolutionary process (not least, human evolution), taking control of it and directing it. This idea has become especially plausible with the rapidly emerging possibilities of manipulating genes and changing the genetic basis of species.

The secularization of the idea of human dominion had a further important result. In stepping outside a religious doctrine of creation, the Western project of dominating nature sidestepped not only the issue of ethical obligation to nature (already abandoned by Bacon) but also that of limits given in the created order of things. Bacon's recognition that nature's laws must be understood if nature is to be exploited (so that presumably nature's laws set limits to the kind of exploitation that is possible) and the Renaissance sense that humanity has unlimited creative power to unleash nature's potentialities have both fed into the modern project, investing science with hugely utopian expectations but also inspiring the hubris that overreaches its capacities and brings unforeseen and disastrous consequences into being. In the late twentieth century it became more and more obvious that the Baconian dream had a powerful element of unreason hidden in its apparent rationality. This 'cunning of unreason', as Leiss calls it, is revealed in the persistent illusion that the undertaking known as 'the mastery of nature' is itself mastered (Leiss 1972: 23).

The secularization of the project of domination has also left it exposed to commercialization and consumerization. It is this that has fatally compromised the humanist ethical goal. The satisfaction of human needs and the curing of human ills have proved too limited as goals for the exploitation of nature. Descartes envisaged 'the invention of an infinity of arts and crafts which enable us to enjoy without any trouble the fruits of the earth and all the good things which are to be found there' (cited in Leiss 1972: 81). But he did not recognize how human desires would have to be manufactured to require the unlimited products of technology. Insatiable desires must match unlimited dominion in a spiral that makes the direction of causality quite obscure. This is where ethical as well as other limits fall away and where disregard of nature's own limits makes them disastrously evident.

An alternative modern tradition: dominion as stewardship

The understanding of the human dominion over nature that has become most popular among Christians, in the context of a new consciousness of ecological responsibilities, is the idea of stewardship. This is often thought to be more rooted in the Christian tradition than it really is. A recognition that the world is God's creation and that this imposes ethical limits on human dominion over it (for example, inhibiting cruelty to animals) has a place in the Christian tradition, however much in tension it might seem to be with the dominant view. But where the mediaeval and even Reformation commonplace that the rest of creation was created by God for human benefit held sway, we cannot speak of stewardship. The idea that human beings have been entrusted by God with the care of creatures not primarily existing for human benefit is not just a restraint on dominion but a different idea of dominion, which it is hard to find clearly expressed before the late seventeenth century.[4]

The stewardship concept seems to have been a response to the growing sense of human control over nature, which had also prompted the Italian humanist and Baconian interpretations of dominion. Consciously or unconsciously, it provided an alternative to the excessively anthropocentric Baconian view in the England of the Royal Society. Those who espoused it shared the contemporary enthusiasm for the extension of human control over nature, but instead of thinking purely of a human right to use nature for human benefit, they maintained also a human responsibility to care for nature, since, as George Hughes (quoted by Thomas 1983: 155) put it, man's rule is 'subordinate and stewardly, not absolutely to do as he list with God's creatures'. In other words, almost for the first time, the dominion was being interpreted in a way that acknowledged ethical obligations arising from nature's inherent value.

Although this idea seems to have been relatively popular in religious writers of the second half of the seventeenth century, it was the eminent English lawyer Matthew Hale (1609–76) who gave it its fullest expression. He presupposes that nature left to itself would be chaotic: fierce animals would render the gentler and more useful animals extinct, the earth would be submerged in marsh and overgrown with trees and weeds. The earth needs a superior creature to keep it in order. Humanity's duty is therefore to keep things in balance. Human beings are to control the earth for the earth's sake as well as for their own sake. The prejudice that nature controlled and managed by humanity is preferable to wilderness, a prejudice from which since classical times few except the hermits had been free, is still dominant here. Human control improves nature. Technology is justified as an instrument of humanity's beneficent stewarding of the world.

The value of the notion of stewardship was that it formally introduced the notion of justice into the human relationship to nature. It is no accident that Hale was a lawyer. As steward responsible to the divine King, humanity has legal obligations to administer the earth justly and without cruelty. Even if the concept of stewardship did nothing to preserve wild nature from human interference, it was significantly linked with an apparently growing Christian sensitivity about cruelty to animals. Matthew Hale himself was one of those who thought it unjustified to chase and kill animals for mere sport. He put his aged horses out to graze, rather than selling them to the knackers. Even the right of human beings to kill animals for food was being doubted by the late seventeenth century, and Hale, though he maintained that right, admitted that the sight of sheep grazing always made him feel God must have intended 'a more innocent kind of food for man'.

The appeal of the notion of stewardship is that it recognizes value in the nonhuman creation other than its usefulness to humanity and gives humanity obligations to treat the nonhuman creation accordingly, while recognizing the unique degree of power over the rest of creation that human beings wield in modern times. However, it should be noticed that it sets human beings over nature just as emphatically as Italian humanism and Baconianism did. In that sense it shares the early modern period's concentration on the vertical relationship of 'superior' humanity to 'inferior' nature at the expense of the horizontal relationship of human beings to their fellow creatures.

In the recent Christian revival of the notion of stewardship, it seems to be a rather flexible term. It is, for example, employed on all sides of the debate about biotechnology. For some deeply involved in developments in genetic science and technology, such as Francis Collins, Director of the Human Genome Project, Donald Munro, and V. Elving Anderson, stewardship seems to be the Christian justification for an uninhibitedly Baconian project (Noble 1999: 194–200). On the other hand, in the recent *Evangelical Declaration on the Care of Creation* (Berry 2000: 18–22), the role of human stewards is portrayed not as improving nature but as preserving and protecting it. The stress therefore comes close to Lawrence Osborn's (1993) preferred image of 'guardians' of creation, Loren Wilkinson's (1980a) 'earthkeeping', or even Andrew Linzey's (1994) 'servants' of creation. Here the emphasis is more on the givenness of the created order than on human intervention to change nature. It is not that nature needs human protection from its own destructiveness, but that it needs protection and healing from human abuse of it. Stewardship has acquired a chastened and humbled aim by comparison with the technological confidence expressed in the seventeenth century. But because, for others, it retains precisely its original force, the idea of stewardship without definition of its relationship to other biblical and Christian themes may not be very helpful.

One problem with the concept of stewardship today may be highlighted by the now widespread agreement that we urgently need to protect wilderness, insofar as any part of nature still remains so. Wilderness can survive only if humans protect it from human interference. But, unlike nature farmed and modified by humans, the value of wilderness is wholly independent of any human part in it. Protecting the last great wildernesses – Antarctica and the depths of the oceans, not to mention the moon – is a serious challenge humans have hardly ever faced before in history. Until recently wildernesses were just always there, feared by most but loved by the remarkable few, the hermits and the monks, who chose to live with wild nature. The question now is whether we can learn to care without interfering, simply to keep away and to keep our hands off, not so that we still have wildernesses to visit as eco-friendly tourists, but actually because God's other creatures have their own value for God and for themselves, quite independently of us. For this purpose it may be that the image of stewardship is still too freighted with the baggage of the modern project of technological domination of nature. Can we entirely free it of the implication that nature is always better off when managed by us, that nature needs our benevolent intrusions, that it is our job to turn the whole world into a well-tended garden inhabited by well-cared-for pets? The problem is in part that stewardship remains, like most interpretations of the Genesis dominion, an image that depicts the human relationship to the rest of creation in an entirely vertical way. It sets humans above the rest of creation, sharply differentiated from it, in God-given charge of it. Stewardship needs to be supplemented by the mediaeval Christian awareness – vividly expressed in many of the stories of saints and animals and never more fully realized than by Francis of Assisi – of mutuality, interdependence, friendliness and confraternity between human beings and other creatures of God.

Dominion in biblical context

Our historical study brings us into substantial agreement with Wybrow's conclusion: '[T]he modern idea of mastery was, from its inception, expressed in Biblical language. And . . . the correct conclusion to be drawn from this fact is, not that the Bible taught modern mastery, but that the language of the Bible was adopted in order to legitimate ideas of human dominion which were not themselves Biblical in origin or spirit' (Wybrow 1991: 163). To a large extent the problem has been that Gen. 1.28 and a few other texts have been interpreted without the aid of their larger biblical context but influenced by ideas drawn from other sources and traditions. We conclude therefore by placing the idea of human dominion in its biblical context, indicating the ways in which it is interpreted by other biblical texts and also that it is only one of at least two other major themes by which the Bible understands the human relationship to nature. These other themes need to be restored to their proper place alongside the theme of dominion, and this will be easier to do when we have also explored the interpretations and limitations that the Bible itself places on the dominion.

1. Human dominion in creation (Gen. 1.26–28; Pss. 8.6–8; 115.16)

There is little disagreement on the fundamental meaning: by virtue of their creation in the divine image, humans represent within creation God's rule over his creation. To object that any such ascription to humanity of a special status and role within creation is unacceptably anthropocentric, as some environmentalists do, is unrealistic. Factually humans do have unique power to affect most of the rest of creation on this planet. We cannot but exercise it, even if we do so by restraining our use of it. We cannot but affect other creatures, even if we do so by sparing them the harm we could do them. What the Genesis mandate does is to recognize this power and to situate it within a framework of God's creative intention, so that humans exercise it responsibly.

That the rest of creation was made for the use and benefit of humans is not the point or the presupposition of the dominion. The Genesis creation narrative is not anthropocentric, but theocentric. The goal of God's creative work is not the creation of humanity on the sixth day, but God's Sabbath rest (Gen. 2.1–3). Creation exists for God's glory. Moreover, the image of rule does not imply that the subjects exist for the use and benefit of the ruler. The Bible is consistently critical of exploitative despotism. If the dominion is a sacred trust in which God delegates some aspect of God's own rule over creation, then it is of course the Bible's portrayal of God's rule that should be the model for humanity's. God's rule is undoubtedly for the good of all God's creatures. 'The LORD is good to all, and his compassion is over all that he has made' (Ps. 145.9); God saves 'humans and animals alike' (Ps. 36.6). God's rule is God's compassionate and salvific care for all creatures.

However, because the model of God's rule has proved so dangerous in the history of the reading of Gen. 1.28, tempting humans to put themselves in a purely vertical relationship to the rest of creation, transcendent over the world on the model of God's creative and sovereign transcendence, it is wise also to consider the only kind of human rule over other humans that the Old Testament approves. Deuteronomy interprets the kingship it allows Israel in a way designed to subvert all ordinary notions of rule (17.14–20). If Israel must have a king, then the king must be a brother. He is a brother set over his brothers and sisters, but still a brother, and forbidden any of the ways in which rulers exalt themselves over and entrench their power over their subjects. His rule becomes tyranny the moment he forgets that the horizontal relationship of brother/sisterhood is primary, and kingship secondary. In the case of the Genesis dominion, the horizontal relationship is that of fellow creatures. It is worth observing that, in the careful schema of the six days of creation, humanity is created on the same day as the other land animals (Gen. 1:24–31). Even though in other respects the creation of humans is distinguished, in this respect humans are classified firmly within the scheme of created animals. The dominion is therefore best understood as authority within creation, not over it. The cure for the hubris, that has so often in the modern period distorted the human dominion into tyranny and destruction, is a recovery of the biblical understanding of creation and the sense of creaturely limits and restraints that comes with a recognition that everything human, not excluding the special human role and responsibility in relation to other creatures, is creaturely. The aspiration to divinity, the dream of liberation from created limits, the illusion of unlimited freedom like God's, still perpetuated both in theological talk of co-creation with God and in biotechnological utopianism, has proved disastrous for both humanity and the rest of creation. Creation in the image of God both assigns a certain likeness to God and at the same time makes clear that this is precisely a likeness in created form. It no more makes humanity divine than the likeness of a painted portrait to its human subject makes the painting human.

Reading Gen. 1.28 in its context within Genesis itself provides interpretation of the human dominion; it is illustrated by Adam's role of serving and preserving the garden (Gen. 2.15, where the Hebrew verbs usually translated 'till' and 'keep' could also be translated 'serve' and 'preserve') and by Noah's conservation of all species (Gen. 6–8). The paradox of identifying rule (Gen. 1.28) and service (Gen. 2.15) can be justified even by an Old Testament understanding of kingship (1 Kgs 12.7), and even more so by the New Testament representation of the divine lordship as service and authority in God's kingdom as service. The same paradox informs the beatitude: 'the meek will inherit the earth' (Mt. 5.5). Not those who aspire to mastery and control, but those who take their human place in creation, with respect for other creatures and recognition of fellow-creatureliness in relation to the one Creator, can legitimately exercise the dominion.

Another aspect of the way the Genesis dominion is interpreted by other material in its canonical context is the limits that legislation in the Torah clearly sets to the exercise of dominion (Exod. 20.10; 23.11; Lev. 25.4; Deut. 5.14; 25.4). The sabbatical laws restrain the use of nature for human benefit, recognizing, of course, that humans, like all animals, must make use of their environment in order to live, but denying that the peculiar human power to exploit the environment excessively should in fact be used in this way. In other words, the dominion is exercised as much in restraint as in use. The periodical allowance of freedom from human interference to wild nature, even within the sphere of Israelite farming (Exod. 23.11; Lev. 25.4), is a kind of symbol of respect for wilderness, reminding both ancient Israel and later readers of Scripture that dominion includes letting nature be itself. Even more of a dissuasive to exaggeration and overinterpretation of the Genesis dominion is God's speech to Job in Job 38–39, which so graphically and incisively draws Job's attention to the creatures over which he plainly does not exercise dominion. The point is precisely that he has no bearing on the value and purpose of their existence for their own sake and for God's sake. The lesson is to teach Job his place as one creature among others (McKibben 1994: 35–42). That lesson is taught by other biblical themes too (see below), but I mention Job at this point because the lack precisely of human dominion is there so clearly implied (especially 39.9–12).

Even with all these forms of input from other parts of Scripture, we have not yet fully put dominion in its place. The vertical relationship in which dominion places humans to the rest of creation on earth is biblically understood only in the closest connection with the horizontal relationship of humans to other creatures. But the latter comes into its own without reference to hierarchical relationship at all, in two other major biblical themes that are as important as that of dominion in defining the place of humanity in creation.

2. Humanity within the community of creation

The Bible fully recognizes the extent to which nature is a living whole to which human beings along with other creatures belong, sharing the earth with other creatures of God, participating for good or ill in the interconnectedness of the whole. In Gen. 9.8–17, the covenant God makes after the flood is not only with Noah and his descendants but also with every living creature; it is for the sake of them all that God promises that there will never be another universal deluge. Psalm 104 treats humans (v. 23) simply as one of the many kinds of living creatures for whom God provides. It depicts the world as a shared home for the many kinds of living creatures, each with its God-given place. In passages which state that God provides for all living creatures (Ps. 147.9, 14–16; Job 38.19–41; Mt. 6.26) there is the implication that the resources of the earth are sufficient for all, provided they live within created limits. When Jesus compares humanity with the birds and wild flowers (Mt. 6.25–34), the effect is to discourage the excessive desires and unrestrained consumption by humans that are presently destroying the earth as a habitat for all creatures.

3. The praise of God by all creation

Most important among the ways of placing us among rather than over the creatures is the creation's worship of God, portrayed in the Psalms (e.g. Pss. 19.1–3; 97.6; 98.7–9; and especially 148) and, with christological and eschatological character, in the New Testament (Phil. 2.10; Rev. 5.13) (Fretheim 1987; Bauckham 2002b). All creatures, animate and inanimate, worship God. This is not, as modern biblical interpreters so readily suppose, merely a poetic fancy or some kind of primitive animism. The creation worships God just by being itself, as God made it, existing for God's glory. Only humans desist from worshipping God; other creatures,

48

without having to think about it, worship God all the time. There is no indication in the Bible of the notion that the other creatures need us to voice their praise for them. This idea, that we are called to act as priests to nature, mediating, as it were, between nature and God, is quite often found in recent Christian writing, but it intrudes our inveterate sense of superiority exactly where the Bible will not allow it (Northcott 1996: 131–34). If creation needs priests, they are the four living creatures around God's throne (Rev. 4: 6–8), only one of which has a human face, acting as our representative worshipper in heaven, whereas the others represent the animal creation with no need of human help. If anything, we should think of the rest of creation assisting our worship (in Ps. 148, the human praise follows the worship by all other creatures, from the angels downwards). But the key point is that implicit in these depictions of the worship of creation is the intrinsic value of all creatures, in the theocentric sense of the value given them by their Creator and offered back to God in praise. In this context, our place is beside our fellow creatures as fellow worshippers. In the praise in which we gratefully confess ourselves creatures of God, there is no place for hierarchy. Creatureliness levels us all before the otherness of the Creator. Christians in the pre-modern period were probably more aware of this, because they more often consciously placed their own praise of God in the context of all creation's worship.

Notes

1. The word *nature* is problematic for a number of reasons, not least because, as generally used, it seems to presuppose that humans are not part of nature (Bauckham 1986).
2. Jürgen Moltmann (1985a: 26–27; 1999: 98–99) sees the fundamental problem as a one-sided emphasis, in nominalism and the Renaissance, on God's absolute power. Human beings as the image of such a God are therefore bound to strive for power and sovereignty over the world. However, if this concept of God were, as Moltmann argues (as an alternative to Lynn White's thesis), the source of the modern project to subjugate nature, why did the latter not arise in Islamic societies? The problem posed for Christian theology by the Renaissance and the modern culture derived from it is not only a matter of getting the understanding of God right, but also of conceiving human likeness to God in a properly creaturely way, such that human self-understanding is formed by contrast as well as resemblance to God.
3. Probably Leiss (1972: ch. 4) is the nearest we yet have to this, though he admits it is no more than a 'fragmental biography of the idea'. The

main concern of Leiss's book is the way in which the domination of nature developed the domination of other humans as a corollary.

4. See Passmore (1974: 28–31). Attfield (1983: ch. 3) argues against Passmore and claims to offer evidence for a strong tradition of stewardship through the patristic and mediaeval periods. But his definition of stewardship seems to me unhelpfully vague, and the fact that he can apparently include even Francis Bacon within a stewardship tradition seems to undermine his case considerably. Calvin's use of the image of stewardship for the way humans should treat all their possessions (quoted in Osborn 1993: 141–42) does not imply the inherent value of these things and does not contradict his belief that God created all things for human use and benefit; it merely limits the individual's use of what God intended for the benefit of all people.

Chapter 3

A Theology for the Earth

Joseph Sittler

Joseph Sittler (1904–87) was a Lutheran pastor who became Professor of Systematic Theology in the Chicago Lutheran Seminary. He was an environmental prophet ahead of his time, a forerunner of the many theologians who have mapped what he pioneered alone. In an anthology of Sittler's writings Evocations of Grace *(Bouma-Prediger & Bakken, 2000), Bakken (p. 18) comments, 'Sittler's loose and allusive style sometimes makes it difficult to determine exactly what he thought or meant by a particular word, phrase or sentence'. This is surely one of the reasons why Sittler has not received the honour due to him for his cries from the wilderness about the misdirections of what he calls 'neo-orthodox theology'. This paper originally appeared in a longer form in* The Christian Scholar *in 1954. In his introduction, Sittler wrote, 'I propose to set down as clearly as I can the substance of what I have missed in the contemporary discussions [on the relationship of Christianity to "culture"]; and to make an effort to articulate a vague but general discontent'.*

As a teacher of Christian theology, I have felt a deepening uneasiness about that tendency in biblical theology, generally known as neo-orthodoxy, whereby the promises, imperatives and dynamics of the Gospel are declared in sharp and calculated disengagement from the stuff of earthly life. And alongside neo-orthodoxy's almost proud repudiation of the earth and the feeling of some profound biblical promise distorted thereby, has gone another feeling that earth – because given of God, capable in spite of all of becoming the cradle in which Christ is laid – is a transparency for the Holy. There is a meaning in the nonhuman world of nature: reason asserts it and all great art bears it witness. When Cézanne paints a barrel of apples, he shows it bathed with a light, which is more like a luminous nimbus than even the softest light of autumn sun. And when Willy Loman in Arthur Miller's play, *Death of a Salesman*, digs and manures and cares for a pathetic patch of sooty earth beside the door of his house in the Bronx, he is seeking for some green and fertile token of meaning in stubborn nature – something that will speak back to the brittle and sterile perdition of his soul. When theology does not acknowledge and soberly come to terms with the covert significance of the natural, the world of nature is not silenced. 'Nature is never spent;' cries Gerard Manley Hopkins in a famous poem.

'There lives the dearest freshness deep down things; ... The world is charged with the grandeur of God. It will flame out, like shining from shook foil!'

When Christian orthodoxy refuses to articulate a theology for earth, the clamant hurt of God's ancient creation is not thereby silenced. Earth's voices, recollective of her lost grace and her destined redemption, will speak through one or another form of naturalism. If the Church will not have a theology for nature, then irresponsible but sensitive men will act as midwives for nature's un-silence-able meaningfulness, and enunciate a theology for nature. For earth, not man's mother – which is a pagan notion – but, as St. Francis profoundly surmised, man's sister, sharer of his sorrow and scene and partial substance of his joys, unquenchably sings out her violated wholeness, and in groaning and travailing awaits with man the restoration of all things.

This theme – perilous if pursued outside Christian faith – when pursued within the context of the faith makes a man sensitive and restless under flashes of insight, which have arisen within the uttered experience of our common life. While I cannot at the moment aspire to shape the systematic structure of Christian meaning out of these insights, I know that I shall as a son of earth know no rest until I have seen how they too can be gathered up into a deeper and fuller understanding of my faith. For these earthly pro-testations of earth's broken but insistent meaning have about them the shine of the holy, and a certain 'theological guilt' pursues the mind that impatiently rejects them.

The inner pattern of this theological guilt is suggested by analogy with a young English poet of the early nineteenth century. In passionate pursuit of a proper poetic idiom for the communication of the crowding and impetuous stuff of his perceptions and feelings, the young John Keats played experimentally on the massive organ of his mighty predecessor, John Milton. He tried desperately to shape the inflammable stuff of his abounding genius to the grave and solemn covalences of the older man. The opening lines of *Hyperion* are an instance of how successfully he actually did contrive to make his muse speak Miltonically. But the poem is unfinished because Keats came gradually to know that what was natural to Milton was false to Keats! – that the sonorous measures of the elder poet were alien to the incandescent lyricism of his own inspiration. His moment of liberation and return is marked by the line, 'The poetry of earth is never dead ...' (from *On the Grasshopper*).

There are, by and large, two ways by which man has sought to do justice to the realm of meaning in the natural world; two forms of relationship by which he has sought to come to terms with what he cannot silence.

First, nature can be subsumed under man. Materially, she is reduced to a resource for his needs; spiritually she is envisioned as only an unreplying theatre for his proud and pathetic life. Nature, that is to say, is divested of her own and proper life and is invested with the goods, the values, and the ends of man. Her life, infinite in richness and variety, is made a symbolic companion of man's life; and all the moods and shadows, the pride and the pathos, the ambiguity and the sudden delight of man's life is read in her mobile face.

Another effort exists alongside of this one and is its exact opposite: man is subsumed under nature. This relationship gains in persuasiveness when man's spiritual powers, confused by their own perplexities, are conjoined with a fresh mastery of natural forces to serve his clamant lusts. In such a case man abdicates and celebrates his shameful abdication by perverse delight in that which overcomes him. Neither of these ways is adequate, and man knows it. For neither one does justice either to the amplitude and glory of man's spirit or to the felt meaningfulness of the world of nature. Christian theology, obedient to the biblical account of nature, has asserted a third possible relationship: that man ought properly stand alongside nature as her cherishing brother, for she too is God's creation and bears God's image.

When, for instance, one reads the 104th Psalm, one becomes conscious that this Psalm speaks of the relationship between man and nature in a quite new way. The poetical naiveté of the images must not blind us to the majestic assertions of the song. In this Psalm nothing in the world of man and nothing in the world of nature is either independent or capable of solitary significance. Every upward-arching phenomenon, every smallest thing, is derived from the fountain of life. Light is a garment the deity wears and the heavens a curtain for his dwelling. The heavy voice of the thunder is his rebuke; the springs are his largesse to every beast of the field. The trees and the birds, the grass and the cattle, the plump vine and wine that gladdens the heart of man are all bound together in a bundle of grace.

Yet this mighty structure of process and vitality, this complex of given creatureliness in which 'the sun knows its time for setting' – all hangs by a slender thread. Natural and mortal life are incandescent with meaning because of their mutual dependence upon the will of the ultimate and Holy one. The Psalm (vv. 27–30) says,

These all look to thee,
to give them their food in due season.
When thou givest to them, they gather it up;
when thou openest thy hand, they are filled with good things.
When thou hidest thy face, they are dismayed;
when thou takest away their breath,
they die and return to their dust.
When thou sendest forth thy Spirit, they are created;
and thou renewest the face of the ground.

53

Here is a holy naturalism, a matrix of grace in which all things derive significance from their origin, and all things find fulfilment in praise. Man and nature live out their distinct but related lives in a complex that recalls the divine intention as that intention is symbolically related on the first page of the Bible. Man is placed, you will recall, in the garden of earth. This garden he is to tend as God's other creation—not to use as a godless warehouse or to rape as a tyrant.

Today, man is no longer related to nature in God's intended way. Nor can he from within himself find his way to the blasted garden of joy. That, fundamentally, is why he plunders what he ought to tend; why he finds in nature sardonic images of his own perversion, and at the same time cannot avert his eyes from his violated sister who is heard groaning 'in pain and travail until now' (Rom. 8.22).

One finds nowhere in the Bible that strange assertion which one hears almost everywhere else – that God is concerned to save men's souls! How richly, rather, is restoration there presented in terms of men's material involvement in the world of nature? Real blindness is given sight, real hands of helplessness are restored, real death is overcome, real legs enable a paralytic to walk. God is the undeviating materialist. 'He likes material; he invented it'. I know no soul save an embodied soul, I have no body save this one born of other bodies, and there is no such thing as a man outside the created context of other men; therefore it is written that 'God so loved the world' (John 3.16).

God—man—nature! These three are meant for each other, and restlessness will stalk our hearts and ambiguity our world until their cleavage is redeemed. What a holy depth of meaning lies waiting for our understanding in that moment portrayed on the last evening of Christ's life: 'And he took bread, and when he had given thanks he broke it and gave it to them, saying, "This is my body." ... Likewise also the wine, saying, "This cup is the new covenant in my blood"' (Luke 22.19–20; 1 Cor. 11.23b–25).

Here in one huge symbol are God and man and nature together. Bread and wine, the common earthy stuff of our life when we have it, and of death when we've lost it. Both in the hands of the restoring God-man!

The problem of material is not a material problem, for man is in it, and he complicates every problem. The problem of enough to eat is not ultimately an economic problem. For as man confronts the marvellous richness of the earth he can use these riches or abuse them. Which of these he chooses is a matter not soluble by mere planning. For there will never be enough for both love and lust.

The largest, most insistent, and most delicate task awaiting Christian theology is to articulate such a theology for nature as shall do justice to the vitalities of earth and hence correct a current theological naturalism which succeeds in speaking meaningfully of earth only at the cost of repudiating specifically Christian categories. Christian theology cannot advance this work along the line of an orthodoxy – neo or old – which celebrates the love of heaven in complete separation from man's loves in earth, which abstracts commitment to Christ from relevancy to those loyalties of earth that are elemental to being. Any faith in God, which shall be redemptive and regenerative in actuality, dare not be alien to the felt ambiguities of earth or remain wordless in the resounding torments of history and culture. For the earth is not merely a negative illustration of the desirability of heaven!

Such positive theological work, it seems to me, must operate with the event of the Incarnation with a depth and amplitude at least as wide and far ranging and as grand as that of the New Testament. We may not be able to go beyond Ephesians, Colossians, and the eighth chapter of Romans; but we dare not stop short of the incomparable boldness of those utterances. For here heaven and earth are held together in the incarnate Christ; here the Scriptures sink both ends of the arc of the Christ-event in ontological footings.

The Incarnation has commonly received only that light which can be reflected backward upon it from Calvary. While to be sure, these events cannot be separated without the impoverishment of the majesty of the history of redemption, it is nevertheless proper to suggest that our theological tendency to declare them only in their concerted meaning at the point of fusion tends to disqualify us to listen to the ontological-revelational overtones of the Incarnation.

> We belong to our kind,
> Are judged as we judge, for all gestures of time
> And all species of space respond in our own
> Contradictory dialect, the double talk
> Of ambiguous bodies, born like us to that
> Natural neighborhood which denial itself
> Like a friend confirms; they reflect our status,
> Temporals pleading for eternal life with
> The infinite impetus of anxious spirits,
> Finite in fact yet refusing to be real,
> Wanting our own way, unwilling to say Yes
> To the Self-So which is the same at all times,
> That Always-Opposite which is the whole subject
> Of our not-knowing, yet from no necessity
> Condescended to exist and to suffer death
> And, scorned on a scaffold, ensconced in His life
> The human household.

> (W.H. Auden, *The Age of Anxiety*)

Chapter 4

Franciscan Conservation versus Benedictine Stewardship

René Dubos

René Dubos (1901–81) was a microbiologist at Rockefeller University in New York; he produced the first commercially marketed antibiotic. He wrote widely about the relationship of humans with their environment (particularly in So Human an Animal, *1968, for which he was awarded a Pulitzer Prize), especially the need for responsible involvement. Together with the economist Barbara Ward, he wrote* Only One Earth: The Care and Maintenance of a Small Planet *(1972), which set the key for the UN Conference on the Human Environment in Stockholm, the first major international conference on the environment. This article is part of Chapter 8 of* A God Within *(1973).*

Francis of Assisi preached and practised absolute identification with nature, but even his immediate followers soon abandoned his romantic and unworldly attitude. Human life was naturally close to nature during the Stone Age, but Paleolithic hunters and Neolithic farmers altered their environment. By controlling and using fire, domesticating animals and plants, clearing forests and cultivating crops, they began the process which eventually humanized a large percentage of the earth. Every form of civilization, each in its own way, has since contributed to the shaping of the earth's surface and thus altered the composition of the atmosphere and the waters. Even persons who thought they were returning to the ways of nature usually transformed their environment more than they knew. 'Sometimes as I drift idly along Walden Pond, I cease to live and I begin to be', Thoreau wrote in his *Journal*. But he used a canoe to drift on the pond and he cleared an area along its shore to grow beans and construct his cabin.

Thus, human life inevitably implies changes in nature. Indeed, man shapes his humanness in the very process of interacting constructively with the world around him and moulding nature to make it better suited to his needs, wishes and aspirations. Stonehenge, Angkor Wat, the Parthenon, the Buddhist temples, and the countless other places of worship created by man before the Judeo-Christian era represent forms of human intervention which exacted as large a toll from nature as did the construction of the

Judeo-Christian shrines or the immense American bridges and industrial plants.

Christianity acknowledged early that human beings differ in their spiritual needs and aspirations; each of its important saints symbolizes a different approach to the human problem. Influentially, Lynn White suggested that Saint Francis's example can help humankind to achieve an harmonious equality with the rest of creation, as if animals, plants, and even inanimate objects were really our brothers and sisters. This doctrine is not quite congenial to me, because I like gardening and landscaping and therefore tend to impose my own sense of order upon natural processes.

Benedict of Nursia, who was certainly as good a Christian as Francis of Assisi, can be regarded as a patron saint of those who believe that true conservation means not only protecting nature against human misbehaviour but also developing human activities which favour a creative, harmonious relationship between man and nature.

When Saint Benedict established his monastery on Monte Cassino during the sixth century, his primary concern was that he and his followers should devote their lives to divine worship. However, he knew the dangers of physical idleness and made it a rule that all monks should work with their hands in the fields and in shops. As a result, the Benedictine monks achieved an intimate relationship with the world around them. One of the still dominant aspects of the Benedictine rule is that to labour is to pray. Saint Benedict had not intended his monks to become scholars. But in the course of time a great tradition of learning and of artistic skills progressively developed in the Benedictine abbeys, along with the continuation of some physical work.

Lynn White, the very historian who advocated that ecologists take Saint Francis as their patron saint, has also emphasized the social importance of the fact that 'the Benedictine monk was the first scholar to get dirt under his fingernails' (White 1968: 65). For the first time in the history of human institutions, the Benedictine abbey created a way of life in which practical and theoretical skills could be embodied in the same person. This new atmosphere proved of enormous importance for the development of European technology and science. The Benedictine abbeys did not immediately launch into scientific investigations, but by encouraging the combination of physical and intellectual work they destroyed the old artificial barrier between the empirical and the speculative, the manual and the liberal arts. This created an atmosphere favourable for the development of knowledge based on experimentation.

The first chapter of Genesis speaks of man's dominion over nature. The Benedictine rule in contrast seems inspired rather from the second chapter, in which the good Lord placed man in the Garden of Eden not as a master but rather in a spirit of stewardship. Throughout the history of the Benedictine order, its monks have actively intervened in nature as farmers, builders and scholars. They have brought about profound transformations of soil, water, fauna and flora, but in such a manner that their management of nature has proved compatible in most cases with the maintenance of environmental quality. To this extent, Saint Benedict is much more relevant than Saint Francis to human life in the modern world, and to the human condition in general.

All types of Benedictine monasteries were involved in technological activities. The monks developed wind and water mills as sources of power on their holdings. This power was used for the conversion of their agricultural products into manufactured goods – leather, fabrics, paper, and even liqueurs such as Benedictine and Chartreuse, which achieved worldwide fame. These mediaeval monasteries prepared the ground for the technological era in Europe.

When practised in the true spirit of the Benedictine rule, monastic life helped the monks to establish close contact with the natural world through daily and seasonal rituals and work which were coordinated with cosmic rhythms. The Benedictine rule also inspired a type of communal organization which was both democratic and hierarchic, because each monk or nun had rights in the monastic organization but also had to accept a certain place in the social order. This complex social structure found its expression in an architectural style beautifully adapted to the rituals of monastic life and to the local landscape. Benedictine architecture, in its several variant forms, thus achieved a functional beauty which made it a major artistic achievement of Western civilization.

Many human interventions into natural systems have been destructive. Technological man in particular uses landscapes and water, mountains and estuaries, and all types of natural resources for selfish and short-range economic benefits. But his behaviour in this regard is not much worse than that of the people whose activities caused erosion in West Pakistan, in the Mediterranean basin, in China, or in Mexico. The solution to the environmental crisis will not be found in a retreat from the Judeo-Christian tradition or from technological civilization. Rather it will require a new definition of progress, based on better knowledge of nature and on a willingness to change our ways of life accordingly. We must learn to recognize the limitations and potentialities of each particular area of the earth, so that we can manipulate it creatively, thereby enhancing present and future human life.

Conservation, according to Aldo Leopold, teaches what a land can and ought to be. Although this aphorism has much appeal, it is misleading because it implies a questionable philosophy of ecological determinism and of man's relation to nature. It assumes that some invisible hand is guiding biological processes to the one perfect state of ecological harmony among the different components of a particular environment, whereas experience shows that different satisfactory ecosystems can be created out of the same set of environmental conditions. The aphorism seems to suggest, more-over, that man should not interfere with the natural course of ecological events, a view which does not square with the existence all over the world of successful parks, gardens, agricultural fields and managed forests.

Francis of Assisi's loving and contemplative reverence in the face of nature survives today in the awareness of man's kinship to all other living things and in the conservation movement. But reverence is not enough, because man has never been a passive witness of nature. He changes the environment by his very presence and his only options in his dealings with the earth are to be destructive or constructive. To be creative, man must relate to nature with his senses as much as with his common sense, with his heart as much as with knowledge. He must read the book of external nature and the book of his own nature, to discern the common patterns and harmonies.

Part II
Criticisms and Exposition

Chapter 5

Stewardship: A Case Study in Environmental Ethics

Clare Palmer

Dr Palmer is a distinguished environmental ethicist, President of the International Society of Environmental Ethics and Founding Editor of the journal Worldviews: Environment, Culture, Religion. *She is a graduate of Oxford University and currently teaches at Washington University in St. Louis. The essay reprinted here was first published in* The Earth Beneath *(SPCK, 1992); it is one of the harshest published criticisms of the commonly understood understanding of stewardship. The ideas expressed in it are discussed by several of the other contributors in this volume, most explicitly by Robin Attfield (pp. 76–91).*

There is no doubt that over the last couple of decades awareness of environmental problems has been growing worldwide. Correspondingly, there has been the recognition that, for those of us in the industrialized West at least, a different language is needed with which to speak about the place of humanity in the natural world.

The search for this new language and conceptuality is difficult and complex, yet fundamental to the way in which humans act in the world. One particular danger of such a search is the tendency to latch on to already existing, familiar concepts, which seem at first glance to solve the problem. In fact, these terms may act as blinkers which block out deeper consideration of the question at issue.

It is this, which I am suggesting has happened with the widespread adoption of 'stewardship' to express the relation of humans with the rest of the natural world. The description of humans as 'stewards' of nature recurs throughout both secular and religious discussion about the environment. Chris Patten MP, when Secretary of State for the Environment, commented in an interview in *The Guardian* (5 February, 1990: 'It's not just a case of bolting on concern for the environment just because it's the flavour of the month or the year. It's a matter of trying to change fairly fundamentally the way you look at things.' What is his proposition for change? He goes on to say, 'I actually think that the best moral case for a pro-active environmental policy is trusteeship and stewardship.' [And see this volume pp. 199–207.]

This view is found even more widely among Christian writers. Pope John Paul II spoke of human 'stewardship over nature' in 1985. The Church of England General Synod in July 1990 called for a statement on 'Christian stewardship in relation to the whole of creation to engage in a critical view of human responsibility to the living environment'. For many, both Christian and non-Christian, stewardship, it seems, has solved the problem of re-examining the way in which humans relate to the rest of the natural world. I want to suggest that this is not the case, and that the use of stewardship can represent an easy retreat to a comfortable concept, which avoids coming to terms with deeper philosophical and theological issues inextricably interwoven with the environmental crisis.

Before embarking on this examination, I would like to add several caveats. I am not intending to suggest that the use of the term 'stewardship' is homogeneous. Clearly, stewardship can mean different things in different circumstances, the most obvious difference being between religious and secular discourse. It may be used with an unspoken biblical, historical or practical association, or even so generally that it has none of these. I want to consider some of the most important associations, which lie behind the concept of stewardship (an investigation that, unfortunately, cannot hope to be exhaustive). I do not intend to suggest by this that stewardship could not be used without intending these associations, or that its use has never been positive. I do wish to suggest that it is inadequate, and that the context from which it arises is an inappropriate one when considering the place of humanity in the natural world at the present time.

The concept of stewardship in the Old and New Testaments

The concept of human stewardship of nature is frequently assumed to have a biblical foundation, and thus to carry particular authority. However, that this is so is by no means certain. When looking at stewardship in biblical writings, there are three areas which need to be considered: first, the use of the term *steward*; second, whether an attitude which might be described as stewardship of nature is advocated or displayed; and third, if this is the case, whether it is found universally throughout the Bible.

In the Old Testament, the term, translated *steward*, usually refers to 'the man over the house', with responsibility to the master for the affairs of the household and his possessions, such as in Dan. 1.11. This is frequently also the meaning in the New Testament, but of particular significance here are the stewards in three of Jesus' parables. It is from these that the concept of stewardship is usually deduced. These parables contain three elements – the master, the steward, and the master's possessions or household, for which the steward is responsible. The focus is upon the relationship of the master to the steward. The 'possession' or 'household' of the master is not important in itself, but only inasmuch as the steward must obey and be faithful to the master with respect to it. It is important to notice that nowhere in the Bible is humanity actually described as a steward of the natural world. In this, more precise sense, there is no 'biblical concept of stewardship of nature'.

Considered in a broader sense there are occasions where humanity's position in nature could be described as a kind of stewardship. In Genesis 2, for instance, Adam is told to dress and keep the garden. The idea of Adam tending the natural world as a garden sounds like stewardship, inasmuch as he is responsible for its welfare and fertility. Yet, on closer inspection, it must be said that Adam is, in this story, a rather singular gardener. The contents of the garden seem to have been chosen for the gardener's pleasure; and the animals created solely to keep him company. This elevates humans to a position where steward seems a rather inappropriate expression.

Even if Genesis 2 is accepted as portraying humans as stewards of nature, there are many other places where stewardship would be an inappropriate expression. One significant passage concerning humanity's relationship with nature may be found in Job 38–41, God's reply to Job out of the whirlwind. Here, God is 'watering a land where no man lives, a desert with no-one in it'. God is directly involved with the land and has no gardener. Humanity is irrelevant. Its position is neither to have dominion over the land, nor to tend and dress it. The 'desolate wasteland sprouts with grass' without human aid. The animals are also completely independent of humanity: the hawk, the mountain goats, the wild ox, the leviathan; they are not made for humanity, not made to be human companions, nor even made with humans in mind. They live their own lives.

From this brief survey, several important conclusions can be drawn. There is no single attitude to the natural world in the Old and New Testaments as different perspectives and historical periods are represented. Even if we were to accept that Genesis 2, for example, put forward something we could happily call stewardship, other passages, like the one in Job, suggest a completely different perspective. There is, therefore, a danger in speaking of a 'biblical concept of stewardship of nature'; it is by no means clear that there is one, and even if there were, it would only represent one view of many displayed in biblical writing.

To return, then, to my original three points: first, the actual term 'steward' is never used in association with nature; second, there are attitudes in Genesis which have some resemblance to the idea of 'stewardship' but which do not share all its characteristics; and third, different writers demonstrate a very different understanding of humanity's position in the natural world.

This all serves to demonstrate that the associations frequently made between the idea of 'stewardship of nature' and the Bible are misplaced. Claiming a biblical pedigree for the idea is at best to oversimplify, and may be largely mistaken. It raises the question of why stewardship of nature is so popular among Christian writers, given the lack of actual biblical support for it.

Stewardship in contemporary use

Part of the explanation for the popularity of the idea of stewardship of nature may stem from the upsurge in the use of the term 'stewardship' in the 1950s and 1960s. At this time stewardship came to the forefront of the churches' campaigns for more resources, largely of money but also of time and talents. (The emphasis on talents may be due to the entirely fortuitous coincidence of translation that the unit of money, the talent, found particularly in the parable of the three servants, is rendered in English to mean something rather different.) *The Christian Century*, for instance, on 22 November 1950 claims: 'There is only one legitimate answer to the financial problem ... to ... teach our people to practice [sic] Christian stewardship.'

Stewardship campaigns took place in many churches, particularly among Methodists and Anglicans; stewardship advisors were appointed in dioceses and districts. All of these focused on the need to recognize that neither money nor time belonged to humanity, but were ultimately God's, and man was responsible to God to make the best use of them. One typical definition of stewardship of this sort is the following:

> We use the word steward in the biblical sense, as a person who has custody of someone else's resources and is responsible not only for its security and accounting, but also for its husbandry – i.e., the maximization of its growth by prudent money management (*The Masonic Tract on Charity Matters*, 1979).

The term 'stewardship' connoting the wise use of money and talents was widely accepted within many churches during the 1960s and 1970s – the time when awareness of environmental problems sharply increased. It was probably this availability of the metaphor that first led to its wide application to the natural world. It could easily be extended from money, talents and human resources, to refer to (so-called) natural resources. These also should be used wisely, treated as God's belongings, not ours; they should not be squandered. In other words, by the use of the term 'steward', the natural world is linked to money and resources. Indeed, it would be no exaggeration to say that the financial world is one of the strongest associations behind the concept of stewardship. When humans are described as stewards of the natural world, the language in which this is embedded is usually associated with money. Again and again, the idea of resources, which we must use carefully, look after as if for someone else, encourage to grow, recurs in both Christian and secular writing. The Church of England report, *Our Responsibility for the Living Environment* (1986), for example, comments:

> The Bible pictures mankind in relation to nature as a shepherd, a farm manager, or a household steward – a role which allows us to make use of resources for our needs, but does not permit us to destroy them, since they are entrusted to us for only a limited period (p. 22).

This idea is seen more strongly in a speech made by Pope John Paul II in August 1985 (quoted by McDonagh 1990: 181):

> Exploitation of the riches of nature must take place according to criteria that take into account not only the immediate needs of people, but also the needs of future generations. In this way the stewardship over nature, entrusted by God to man, will not be guided by short sightedness or selfish pursuits; rather it will take into account the fact that all created goods are directed to the good of all humanity.

Here the Pope speaks of nature as 'riches' to be 'exploited', but with a view to the future well-being of humans. Nature resembles a trust account, which must be allowed to accrue interest for future generations, rather than be selfishly spent in an orgy of present luxury.

Chris Patten MP, in a secular context, is even more explicit. In the interview already cited, he comments: 'I think being prudent about the environment has, frankly, some relationship to being prudent about money.' These are just a few examples of the common link made between stewardship of nature and of money. One could almost compare the natural world to a giant, all-embracing bank account, containing food, clothes, riches, medicines, companions, leisure facilities, landscapes, views and climate regulators! We are here to look after it, cultivate it, develop it, use it – but prudently, as we have it in trust. We must not destroy it by 'spending it all at once'.

This perception of stewardship portrays God as a rich man who has handed his riches over to humanity to use to its greatest advantage. Thus humanity is a kind of investor – intended to use the resources to the master's and its own best advantage, to make them grow. The master is thus no longer actively involved with his possessions, although there will ultimately be a reckoning when the steward has to account for the way in which he has used the finances entrusted to him. The primary emphasis is on the steward and the use of the resources, rather than on the relationship between the master and the steward.

However, as I commented earlier, stewardship can be perceived in different ways. Sometimes it is viewed in a more traditional way: the relationship between God and humanity is like that between master and servant on a feudal estate. A steward in this sense would be expected to demonstrate unquestioning obedience to his master due to his lower rank in the social hierarchy, and to demonstrate a probably equal degree of control over those beneath him. His actions could only be questioned by the master. God is the ultimate power and authority; he issues commands, and his will is absolute. The steward, humanity, is in a position of delegated power and responsibility. Here, the focus is very much on the relationship of the master and servant. The possessions of the master, in this case the rest of the natural world, appear to be in a powerless position. Owned by one, and managed by the other, they are at the lowest end of this hierarchy. It seems to me that both of these perceptions of the relationships between God, humanity and the rest of the natural world are deeply flawed, theologically, politically and ecologically.

Stewardship: a theological problem

Both the above perceptions of stewardship have great difficulty in accommodating the idea of God's action or presence in the world. God is understood to be an absentee landlord, who has put humanity in charge of his possessions. In itself, this excludes the presence of God in humanity or in the natural world: it is absurd to speak of a master 'indwelling' his steward, or his possessions. Within the framework of the model, God's action and presence in the world are largely mediated through humans. This is so of both the feudal perception, where God the master leaves man in charge of his estate, and also of the financial perception, where God, the owner of financial resources, puts them in the trust of humanity, the investor, to use for him as best it can. This separation of God from the world was one of the criticisms of Christianity brought by Lynn White in his famous article in 1967, 'The Historical Roots of our Ecologic Crisis'. White contests that in destroying native religions, with their beliefs in God or gods dwelling in the world, Christianity desacralized the natural world, and laid it open to exploitation. White's article has frequently been criticized on historical grounds. None the less, it seems likely that a theology which separates God from the natural world is less likely to respect it than one which sees God as indwelling – a pantheistic or panentheistic model.[1]

The problematic nature of this view of the nature of God is increased by the tendency of Christians to accept theological models as absolutes,

or the 'way things are'. Once stewardship is believed to constitute the God/
humanity/rest of the natural world relationship, holding a different model
alongside (such as that of God indwelling the world) becomes difficult. In
this respect also, stewardship poses yet another theological problem.

Political implications of stewardship

Although the term 'steward' has now been adopted in the West as a convenient way of expressing man's place in the natural world, its implications
are not only ecological. The feudal perception in particular has political
consequences since it is based on a power hierarchy of control and obedience. As we have already seen, God is ultimately in control, as a benign
dictator. It is against this model of the God–human relationship that many
branches of recent theology – liberation theology, feminist theology, process theology – have been reacting. These theologians argue that it is the
triumphalist models of God as sovereign and ruler, dominating the world,
that help to sustain, if not to create, the oppressive, hierarchical societies in
which we live. Feminist theologians reject the stress on the divine as
'masculine', with its accompanying characteristics of control and emotional
detachment. Liberation theologians, such as Gustavo Gutierrez and Juan
Luis Segundo, argue that God suffers, is in solidarity with the poor, lib-
erating them from the oppression in which they live. Moltmann (1985)
goes so far as to say: 'The one who knows God in the lowliness and
weakness of the dying of Christ, does not know him in the dreamed-of
exaltation and divinity of the man who seeks God, but in the humanity
which he has abandoned, rejected and despised.'

'Stewardship' sits very uneasily with these theological standpoints, which
both emerge from and address the political and social conditions in which
the majority of the world's population are forced to live. 'Stewardship'
originates from a human relationship, which has now, consciously at least,
been condemned: slavery. The political message encoded in stewardship is
one of power and oppression; of server and the served. Its popularity in the
Western world could be said to reflect the dominant positions that the rich
economies have over the struggling nations of the Third World. For those
who lead and benefit from these economies, stewardship can be used
without mounting a challenge to the status quo.

While to this extent acceptable in the West, at another level, 'stewardship' fails to correspond to political structures, which we ourselves
advocate. We no longer respect societies based on the model of the benign
dictatorship. Political values over an increasing proportion of the earth's
surface at least advocate political freedom, democracy and consultation
(even if their actions belie their words). We would not respect someone for
unquestioningly obeying the orders of a dictator, however convinced they

were that she or he was good, nor would we respect a leader that expected it. Dorothée Sölle (1978) makes this point when she says:

> How can we stand a God-talk based on the refusal of democratisation and self-determination? If God is not ready to give up his power, if he does not want us to determine our fate, we cannot trust him. He is then nothing but a somewhat liberal capitalist, and our trust in that end makes us more childish than we are. The God we are in need of is not a private owner, nor a capitalist with a human face. There is only one legitimation of power, and that is to share it.

Of course, God is not a political leader in the normal sense (for instance, elections are impossible!) but the language used to speak about him or her is important. If slaves of God, then being slaves of a 'representative on earth' is made more acceptable; if unquestioning obedience to God, then an inability to exercise independence of thought in other matters is made more likely. A model of God which engages with the political concerns with which we are surrounded must resemble democracy rather than dictatorship (Nicholls 1989).

The idea of stewardship originates in a society which is based on slavery or serfdom, and represents a despotic and autocratic form of government, a fact which is particularly clear when considering it in the feudal context. In this respect alone, the term is unsuitable for use in modern society.

The ecological implications of stewardship

Speaking of 'stewardship of the natural world' has important ecological consequences. Certain assumptions seem to lie behind or to be associated with it. Firstly, there is a strong sense of humanity's separation from the rest of the natural world. Following on from this there may be a cluster of other beliefs: that the natural world is a human resource, that humans are really in control of nature, that nature is dependent on humanity for its management.

These are, of course, complex and difficult questions. The question of how far humanity is separated from nature has been asked for thousands of years. In a very obvious, although perhaps underestimated sense, humans are entirely part of, and dependent on, the natural world. Humanity evolved within the natural world. We share part of the genetic codings of all living species, especially other mammals. We are part of the food chain; we eat and are eaten; our bodies are the hosts of bacteria, yeasts, parasites; when we die, our bodies form the parts of other living creatures. We are, as are all living things, dependent on the natural cycles of water, nitrogen, carbon dioxide. If the rains fail, as they frequently do, we starve. Yet, in an equally obvious sense, humans seem to be different from the rest of the natural world. Humans have the most developed cerebral cortex of all animals; they are more intelligent, although not unique in possessing intelligence. This enables a greater control over their environment than any other species; witness the construction of amenities to better the human condition: houses, roads, schools. To this extent, humans exercise a degree of dominance over the natural world unsurpassed by any other species.

It would be foolish to claim that humans are not the dominant species at present existing on this planet. However, this is not evidence that humanity has been in some theological or even philosophical sense 'set apart' as manager or governor, God's representative on earth. Humans have evolved with unique characteristics, as have all species, and this difference has enabled them to move to a position of control. But if, for instance, there was abrupt climatic change, humanity could easily become extinct, while other species, better equipped for such an event, could gain the ascendancy. In the light of evolution, the idea of human metaphysical 'set-apartness' becomes impossible to justify. However, the concept of stewardship continues to support this set-apartness.

The other ecological beliefs which cluster around stewardship are of a similar nature. The contention that man is needed to look after the earth stems from a pre-evolutionary understanding of nature. It is perhaps influenced by the idea that nature is 'fallen' and imperfect. In the light of evolutionary science, the idea that the earth 'needs to be managed' by humans is obviously a nonsense, although still maintained by some theologians. The earth existed for millions of years without humanity, life flourished, evolution continued. If humanity should become extinct, as all species ultimately seem to do, then life on earth will continue to flourish, as it went on after the dinosaurs and after the dodo. There are parts of the earth where humans have never seriously lingered (although perhaps will do): the heart of Antarctica, the inner rainforests. These are not 'managed' or 'stewarded', and they do not lack anything. Stewardship is inappropriate for some of the planet some of the time, some of it for all of the time (the deep oceans) and all of it for some of the time – that is, before humanity evolved and after its extinction.

The work of the scientist James Lovelock (1979), although by no means unanimously accepted among the scientific establishment, brings a new dimension to this insight. He considers that the planet acts as one huge, self-regulating organism, keeping the atmosphere and temperature of the planet capable of sustaining life. He points out that, for instance, solar energy has increased by 25% in the time that life has existed on the planet, yet the temperature has never increased or fallen by more than five degrees. The crucial regulatory organisms, he argues, are the tropical rainforests and the algae growths of the deep oceans. It is these which act to control the conditions of the planet, and it is these which are most important to the continuance of life on earth. Seen from this perspective, humanity is no manager, nor steward; in fact its position is less central to life than that of many other organisms – which, at present, humans are intent on destroying.

It is this very destruction that brings me to question another, associated belief: that man actually is ultimately in control of the natural world – or, to phrase it another way, that man is able to be a steward. To be a successful steward, either in the feudal or the financial sense, it is necessary to understand that which is being controlled. But the natural world is not like an estate, nor like money in this respect. It is composed of complex eco-systems and atmospheric conditions that we do not understand and cannot predict. The depth of uncertainty about global warming is one illustration of this. Scientists are neither sure that it is happening nor sure of what will happen if it is. The immunity developed by so-called pest species to poisons such as DDT is another example; malarial mosquitos cannot be eliminated by this pesticide. The greatest chemists and biologists alive are quick to point out how little we understand the natural world in which we live. Can we then be stewards of the natural world? Saying this leaves me open to the criticism that I am both asserting human helplessness and simultaneously arguing that humans bear responsibility for the preservation of the natural world; that I am both urging that humans do something, and then claiming that they are unable to do it. This is not my intention at all. I am not, as I have said, suggesting that humans are completely helpless. We may not have the regulatory effect on the world's environment of the deep sea algae, for instance, but we are capable of causing vast environmental devastation (while probably not extinction of life). I am suggesting that our control is only partial and that we must see it in the perspective of the many things we do not know and perhaps will never know. It is surely the case that when humans admit their partial knowledge they will take their responsibilities more, rather than less, seriously.

The final belief associated with stewardship of the natural world which I wish to question is perhaps the most pervasive and powerful: that the rest of the natural world is there for us to use. It is our resource. This attitude is implicit in the feudal perception of stewardship, in that the natural world is regarded as an estate, to be treated as the master chooses, but is explicit in the financial model of stewardship, which sees the rest of the natural world as it sees money.

Money is, obviously, a human invention, created by us and for us. It has no function outside human society, and is entirely a human resource. Accumulating more of it, and using it prudently, is one of the aims of Western society at least. But the natural world around us is not a human creation. It does function outside human society. It existed for millions of years before humans evolved, and, as I have said, it will exist after we have become extinct. In this fundamental respect, it is not like money. Yet the language of financial stewardship persists in treating it so.

Everything that lives must use other, living and non-living materials in order to survive. Humans, of course, must do this too. However, the model of stewardship of the natural world contains the implicit idea that this is what they are there for. The reason for the existence of minerals in the soil, trees in the forest, fish in the sea, is for the benefit of humanity. Thus Pope John Paul II could say, 'all created goods are directed to the good of humanity'. It is this idea which is the most dangerous assumption contained within the concept of stewardship. Its implications are immense. If the natural world is like a huge bank account, which we may use, however prudently, the environmental ethic that flows from this is entirely human-centred. Provided that something can be justified as benefiting humanity, or some of humanity, it is morally acceptable under a stewardship ethic.

There has been little criticism of the implications of this idea of stewardship. However, the environmental philosophers, Richard and Val Routley (1980) comment in their essay, 'Human Chauvinism and Environmental Ethics' that stewardship is

> inconsistent with a deeper environmental ethic because it implies policies of complete interference ... [stewardship] would, in fact, prefer to see the earth's land surfaces reshaped along the lines of the tame and comfortable, but ecologically impoverished European small farm and village landscape ... man's role, like that of a farm manager, is to make nature productive by his efforts, though not by means that will deliberately deplete its resources.

Cultivation of all practicable land for use is reasonable, and even desirable in terms of a stewardship ethic. The destruction of wildwood or wilderness for agriculture to feed an expanding human population would be quite acceptable. The flooding of river valleys, such as the Loire project in France, to produce hydro-electric power could be defended on a stewardship ethic. Indeed, stewardship would not only allow but actually encourage total use or cultivation of the natural world for human benefit. That nature should be productive by our standards is built into the stewardship assumption.

These assumptions, which lie behind most uses of stewardship, demonstrate that stewardship is an anthropocentric ethic, which considers it to be better not only for humans, but for the rest of the natural world, for nature to be managed and made fruitful by human standards.

Stewardship in secular political discourse

Although the concept of stewardship of the natural world originated in religious discourse, it has since been abstracted into international political discussion, usually losing its ultimate religious referent, God. This is not always the case. Margaret Thatcher commented in a speech to the United Nations made in 1989, 'We are the Lord's creatures, the trustees of life on this planet, charged with preserving life itself.' Although the word 'steward' is not used, 'trustee' has here a similar ring – a divine charge to preserve, to look after the planet. It has not yet been extracted from a religious context. However, in most political language, 'steward' is used without reference to God. This goes on to pose problems of interpretation, since steward, by its very nature, implies that someone else's possessions are being looked after. Yet if not for God, for whom could we be stewards? This question was addressed rather flippantly by the naturalist Richard Mabey (article in *The Guardian*, 7 July 1990):

> On whose behalf are we stewards of the planet? Not presumably its literal owners. God then, or Gaia? I suspect that most of us who use the word might answer 'the planet itself' which is, at best, a piece of sophistry, and at worst, a reworking of the patronising view that nature needs to be in human custody for its own good. This is asking for a warder, not a steward.

He does, however, raise an important question: is non-theistic stewardship exercised on behalf of the planet? For future generations? Or is there no particular referent at all? It has been used in all three senses, but all have problems. If humanity is the steward for the planet, or Gaia, as Mabey says, this carries the suggestions that the earth has a will, or can give commands, or has preferences as to how it develops; that the earth needs humans to manage it, and from this, that humans are separated from it. All of these are open to question.

There are fewer obvious difficulties in envisaging humanity as the steward of the earth on behalf of future generations, as encapsulated in the environmental phrase, 'we do not inherit the earth from our ancestors, we borrow it from our children'. It has the advantage that, unlike Gaia, future generations will possess wills and preferences. However, as with all models of stewardship, humanity is still separated from the rest of the natural world, and the implication still is that it needs to be managed. Further it suggests that future generations actually own the natural world.

Having said this, stewardship often seems to be used in political discourse without corresponding to a 'master'. This can mean either or both of two things. 'Steward' may become a vague term, with no real meaning, but suggesting the idea of responsible use; or 'steward' and 'master' may become telescoped into one, and when spoken of, stewardship actually means a form of mastery, in that we decide when the rest of the natural world should be used, and for what.

Stewardship of the natural world, whether Christian or otherwise, then, remains profoundly anthropocentric and un-ecological, legitimating and encouraging increased human use of the natural world.

In conclusion

I suggested at the beginning that the idea of stewardship can act as a comfortable concept blinkering us to the deeper philosophical and theological problems raised by the environmental crisis. Stewardship allows humanity to continue with exploitative attitudes towards the natural world, often with the justification that God has given this authority; it certainly softens existing attitudes of domination and triumphalism towards the rest of the natural world, by adding an element of responsibility. However, it fails to change the fundamental human centredness of the original premise. It is this concept of stewardship which allows Chris Patten MP to accept the building of a theme park on Rainham Marshes and a marina in Cardiff Bay, both wildlife reserves, in order to serve human recreational and aesthetic ends. It allows the Church of England to make the statement advocating stewardship quoted earlier, in order to avoid passing legislation to ban intensive farming and fox hunting on church-owned land. Perhaps James Lovelock (1979: 145) is right to comment:

> From a Gaian viewpoint, all attempts to rationalise [domination of the planet] with man in charge are as doomed to failure as the similar concept of benevolent colonialism. They all assume man is the possessor of this planet; if not the owner then the tenant ... All human societies in one way or another regard the world as their farm.

Note

1. However, there are also problems with pantheistic and panentheistic views, in that the natural world is revered for the spirit it contains, rather than for itself.

Chapter 6

Environmental Sensitivity and Critiques of Stewardship

Robin Attfield

Robin Attfield is Professor of Philosophy in the University of Wales at Cardiff. His book The Ethics of Environmental Concern *(first published in 1983, revised edition 1991) quickly became a classic. In this paper, Attfield critiques a range of environmental views, including those of Clare Palmer (see pp. 63–75), Matthew Fox and John Passmore. It is an amended version of Chapter 3 ('Trustees of the Planet') from his book* The Ethics of the Global Environment *(1999). It was one of the papers given at St George's House, Windsor in 2000 (see p. xi).*

An ethic of environmental sensitivity can derive support from the tradition of stewardship, which has long been central to Judaism, Christianity and Islam. This support importantly means that adherents of these major religions can uphold this ethic through appeal to their own traditions; and if so, in order to be environmentally sensitive in a consistent way, it is not necessary for believers (as is sometimes suggested) to discard their religion. These religions have usually maintained that humanity is answerable to God, both for the use and for the care of nature, rather as the steward of an estate is answerable to its owner or as trustees are answerable before the law for the goods which they hold on trust. They have also standardly maintained in consequence that our dealings with nature are subject to ethical constraints. Whatever our laws may say about property, another implication is that humans do not own the Earth, nor its lands nor its oceans, but hold or possess them on a provisional basis; hence their answerability.

However, some writers represent the role (and the model) of stewardship as objectionably anthropocentric, managerial, aloof from nature, and thus no useful guide in environmental ethics; others represent it as enlightened and heedful of nature as intrinsic value, but unrepresentative of traditional religion.

While some of these criticisms may seem far-fetched, and not all the critics can possibly be right (for they clearly contradict one another), addressing the criticisms elicits some important implications of stewardship.

I have developed views elsewhere about how best to theorize the concept of environmental sensitivity (Attfield 1983 [1991], 1999). For the present purpose, the only required assumption is that environmental sensitivity is present when independent value is recognized as present in nonhuman life or flourishing as well as in human life. This assumption, however, turns out to underpin some of the would-be criticisms of stewardship and thus ensures that stewardship will not be vindicated too easily.

Ethical and theological concerns

One of the critics of stewardship is Matthew Fox, a theologian who suggests that belief in stewardship represents God as an absentee landlord and humans as serfs, as if this belief deprived people of their freedom and spontaneity. That would be a serious defect, if true; but in fact neither tenant farmers nor trustees (who are both answerable to others, and thus analogous to the stewards of the biblical parables) are remotely as unfree or inhibited as this view suggests. Belief in stewardship does not abrogate freedom, or render the stewards serfs, or, come to that, make God an absentee landlord. Meanwhile, belief in the answerability of human individuals and their communities conveys that we are ethically unfree in one significant way – to treat the Earth just as we please; ethical limits to human transactions with nature are real and ought to be recognized. It is not these beliefs about answerability but their absence which contributes to ecological disasters.

Some related criticisms have been supplied by Clare Palmer. Her first suggestion is that the stewardship model separates God from the natural world, and makes respecting the world of nature less likely than a pantheistic model or a panentheistic (or 'immanence') model would (Palmer 1992). Pantheism holds that the world is identical with God and that God has no existence other than as the world; this view precludes belief in the world being created by God, and respect being due to fellow-creatures as God's creatures. Quite apart from being incompatible with the great theistic religions, it removes an important basis for respect for nature. Panentheism, the belief that God is present or abides (or is immanent) in the world without being identical with it, is different, as it implicitly recognizes God's transcendence, although, as Palmer recognizes, it could lead to respect being focused not on nature but on the deity within it. But in any case the assumption that the stewardship model is incompatible with the immanence model should be questioned, because the former is entirely compatible with belief in nature's independent value, a belief which has often fostered panentheism, as, for example, in the thought of Augustine (Glacken 1967: 196–202; Santmire 1985: 55–74).

Palmer's second suggestion is that if the stewardship model is held in an absolutist manner (by which I take her to mean an uncompromising manner), it is difficult to accept the immanence model. If this were so, the obvious solution would be to avoid absolutism about stewardship; for on any account it is implausible that stewardship encapsulates every facet of the relation between God, nature and humanity. But believers in stewardship need not in any case reject the belief that God indwells the world. For governments and owners (or any to whom stewards are answerable) typically live in the lands they rule or own, and so the stewardship model need not convey God's separateness; if creation is continual (rather than a past event), divine activity might in any case be expected to pervade the natural order, rather than somehow to pass it by. Nor need belief in divine immanence deter its adherents from using resources; sculptors, joiners and miners who become panentheists need not abandon their trades.

This discussion throws light on further criticisms from Fox, who declares: 'I reject the stewardship model [that God is an absentee landlord and we humans are serfs, running the garden for God]; ... We need mysticism ... God IS the garden' (Fox 1990). For while love of nature may take the form of mysticism, which is sometimes inspired by panentheist beliefs, Fox's position is clearly pantheistic, and the pantheist attempt to identify God with nature stipulates that there is no creation and no creator, and that the respect which might be due to fellow-creatures has no religious underpinning as such; any respect for natural entities has to depend on some other basis (or on nothing). Later, I shall return to the question of whether stewardship beliefs can be held by non-believers in God. But for present purposes it should be concluded that the suggestion that pantheism supplies a more adequate account of either religion or religious ethics or respect for nature than belief in creation and in stewardship is unconvincing.

Stewardship: a fuller statement

Before turning to political, economic and historical criticisms of stewardship, it is appropriate to consider a more detailed expression of such beliefs.

> We all share and depend on the same world, with its finite and often non-renewable resources. Christians believe that this world belongs to God by creation, redemption and sustenance, and that he has entrusted it to humankind, made in his image and responsible to him; we are in the position of stewards, tenants, curators, trustees or guardians, whether or not we acknowledge this responsibility. Stewardship implies caring management, not selfish exploitation; it involves a concern for both present and future as well as self, and a recognition that the world we manage has an interest in its own

78

survival and wellbeing independent of its value to us ... Good stewardship requires justice, truthfulness, sensitivity, and compassion. It has implications ... for individuals, organisations, and states (*Christians and the Environment*, 1991).

This statement from the Board for Social Responsibility of the General Synod of the Church of England involves claims that go well beyond the scope of this paper, which is not concerned with claims about redemption. However, its acceptance of the independent value of nonhuman interests is significant, cohering with the assumption about environmental sensitivity mentioned above. Of greater immediate relevance is the range of metaphors used in this statement; it shows that belief in stewardship need not cast humanity in the role of a task-master of slaves or in that of a mediaeval bailiff set over serfs, not least because the contemporary metaphors of curators and of guardians are at least equally in place as those of an ancient or mediaeval estate-manager. (Besides, by no means all ancient stewards would have had charge of slaves in any case.) The belief that the world belongs not to humanity but to God will also be seen to be particularly significant, while the whole statement shows how, in combination with other appropriate convictions, stewardship beliefs are well capable of generating not only assent but enthusiastic commitment as well.

Political criticisms

Yet the charge continues to be made that stewardship presupposes a hierarchical social order of control and obedience, symbolizing and inadvertently teaching despotism rather than democracy (Palmer 1992: 75–77). Undeniably the metaphor of stewardship in matters of resources derives from the teaching of Jesus, who deliberately drew on contemporary social life in his parables, and thus unavoidably it was influenced in its earliest use by the hierarchical social structure of the Roman Empire, as well as the more socially radical traditions of Judaism. But none of this has prevented the teaching of Jesus, nor related beliefs such as the priesthood of all believers, taking root in societies with very different forms of social order, including democratic and (sometimes) egalitarian ones. Such societies, like hierarchical ones, need to appoint officers answerable to government and specifically charged with the care of nature and the use of natural resources, and have proved able to interpret the stewardship model accordingly.

So the issue concerns not the origins of the metaphor of stewardship, but its current message: need it convey despotism or at least unrepresentative social arrangements? If so, it would clearly be ill-fitted for coping with the global environmental problems of a new millennium. But depicting humanity as in a position of trust with respect to nature does not involve understanding society or government as either undemocratic or un-representative; if anything, it commends democratic debate, so that the members of society can jointly discover or decide how to exercise their role. Certainly the best kind of exercise of stewardship would involve expertise; but this does not make the stewardship model elitist, since every human group can acquire enough expertise to perform its stewardly role, if empowered to do so – and arguably has responsibilities, where circumstances make it possible, to come by this degree of understanding. No human group can be regarded as excluded from the role of stewardship, or as entitled to deprive any other group of that role. Indeed, no relations of domination within humanity receive the least support from the stewardship model.

Trustees, however, are subordinate to the authority to which they are answerable; which, in the case of traditional stewardship beliefs, is God. Is this kind of subordination or answerability objectionable? Certainly if God is not believed to exist there would have to be some other form of answerability (see below), or else none at all. But if there is a creator, the suggestion that humans are not God's creatures and subjects cannot arise, unless being God's subject is equated with subordination to some hierarchical form of society or to some human bearer of divine authority (and here it is the supplementary beliefs about hierarchy or divine authority which need to be contested). Belief in humanity as nature's stewards, however, implies not a need for social hierarchy but answerability (as opposed to ownership) with regard to the natural world; this belief makes neither humanity nor God a despot, but teaches a salutary humility, especially to people intent on remoulding the planet solely for human benefit.

The related charge has sometimes been made that stewardship makes humanity a despot over nature. In particular, stewardship has been designated (by Palmer among others) as an 'anthropocentric ethic', capable of advocating interference with the entire surface of the planet to enhance nature's productivity (Routley and Routley 1980; Palmer 1992: 77–82). The charge of despotism is paradoxical, as the classification of traditional attitudes to nature by John Passmore contrasts despotic attitudes and stewardly ones (Passmore 1980 [1974]); yet if stewardship authorizes changing the face of the entire planet in the interests of (say) productivity, then it could justifiably be considered not only anthropocentric but despotic too, and Passmore's definitive contrast between despotism and stewardship would be annulled.

This objection is partly an economic one, and would apply by extension to secular versions of stewardship beliefs if it fitted religious ones in the first place. But it clearly does not fit any religious versions like that of the General Synod, which recognizes the independent value of the natural world, thus rejecting instrumentalism, and urges caring management as opposed to selfish exploitation. While caring management is undeniably a form of management, it is not managerialism, which implies a pre-occupation with instrumental aims and values to the exclusion of all others. Caring management also implies recognition of constraints on instrumental approaches, and concern for future needs as well as present interests, and thus, effectively, some amount of letting-be for both species and ecosystems; or, in other words, some amount of forbearance from management. Stewards and trustees need not be perpetually intervening where the good of what is in their charge would be better served by non-intervention. Peter G. Brown has argued along parallel lines that a stewardship or trusteeship conception of the role of humanity (whether religious or secular) diverges markedly from the instrument-alism of conventional discounting and conventional cost-benefit analysis (Brown 1998).

The objection is also implicitly historical, and certainly some advocates of stewardship, such as John Calvin, have held an anthropocentric view of creation.[1] Yet even Calvin held that the beasts were to be treated with respect and not misused, but nourished and cared for, being creatures of God (Thomas 1983: 154). While these beliefs recognize animals as mattering simply for the sake of the creator, they are far removed from managerialism, and are close to the view that animals matter because of what they are. Indeed other advocates of stewardship, such as John Ray, Thomas Tryon and Alexander Pope, were soon adopting a more biocentric view of nonhuman creatures (Singer 1976: 221; Thomas 1983: 155, 166–67);[2] and this supplies further strong evidence against stewardship being essentially anthropocentric. (It is not essentially non-anthropocentric either, and is still sometimes found in anthropocentric versions; otherwise the criticisms of Richard and Val Routley (1980: 113, 121–25) would not begin to be coherent. Yet the suggestion of such criticisms that it is either essentially or characteristically anthropocentric emerges more and more clearly as misguided.)

Similar lessons emerge from the tone of the seventeenth-century figure who first explicitly applied the language of stewardship to the natural world, Sir Matthew Hale. For Hale, man is God's 'Steward, . . . Bailiff, or Farmer of this goodly Farm of the lower World', the justifications of whose authority include 'to preserve the face of the Earth in beauty, usefulness and fruitfulness'. While humanity is to enjoy the fruits of nature, people are also to preserve species (and improve them), and, in addition to all this, to prevent the destruction of natural beauty (Hale, quoted by Black 1970: 56–57). There is no suggestion here that beauty is to be preserved just for the sake of humanity, and thus Hale's position seems to have been neither managerial nor anthropocentric. True, the mandate of humanity includes 'to limit the fiercer animals' rather than to respect their wild habitats. Nevertheless the charge of managerialism is off-target for Hale and his successors, let alone the charge of supporting planet-wide interference with nature in the human interest.

Stewardship can thus be defended against a range of ethical and political objections. The role of steward can even be reconciled with that of shop-steward, speaking on behalf of voiceless creatures, as James Lovelock (1991) has suggested; thus stewardship could foster attempts to represent voiceless interests, such as future generations and nonhuman creatures, in decision-making bodies and legislatures.

Stewardship in history

Implicit as the message of stewardship is in the parables of Jesus, explicit advocacy of the stewardship of possessions and resources began with Calvin in the sixteenth century, and its first direct application to animals, plants and the rest of nature can be credited to Hale in the seventeenth century. However, this does not mean that stewardship beliefs both about resources and about nature were not substantially present in the Bible and in the intervening centuries, albeit in different language; the key components of these beliefs have roots much deeper than the early modern period.

Thus in Genesis 2, Adam is told to dress and keep the garden, apparently a role both of productive use and of conservation or protection. Palmer's suggestion that the contents of the garden and the various animals are represented as created solely for the sake of the gardener conflicts both with the mandate to keep the garden (which suggests it has some kind of value of its own) and also with the other creation narrative (Genesis 1) (Palmer 1992: 70). In this narrative everything that has been created is seen by God to have been 'very good', and that not only for human purposes, since the plants are given as food to all the animals.

Elsewhere the Earth is understood as belonging to God (Psalm 24), and the land as not owned by humanity but as a leasehold (Lev. 25.23), and as held subject to ethical requirements concerning the support of the poor (Lev. 25.25–55; Deut. 15.1–11). Hence the passages about human dominion (Gen. 1.26–31; Psalm 8) have to be understood as concerning a conditional tenancy, and not unconditional domination. As Palmer stresses, passages such as Job 38–41 imply that the animals were not made for humanity, and that the wilderness is sufficient to itself and needs no gardener. Yet none of this suggests that the authors of Job would reject human responsibility with regard to the beasts (recognized elsewhere in the corpus of wisdom literature at Prov. 12.10) or for letting the wilderness remain intact for them (as intended by the Creator, according to Psalm 104). While different passages have different emphases, the various strands still form a coherent picture.

The same applies to the New Testament. The teaching of Jesus about lilies and birds (Mt. 6.26–28; Lk. 12.24, etc.) and about domestic animals (Mt. 12.11–12; Lk. 13.15–16; Lk. 14.5) presupposes their independent value and moral standing, while his parables about stewards and accountability (Mt. 21.33–41; 24.45–51; 25.14–30 and the corresponding passages in Mark and Luke) concern not only the Church, as Passmore suggests, but implicitly the use and deployment of resources too. Paul taught that terrestrial bodies of different kinds (humans, beasts, fishes, birds) have their own glory, comparable with that of celestial bodies (1 Cor. 15.39–41), and, like other New Testament writers (see, for example, Jn 1.1–14; Hebrews 1.2–3), he includes the whole created order in God's plan of salvation (Rom. 8.19–22). Granted also that Jesus and the New Testament writers took for granted Old Testament teachings about creation, the land and the natural world, Passmore's view that there is little evidence for a stewardship interpretation of early Christian teaching cannot be accepted. Stewardship is the clear message of the Old Testament, and consistent with the passages about human dominion there (Genesis 1; Psalm 8), as Eric Katz (1993) remarks, conveying also the standard interpretation adopted within Judaism, while Clarence Glacken (1967: 168) in his masterly survey of historical Christian attitudes to nature, readily interprets both testaments in this sense.

Passmore identifies as a distinct tradition the approach of cooperation with nature, in which the role of humanity is 'to perfect nature by cooperating with it', but finds few if any traces of this tradition between pagan antiquity and the German metaphysics of the romantic period (Passmore 1974: 32–34). Yet the belief that the creation was deliberately left incomplete with a view to a challenge to human creativity and to scope for human improvements to nature pervaded the early centuries of Christian thought, from the time of Lactantius in the West and Origen in the East (both living in the third century AD), and was resuscitated in the seventeenth century by writers such as John Ray, William Derham and others) (Glacken 1967: 181, 185, 423–24, 485).

Passmore is on surer ground when he writes of this and the stewardship tradition coalescing; a good example is supplied by the Benedictine monasteries, which, throughout the period from Benedict (sixth century) to Bernard of Clairvaux (twelfth century), sought to enhance both the beauty and the fertility of their lands. These Benedictine attempts to improve the land also form a constructive example of stewardship, which René Dubos has aptly characterized as a paradigm of environmental responsibility. Granted the pervasive human need to derive food and shelter from the environment, as well as to conserve it, and the impossibility of preserving much of it untouched, Benedict is, for Dubos, a fitter patron saint of environmentalism than Francis of Assisi (Dubos 1974).

Similar attitudes to the enhancement and adornment of nature, combined with strong opposition to pantheism, were held by the fourth-century founder of Orthodox monasticism, Basil the Great, and have persisted throughout succeeding centuries in the Eastern churches; his conception of humanity as partner of God in improving the Earth was popularized in the West by Ambrose, whose teaching probably influenced Benedict, among many others. This is not the place to discuss the history of attitudes to nature of the Christian centuries in further detail (a summary is given by Attfield 1994); it is already clear that the stewardship tradition, often associated with ideas of cooperative improvement of the land, has been a central approach throughout these centuries, and not just a modern development.

A further strand among Christian attitudes to wild creatures is found in a New Testament passage about the forty days spent by Jesus in the wilderness: 'and he was with the wild beasts ...' (Mk 1.13). This sojourn amongst the desert animals is symbolically significant, because of long-standing expectations that the Messiah would make peace with the beasts. What is more, because this expression of acceptance and confraternity with wild creatures concerns neither conservation nor management, it supplements the message of stewardship. Richard Bauckham (1994) writes in this connection of 'peaceable companionship' with the wild creatures, a posture which seems to have been consciously imitated by saints from St Antony (third century) to the Celtic saints, to Cuthbert (seventh century) and to Francis of Assisi (Bratton 1988). While no one has suggested that the generality of believers should also imitate Jesus in this respect, awareness of this aspect of the lives of the saints has kept alive a recognition that wild creatures deserve respect, and is likely to have been as influential as the largely anthropocentric teachings of theologians such as Aquinas and Luther. It has also served as a reminder that nature does not just consist in resources, and that stewardship is best understood in a non-anthropocentric sense. As Dubos says, 'Reverence for nature is compatible with willingness to accept responsibility for a creative stewardship of the earth' (Dubos 1974: 136).

However, confraternity, like cooperation with nature (and the corresponding theological belief in partnership with God) is not identical with stewardship, even though these positions are usually compatible. When necessary, they can be contrasted with one another, and could support different approaches to conduct. From this it emerges that stewardship is not being presented as the all-inclusive Christian view, nor as a stance that is necessarily right in all circumstances. For that approach, the rightness of stewardship would be a tautology, there would be no credible alternatives, and the notion of stewardship would have become all-inclusive. But none of these implications arise from the approach presented here.

Islam too has rediscovered ancient doctrines closely resembling the stewardship tradition of Judaism and Christianity. For Islam, the world belongs to God, and humanity is God's servant, *Khalīfah* (caliph or vice-gerent) and trustee of the Earth, accountable to God for its use and its care. The related responsibilities apply to all believers and all their activities, including all use of resources (Hassan, forthcoming). An example of this teaching consists in the provision of Islamic law for 'himas', tracts of land set aside to remain undeveloped in perpetuity, of which thousands remain to this day (Dutton 1992: 54–57). While it is sometimes held that the world was created solely for human use, Al-Hafiz Masri (1992:6) maintains that according to Islamic law the natural elements are the common property of all creatures, and not only of human beings. Thus the view is tenable that environmental problems in the Muslim world result from too ready an abandonment of Islamic insights and adoption of Western technology and beliefs about progress (Wersal 1995). It is worth adding that other non-Trinitarian theists, such as Unitarians, are equally free to endorse stewardship beliefs, and often interpret the Bible in this sense, with no less enthusiasm than Trinitarian, Jewish or Islamic theists.

Another criticism of stewardship is that stewardship is liable to ignore social justice, and might become 'reduced to a reasonable way of managing time, talent, and treasure', all in the name of the kingdom of God (Jegen 1987: 102). Certainly if stewardship is reduced to this, or to the management of natural resources simply to maximize profits, then it falls short, and this has often happened in practice. But what it falls short of is the teaching of the Bible, and also of the mediaeval church, for, as John Black (1970: 64–66) points out, the teaching of Aquinas (thirteenth century) was that property beyond a man's necessity was owed, as of right, to the poor for their sustenance. Such teaching was resuscitated and applied to the international stage by Pope Paul VI, who stated in *Populorum Progressio* (1967) that 'the superfluous wealth of rich countries should be placed at the service of poor nations ... Otherwise their continued greed will certainly call down upon them the judgment of God and the wrath of the poor ...'

In general, while social justice and stewardship comprise independent commitments, twentieth-century Christian adherents of stewardship reject versions of stewardship unrelated to justice and provision for the poor. Indeed Jegen's criticism does not condemn stewardship as such, but only reductionist versions. I have elsewhere defended early modern exponents of stewardship such as William Derham against related criticisms from William Coleman of too uncritical an endorsement of capitalist enterprise; greater selectivity on Derham's part about contemporary commerce would have been in place, but longstanding Christian condemnations of greed and self-aggrandisement were never abandoned, and well cohere with stewardship (Attfield 1994: 32–34; Coleman 1976). As with Islam, problems arise when ancient values are forgotten, rather than from remembering them.

One last charge against stewardship should be considered here, concerned as it is (in part) with history. Palmer suggests that stewardship presupposes a pre-evolutionary view of nature, and envisages humanity as set apart as God's manager on Earth (Palmer 1992: 78–79). While this point may well require a revision of the position of some anthropocentric adherents of stewardship, the view that everything was made for humanity conflicts, as we have seen, with the Bible. Where this view is rejected, humanity cannot be supposed to be called on to settle everywhere or to manage everything (and thus potentially to redeploy it), including the habitats of all the other creatures for whom the created order has (from this perspective) been made, despite Margaret Thatcher's claim that 'All we have is a life tenancy [sc. of the Earth] with a full repairing lease' (*This Common Inheritance* 1990: 10).

Palmer goes on to point out (rightly) that the idea of universal management is a nonsense. Her point tallies with James Lovelock's remark that nothing worse could befall humanity than our becoming or trying to be stewards or managers of the planet. But her conclusion can still be questioned: 'Stewardship is inappropriate for some of the planet some of the time, some of it for all of the time (the deep oceans) and all of it for some of the time – that is, before humanity evolved and after its extinction' (Palmer 1992: 79). For one thing, stewardship is not synonymous with interventionism, and is compatible with letting-be (for example, in Antarctica). There again, granted that there was no human responsibility before there were human beings and there will be none (in terms of new human actions) after human extinction, responsibility remains possible for the entire sphere of nature which humans can affect (and not only for the sphere of human settlement or appropriation), and in the twentieth century this includes, for better or for worse, the deep oceans, the solar system, and much of outer space beyond it. Unless this extensive power is exercised with responsibility, global problems will be intensified. Thus the choice is between power exercised responsibly and power without responsibility. So, far from evolutionary theory making stewardship obsolete, twentieth-century technology actually makes an attitude akin to stewardship indispensable.

This remains the case whether believers in God believe also in revelation (as theists usually do) or not (the position of deists such as Rousseau). Indeed, unless strong grounds can be given for accepting one or another revelation, the combination of deistic beliefs and attitudes of stewardship should not be written off as *a priori* erroneous. But whether an attitude of stewardship can be held in the absence of religious belief is a question which has to be tackled.

Stewardship without God

Are beliefs in answerability possible where belief in God has disappeared? Belief in responsibility need not lapse in these circumstances; some acts and some omissions remain unacceptable, in view of their contexts and consequences, even if belief in the Kingdom of God is absent. Thus Martin Heidegger wrote of 'dwelling' (*das Wohnen*) with the things which comprise the natural environment; such heedful inhabitation implicitly involves the role of 'care-taker' (in the full sense of one who has '*Sorge*' or 'care') (Heidegger 1971: 47). Yet motives such as love and loyalty reinforce responsibility, and are prone to accompany answerability; so the question with which this section begins remains worth asking.

To whom, then, or before whom would secular stewards be responsible? In 1990, the Conservative government of Britain espoused the view that stewardship is an ethical responsibility, 'an imperative' which must 'underline all [the nation's] environmental policies', requiring us 'to look after our planet and to hand it on in good order to future generations' (*This Common Inheritance* 1990). Admirable as was the global scope of this statement, its readers could be excused some unease about how far 'in good order' implies managerialism. Also, while it makes good sense to talk of obligations with regard to future generations, and such talk could comprise part of the basis of secular stewardship, we could not actually be answerable to generations which do not yet exist. Another possible answer is supplied by David Pearce and fellow-authors, when in *Blueprint 2* they write that 'Humans should act as nature's stewards and conserve natural resources and the environment, for their own sakes and to preserve the interests of other creatures.' While the motivation which they applaud for conserving 'natural assets' is concern for human interests, they remark that this 'also conserves the environments of sentient non-humans and non-sentient beings' (Pearce *et al.* 1991). Despite differences at the level of theory, this position (which also explicitly rejects the ethic known as 'ecocentrism') in practice comes close to the consequentialist and biocentric position which I commend elsewhere (Attfield 1991, 1999). Even so, the question about answerability remains unanswered, and this might be held to undermine talk of stewardship, except as a term for an ethic of this kind.

A less explicit but possibly more significant expression of stewardship forms the basis of the 1990 Code of the G7 nations, which speaks of 'stewardship of the living and non-living systems of the earth in order to maintain their sustainability for present and future, allowing development with forbearance and fairness' (see Berry 1993: 253–62). It may be that the anodyne nature of these words is what allowed the Economic Summit Nations (the G7) to adopt them. Yet their adoption genuinely commits the world's leading economic powers to efforts to tackle disruptions of natural systems, such as global warming, acid rain and ozone depletion. However, answerability to natural systems is clearly out of the question.

More light is shed on secular stewardship from an unexpected quarter. For Karl Marx, while discussing the need to sustain the soil across the generations, wrote as follows about the impossibility of owning the Earth:

From the standpoint of a higher economic form of society, private ownership of the globe by single individuals will appear quite as absurd as private ownership of one man over another. Even a whole society, a nation, or even all simultaneously existing societies together, are not the owners of the globe. They are only its possessors, its usufructuaries, and, like *boni patres familias*, they must hand it down to succeeding generations in an improved condition (Marx 1967: III, 776).

In this striking (albeit anthropocentric) passage, 'possessors' can be translated as 'occupants', 'usufructuaries' as 'tenants', and the Latin phrase '*pater familias*' which Marx uses can be translated 'head and representative of household'. So his words convey that the current generation must bequeath the Earth to succeeding generations in the way that good representatives of family lineages hand down family resources. Marx seems to be saying not only (as Leviticus does) that the Earth cannot be owned, at least not by any one generation, but also that the reason why the current generation must bequeath it in an improved condition is that this generation comprises representatives of humanity, conceived as a transgenerational community.

While this passage can be held to show ecological awareness, it is as limited as *This Common Inheritance* with regard to the value of nature; there is no awareness that the natural world consists in more than resources. Nevertheless, in accepting that people now alive do not own the Earth but hold it on trust for their successors, it comprises an early secular expression of stewardship (albeit of the anthropocentric variety); and it also evokes an answer to the problem of answerability through hinting that the current generation is answerable to the transgenerational community of humanity. Because this community, unlike future generations, has living members, it is not absurd to talk of answerability to such a community. Furthermore people's widespread sense of obligation to past members or to their memory makes this all the more credible, at least where living people are regarded as continuing the projects of the dead. Marx did not, of course, hold that responsibility or answerability attach equally to all current humans, since he was acutely aware of inequalities of resources and of power. But his position still conveys the stewardship of humanity as a whole.

An alternative way of thinking about answerability focuses on those who share (or have shared or will share) in the task of caring for the biosphere and the planet. For we may all be held to be answerable to the others for our share in this task; if some default, the greater becomes the burden on the others. Here, the relevant class includes all moral agents: once again, a transgenerational community, consisting of all the individuals and organizations capable of responsible action and of making a difference to the world and its value. Humans now alive would, on this basis, be stewards and trustees of the planet, answerable to the ampler company of predecessors, contemporaries and successors combined (Attfield 1994: 59–60) and this approach has the advantage of making us responsible to agents entitled to complain if we shirk our part.

However, the scope of the community of moral agents is virtually co-extensive with that of the transgenerational community of humanity (except that moral agents would also include God). Hence little practical difference is made whichever of the two communities is invoked with relation to a secular theory. In either case, answerability remains a characteristic of stewardship, which turns out to be not simply an ethic, but capable of being understood as involving an appropriate metaphysical backdrop, and an implicit awareness of the company of those to whom our trusteeship is owed. Against this backdrop, obligations with regard to future generations come to appear more significant, since we, the current generation, are now seen to depend on the beneficiaries of our responsibilities for the continuation and in some cases completion of our tasks, just as we continue the projects and tasks of previous generations.

This also helps to bring out some of the motivations of secular stewardship. People are frequently prepared to make efforts and sacrifices for the sake of future generations, particularly to ensure the continuation of practices and commitments in which they share – love of nature and its diversity included. While the motivations of secular stewardship sometimes include not only love of humanity and of fellow-creatures but also self-interest (for example, through concern for a good reputation), love of humanity and fellow-creatures are typically no more dependent on self-interest than religion and love for God usually are. The motivation of being fruitful through leaving numerous progeny (sometimes suggested as crucial and inescapable) need not be all-pervasive among human stewards any more than self-interest need be, pervasive as it is sometimes held to be in nature. Many seekers after truth, justice and freedom (like benevolent people such as the Good Samaritan, as Holmes Rolston points out [1999: 249–69]) show little or no tendency to be motivated by their own interest alone, having motives enough in the form of compassion, or (as just mentioned) of love of humanity and/or fellow-creatures, plus regard for successors.

This is the place to consider Murray Bookchin's suggestion about the scope of the secular stewardship of humanity. Besides stressing the responsibility for the natural world conferred on human beings by evolution, and the distinctive attributes which facilitate this responsibility, Bookchin also claims that stewardship can take the form of intervention into natural processes, intervention as creative as the creativity of nature itself, of which it comprises a realization (Bookchin 1987). To the extent that this means accepting responsibility for ecological impacts (including global environmental problems), and for taking steps to ameliorate or even cure them, this is a welcome suggestion. But if it involves either total management of the surface of the Earth or attempts to redirect the evolutionary process, despite our abiding ignorance of its workings, it resembles rather a secular counterpart of the religious-based managerialism castigated by Palmer and others.

Thus my verdict on the scope of stewardship consists in welcoming accounts which recognize a trusteeship extending to the impacts, actual and possible, of human action and inaction (and which thus cohere with the scope of the normative ethic of consequentialism, and, in my application of that ethic [Attfield 1999], with policies of promoting sustainability and sustainable development); but rejecting interpretations which represent humanity as authorized to act as if everything were made for itself, or as authorized to be continually and ubiquitously active across the entire natural world. Such accounts, in my view, overstretch stewardship in the direction of human domination of nature, the approach with which (as has been seen above) Passmore expressly contrasts it. They also show how secular stewardship (like religious stewardship) has its limits, cannot be used to justify whatever its adherents happen to favour, and thus cannot be stretched indefinitely.

Afterword

Effectively the same issue, of whether secular stewardship opens the way to exploitation of nature, is sometimes raised in the form of the suggestion that, historically, stewardship has 'desacralized' nature, authorizing its investigation and its unlimited appropriation and use. Where 'desacralization' concerns rejection of the worship of nature, theistic religion has indeed been a desacralizing influence throughout its history, fostering worship of God alone, and (in recent centuries) the secular study of the natural world. But where 'desacralized nature' means representing nature as having no independent value of its own, neither theism nor stewardship implies anything of the kind. In the words of the General Synod (*Christians and the Environment* 1991), it can recognize that the world has 'an interest in its own survival and well-being independent of its value to us' or rather that its living creatures do (as the books of Job and the Psalms attest). Both traditional religious stewardship and secular trusteeship imply that the sphere of our responsibility is as extensive as our powers, but that the scope of management has strong ethical limits. Some of the resulting dilemmas are discussed in my book, *The Ethics of the Global Environment* (Attfield 1999).

Most non-theistic religions (as well as theistic ones) include strands conducive to environmental sensitivity, and this makes possible the advocacy of an interreligious global ethic concerned in part with such sensitivity (e.g. Küng and Kuschel 1993). I have argued here that the stewardship tradition of theistic religions well equips them to endorse and foster a biocentric environmental ethic, both in theory and in practice, and to offer reasons why it is important. I have also sought to show that secular versions of stewardship can be embraced without adherence to these religions, harnessed rather to a secular metaphysic and matching secular motivations.

Notes

1. I have in mind here both teleological anthropocentrism, the view that everything was made for the sake of humanity, and axiological anthropocentrism, the view that nothing but human concerns and interests have value of a non-derivative kind, and that only these concerns and interests are to be taken into account in decision-making. Many adherents of stewardship have consistently rejected both these views. Admittedly they, like everyone else, perforce accept what Mary Midgley has called 'perspectival anthropocentrism', the view that all judgments of value (except those made by God) are made with human faculties. But acceptance of perspectival anthropocentrism commits us neither to teleological anthropocentrism nor to axiological anthropocentrism; for human reasoning is free to conclude that humanity is not the sole concern of the creator, nor its good the sole concern of ethics; and bearers of human faculties are free to judge and act accordingly.

2. Here I have in mind both teleological biocentrism, the view that all living creatures are of concern to the creator, and axiological biocentrism, the view that the interests of nonhuman creatures matter as well as human interests, and should be taken into account in decision-making, where relevant.

Chapter 7

The Dominion of Man

John Black

This essay was originally published in The Dominion of Man *(Edinburgh University Press, 1970), which was derived from a series of lectures in Conservation given at University College London the previous year. At the time John Black (1910–81) was Professor of Forestry and Natural Resources in the University of Edinburgh. He later moved to become Principal of Royal Holloway College in the University of London.*

The concept of stewardship

A society which includes amongst its earliest and most tenaciously held beliefs a concept of its right to dominion over nature is faced with a paradox: the fullest exploitation of nature involves its eventual destruction. The destruction of nature involves, too, the destruction of that society itself. Man's belief in his right of dominion over nature may be based on the role of the rest of nature as providing the resources needed for his own survival, but when this attitude is expressed in terms of a direct injunction that nature is his, to be subdued and conquered, the need for a system of contrasting beliefs which would operate to hold exploitative policies in check becomes urgent. There is thus set up a pair of opposite and contradictory positions which must in some way be reconciled if a society is to be maintained in equilibrium with its resources, and may be epitomized as a conflict between long-term and short-term interests.

It is as well to recognize the fundamental knife-edge on which the management of all biologically based resource systems must rest. If successful management is deemed to be that level of exploitation which permits a steady flow of products over the longest possible period of time visualized by the society (possibly stated as 'in perpetuity', but usually considered unconsciously in terms of finite periods), it is possible to maintain a level of production which does not involve a deterioration in the system itself, and may even improve it. This rate of flow could, on the other hand, be greatly increased if the concept of sustained yield over long periods of time is abandoned, and a much higher rate of production achieved in the short term. This would result in a reduction in the productivity of the resource system, perhaps even to zero if the process were to be continued long enough. A simple analogy can be made with money in the bank: either you can live off the interest, leaving the capital intact, or you can increase the flow of money from your account by removing interest and a proportion of the original capital with obvious implications for the future of that particular resource system. If the exploitative process is arrested before the system is completely ruined, a period of rest may permit a return to a fully productive condition, but this must by no means be taken for granted. For most, probably all, ecosystems there is a point of 'no return' beyond which restoration is no longer possible.

The risk of over-exploitation is particularly serious in those environments frequently referred to as 'fragile' or as 'ecological tension zones', where the ecosystem is so delicately balanced that a level of human intervention that would be appropriate and harmless in more favoured circumstances quickly becomes disastrously disruptive. Western civilization was cradled and developed in just such tension zones in the Near East, under semi-arid conditions, dependent on low and erratic rainfall, with high rates of evaporation and a sparse vegetative cover, quickly eaten out and slow to recover from even moderate exploitation; and on the erosion-prone landscapes of the Mediterranean area, where the hot dry summer is followed by heavy rains which wash the soil from unprotected hillsides. These fragile environments in 'problem' climates are, above all others, in need of protection from uncontrolled human exploitation; the survival of societies then depends in large measure on the philosophical and technical means, which can be developed to ensure the necessary degree of protection.

The essential paradox remains; dominion over nature is incompatible with long-term sustenance. Only if the subjugation of nature is not permitted to proceed all the way to complete domination can a system of secure management be perpetuated. How can such subjugation be held in check; how can the claims of moderate, long-term production be maintained against those of higher production obtained by 'mining' the resource system itself? The life and thought of a society may involve a number of uneasy compromises between what is ideal and what is possible, and its world-view has to face up to many contradictions; in our civilization, the conflict between short-term and long-term concepts of management is just one such contradiction. If society is to continue to function, such contradictions have to be avoided or resolved, and if it is not permissible to state explicitly that the ideal is not possible (and it may be considered unwise to formulate such a view, however obvious it is), it may have to be wrapped up in mythological terms and an acceptable reconciliation of opposing and contrary positions thus put forward.

The Hebrews achieved this reconciliation by evolving a concept of man's responsibility to God for the management of the earth, a concept which was duly carried over into Christianity, becoming part of the Western heritage. If a view can be inculcated that man is only looking after the world on behalf of some extra-terrestrial presence such as a God or Gods, the contradictions in the concept of dominion over nature can be softened by a feeling of responsibility, and a reason provided for holding exploitative tendencies in check. Responsibility for managing the world is thus a mediating factor, in the mythological sense, providing a fulcrum between two opposing positions, and was readily acceptable within the context of the rest of the world-view of Hebrew and Christian society ...

It is interesting to note here that the concept of man as a steward of the earth, acting there on God's behalf, has a central place also in the Islamic faith. In the Qur'an (Sura 2.30), God says to the angels (who are initially rather hostile to the suggestion) 'I am going to place a *khalifah* on earth' before creating Adam. The proper rendering of *khalifah* into English is not easy in this context: one rendering would be 'substitute', but 'vicegerent' or 'deputy' would appear to be more acceptable translations. The political implications of this phrase have been discussed by Watt (1963) and it is clear that the sense of viceroy is intended; he refers also to Sura 38.26, where God says to David, 'We have appointed thee a *khalifah* on the earth: judge therefore between men with truth'. It is clear that God was seen to place man on earth in order that he would rule it as God's deputy. Concerning this interpretation, Cragg (1965) comments, 'This is the charter of man's responsible dignity, his call to mastery linked with the acknowledgement of accountability. All things are under man and he is under God.' It seems to me that, in this instance, the Qur'an has expressed one of the basic tenets of the western world-view more explicitly than did Genesis, though the essence of responsibility is implicit in 'dominion' also. To quote Cragg again:

> Yet insofar as that *imago Dei* concept is fulfilled in this awareness of man as having creativity within nature and a dominion for God's sake, the absence of the term and the silence about its other Biblical significance need not be over drawn. Much of the intention of the phrase is already here. In effect the caliphate of the Qur'an is the dominion of the Bible: in practical senses the larger, bolder terminology of Genesis may be said to be implied. Mastery and control in due subordinate order within the Divine will are the essential quality of 'man made in the image of God'. .... The place left for man in the scheme of things is seen to be a vice-gerency, where the feasibility of conquest and control is discovered to be a delegated trust.

This argument can best be summed up by stating that, in relation to the resources of the earth, the people of western civilization inherited a picture of God as an absentee landlord, with themselves as His steward. The introduction of the term 'resources' in this context is not unreasonable. A component of the human environment is transferred from a neutral category to the 'resource' status when it is perceived to be incorporated through appropriate cultural manipulation into the life of man, and as a factor in his survival. Although the term 'resources' is, not surprisingly, absent from the early records of western civilization, the concept of certain plants and animals as being set apart for the particular use of man is clearly set out in Genesis. It is perhaps a little surprising that there is no explicit reference to man as God's steward in the management of the earth; possibly the concept was too important, too central to the way of life, too obvious to require any precise statement or reiteration ...

The idea that man was responsible to God for the use of the earth remained – and remains – a central part of Judeo-Christian thought, so much so that the need to formulate it in precise terms seems to have been infrequently felt. The clearest statement known to me comes from the unlikely pen of Sir Matthew Hale, the distinguished seventeenth-century Chief Justice of England. In the introduction to *The Primitive Origination of Mankind*, published in 1677, he informed his readers that it had been written in odd moments over a long part of a busy professional career, in order to show that the essential truths of religion did not need to depend on revelation, but could be derived from a consideration of natural phenomena alone. Towards the end of his long book occurs the following passage:

In relation therefore to this inferior World of Brutes and Vegetables, the End of Man's Creation was, that he should be the VICE-ROY [*sic*] of the great God of Heaven and Earth in this inferior World; his Steward, Villicus, Bayliff, or Farmer of this goodly Farm of the lower World, and reserved to himself the supreme Dominion, and the Tribute of Fidelity, Obedience, and Gratitude, as the greatest Recognition or Rent for the same, making his Usufructuary of this inferior World to husband and order it, and enjoy the Fruits thereof with sobriety, moderation, and thankfulness.

And hereby Man was invested with power, authority, right, dominion, trust, and care, to correct and abridge the excesses and cruelties of the fiercer Animals, to give protection and defence to the mansuete and useful, to preserve the Species of divers Vegetables, to improve them and others, to correct the redundance of unprofitable Vegetables, to preserve the face of the Earth in beauty, usefulness, and fruitfulness. And surely, as it was not below the Wisdom and Goodness of God to create the very Vegetable Nature, and render the Earth more beautiful and useful by it, so neither was it unbecoming the same Wisdom to ordain and constitute such a subordinate Superintendent over it, that might take an immediate care of it.

And certainly if we observe the special and peculiar accommodation and adaptation of Man, to the regiment and ordering of this lower World, we shall have reason, even without Revelation, to conclude that this was one End of the Creation of Man, namely, to be the Vice-gerent of Almighty God, in the subordinate Regiment especially of the Animal and Vegetable Provinces.

In Hale's view there was clearly no escape from man's responsibility to God for the proper management of the earth, to control the wilder animals and to protect the weaker, to preserve and improve useful plants and to eliminate weeds and, be it noted, to maintain the beauty as well as the productivity of the earth. Was it entirely a coincidence that, like the author of Genesis, he put beauty before utility? Man's ability to carry out these duties appeared to him as evidence for the purpose of his creation, and, given Hale's legal training, it is not surprising that he viewed the situation within the contractual framework with which he was in everyday contact, 'steward, villicus, bailiff, or farmer'. The elements of contract – rights and obligations, responsibility and accountability – are inherent in the Judeo-Christian attitude to man's role on earth, even if there is little explicit statement of this general theme, although there is a parallel system in a man's individual responsibility for his personal property, and the obligations imposed thereby.

Chapter 8

The Fellowship of All Creation

Ruth Page

Before her retirement, Ruth Page was a Senior Lecturer in Divinity at New College in the University of Edinburgh. She has had a long interest in the relationship of theology and ecology. This article was first published in Theology in Green 7 *(1993); Dr Page later expanded it into a book* God and the Web of Creation *(1996). Her argument is that the popular understanding of stewardship is inadequate, particularly in its anthropocentricity; she wants to include in it a notion of humanity in creation as well as over creation. It is reprinted here with permission.*

Stewardship is undoubtedly a good and useful model for the relationship between humans and the rest of creation, and it is one which recurs in the Bible. But on the one hand it is not all the Bible has to say on the subject of the interrelationship of creation, and on the other hand, like all models, it has to be used with care. On examining the model of stewardship it becomes clear that the human attitudes and behaviour implied by it are those concerned with the wise and humane management of resources by divinely delegated authority. Thus, for instance, the Sabbath rest for farm-working animals prescribed in the Old Testament is not only good for the animals but also makes them more able for the following week's work. Similarly, land is refreshed for further use by lying fallow for a Sabbath year. In this way the land and the animals were brought into the covenant relationship with God not, so to speak, in their own independent right, but as resources for humans to manage with care.

The kind of relationships implied by management – even at its most humane – is the area where there is a danger of one-sidedness in the exclusive use of the stewardship model. A steward is necessarily something other than the 'objects' of stewardship, so this model constantly implies distance and difference between humans and all the rest. This is a critical point, for it was this very sense of distance and difference – the otherness and superiority of humanity – which made manipulation, indeed exploitation, possible in the first place. They remain dangerous possibilities since hierarchy is built into the model with stewards 'over' their charges. In a sense stewardship, even when enlightened by modern knowledge, chastened by past excess and Christianized, is still basically about the manipulation of the natural world, although it substitutes a kindly paternalism for egocentric tyranny. The notion of managing others for their own good is reminiscent of Victorian ideals of colonialism, with the same implicit assumptions of superiority over inferior beings. It is undeniable that, in the crisis we have brought upon ourselves, resources must be managed as wisely as possible. But to prevent that management from becoming anthropocentric and as manipulative as the practices that gave rise to our problems, stewardship needs to be tempered by a different model, in and beyond the Bible, which observes no critical differences between humanity and the rest, involving the role of creation equally and together.

> All creatures of our God and King,
> Lift up your voice and with us sing,
> Alleluia!

This popular hymn by St. Francis of Assisi is probably the best-known expression of an alternative vision of the world from the pragmatic needs of stewardship, for here all creation is joyfully united in the praise of God. In the hymn sun, wind, water, fire, earth, humanity and even death combine in an out-flowing of thankfulness from all that is to the Creator God. In writing it St. Francis was drawing on a tradition from the Psalms, where the same community of thanksgiving appears. Psalm 150, for instance, concludes on a universal note: 'Let everything that breathes praise Lord.' Thus the greatest offering creation can make to God is when in fellowship together it worships its creator, expressing joy and thankfulness of being to the one who let it all be.

There seems to have been no doubt in the Psalmist's or St. Francis' mind that non-human creation is as capable of praise in its own way as articulate *Homo sapiens*. Every particle of creation is involved – even those members which humanity has not yet discovered, those it finds more appalling than appealing, and those for which it has no self-regarding use. In this totality and equality creation does not need humanity to speak in its name or on its behalf. There is a direct and unmediated relationship between God and creation, just as there must have been for almost all evolutionary history when there was no humanity present to express anything. We may not be able to hear or understand the praise given by animals, insects or plants, but then, for all our abilities, we are limited humans and it is to God that the thankfulness for being is expressed. 'All your works shall give thanks to you, O Lord' (Ps. 145.10). Moreover in this common response of praise the variety of creation is affirmed but no hierarchical distinctions are made. What unites is that every living thing is equally a creature of God and owes God thanks on that account. As Weiser puts it in his commentary on the Psalms: 'In praising God the meaning of the world is fulfilled' (Weiser 1962: 841).

Against this account it could be argued that the orderly picture of creation painted in the Psalms and the cooperative account of human and non-human nature in St Francis are too idyllic. Real life on earth includes food chains, while often the flourishing of one individual or species is at the expense of others. 'Nature red in tooth and claw' (Tennyson) may not be the whole story but it is part of it. Yet what is being celebrated in praise is life, however competitive or transitory, as a gift from God. Whatever its limitations life is seen to be something worth having and perhaps by their very being, their existence, creatures express praise of God. Nevertheless there is another strand in the Old Testament, aware of troubles and conflict in the present, which describes harmony among all creatures not as a present reality but as a final hope. Thus Isaiah envisages a just state when 'the earth will be full of the knowledge of the Lord' which is also a time when

The wolf shall live with the lamb,
the leopard shall lie down with the kid,
the calf and the lion and the fatling together,
and a little child shall lead them ...
They will not hurt or destroy
on all my holy mountain

(Isa. 11.6–9).

The same comprehensiveness of final hope is expressed again in the New Testament in the visions of Revelation where 'every creature in heaven and on earth and under the earth and in the sea and all that is in them' will join in praise of the Lamb of God (Rev. 5.13).

From all this we may say that there is at present praise from all creation that there should be a world at all and that life is possible, even though that life may be harried by others, parched by drought or threatened by loss. In a real sense stewardship exists only in the service of this praise, being concerned with making it possible by creating conditions for life rather than managing life. 'The meaning of the world is fulfilled', in Weiser's comment, not when humanity has control of it all, but 'in praising God'. Although that is to happen completely and spontaneously at the end of time in the equal community of thanksgiving, it can happen imperfectly but really in the present. Men and women are in a position to enhance or obstruct that praise.

There is a further reason in the modern world for thinking in terms of the fellowship of all creation rather than exclusively of human stewardship over the rest with its temptation to human pride. We are all evolved species and the organization of human DNA is not very different from that in other

99

creatures. We share, with variations, the basic building blocks out of which everything in creation has evolved. The variations may be enjoyed in their diversity, as God surely enjoys the diversity of the world, without a sense of specialness always setting us at a distance from the rest.

Our familiar environments of stone, water, air, earth, grass, birds, animals and so on, are seen to share with us common molecular structures and to be stages in a common development in time. The very stuff of which we are made and the way it has become organized as ourselves is an inherent part of the ongoing development of the physical cosmos, which we survey. We, and all other living creatures, have evolved in time out of the non-living world of water, air and rocks, which seem so distinct and different from us (Peacocke 1975: 135).

This knowledge of our kinship in evolutionary history reinforces from another angle the perception that in stewarding creation we are not dealing with alien beings, objects that we may dominate for their and our good, but rather we are relating to fellows – indeed in St. Francis' terms to our brothers and sisters.

The interrelationship of creation which fellowship implies is also at the moment the subject of a serious scientific hypothesis which has caught the imagination of many without any scientific expertise, partly because it goes under the highly suggestive name of Gaia. The scientific hypothesis holds 'that the Earth's climate and surface environment are controlled by the plants, animals and micro organisms that inhabit it' (Joseph 1990: 1). Whereas it had previously been unanimously agreed that all significant environmental development had been dictated by *geological* features, such as the state of the Earth's crust, scientists persuaded by James Lovelock and Lynn Margulis are collecting evidence for the influence of *biological* features (Lovelock 1988; Margulis and Sagan 1986).

The Gaia hypothesis is far from being wholly accepted in the various scientific disciplines it embraces, but it has won its way to relative respectability as something which may be tested and which throws out interesting possibilities for research (q.v. Joseph, *loc. cit.*). It is an attractive hypothesis to Christians – but that, of course, does not add to its scientific credibility. If it were accepted, however, it would show that there was more unconscious stewarding going on than the deliberate human variety, for the Earth is in that case kept habitable by millions of tiny interactions. There is no need for Christians to invoke Gaia, the ancient Greek goddess of the earth to represent that interactive unity, for the idea is there already in the Psalms which declare that God is directly related to everything in the world as it plays its own role within the whole. That is a part of the Christian tradition, which needs to be recalled and given greater prominence today – a matter to which I shall return.

The Gaia hypothesis involves all creatures, and perhaps for the first time microbes are being given their real importance! The life-giving process of interaction it posits was in place long before humans appeared on the scene and therefore it gives humans no effective role except the possibility of destroying it all. Yet the Gaia hypothesis, as opposed to the unconscious ecological action it describes, could only have been formed by humans. Thus there remain, of course, great differences between humanity and the rest of creation, and it is only because these have formed a dis-proportionately large part of past Christian thought on creation that I am concerned to put the other side of the case. Clearly this article also could not have been written by any creature other than a human, capable of wide-ranging review and the possibility of rational argument couched in the syntactical language which makes communication more effective, while the whole project is made known via the technology developed for its transmission. These are uniquely human capacities and achievements on Earth.

At the same time, however, these differences, although real, should not be made too absolute. There are great continuities, for example, between humans and animals. As C.W. Hume has argued, animals have sensations such as sight or the experience of pain, sentiments like hatred or affection, self-consciousness and the capacity to perceive objects and persons as such, as well as sharing with us emotions, instincts, curiosity and the love of play (Hume 1967: 11f.). He suggests that one difference may be the capacity for abstract thought. That may indeed be right, and humans can certainly produce the results of their abstract thought intelligibly to each other. But it would be hard to demonstrate that animals lack all capacity for abstract thinking. There is no particular behaviour which characterizes such thinking and it is largely through their behaviour that we understand species other than our own. They may, for all we could show, have abstract thought we are unable to perceive. Whales and dolphins have larger brains than humans and who but God knows what abstract thought they may pursue? What is clear is that their way of living is far less greedy and destructive than ours. Through continuities with animals humans are included in a totality of creation yet again, although our cleverness and complexity of organization has permitted this comparatively small, slow and weak species to dominate the planet.

One way of giving religious expression to human specialness has been to invoke the language of Genesis concerning the 'image of God' in which men and women are made. There is certainly specialness here, but the point of the image in Genesis is for man and woman to be endowed as the responsible representatives of God on earth.

The emphasis on responsible action, however, was lost in the history of theology, for the image came to be expressed solely in terms of what made humanity superior to everything else. Very occasionally this was still con-ceived in physical terms. John Milton, for instance, in *Paradise Lost*, Book IV, describes Adam and Eve as 'Godike erect' since no other creature stood up straight on two legs and God was thought in personal terms. But Milton continues:

> In their looks divine
> The image of their glorious Maker shone,
> Truth, wisdom, sanctitude severe and pure

and it was in the spiritual, but even more the mental capacities that the image was predominantly sought. Augustine fathered a tradition of finding the image of God in human reason. That tradition set the pattern of believing in a divinely ordained gulf between humans and 'unreasoning beasts'.

Human superiority over the rest of creation was seen as a pale reflection of God's superiority over all, for the divine–human relation is the model and inspiration for all Christian relationships. It is no accident that when humans could see only their superiority over the natural world God was thought of only as transcendent, as a sovereign acting from a distance. Recently, however, we have come to see how cold and partial a picture of God that is. Douglas Hall, for instance, reinterprets the image of God in terms of relationships and takes as his guide the kind of relationship typified by the servanthood of Jesus Christ. The Jesus who washed his disciples' feet is not the incarnation of a God who is adequately described as a distant absolute sovereign. There is more emphasis today on God's proximity, accessibility and sharing in all that is going on. God indwells creation (as well as transcending it infinitely), companioning it all, rejoicing and grieving at what happens to any part of it. God is vulnerable and suffers with the suffering on earth when the divine purposes of freedom and love are thwarted (Page 1991: 1–11). With that understanding of God's relationship with creation the human calling to image God includes companioning the world accessibly in the fellowship of all creation as well as using our freedom in love for the increase of freedom and love.

It is within that general picture of God, humans and the world that the role of steward takes place, including the husbanding of resources and the need for hardheaded decisions on the assigning of priorities in a finite world. Humanity has a task before it which will require all its intelligence and managerial efficiency. Our present behaviour, prodigal with energy and careless of waste, has to be changed; our whole vision of the world, and of God in relation to the world, requires a kind of conversion to see us all in interrelationship rather than humanity in isolation, or alone with God. There remains the danger that notions of stewardship on their own will not effect this conversion, changing only the mode of action without addressing the change of heart. Such stewardship will in the end be inadequate. An example may make this clear.

After the First World War a need was perceived for a strategic reserve of timber in Britain. By now more than 12% of Scotland is devoted to productive woodland and more than 90% of all new planting in Britain takes place there. Earlier planting schemes 'matched species to site characteristics of the area: larch for dry knolls, Norway and Sitka spruce for wetter soils, Scots pine for podzols and other species for better soils' (Mowle 1991: 121). But as the financial return on upland afforestation was poor, a strategy for lowest cost planting came to be implemented during the 1970s. 'Sitka spruce offers the highest yields for the lowest expenditure and our hills are now covered with this tree as a direct result' (Mowle, *loc. cit.*). Modern forestry is as intensive as modern farming. The close planting of sitka spruce all at the one time creates a dark, sterile habitat below the trees and is a uniform 'dark tide' to look at. Areas of moorland have been lost, reducing the habitats of such birds as the merlin. In the Caithness Flow Country, a peaty, boggy area deemed by many unsuitable for private forestry in the first place, undisturbed habitats were put at risk. Since then sample surveys have 'suggested that some 640 pairs of Golden Plover, over 300 pairs of Dunlin and, rarest of all, over 120 pairs of Greenshank had their unique habitat destroyed' (Minns 1991: 66). Clearly ecological disasters have accompanied the drive to afforestation although in some respects matters have improved in the last few years.

If this is taken as a test case for Christian thinking (setting to one side for present purposes resources, concerted action and effectiveness) it could be argued that this entire example could have been covered by the application of the model of stewardship. Thus one could begin by saying that timber is a necessary resource whose planting is to be encouraged (although sitka spruce is soft for a conifer, yielding only pulp paper and board). Trees moreover trap carbon dioxide, a greenhouse gas, and thus help to lessen the impact of global warming. Stewardship will assess both the positive and the negative results of the plantings: on the one hand the productiveness of the land, most of which had been bare before, and the value of the crop; on the other the possibility of flash floods and the acidification of soils and rivers which in turn kills off fish eggs and fry. Moreover, as stewardship is stewardship over *all* creation, those animals, insects, plants and birds which may lose their habitats are part of the total consideration.

That analysis in terms of stewardship is all right as far as it goes. The difficulty, however, is that like is not being compared with like. Trees, fish and soil may be regarded as resources and compared with each other on that basis. But the merlin and the greenshank are not; they are not useful to humans. If they are to enter human calculations concerning a pragmatic outcome it must be because they have a value which is independent of their usefulness. In ethical terms this is called intrinsic value, the value of their very being, as opposed to instrumental value, which is the value of usefulness. Most decisions on land-use are particularly difficult because they involve a blend of instrumental and intrinsic values, and unless the 'green' party to the debate is clear about the value of what is not useful the pragmatic lobby will always win. It takes a kind of conversion away from self-love or species-love to see the intrinsic value of the greenshank. Humanity's interests are not necessarily the only thing that matters. For many people of no particular religious persuasion it is simply a good thing that such birds should be and should live in peace. Christians would want to say more. What are their reasons?

I have been giving the reasons in this article by describing a God who has a direct relationship with all creation, and a creation whose meaning is fulfilled in praising God. Humans and birds are part of a fellowship through evolution and in the community of thankful creation. On account of both the fellowship and the relation to God, dunlins and golden plovers have intrinsic value. For that reason, as a second stage, they enter into the concerns of stewardship. In matters of land-use it is always more difficult to argue the case for what is not useful. Unless we are convinced of the intrinsic value of other species and have caught a vision of the Earth as a fellowship of creation, we are less likely to be tenacious in advancing the interests of creatures who cannot speak for themselves.

My example, however, has not yet gone quite far enough. One might suppose from what has been written so far that only what cannot be subsumed under instrumental value is to qualify as having intrinsic value. But that will not do, for it could lead to humans using what is useful to them as they like without any of the respect and fellow-creaturehood which finds golden plovers valuable. Instead of that, *all* creation praises God, *all* creation is in fellowship. And that includes the sitka spruce. So even those creatures which have instrumental value, without which we would not be fed, clothed, sheltered, kept healthy and so on, have intrinsic value as well, being part of the fellowship of creation.

Humanity has the unenviable task of having on occasion to choose among members of the fellowship what will flourish and what will not, for all creatures cannot flourish equally. That variation in flourishing can be seen in entirely natural terms by the regulation of populations within an ecological system. There are checks and balances, such as the availability of food supply, for any population which grows too large. Similarly, in human decisions on land-use between bird and tree, both are within the fellowship of creation, but both cannot flourish equally. After all the valuing has been done, decisions usually have to go one way or the other unless a good compromise (nature reserves?) can be found. But whatever part of creation loses out in any decision it is still of intrinsic value, still related to God and part of the fellowship, and therefore still worthy of respect, gentleness and the fellow-feeling of grief.

In these ways, then, stewardship requires the model of fellowship, so that creaturely existence of every kind may be given its true value before decisions have to be made on its future, while stewardship itself is less about control and management, though these may be the means, and more about creating the best possible conditions of life in the circumstances, in which God may be praised.

Let all things their Creator bless
And worship him in humbleness,
O praise him, Alleluia.
Praise, praise the Father, praise the Son,
And praise the Spirit, three in one.
Amen.

Chapter 9

The Fallible Concept of Stewardship of the Earth

James Lovelock

Jim Lovelock, CBE, FRS, CH is a physical chemist and inventor. One of his claims is that he precipitated environmental concern by his invention of an electron capture detector, which for the first time allowed the recognition of trace pollutants in the atmosphere. He is best known for his proposal that the living and non-living constituents of the Earth (including the atmosphere) constitute a single positive feedback system, which he has called 'Gaia'; he drew up the concept as a result of ideas he got while working as a consultant to NASA. Lovelock has described Gaia and its properties in several books (Lovelock 1979, 1988, 1991). He is a visiting Fellow of Green College, Oxford. This paper was one of those given at Windsor in 2000 (p. xi).

You may believe that, as the only organized intelligence, we have the duty as well as the right to be stewards of the Earth, to take charge and govern it responsibly. But first, we must ask, what is the Earth? This is not a trivial question because the Earth, like the Universe, is something we do not yet understand. We take the Earth for granted – almost as if the planet in our minds were one of those schoolroom multicoloured political spheres mapping the territories of tribes and nations. The real Earth, that stunning blue and white sphere, is in danger of becoming a visual cliché, no longer inspirational, a banal image advertising soap on satellite television. As a scientist, I know that we are far from understanding our planet and ourselves.

Most scientists, even though they are beginning to see the Earth as a system, still act as if it were no more than a ball of white hot, partially melted rock with just a cool crust moistened by the oceans and enclosed within the atmosphere. On the surface, they see a rich spread of life and think that the organisms have simply adapted to the material conditions of the planet. With such a view go metaphors like 'The Space Ship Earth'. As if humans were the crew and the passengers of a rocky ship forever travelling an inner circle around the sun. As if the four billion years life has existed on Earth were just a preparatory period before it could serve as our life support system when we happened to come aboard. Seen this way, the Earth system might appear fragile, like one of those great greenhouses in Arizona or Cornwall, and in need of our care as its stewards.

A flaw of twentieth century science was the unshakeable belief that life merely adapts to its environment and does not change it. It allowed the Life and the Earth sciences to separate and divide into a range of narrow reductionist specialties. Practising scientists are often unaware how narrow is their view of the world when seen through the tiny window of their specialty. We all read the latest news of scientific advances and brief reviews of the other sciences in the *New Scientist* or the *Scientific American* but back in the laboratory, where we do serious science, we continue to follow the narrow paths of our own research. The focused reductionist approach to science has been so successful in the last century that we have forgotten the need for a top-down physiological view of the whole Earth. We have truly lost sight of the wood for the trees.

A small number of scientists, who call themselves geophysiologists, are not wholly reductionist and see the Earth as a superorganism, or if you prefer, a planetary-sized ecosystem called 'Gaia'. We postulate that this system automatically regulates such important properties as climate and atmospheric composition, so that they are always more or less comfortable for life.

An increasing number of scientists are moving towards this minority view and see life and the environment as a single system. Some of them are Gaians without realizing it, while others agree that the presence of life affects the composition of the air, the ocean and the rocks, but are not yet convinced that the Earth self-regulates to sustain a comfortable environment.

Biologists find the greatest difficulty in understanding this view but in the past few years a few of them have accepted that there is some evidence for self-regulation on a global scale but they still do not see how it could happen by Darwinian natural selection. It took that great biologist William Hamilton to take this as a challenge not an objection (see, for example, Hamilton and Lenton 1998), which makes his premature death so sad. William Hamilton changed, from being a strong opponent, to seeing Gaia theory as a new Copernican revolution; without his wisdom I think it will take many years to disentangle the links between organisms, their ecosystems and large-scale climate and chemistry. I see it as rather like the problem faced by supporters of natural selection in the last century when asked 'How could anything so perfect as the eye evolve by a series of random steps?'

Most Earth scientists now recognize the need for interdisciplinary research and are the force behind the global scientific programmes to model, monitor and measure the Earth. Bodies such as the Intergovernmental Panel on Climate Change, and the International Geosphere-

Biosphere Programme show an impressive degree of international co-operation, and are concerned with both the climatic effects of greenhouse gas accumulation and the changes in land use as more and more of the natural ecosystems are converted to farm land. They are beginning to provide a physiological understanding of the Earth but are still far from understanding it as a system. It may be some time before we know if, or how strongly, the Earth self-regulates as proposed by Gaia theory.

It may be that we will find that the Earth is truly no more than a ball of rock and is in no way a self-regulating system. In that case, we would be like colonists on the Moon or Mars and I would agree that stewardship is right and proper and necessary for our survival. If on the other hand the Earth is a superorganism made up of the material Earth and all of life, and one that sustains a favourable environment and has always done so, then we are not separate from the Earth but a part of it. In these circumstances, the concept of stewardship is unhelpful. It requires us to be wise enough to regulate the environment for the common good and to be better at doing this than the evolved system that has kept the Earth fit for life for nearly four billion years.

So what can we do when science is still decades away from telling us what the Earth is? Should we wait for the deliberations of the plenary session of the all-science interdisciplinary congress? Or should we listen to thoughtful environmentalists, such as Jonathan Porritt, who often ask: Can we afford to wait for scientific certainty before taking action on environmental affairs?

Governments throughout the world acknowledge that the massive changes we are making to the atmosphere and surface of the Earth are a threat to humanity. Legislation is growing to regulate the emissions of harmful gases and restrict land use. So far, these good intentions have been so restricted by politics that only minor changes in land use or greenhouse gas emissions have taken place.

Common sense tells us that in the absence of a clear understanding of the consequences of what we are doing to the Earth we should cut back our pollutions and land abuse to the point where at least there is no annual increase. But we are like an addicted smoker and it is very easy to continue our pleasant pollution until there are unmistakable intimations of mortality. By then it may be too late. Just as in peacetime, the prospect of war is rarely taken seriously, so with the threats from the environment, not enough will be done before events force action.

As a young man, I was proud to be a subject of a great empire and even now, although it is largely history, I still see it as something that, like the Roman Empire, left behind a beneficial legacy. But I sense that stewardship is an imperial concept that assumes an automatic superiority invested in those in charge.

Even if such a conviction justified stewardship we, the United Kingdom, are no longer in charge and stewardship is therefore now the right and duty of the greater powers. Do we trust them to exercise their power justly and sensibly? Do we think that the United States or China or a body like the UN could be trusted to regulate climate or the oxygen level of the atmosphere? National legends are revealing and the galactic scale imperialism expressed in the Hollywood legend *Star Trek* and the more serious talk of colonizing Mars should warn us that imperial leopards do not change their spots. The danger of these new imperial legends comes from lack of hands-on experience and leads, when there is danger to the Earth, to such breathtaking hubris as the technological fix. Too much CO_2 in the air – send out the tankers full of iron chloride to feed the algae that will then remove the CO_2. This is the environmental equivalent of gunboat diplomacy. Occasionally it might be the right thing to do but more often it is the harbinger of a gaudy and costly mess.

I would like to put some alternatives to stewardship.

Firstly, it might help if we saw ourselves as planetary physicians. In the nineteenth century, environmental problems just as serious as our own today faced the Victorians. There were epidemics of water-borne diseases like cholera and typhoid that caused the death of a third of the inhabitants of a city in a few months. Science was not then organized as a powerful lobby and was prepared to admit that it did not know the cause of the diseases. Physicians at the sharp end of this battle suspected from the epidemiology of the diseases that infection was water-borne or came from the bad odours of the primitive sewerage systems then in use.

Our sensible forefathers did not pour funds into the infant science of microbiology and wait until it proved that cholera and typhoid were water-borne bacterial infections. They acted promptly and empirically by installing clean water supplies and efficient sewage collection and disposal plants. In those days engineering was a proud profession and triumphantly displayed its self-confidence in those amazing gothic pumping stations which are now a place of pilgrimage for students of architecture.

If we emulate our Victorians ancestors and develop an empirical approach to planetary problems, we might find it helpful, even if only notionally, to introduce a new profession, that of planetary medicine. It would stand to specialist Earth science in the same way that medicine stands to biochemistry and microbiology and would be the environmental equivalent of the practice of medicine. Its general practitioners would be concerned with the health of the planet and an important part of their practice would be planetary preventative medicine.

It may be that nothing we do can prevent environmental changes severe enough to destroy our present civilization and move us into a truly dark age. I think it would be well worth our while to insure against this gloomy possibility by making sure that our successors who survived the collapse of civilizations knew what mistakes we had made and also have a condensed account of all the important and hard-won things we had achieved – such as that micro-organisms caused infectious disease and that the Earth was not the centre of the universe.

Lastly and perhaps most important is a change of heart and mind. There are ethical consequences of thinking of the Earth as a self-regulating system. Strangely, a statesman led me to think this way. That noble and brave man, Vaclav Havel, stirred me to see that science could evolve from its self-imposed reductionist imprisonment. His courage against adversity gave his words authority. When Havel was awarded the Freedom Medal of the United States he took as the title of his acceptance speech, 'We are not alone nor for ourselves alone'. He reminded us that science had replaced religion as the source of knowledge but that modern science offers no moral guidance. He went on to say that recent holistic science did offer something to fill this moral void. He cited Gaia as something to which we could be accountable. If we could respect and revere our planet it would be to our as well as the Earth's benefit. Perhaps those who have faith might see this as God's will also.

I do not think that President Havel was proposing an alternative Earth-based religion. I take his suggestion as offering something quite different. I think he offered a way of life that agnostics and those with faith could share.

Gaia has ethical implications that come from its two strong rules. The first rule states that stability and resilience in ecosystems and on the Earth depend upon the existence of firm and binding rules that limit the growth of organisms. The second rule states that those who live well with their environment favour the selection of their progeny. With these rules in mind, we should make living well with the earth our priority and see that the good of humankind is conditional upon our good behaviour. This applies to us as individuals as well as in our collective responsibility as a species. Our planet is one of stunning beauty and made of the breath, the blood and the bones of our ancestors. We need to recall our ancient sense of the Earth as an organism and revere it again. Gaia has been the guardian of life for all of its existence; and we reject her care at our peril. If we put our trust in Gaia, it can be a strong and joyful commitment like that of a good marriage where the partners put their trust in each other. The fact that, like us, she is mortal makes that trust even more precious. Gaia should never become a religion, for being of science, it is always provisional; but the Earth, which is its embodiment, is something real for us to respect and revere. It is something much larger than we are and, unlike imaginary goddesses, can truly reward or punish us. What she does offer is an evolving world-view that requires an interactive trust, not blind faith; a trust that accepts that, like us, Gaia has a finite life span. Gaia is not an alternative to religion but a complement. The great religions have already given us their prescriptions for living with each other in their

110

parables. The Earth's parables are about the mortality of Gaia and that for every change we make to our environment there are consequences. We must learn to live with the Earth in partnership; otherwise, the rest of creation will unconsciously move the Earth itself to a new state, one where humans may no longer be welcome.

Chapter 10

Tensions in a Stewardship Paradigm

Bruce R. Reichenbach and
V. Elving Anderson

Bruce Reichenbach is Professor of Philosophy at Augsburg College, Minneapolis, Minnesota; Elving Anderson is Professor Emeritus of Genetics at the University of Minnesota at Minneapolis. This chapter has been written especially for this publication, following the themes developed in their book On Behalf of God *(Eerdmans, 1995) which is an extensive exploration of the outworking of stewardship in a range of biological disciplines. In their treatment here, they show that a biblically based practice of stewardship can (and should) be an effective enterprise, not the mere aspiration that some consider it.*

Stewardship is one of the first paradigms readers encounter in the Bible, and in one form or another it continues throughout scripture. From Genesis 1 and 2 we learn that humans are stewards for the Owner of the world, to fill, rule over, and care for creation. As stewards we are to *fill* the world. We direct our ethical attention to our obligations to change the world for the better. We are concerned not merely for quantitative change, but also (and especially) for the quality of what we produce or bring about. As stewards we are to *rule over*; God gives us dominion. We direct our ethical attention to the extent of our power and the relations that hold between Ruler and subjects, and between stewards and what we are stewards over. As stewards, we are to *care for* the earth. We pay ethical attention to the ways we use our powers over nature. We have obligations to God and to the persons and things over which we are stewards, not only to profit the Landlord but also to benefit and do justice to other stewards and the creation. Ethicists carefully consider the moral obligations that arise as the paradigm is applied to diverse ethical issues, including those addressing the environment, a task that we have performed elsewhere (Reichenbach and Anderson 1995). Here we want to focus on perhaps one of the most significant paradoxes of being a steward.

A paradox of stewardship

Stewards are charged with a seemingly contradictory obligation: they are to promote the good of the Landowner through conservation and through change. On the one hand, stewards are to preserve what is valuable and essential; on the other they are to profit the owner through risking the estate, by making changes in what is entrusted to their care. How can they do both – preserve and change; conserve and risk?

Interestingly enough, we find biblical precedent for this very contrast. Jesus tells a parable (Mt. 25.14–30) about a householder who, intending to go on a journey, summons his servants and entrusts some of his capital to them. As stewards, they are faced with the problem of what to do with the property assigned to their care. One servant takes seriously the steward's preservative role, knowing that his master is a hard man. Not willing to risk what was entrusted to him, he hides it in the ground, so that when the master returns, nothing over which he was given charge will be lost. The steward expects praise for preserving the owner's resources. But to his shock and dismay, the mere preserver receives condemnation. Why has he not invested the capital, expanded the owner's possessions, and enriched his master? He has failed as a steward and is immediately relieved of his position. What the owner entrusted to him is turned over to the other two stewards who achieve a profitable return on their investment of the owner's property. One point of the story is that stewards who never risk the trust, but merely preserve, fail in their office. Stewards are obligated to both preserve and change (and thereby profit).

As God's stewards of the biosphere, we likewise must both preserve and change. And this raises five important and difficult questions.

Key questions

(1) What are we to change? This question faces any steward engaged in the task of improving the prospects of the Landlord. Though the universe is ordered, the order is not always beneficial either to humans or to their counterparts in nature. The environment that makes agriculture possible can also threaten its bounty. The earth-watering rain may cause floods; the life-giving sun warms the crops but also creates conditions ripe for devouring insects to multiply. Though we are not faced with the unmitigated disasters pictured by Voltaire in *Candide*, neither do we have Leibniz' best of all possible worlds.

It would seem, then, that change appropriately ought to begin with what negatively affects human existence. We ought to search for cures for ravaging diseases and for treatments to mitigate dysfunctional conditions. The environment should be tamed and transformed to be more inhabitable and hospitable. The Green Revolution and genetically modified foods are legitimate because they prevent malnutrition and starvation. It would seem that we are obligated to change either what does not benefit us or what has a potential to harm us, in order to make our planet a better place for humans to live.

But why should we change the environment to benefit humans? Is this not a kind of hubris, contradicting the basic intent of the original paradigm according to which stewards were to profit the Landowner and not themselves? In the Genesis story, God sees that what he creates is good. The good is for God as the valuing Landowner. But now we speak of changing the creation to benefit human beings, the stewards. Have we not unwarrantedly switched the valuer?

Not really, for both Genesis creation stories indicate that God meant creation to be not only for himself but for humans as well. In the first account, God's creation of humans caps the long creative process before God rests. In God's final creative act, he forms something to bear his image and to rule over the rest of creation. True, the humans are made from and return to the dust of the earth, as do the other creatures. Yet we have a transcendent aspect as well, for only of humans does the author attribute a being made in God's image and likeness. In the second Genesis story, God specially breathes into the man his divine breath. He places him in a fertile park, allots him the fruit of the trees for food, and even marshals the animals for him to name. To hold that change should benefit humans as well as the Landlord is not hubris. Our paradigm has a precedent.

But is it always better to change the environment for human benefit? It is often the case that when humans are benefited by changing the environment, more harm than good results overall. We may so alter the environment that it cannot recover: gone are the white and red pine forests of the northern American Midwest, turned into frame houses and railroad ties; gone is the American prairie, converted into endless corn and wheat fields; mined for their energy-producing coal, the hills of Pennsylvania and Wales lie buried under slag heaps; the pristine lakes of New England and Scandinavia are polluted with heavy metals from our industries. Would it not be more effective, if not more right, to exercise our new power, where appropriate, to alter humans themselves to adapt to their environment, rather than always altering nature?

In the past, change was directed almost exclusively to the environment; alterations of humans were minor. Yet it would appear that we should alter ourselves as well. But in what ways? Perhaps the most obvious concern our lifestyles. This injunction can be directed to a variety of aspects (helpful examples are given by Wilkinson 1980a: 261–62).

(a) It is easy to confuse wants with needs. Yet a life of simplicity, in which we meet our basic needs but creatively rechannel many of our desires, can be both personally satisfying and ecologically sound

(Sider 1977). In place of our emphasis on individual ownership, we might share resources with our neighbours, so that fewer possessions are needed to live comfortably.

(b) We can alter our current pattern of energy consumption, to consume less energy and to decrease reliance on those resources that are most destructive to extract and polluting to use. The initial cost, though high, of more environmentally friendly energy production is insignificant when compared to the long-term value of sustaining our environment.

(c) We can alter our habits and behaviour: how we use transportation, what and how much we buy, where we live and what kind of living space we make. By eating more grains and vegetables we can reduce our dependence on livestock that have a destructive impact on their environment. We can alter the way we use materials, what materials we use, and what we do with them after we are done. The recent emphasis on recycling illustrates the significant changes we can make to our ways of doing and disposing of things.

(2) Is change permissible or obligatory? The reader may think that it is enough to hold that changing the environment and human persons is permissible. But is it also obligatory? Ethicists distinguish being permitted from being obligatory. For example, a thoughtful defender of capital punishment maintains that capital punishment ought to be permitted without holding that it is obligatory to impose it. Or again, risking my life to attempt to save someone from drowning is permitted but might not be obligatory, especially if I possess marginal swimming skills.

Which of these – permission or obligation – applies to our acts of changing our environment and ourselves? If one takes the injunctions of Genesis and Jesus' parable seriously, not only are we permitted, we are obliged to change things for the better. The steward in Jesus' parable was not merely permitted to invest his trust; he was obligated to do so and in failing was roundly condemned. As stewards, investing in change to improve our world is our mission, our business, our vocation. But what about changing ourselves? We have noted that our normal reaction to the obligation to improve is to change something else to fit our own needs, wants and behavioural patterns. This, it is argued, is less risky to us, not to mention being often cheaper and easier. But this normal reaction often runs counter to our stewardship ethic, for we have obligations to benefit not only the Landowner but also that over which we rule. And to change what we rule over to benefit ourselves might violate this trust. Thus, we reject the easy, non-sacrificial route of always changing what is around us instead of directing attention to changing ourselves – our desires, habits, lifestyle and behaviour.

(3) For what purpose are we to change? We have the injunction to rule over the trust for the profit of the Landlord. But how will the Landlord gain from our investments? What is God's profit? This poses a difficult

question, for the traditional Christian approach to creation has been to argue that a perfect God freely created the world out of his goodness and plenitude, not out of any need. 'He intends only to communicate His perfection, which is His goodness ... Therefore divine goodness is the end of all things' (Aquinas, *Summa Theologiae*, I, 44.4), not in the sense that things add to God's goodness, but in that the good they achieve emulates it. On this interpretation, God's relation to the creation is unilateral, not reciprocal. It would not exist without him and his continuous, sustaining power. But since nothing can add to his infinity, all that happens does not affect him; it neither fills a lack in him nor adds anything to him. But if creation makes no difference to God and his existence, one has to wonder what the significance of the creative act was from God's perspective.

Because of this and other difficulties, we side with those who see the relation between God and his creation as reciprocal; each contributing in significant ways to the other. God's own self-realization is found partly in the realization of his creation, just as the realization of the creation is found in achieving the good for it determined by God. Our response to God has significance for his life, just as his response to us has significance for ours.

Returning to our original question, we ask, what profit ought we bring to God? On the classical view, God as the Landlord gets from his creation nothing that he needs; nothing can contribute to him and his existence. He receives praise or glory, but the praise, as it were, only adds to an already overflowing cup. One cannot add meaningfully to the infinite. On our revised view, however, the Landlord gains a great deal from his creation. The creation contributes to God's ongoing life. His good is achieved partly by and through the goods realized in the universe. Some of these goods will be moral and spiritual goods, realized through the right actions, motives and virtues of his created stewards. Others will be goods of self-realization, where the creation and the stewards realize the potentialities that fulfil them. These goods will also include aesthetic goods such as order, harmony and beauty. In sum, we should change what detracts from meaningful existence and overall goodness and beauty, as well as what has been affected by our sinful acts, for the good that we achieve contributes both to God's and to our own good.[1]

In a backhanded way, the obligation to change the world for the better not only legitimizes both science and technology; it also saddles their practitioners with moral obligations, for in knowing and changing the world they are faced with obligations to realize the good. Their endeavours have, as their end, the profit of the Landlord, his stewards, and the earth that they care for. Likewise, their practitioners should be concerned about the appropriate ways to realize these goods (the means). Put another way, the steward-paradigm invokes both teleological and deontological concerns.

According to this model, science and technology are not value-neutral.

They must address concerns about what is worth knowing in light of human needs, about what is worth doing in light of potential human and environmental good, and about what scientists should be doing in light of the development of their own moral character. In all of this, stewards answer not merely to themselves and their peers, but to the God who charged them to care for the world. If we are God's stewards, we are not our own but have obligations to bring about God's good. Thus, scientists as human beings are held to the same accountability as all other stewards, while at the same time, because of their unique knowledge, power and technical abilities, they have a special accountability for what they have done.

(4) What are the limits of the change? If we are obligated to change, are we permitted to change absolutely everything? Or are there things that should be preserved, left unchanged? To answer this, let us return to our biblical paradigm. In the first Genesis creation story, we are told six times that God sees his creation as good. One common but problematic way of understanding goodness in this story is to connect it with human happiness and well-being. God's creation contains no evil, either moral or natural. Moral evil, in the form of sin against God, is introduced in a subsequent story, where humans, seeking to be like God, violate the divine command. Natural evil enters as a punishment for human disobedience. The disobedient now suffer pain in childbearing, difficulties in farming, and mortality. According to this view, goodness was present in the beginning, reflecting the goodness of God. The creation of finite creatures did not introduce evil, only its possibility. Only when humans act in defiance of God does evil actually begin.

Another, more likely, interpretation of the goodness in the story is that God sees the creation as good in that it is capable of doing what God intended it to do. The universe is ordered and functional. The light is good because it divides day and night. The separation of the waters from the land is good because it facilitates development of vegetation on land and creatures both in sea and on land. All in all, God finds a fit harmony of means and ends, of order and purpose. Everything has value because it has a place in and contributes to the whole.

What would happen, for instance, if all animals were capable of interbreeding, if there were no natural species barriers? Put another way, what if there were no species, only individuals? Then individuals that had successfully adapted to their environment could breed with others suited to another environment, possibly producing offspring suited to neither. The superior genotype for that particular environmental niche could be lost if combined with entirely different ones. Under this scenario there could be no environmental stability upon which organisms could depend.[2]

Because it is ordered, nature is also intelligible. If it were an indeterminate chaos, it would be impenetrable to human reason. The concepts

117

through which we know the world are universals covering numerous particulars that are alike in relevant ways. Knowledge of biology depends on knowledge of such things as cells, chromosomes, strands of DNA, genes, and proteins, and of such processes as cell division, gene expression, and cloning. It would be humanly impossible to know these things and processes if each thing or event were unique and uncategorizable, for then to know something about one object or process would tell us nothing about other things or processes. Generalization, induction, and hypothesis and theory formation would be impossible. Order and repetition are necessary for knowledge, and as knowable, the created world is a 'fit object for human inquiry, understanding, and control' (Gilkey 1965).

So what then is to be preserved? If we are to contribute to human wholeness and benefit from what exists in the universe, the structures that already serve to foster those possibilities ought to be preserved. This includes, among other things, preserving the conditions for genetic stability as well as genetic variability, the integrity of ecosystems, the viability and integrity of human life that make possible the enjoyment of quality of life, freedom of choice that makes for moral responsibility, the conditions necessary for attaining spiritual growth and maintaining a relationship with God and other humans, and the order and balance necessary for realizing aesthetic ends.

Undoubtedly the limits of the conservator will be the sorts of things that scientists continually bump up against. Just as scientists continually push at the borders of the 'knowable' and the 'doable', they push at the borders of the 'ought to be known' and the 'ought to be done'. The debate in the 1970s over whether scientists should proceed with certain kinds of recombinant DNA experiments illustrates the tension. In July 1974 the Committee on Recombinant DNA Molecules of the National Academy of Sciences published a letter in the journals *Science* and *Nature* that called for a moratorium on certain recombinant DNA experiments because of the uncertainty about what could result from laboratory accidents. What would result if the genes of *E. coli* bacteria were combined with those from a tumor virus; could the resulting organisms become carcinogenic? Could the bacteria colonize human intestines and cause cancer? Would we be able to control a humanly manufactured scourge that, made resistant to certain antibiotics, might escape from the controlled laboratory environment? With the moratorium, 'oughts' for the moment controlled the 'cans'.

Yet the self-imposed moratorium lasted less than a year. Safety guidelines for continuing experiments with recombinant DNA, developed at the Asilomar Conference in February 1975, replaced the moratorium; the desire to know and do could not be restrained. As one researcher put it, 'If you're dedicated to the truth, you have to say that there are no truths not worth seeking' (*Newsweek*, 12 January 1976). Today, as scientific research proceeds, new boundary-pushing issues, such as genetically modified foods, human cloning, transgenic modification and embryonic stem cell research, have arisen.

(5) What are the risks of change? Being a landowner and entrusting the estate to stewards involves risks. Does our imperative to change create risks, and are there limits to the risks God takes?

According to classical theology God is not a risk taker. Even before he created the world he knew everything that would happen to it. Indeed, some theologians hold that God, as omniscient, knew not only what would happen (the actual) and what could happen (the possible), but also what would happen if certain other things happened that never did (called middle knowledge). That is, God knew that I would get up this morning at 6:20 (the actual), that I could have arisen earlier (the possible), and that had I decided to arise at 7:13 I would have chosen hot rather than cold cereal for breakfast (middle knowledge). Hence, he was in a position to create those beings that, by their already-known choices, best suited his purposes. Reformed theology goes even further. God did not create on the basis of his knowledge, but actually foreordained the existence of every creature and the performance of every action (Calvin, *Institutes of the Christian Religion* 1.16.2; 3.21.5). The world, its contents, and all its events are predestined by God. In these theologies, then, God risks nothing in creation; he faces no surprises because he either foreknows or foreordains all.

Yet neither of these theological positions captures the drama of the biblical narrative. God expresses a profound sense of disappointment in the questions he poses to the first sinners. To the hiding Adam, whom he often encountered as he walked in the cool of the day, he asks, 'Where are you?' Of the murderer Cain he inquires, 'Where is your brother?' The wickedness of the recalcitrant humans becomes so great that God is sorry he created them and threatens to destroy them all. Saving only Noah and his family, he tries his experiment with humans a second time, with a similar, unsatisfactory outcome. Later on, he chooses Saul as the first king of Israel, and then when Saul disappoints him he repents of having chosen him and has to restart the kingly lineage with David. We could go on, but the evidence is clear: God is a risk taker. The creation, especially insofar as it includes free human beings who can choose to obey or disobey, to improve or to destroy the world, is fraught with risk. But if he is a risk taker, what does the Landlord entrust to his stewards to venture, to risk?

One answer is that God has given to us everything within our reach to risk. Whatever we can touch we can affect, for good or ill. We have the power to create and to destroy, to benefit and to despoil. Yet the biblical story suggests that God has imposed limits. In the Genesis account, following their disobedience, God drives the man and the woman from the divine park, Eden. Although they attain knowledge, God withholds immortality from them. This suggests that God withholds certain things that are his to give and not attainable by human technology.

119

It is difficult to discern what those limits on our power are. Yet even with limits, much (though not all) of the earth is at risk. (Though the great natural catastrophes of the geological past destroyed a great many species, they left the earth with life.) The extent of our power means that science is serious business. This is no reason for opting out of science and technology. To the contrary, science is legitimized by the injunction for change. In doing what we do, we must be concerned with the good that benefits the earth we are to care for, the stewards for whom the earth was created, and God who created both the earth and its stewards.

Does nature need stewards?

Our stewardship paradigm neither lacks critics nor stands free of problems. We must address one particular objection here. Simply put, why should one think that nature needs stewards? Why does nature have to be taken care of at all? If nature has existed for over three billion years without human supervision, cannot it continue to survive well without humans? Stephen Jay Gould puts the objection this way:

> The views that we live on a fragile planet now subject to permanent derailment and disruption by human intervention [and] that humans must learn to act as stewards for this threatened world, ... however well intentioned, are rooted in the old sin of pride and exaggerated self-importance. We are one among millions of species, stewards of nothing. By what argument could we, arising just a geological microsecond ago, become responsible for the affairs of a world 4.5 billion years old, teeming with life that has been evolving and diversifying for at least three-quarters of that immense span? Nature does not exist for us, had no idea we were coming, and doesn't give a damn about us ... We are virtually powerless over the earth at our planet's own geological time scale ... On geological scales, our planet will take good care of itself and let time clear the impact of any human malfeasance (Gould 1990: 30).

This objection directly challenges our paradigm and indirectly the analogy, underlying the Genesis text, that likens God's employment of stewards to that of a secular monarch (Reichenbach 2003). Without proper supervision and administration, the secular monarch's kingdom would go to wrack and ruin. The laws have to be enforced; taxes collected; revenues disbursed; infrastructure constructed and maintained; disputes settled; criminals caught, prosecuted and punished; the citizenry protected and defended against both internal and external threats. Since the kingdom cannot run effectively on its own and since the monarch cannot be everywhere, he places his representatives or stewards throughout his vast empire to administer it and guard against disruption and social turmoil.

But the earth is different. Through stasis and catastrophe, life persisted and evolved long before any monarch placed stewards throughout the land. Since it functioned well on its own for many geological eras, why should one think that if God had not recently placed his stewards throughout his kingdom, the place would have gone to wrack and ruin? Of course, in nature not every individual thrives. But not only is continual thriving not required, it is not desirable. Without death there is no birth or life; without decay no renewal.

Even the powers of the stewards in the analogy are greatly limited. Through their actions or inaction, the monarch's stewards significantly affect the kingdom's ability to survive and flourish. Their wisdom, perseverance and selfless concern for the people often furnish the glue that holds the kingdom together; their inept economic policies, lack of military preparedness, dishonesty or selfish greed could spell its quick demise. But not so for human stewards of the earth; nature's immense residual powers dwarf human power. 'All the megatonnage in our nuclear arsenals yield but one ten-thousandth the power of the asteroid that might have triggered the Cretaceous mass extinction. Yet the earth survived that large shock and, in wiping out dinosaurs, paved the road for the evolution of large mammals, including humans' (Gould 1990: 30). Even if we initiated a catastrophic nuclear war, though humans may be annihilated, some forms of life would survive to continue nature's evolutionary process.

This poses a serious objection. To construct a response to the question – does a stewardship paradigm entail that nature cannot take good care of itself? – we need to inquire about the view of nature that the objector presupposes and to note the context in which the question is raised.

First of all, the objection assumes that nature has operated and continues to operate on its own. No omnipotent potentate reigns over nature; no being guided its fantastic development from eukaryotes to conscious animals or was involved in preserving it through its catastrophic collisions with asteroids. On such a view, the concept of stewards who act on behalf of someone greater than nature does not connect with any other thesis. Gould is no theist.

Yet our stewardship paradigm assumes from the outset that there is a God who is the original and continuing source of nature, its creative and sustaining cause, a being who can act and has acted in geological as well as in human history. As omnipotent, God can act directly on or indirectly through his creation. This claim forms the heart of our Christian worldview. Thus, Gould's presupposed claim that nature has been on its own over the geologic eons reveals a critical difference between our world-views.

Admittedly, ours is not a scientific hypothesis. It can, however, be argued on scientific grounds that the conditions of the universe necessary for the existence of living, knowing, valuing beings are so unlikely as to be staggering. For example, had the 'Big Bang expanded at a different rate, life would not have evolved. A reduction by one part in a million million at an initial stage would have led to recollapse before temperatures could fall below ten thousand degrees. An early increase by one part in a million would have prevented the growth of galaxies, stars and planets' (Leslie 1982: 141). Or if the gravitational force were slightly greater, all the stars would be blue giants whose life span would be too short to allow the evolution of intelligent life. But if it had been slightly less, the universe would be devoid of many elements essential to life. In effect, what is *a priori* unlikely is necessary not only for what exists now, but for the very possibility of consciously understanding its purposefulness. At the same time this theistic thesis cannot be empirically tested, for we do not know the manner in which or the conditions under which God acts. For the Christian, the belief that God exists and is active in human history is engendered by the acceptance of revelation, which is itself held to be the result of divine interaction with creation.

A second consideration raised by Gould's objection is: What is meant by 'take good care of itself?' The objection presupposes that nature is a complex system composed of many individuals or parts. In the geological long run the parts are insignificant; whether any particular organism, species or ecosystem survives or thrives is irrelevant.[3] What matters is the 'survival' or continuity of nature, with earth's 'prosperity', reasonable 'stability', diversity, and the possibility of 'paving the road' for the development of more complex forms of life.

Given this interpretation of 'take good care of itself', the answer the stewardship paradigm might give to Gould's objection depends upon the context in which the question is raised. If it is raised outside the context of the existence of human beings, then clearly the answer is, no, a stewardship paradigm does not entail that nature cannot take good care of itself apart from humans. Before humans existed on earth, nature procreated, manifested ecological stability and diversity, and developed, as the biological-geological history of the world shows. (At the same time, we do not affirm that nature can take good care of itself apart from God, who is the creator and conserver.) As such, the primary reason why God created human beings cannot be that God needed stewards to preserve the environment. It was not as though nature, failing in its purpose or structure, and in a state of chaos and dissolution, required that God create stewards to enable it to survive and prosper or to restore order.

The fundamental reason why God made us is well stated in the answer to the first question of the Westminster Catechism: our 'chief end is to glorify God, and to enjoy him for ever'. People were created to return love and glory to their creator in a way that supersedes the response to God that nature makes. Nature gives glory to God by doing what it does naturally

(Ps. 19); people give glory by their free, loving response to the love God shows them. Just as we desire the free return of love from those whom we procreate and just as we prefer this love over any programmed responses of affection from a robot, so God desires that we freely return love to him. The first and greatest commandment, that we should love the Lord our God with all our heart, soul, mind and strength (Mk 12.29–30), provides the reason for our being.

Since stewardship does not provide the primary *raison d'être* for the existence of humans, the stewardship commands must be seen in the context of the existence of human beings who are created by God, whose very existence is valued by him, and whose free love is sought in return. In the context either of the existence of humans or of God's intention that there be humans, the answer to our question – Does the stewardship paradigm presuppose that nature cannot take good care of itself? – is Yes, for with the introduction of powerful, conscious beings who can radically affect their environment, nature itself lies in jeopardy. Its stability, diversity, and ability to evolve and prosper are under possible attack. To return to our kingdom analogy, the very creation of inhabitants who could function as stewards created the problems that the kingdom faces. The stewards are possible catalysts for social and environmental disruption. At the same time, the existence of the stewards is so valuable that it is worth risking the kingdom to create them. Hence, we derive the paradoxical conclusion that the existence of humans requires stewardship as one of their primary charges.

One might liken the situation to commanding my son to keep his room orderly. Does my stewardship command presuppose that his room cannot be ordered without him? No. Without him things would stay as they are. I did not bring him into the world to keep his room orderly. At the same time, having my son is more valuable than not having him. But having a son means there will now be disorder in his room that must be addressed. Hence, it is meaningful to give him the injunction to keep his room orderly; room stewardship becomes one of his assigned tasks.

As Gould correctly notes, we might not be capable of jeopardizing the ultimate existence of nature, but God's plans for nature might well extend beyond nature's mere survival of any humanly contrived holocaust. Gould sees nature not merely surviving, but prospering and providing a base for future evolution. But the theist may well hold that nature has a greater purpose than this. Nature is so important that God seeks to renew and recreate it.

The New Testament speaks about creation groaning in the pains of childbirth, waiting for its redemption. The human Fall negatively impacted nature. Nature, 'frustrated', in 'bondage to decay', waits in 'eager expectation' for its liberation (Rom. 8.18–25). This liberation began with the death and resurrection of Christ and will be fulfilled in the eschaton with

123

his return. We admit we do not know what this theological affirmation means in practical, ecological terms. Theological descriptions of the renewal are exceedingly vague and at times biologically naive (Wise 1991) Morphologically, it is difficult to conceive of the lions eating straw like the ox (Isa. 11.7). Or again, some suggest that in the new kingdom there will be no more death in nature: 'The abolition of the present world form will show itself negatively in that the rigid, fundamental law, to which all life in the present world is subject ... will be cancelled – the biological principle that life can only increase and multiply by a process in which other life is suffocated and destroyed with pain and deadly torture' (Taylor 1958; cited in Wise 1991: 127). But since death and decay were present in the natural world long before humans came on the scene, and since death – whether of plants, animals, or other organisms – is necessary for life, the changes envisioned for nature must encompass something other than death's elimination if the future kingdom is to be structurally continuous at all with this one.

What the redemption of nature will be like, precisely how nature will be made anew, how it will find itself in a new harmony with God, and how the curse brought about by Adam's sin is reversed (Rom. 5.12–19), remain divine mysteries. The same openness that was present before the original creation still exists about what will result from God's recreative and restorative acts. No one beforehand could have predicted or surmised what God would create. Yet, as the New Testament affirms, just as God in Christ made the universe (John 1.3; Heb. 1.1–3), so in Christ God will renew heaven and earth (Rev. 21.1–5; see also Isa. 65.17). In Revelation, 'the garden has become the city, but the city is reminiscent of the garden' (Manahan 1991; Zerbe 1991). But we cannot even speculate about the ecology of either.

What can be said is that because our presence and increased footprint on earth puts the kingdom at risk, the stewardship commands to fill, rule over, and care for take on greater importance and urgency. God's creation of us to love and worship him involved his giving to humans significant freedom to use well or to misuse. History records our repeated failure to be good stewards, not only for each other when we ignore the common good, but also for the environment over which we have some control. Our past record thus makes it more urgent that we discern and fulfil the divine command to be responsible stewards on behalf of God.

Notes

1. The obligation to change what we have destroyed by our sin is consistent with the redemptive motif that runs through Scripture. The Apostle Paul speaks about creation, along with us, groaning, waiting

for redemption (Rom. 8.22–23). Together we desire God's redemptive and renewing acts. We are not contending that humans merely by themselves are able to provide creation's needed redemption. However, in our stewardly role we can be representatives of God as he works out his redemptive plan for creation.

2. We should not be misunderstood as advocating a doctrine of the 'fixity of species'. We also recognize the shortcomings of defining 'species' in terms of inability to interbreed.

3. Gould takes pains in his article to show that the long-run view need not apply in the short run. In the short run, which encompasses the human time scale, it is reasonable to try 'to preserve populations because the comfort and decency of our present lives, and those of fellow species that share our planet, depend upon such stability' (1990:26).

Part III
Consolidation

Chapter 11

Stewardship as Key to a Theology of Nature

Douglas J. Hall

Douglas Hall can be regarded as virtually the founding father of modern interest in stewardship. He has written extensively on the characteristics, implications and biblical basis of stewardship. This article is a shortened version of Chapter 7 of his 1990 book The Steward: A Biblical Symbol Come of Age, *itself a revised edition of a book first published in 1982. In it, Hall develops his ideas of stewarding with nature as well as over nature. Professor Hall was Professor of Christian Theology at McGill University in Ottawa from 1977 to 1995; he is now Emeritus Professor. He is a member of the Order of Canada (CM).*

The integrity of creation

Wisely, in view of the growing threat to the natural order, the World Council of Churches at Vancouver in 1983 added to the two existing concerns (justice and peace) on which most of the member churches had been working for years, a third: 'the integrity of creation'. The term was new; for a discussion of the theological and biblical connotation of the term, see the WCC Paper, *Reintegrating God's Creation* (1987 – this was incorporated into a description of the whole Justice, Peace and the Integrity of Creation (JPIC) process, see Niles 1992). In explaining it, Premen Niles, secretary of the JPIC process, draws the connection with stewardship:

> The term includes ecological and environmental issues, but goes beyond them. Its central thrust is on a caring attitude towards nature – an emphasis that is more evident in the German *'Bewahrung die Schopfung'* and in the French *'sauvegarde de la création'*. The English 'integrity of creation' says more. It tries to bring together the issues of justice, peace and the environment by stressing the fact that there is an integrity or unity that is given in God's creation. What this means

129

will become clearer as we continue in the various struggles for life, and realize more fully that we live in an interdependent world of complex relationships and delicate balances. To realize, for instance, that justice for the poor and the hungry is tied up with the issue of justice for the land. To ignore the integrity of creation is to destroy finally all that sustains us. In essence, it is a call for a new life-style that is based on stewardship and compassion rather than on mastery and exploitation.

Similarly, Professor Charles Birch, noting that 'the phrase Justice, Peace and the Integrity of Creation recognizes three momentous instabilities of our time', writes:

Integrity has to do with wholeness, completeness, the notion of organic unity which is more than an aggregate, and the reciprocal relation of the individual elements to the ensemble. We may understand the meaning of integrity better if we think of its opposite: fragmentation, separation, alienation, estrangement.

While Christians have absorbed the concerns expressed openly by scientists as early as 1960, we are not permitted quickly to leap in with our solutions; we have a good deal of internal house cleaning to do before we may legitimately claim to be keepers of ancient wisdom that may be useful to the world at this critical juncture. If our theology of stewardship is to be credible in the face of dire crises such as 'the greenhouse effect' and the depletion of species ('every hour a score of nonhuman species becomes extinct'), we have first to take seriously the criticism that is levelled against our religious tradition. The Christian faith, the official 'cult' of the majority of postindustrial societies, stands accused of being the primary spiritual sponsor of technocratic humanity's plunder of the earth. It benefits us therefore, first, to come to terms with our own culpability.

Christian culpability

'Nature is the enemy! She must be brought to her knees!' Such were the triumphant words of the narrator of an unforgettable documentary film that I saw in the early 1970s. The screen pictures to which these words corresponded as a kind of litany depicted a vast upheaval, an explosion caused (one supposes) by tons of dynamite: rocks and trees and water and (in all likelihood) several thousands of little animals went rushing pell-mell heavenwards. And when the dust settled the earth movers and the heavy machinery moved in, ready to turn the wilderness of the north into one of the great hydroelectric projects of our continent. This undertaking, the actual need and worth of which has been seriously challenged by many scientists, economists and politicians, is a monument to the technocratic mentality.

But what was so vexing to me was that the same script was studded with quotations from the Bible. I do not remember all of them, but some of the following texts were certainly used in this carefully written film script:

> And God said to them, 'Be fruitful and multiply, and fill the earth and subdue it; and have dominion over the fish of the sea and over the birds of the air and over every living thing that moves upon the earth'. (Gen. 1.28).

> And God blessed Noah and his sons, and said to them, 'Be fruitful and multiply, and fill the earth. The fear of you and the dread of you shall be upon every beast of the earth, and upon every bird of the air, upon everything that creeps on the ground and all the fish of the sea; into your hands they are delivered. Every moving thing that lives shall be food for you ... I give you everything (Gen. 9.1–3).

> What is man that thou art mindful of him? ...
> Yet thou hast made him little less than God,
> and dost crown him with glory and honor.
> Thou hast given him dominion over the works of thy hands; thou hast put all things under his feet (Ps. 8.4–6).

> Look at the birds of the air ... Are you not of more value than they? (Mt. 6.26).

> But these, like irrational animals, creatures of instinct, born to be caught and killed ... will be destroyed in the same destruction with them (2 Pet. 2.12).

Some time later, when colleagues in the life sciences at the University of Saskatchewan began to demand of me why we Christians have such a deplorable view of nature, I understood something of their meaning. They showed me the then newly published essay on 'The Historical Roots of our Ecologic Crisis' by the historian, Lynn White (White 1967).

Professor White's article makes a clear-cut case: Behind the modern pillage of planet earth there stands the Hebraic–Christian religion with its too lofty estimate of the human species, its frank denigration of the animal and vegetable kingdoms, and its insistence that humanity has both the right and the duty to rule. Have dominion! Subdue! These two words are in Hebrew very strong ones: *Kabash* (subdue) comes from a Hebrew root meaning 'to tread down'; it conveys the image of a heavy-footed man making a path by smashing everything in his way. The connotation of *radah* (dominion), 'is no less harsh: it also conveys a picture of "treading" or "trampling" and suggests the image of a conqueror placing his foot on the neck of a slave' (Wilkinson 1980b: 27).

What are we to make of this? Is biblical faith especially culpable in connection with the industrial oppression of the natural world? How can we reconcile (or can we?) the apparent contradictions of a religion that on the one hand clearly makes the world – God's good creation – the very object of the divine *agape*, and on the other seems to give to greedy *anthropos* all the justification needed for turning the beautiful place God made into a pigsty?

One thing is certain: The technocratic approach to existence has evolved within a civilization whose most influential religious background has been one that called itself Christian. This connection we cannot deny. It is in particular the anthropology of our Christian West that E.B. White (quoted by Rachel Carson 1962: vii) had in mind when he wrote: 'I am pessimistic about the human race because it is too ingenious for its own good. Our approach to nature is to beat it into submission. We would stand a better chance of survival if we accommodated ourselves to this planet and viewed it appreciatively, instead of skeptically and dictatorially.'

Does beating nature into submission actually express the meaning of 'dominion'? Are skepticism and dictatorship authentically Christian attitudes towards the planet? Or does Christianity somehow, even unwittingly perhaps, encourage such attitudes? How, in the face of much ecological bitterness directed at the Judeo-Christian world-view, can Christians describe the relation between humanity and extra human creation – if not to exonerate ourselves from past guilt, at least to contribute something better to the future?

A. Humanity above nature

One way of conceiving this relation is to place *Homo sapiens* on a very high rung of the ladder of being, and to insist that nature is simply there for human usage. At the outset of the modern period, Western philosophic literature was crammed full of this sentiment. Indeed, the sentiment is of the essence of modernity, the very cornerstone of the religion of progress. One of its most straightforward statements comes from the pen of the English philosopher Thomas Hobbes, who over against the mediaeval propensity to regard nature cautiously, as a realm of immense mystery, wrote:

She is no mystery, for she worketh by motion and geometry . . .
[We] can chart these motions. Feel then as if you lived in a world
which can be measured, weighed and mastered and confront it
with audacity (quoted by Basil Willey 1953: 95–96).

Another architect of modernity, René Descartes ([1950]: 40), put the
matter in somewhat gentler terms, but his claim for humanity is, if anything, even more extravagant than Hobbes:

I perceived it to be possible to arrive at a knowledge highly useful in
life, and in room of that speculative philosophy usually taught in the
schools, to discover a practical [philosophy], by means of which,
knowing the force and action of fire, water, the stars, the heavens, and
all other bodies that surround us, as distinctly as we know the various
crafts of our artisans, we might also apply them in the same way to all
the uses to which they are adapted, and thus render ourselves lords
and possessors of nature.

Maître et posseseur de la nature! Francis Bacon reduced the sentiment to a
slogan: *Scientia est potestas* ['science is power'] (see discussion in Moltmann, 1985a: 27f.). We achieve knowledge (*scientia*) of our world, not for
the beauty of knowing, not for the joy of discovering truth (that was the aim
of the ancients), but for power (*potestas*).

This has been the dominant attitude of modern Western civilization into
our own time. You can hear it still, chanted on every television adver-
tisement, inserted openly or implicitly into nearly every election speech.
Knowledge, not wisdom (*sapientia*), is the goal of human reason and (the
sacred word of the modern university) research. Science is power. 'Modern
technique,' wrote Bertrand Russell in the late 1920s,

has given man a sense of power which is rapidly altering his whole
mentality. Until recent times, the physical environment was something which had to be accepted and made the best of . . . To the
modern man his physical environment is merely raw material, an
opportunity for manipulation. It may be that God made the world,
but that is no reason why we should not make it over (Russell 1931:
151–52).

It is interesting to note that the same Bertrand Russell, near the end of his
long life, confided in a BBC radio interview that he was pessimistic whether
we would see the end of the present century.

However we may feel personally about the 'humanity above nature'
world-view, we are part of a society that has been built upon that premise.
The idea that humanity is nature's lord and possessor, capable of making

over what God rather thoughtlessly put together in the first place, is an almost exact description of the North American attitude towards the natural universe. It is our very birthright. We are, as the late George Grant, Canadian philosopher and theologian, so ably stated, the children of the modern epoch; we have no other past than the modern past:

> It is hard indeed to overrate the importance of faith in progress through technology to those brought up in the mainstream of North American life. It is the very ground of their being. The loss of this faith for a North American is equivalent to the loss of himself and the knowledge of how to live. The ferocious events of the twentieth century may batter the outposts of that faith, dim intuitions of the eternal order, may put some of its consequences into question, but its central core is not easily surrendered (Grant 1959: vi).

It is ingrained in our most rudimentary thinking as a people that nature, which has been exceptionally bounteous in our case, if not precisely the enemy, is at least there for the taking, the making, and the breaking. As Ogden Nash lamented:

> I think that I shall never see
> A billboard lovely as a tree;
> Indeed, unless the billboards fall,
> I'll never see a tree at all! (from *Song of the Open Road*)

There are also those who rejoice over our increasing capacities for controlling life processes at their most basic – in the field of genetic engineering. The case of the turkey is symptomatic of far more subtle changes that are in the offing:

> When Audubon painted it, it was a sleek, beautiful, though odd-headed bird, capable of flying 65 miles per hour. Benjamin Franklin said that it should be adopted as America's national bird, thinking it a 'more respectable bird' than the 'poor and often lousy' Bald Eagle. Today, the turkey is an obese, immobile thing, hardly able to stand, much less fly. As for respectability, the big bird is so stupid that it must be taught to eat, and so large in the breast that in order to breed, a saddle must be strapped to the hen to offer the turkey cock a claw-hold. The modern bird is not so much a turkey as it is a mutation, a commodity manufactured rather than a bird hatched ... [It sports] 60% of its flesh in the breast and wings. Americans like white meat, and the American poultry industry, using methods that may harm you, is happy to remodel its birds in order to comply (*Conservation Society Notes*, December, 1975, p. 15).

By comparison with what is now envisaged, the case of the turkey is primitive indeed:

> Bioengineering is the manipulation of the becoming process of living organisms in advance. For the first time, it is possible to envision the 'engineering' of the internal biology of an organism at conception so as to control its entire future development. When scientists engineer changes in the genetic code, they are programming the life cycle of the organism before it unfolds ... We are engineering organisms to make them compatible with an environment we have created ... We have managed to construct a concept of nature that is remarkably sympathetic to the way we happen to be managing nature (Rifkin 1983: 219).

Is all of this really the product of the Judeo-Christian tradition? Is 'the nihilism practised in our dealings with nature' (Moltmann 1985a: xi) finally to be laid at the doorstep of biblical faith?

The accusation must at very least be clarified. In its typical form (including Lynn White's essay) it represents a rather naive understanding of the Scriptures of Israel and the church, however it may be justified in other respects. There are in fact many things in the biblical tradition that go straight against the grain of a manipulative approach to nature. Nature suffers, not when human beings are doing what they are meant to do in God's intention, but when they sin:

> The earth mourns and withers, the world languishes and withers; the heavens languish together with the earth. The earth lies polluted under its inhabitants; for they have transgressed the laws, violated the statutes, broken the everlasting covenant. Therefore a curse devours the earth, and its inhabitants suffer for their guilt; therefore the inhabitants of the earth are scorched, and few men are left. The wine mourns, the vine languishes, all the merry-hearted sigh ... The city of chaos is broken down, every house is shut up so that none can enter. There is an outcry in the streets for lack of wine; all joy has reached its eventide; the gladness of the earth is banished (Isa. 24.4–11).

Even on strictly historical grounds, it is simplistic to trace the idea of humanity above nature in an undialectical way to the biblical tradition. Mediaeval Christians were for limiting human power. They did not look upon *scientia* as *potestas* but as *veritas* (truth). They wanted wisdom, not control.

In the sixteenth century a new feeling for human autonomy and potential arose within the soul of European humanity. Perhaps it was the consequence of the preceding apocalyptic age, with the ravages of the bubonic plague, the breakdown of institutions, and the general demise of the mediaeval vision. Perhaps in the darkness of that age the idea began to dawn upon the sensitive that human beings need not wait passively for death and destruction, but might take their destiny into their own hands – 'change the world', in the famous dictum of Karl Marx. With such a spirit (*Zeitgeist*) brooding over the face of history, men and women will make use of whatever is at hand to construct the image of humanity that is required for the articulation and employment of that spirit: humanism, Protestantism, nominalism, empiricism – whatever can contribute to the ascent towards an imagined light. And who, whether from a sacred or a secular perspective, will dare to blame them for that? All the same, it meant that something had begun to be lost – something that belonged to both the tradition of Jerusalem and the tradition of Athens, namely, the sense of our essential smallness before 'the Real'.

The conception of human nature and destiny that emerged from this crucible contained many elements of Constantinian Christianity. But it also left something out: the darker side of the mediaeval analysis, which in spite of theological triumphalism and ecclesiastical imperialism, bore the ancient insight of the prophets and apostles that humanity's use of power is frequently if not habitually directed towards ambiguous or straightforwardly evil ends. In addition, as we have said above, modernity left out the mediaeval Christian respect for nature, exemplified in a highly positive and spiritual manner in the mysticism of Tauler and Eckhardt and others, and in a no doubt more primitive and superstitious way in the popular fear of nature's grandeur and unpredictabity.

While both biblical and historical analysis necessitates locating the historical roots of our ecologic crisis at the beginning of the modern epoch, however, this does not exonerate the Christian church. For one must ask why the Christians at the turn of the modern epoch permitted their faith and their sacred texts to be used in this way. Why were they not more diligent in saying to the Bacons and Descartes and Eric Hoffers and B.F. Skinners of this world that the name our religious tradition has given to the human quest for power without love is *sin*?

In fact, instead of maintaining a prophetic vigilance against being co-opted by modernity, Christianity on the whole aided and abetted the whole process by openly supporting the notion of human mastery. For the most part, Christians, including Christian intellectuals, have announced 'Christian truth' with very little regard for the manner in which it could be heard and used.

The following statement is typical: 'Man is a creature divinely endowed with gifts which set him above all other creatures: he is made in the image of God' (Whale 1941: 44). A more contextually aware theology would think twice before making such a statement. To affirm the radical distinction between humanity and all other creatures in an age which was already in the grip of a Promethaean image of the human is to be wholly innocent of prophetic vigilance. A theology in dialogue with the whole of the tradition would, in such a cultural context, feel the need at least for a more nuanced definition of the image of God.

Of course, what is really at fault in this whole approach to the relation between human and extrahuman being is signalled by just this kind of definition. If one thinks of the human creature as a possessor of superior endowments such as intellect and will, and locates the relationship between this creature and the others on a scale or hierarchy of being which is determined by such gifts, one is bound to end up with the humanity above nature alternative. But if the image of God does not refer to a quality that we possess (making us superior to other creatures), but to a relationship in which we stand vis-à-vis our Creator, and a vocation to which we are called within the creation, a very different conception of the humankind/other kind relation follows. The symbol of the steward assumes the latter arrangement.

B. Humanity in nature

The second possibility for conceiving of the relation between human beings and the natural world is to think of *Homo sapiens* as one of a myriad of creatures. This conception of the place of the human species is a modern one although it is possible to find hints of it here and there in earlier civilizations and religions – for example, in Epicureanism. One can discover such hints also in the Scriptures of Israel and the church. Amongst these, none is more significant than that picture of Adam provided in the second of the two creation sagas of Genesis: *Adam* is taken from *adamah*, the man from the ground, or, as Loren Wilkinson (1980b: 27) translates the Hebrew pun, 'God made humans out of humus'.

Yet in the literature of the Bible, as in other ancient sources, humanity is hardly ever just this. There is a mystery which prevents the ancients both of Jerusalem and of Athens from regarding *anthropos* as 'just another animal'. To be sure, the creature is animal. But it is a thinking animal, a 'rational animal' (Greece), a 'speaking animal' (Jerusalem). Its thinking and speaking are not always good for it. Thinking does not make it happy most of the time. Evil flows from its tongue. And 'no human being can tame the tongue – a restless evil, full of deadly poison' (James 3.8). Imagination regularly begets evil, and human ambition is 'vanity' (Ecclesiastes). Yet thought and the articulation of thought do render this creature somehow transcendent.

Naturalizing the human species must be regarded as a clear reaction to placing it above nature. It is the reaction of a protesting element against the spirit of the Enlightenment and the industrialization and technicalization of existence that flowed from the Enlightenment mentality. Against the elevation of the human species along the lines of an almost divine rationality, the romantics rebelled on the side of the heart – on the side of nature. From Rousseau onwards, they saw that this supposed elevation of the human species above nature was at the same time a denigration of the species. Turning humanity into nothing but mind could lead to a situation in which everything about *Homo sapiens* itself that is not mind (feeling, love, emotion, the body, sex, suffering, etc.) would have to be repressed or, if possible, eliminated. The ironic thing about humanity being above nature is that it has to eliminate all that is natural in human beings themselves, finally, in order to seem plausible. So by now, as Abraham Heschel has reminded us, the efficient machine is a more acceptable model for human beings in the modern image than is Aristotle's category, the 'rational animal' (Heschel 1965: 30).

Sometimes, however, when the pendulum of history swings, it goes too far. Extremes beget extremes, and we find ourselves caught between one absurd reduction and a polarity that is equally absurd. Thus in the past few decades, and in the face of a technocracy that has gone much farther than ever Bacon or Descartes envisaged, a countercultural movement in the Western world and especially in North America has happened that carries the idea of humanity being in nature to sometimes ridiculous conclusions. It is now possible to hear even Christians speaking as if the only way of saving the planet were for the human species to plan itself out of existence. To become, so to speak, as 'natural' as the dinosaurs!

No doubt the human species has created more trouble in the world than any other creature. Christians affirmed this long ago when they made the fall of creation consequent upon the fall of Adam and Eve. But is the 'mending of creation' to be achieved through the extinction of the troublesome human component? Not as I read the story of our redemption. Besides, Yahweh already thought of that solution, as the story of the great flood mythically tells us.

It is not only a counsel of despair but patent nonsense, in my opinion, to assume either that humanity is or that it ought to be simply 'in' nature. Even the limiting of our powers, even the entire sacrifice of our powers, presupposes that we are after all unique creatures, who do not simply do 'what comes naturally'. As a corrective to the pretention of humanity above nature, this second approach is necessary and true. But as a permanently valid approach it is without foundation in reality, and under certain conditions – especially in contexts where there is already a propensity towards apathy and irresponsibility on the part of whole segments of human society – it can be positively dangerous. Many would argue that ours is precisely such a context.

C. Humanity with nature

Using the two previous approaches for purposes of contrast and definition, we are led to a third possible way of conceiving of the relation between humanity and the natural order. It is probable that this must be regarded more as a possibility than as an approach that has actually been given a chance in history, although it is without doubt the approach that belongs in our religious tradition. Here humanity is neither superior to the rest of creation (above) nor simply identical with it (in), but the human creature exists alongside the others, in solidarity with them, yet also distinct.

Those who read the Bible with any frequency will have noticed the prominence of the preposition 'with' in this literature. Husbands are with their wives, wives with their husbands. Friends are with one another – as Jesus' disciples are described as being 'with' him in this or that place. Even God is depicted in these terms: Emmanuel – 'God *with* us.'

This predominance of the preposition 'with' is not accidental. The language of the Bible is determined by its ontology, that is, its assumption concerning the nature of what 'is'. And in the tradition of Jerusalem we have to do with a quite distinctive understanding of reality. Here there is on the one hand a strong sense of the interconnectedness of everything that 'is'.[1] This is present both in the creation theology of the Genesis writers, where all creatures share a common origin and life principle, and in the New Testament's redemption theology, where the unity and reunification of all informs both the doctrine of the church and of the consummation of all things.

At the same time, this feeling for the interconnectedness of everything is held in creative tension with an equally important emphasis upon the uniqueness of each creature. This is true of God, who despite being the 'ground' of all that is, is nevertheless distinct and not to be confused with creation. Likewise the human individuals who make their appearance in this long story are all unique. Jacob and Esau are brothers – but very different from each other. Peter is a human being like John, but he is not just a carbon copy of John, and has to be told in no uncertain terms that John's destiny is not to be confused with his own (John 21.21–22). Eve is so close to Adam that he names her 'bone of my bones, flesh of my flesh'. But already this ancient saga of creation and Fall gives distinctive characters to the two who are at the centre of it. So also with the animals. According to Genesis 2 they are all created out of the same 'dust' as the 'earth creature' Adam. But they differ markedly from Adam, and will not do as his partner. They differ also from one another, as the flood story demonstrates in a subtle way.

Given this dialectical tension between participation and individuality, commonality and uniqueness, 'with' is the only preposition that will serve with any accuracy. The underlying theory of reality, which with Joseph

Sittler (1970) I should like to call Jerusalem's 'ontology of communion', requires a language that will do justice to the nuanced combination of seemingly antithetical characteristics found in biblical thought. 'With' is perhaps the only preposition that will serve this purpose, for it contains both the idea of sameness and the idea of difference, both being together and being apart, both participation and particularity.

Or, to put the matter more succinctly still, 'with' is the preposition that belongs to the language of love. And love, to state the biblical ontology in its most direct and un-technical form, is the reality that the Bible wants to describe.

Love means difference: I am not you, you are not me. If we love each other, it does not mean (what it means in some ancient and also modern types of mysticism) that we simply merge into an ontic unity (John and Mary when they are married and are pronounced one flesh do not become a hybrid 'Jarry'). Love means that I am with you and you are with me in a special sense. We do not disappear into each other's being. Rather, we become all the more real and solid as persons in the process of our being united with one another. What is forfeited in our relatedness is not our individual 'thou-ness' (on the contrary, that is what is gained!), but the hostility, the suspicion, the bid for self-sufficiency that belong to the distortion of our personalities in their separation from the other, the counterpart.

Love, as the fundamental ontology of the tradition of Jerusalem which incorporates even this tradition's doctrine of God (for 'God is love'), positively needs something like the preposition 'with'. If this preposition did not exist, love as it is understood in this tradition would have to invent it. For neither 'beside', nor 'within', nor 'in', nor 'to', nor even 'between' and certainly not 'above' – is suitable for delineating what is intended in this most basic category of being.

In fact, the term 'being' as such is misleading. The tradition of Athens could employ the language of being (*ontos*) honestly enough; but Hebraic thought has a different preconception of the nature of being. Everything of which it may be said that it 'is' stands in relationship with everything else that is. The whole of reality, in other words, presupposes this dialectical interaction of sameness and difference, identity and distinction. Being itself is relational – or, to employ an awkward term: being for this tradition itself implies *with-being, being-with*.

What this implies about the relation between theology and ethics is very important. It means that the Christian's ethic, whose summation is the commandment 'to love', is absolutely grounded in the basic Christian assumption about reality itself, which is what theology tries to describe. The ethic (love) is nothing more nor less than the theology (God loves) stated in the imperative mood. The ethic is not derived from the theology but is already present in the theology; the only reason why it has even to be made explicit as commandment (love your neighbour) is that our hearts are hard and our wills bound to patterns of behaviour that resist the gospel of divine love.

Both the theory and the practice of faith, both theology and ethics, presuppose this ontology of communion. All that *is* exists under the mandate of its Creator that it should seek out and dwell 'with' (that is, and love) everything else that *is*. Our very being as human beings, as God intends it, is a *being-with*. The distortion of our being (sin) is nothing more nor less than our alienation from all that we are created to be with. Sin, we could say, is a resolute 'being-alone', which implies also 'being against'.

In their better expressions, Christian theology and ethics have known how to express all this with respect to two of the dimensions of our human relatedness: God, and our human partners (the neighbour). But Christian theology has rarely explored the meaning of this fundamental ontological assumption for the third major dimension of our threefold relatedness as creatures, namely, our relation to the extra-human world, the inarticulate creation. This is now what must be explored under the heading of 'Humanity with Nature'.

As the 'being-with' of the ontology of communion applies to our human relation to the extra human world, it contains the same two polar movements that are found in the other dimensions of our relatedness. One pole of this dialectic contains the thought of human difference from the other creatures. We cannot escape this, no matter how romantically attached we may be to the idea of humankind's being simply part of nature. According to the biblical witness at least, we are different. This does not mean superior but it does mean that we human beings are more complex, more versatile, and also more vulnerable than most other creatures. But why? Not, certainly, in order that we can lord it over them! Rather, so that we can exercise a unique responsibility towards them, a unique answerability for them. We are – yes, why should we not use this word? – to 'have dominion'.

But what does that mean precisely in the full perspective of biblical religion? When we hear the words 'have dominion', what or whom should we think of? Not, surely, of Caesar, or Pharoah, or Herod. Not even of Cyrus, the divinely approved king. Surely dominion as it is exegeted by the biblical story itself is to be interpreted on the model supplied by the Bible's description of the one, the only one, who really is Lord: 'Hear O Israel, I am the Lord thy God'. And for Christians what is already implicit in that 'I am' is made explicit in the one who is sent. 'Jesus Christ is *Dominus*' (1 Cor. 12.3), whispered the early Christians to one another; and Paul added, 'and him crucified' (1 Cor. 1.23; 2.2).

We are different, then, from the beasts of the field and the birds of the air. Let us not be naive and imagine that we can just melt into nature. But the purpose of all this is that we should 'have dominion': that is, that we should be servants, keepers and priests in relation to the others. That we should represent them before their Maker, and represent to them their Maker's tender care.

But more importantly, we are *Homo loquens*, the speaking creature. We do not speak for ourselves only (using the phrase in both its literal and its figurative sense). When we are true to our own essence, to the ontology of communion and community, we speak for all our fellow creatures. And when we really do speak for them, and not just to hear ourselves talk, what we say is simply 'thank you'. *Eucharistia!* That is to say: gratitude alone authenticates any human claim to dominion. Until that gratitude has wholly and unambiguously permeated our being, 'the whole creation groaneth' (Rom. 8.22, KJV).

But the other side of this dialectic of our being with nature must also be well remembered. We can be the keepers and priests of the others only if we are in some sense also the same as they. Of course, we do in fact share their being: their mortality, their limitations of power, their finitude, their reproductive capacities and incapacities, their need for air and food and water, their subjection to the laws of gravity, thermodynamics, and all the rest. But our temptation and possibility is to deny our solidarity with them, to seek to be above; and so (like the Prodigal envying even the swine he fed) regularly we fall into a degraded contradiction of our creaturely reality that animals never know. We have to affirm and reaffirm our real identity with nature. Indeed, what is redemption in this tradition if it is not precisely that grace-given transformation in us, that *metanoia*, which gives us the courage to affirm our own creature-hood, and therefore our co-creature hood? Not the overcoming of our creature-hood, but its joyful acceptance: this is salvation!

And this is the only condition under which we may represent the other creatures. Accepting our rudimentary solidarity with them, our difference from them is not a boast; it is only a means to the end of our serving both God and them. Our so-called endowments – thought and will and speech, for instance – are not ends, but necessary means to our peculiar service within the general creaturely sphere. 'We perceive in order to participate, not in order to dominate' (Moltmann 1980: 59). Our representation of the unspeaking creation depends upon perception, thought, reflection and imagination. But it also depends upon participation. One side demands the other.

And this brings us back at last to that symbol we have hardly named in this discussion of the relation between humanity and nature. There is no other symbol in biblical faith – perhaps there is no other symbol in all of human literature – that so appropriately catches the two sides of this dialectical tension about which we have been thinking. The steward symbol is in the realm of the metaphoric what the preposition 'with' is in the realm of the linguistic.

On the one hand, the steward is singled out for special responsibility. Unlike the other servants, the steward is truly answerable for what happens in the household. All the same, the steward is one of the others, having no absolute rights over them, but liable to judgment because of his treatment of them. The steward is different, but the steward is also the same. Like all the others, the steward is recipient of that which can never be his or hers to own.

It is no wonder then that an increasing number of persons, many of whom have no personal relation to the Christian faith, find in this Judeo-Christian symbol a profound metaphor for expressing a viable Western alternative to the status quo in our relation with nature. For example: 'Although much in Christianity has rightly been found by critics to be ecologically objectionable (in that nature is almost completely de-sacralised and man given quasi-total dominion over creation), others point out with equal correctness that stewardship and other Christian virtues could easily form the basis of an ecological ethic' (Ophuls 1997: 242–43).

From symbol to political necessity

When we speak about stewardship as the key to the relation between humanity and nature, we are speaking of a vision. Under the conditions of history, this vision is never fully realized. It is an eschatological vision in which the enmity between creature and Creator, creature and creature, and creature and creation will have given way to true mutuality and unconditional love: 'being-with'.

It was this visionary aspect of our stewardship that the great American painter Edward Hicks (1780–1849) tried to express in his work, 'Peaceable Kingdom'. As James Thomas Flexner (1962: 34) writes, Hicks 'painted many Peaceable Kingdoms illustrating the biblical prophecy that the lion and the lamb shall lie down together. Not the lax sermons of conventional moralists, these pictures do not ignore the problem of evil. Hicks, who fought daily engagements with his own passions, knew that it would not be easy for the lion and the lamb to lie down together.' And, we might add, it would be even more difficult for the child of Adam and Eve to lead them.

But while this is and remains an eschatological vision, it is not merely an impossible dream. Today it has become the only real and practicable alternative. To continue trying to be nature's lords and possessors can only mean the premature end of the experiment, for our lording and possessing has become increasingly bellicose and vengeful. On the other hand, to adopt the solution of the bourgeois romantics and disappear into nature (while ensconced in the comforts of a California bungalow by the sea or a New England classroom) may solve some of the problems of the cockroaches, but what about the future Mozarts? Stewardship is no longer just a nice ideal. It has become a social and political necessity.

That is why such statements as that of the WCC on 'the integrity of creation' which could once perhaps be received as ecclesiastical rhetoric, ought now to be heard by serious Christians as aspirations that challenge us to approximate the divine love that we have said, these many centuries, saves and surrounds us: 'Through the One who loved 'the world' (John 3:16), we are called and enabled to love and to embrace with compassion the whole creation. Like the love of God by which it is enabled, love also involves suffering for 'the other' – and 'the other' understood, now, as inclusive of other species, not only of our own kind. In this solidarity with the whole, in the love of Christ, we shall find our own human fulfilment as well.'

Note

1. Christianity shares this sense of the integrity of all that is with some other religions of the world, especially Buddhism. When I asked the renowned Buddhist scholar Masao Abe what as a Buddhist he felt it most important to preserve, he answered immediately, 'the interconnectedness of all that is'.

Chapter 12

Stewardship: Responding Dynamically to the Consequences of Human Action in the World

Calvin B. DeWitt

Calvin DeWitt is Professor of Environmental Studies at the University of Wisconsin-Madison and founder and now President of the Au Sable Institute of Environmental Studies. He has been a pioneer and inspiration of Christian environmentalism in North America for many years. He has written or edited many seminal works, including The Environment and the Christian *(1991)*, Missionary Earthkeeping *(1992, with Ghillean Prance), and* The Just Stewardship of Land and Creation *(1996). This paper was one of those given at Windsor in 2000 (see p. xi).*

The interwoven living fabric that envelops our planet – the Biosphere – is the life-giving and life-sustaining system upon which all living things depend. It is the manifest integration of interacting biotic and abiotic elements, structured and ordered in ways that maintain the conditions for its own systemic sustainability and for the ongoing lineages of its prolific and highly textured abundant life. Human beings, along with all other living creatures, are wholly dependent upon this system for their biological existence and support. Yet human beings, even as they know their absolute dependence on the biosphere for their lives and livelihoods, are degrading and threatening its life-support processes, threatening not only the earth but also themselves.

How can we address this problem in our time? Do we have the means available to help us deal with it effectively and successfully? More specifically, can the stewardship model that has been practised from antiquity up to the industrial revolution be re-instated, refurbished and returned to effective service? Can it be made sufficiently robust for a highly dynamic earth at a time when human beings have become a major biological and geological force?

This paper addresses these questions and the necessity for right living on earth.

Stewardship from antiquity to the present

From antiquity to the present there is a continuing stream of writing that documents the dynamic interaction between people and the earth directed toward applying lessons learned from Creation toward (1) improving the earth for human use and habitation and (2) correcting adverse environmental consequences of human actions in the world. In his definitive treatise, *Nature and Culture in Western Thought from Ancient Times to the End of the Eighteenth Century* (1967), Berkeley professor Clarence Glacken describes how ancient peoples observed the ordered cosmos and, in their desire to respect and emulate this order in their lives and landscapes, correspondingly ordered the land for human habitation. He reports that 'the writers of the Roman period, like Varro, Columella and Pliny, were deeply interested in the improvement of soils, methods of plowing, irrigation, removal of stones, clearing away of thickets, winning of new lands for cultivation, manuring and insect control ...' (Glacken 1967: 137) He shows how fusing these classical ideas with their later expression in Christian theology and the writings of the early Church Fathers 'produced concepts of the earth as a habitable planet' – concepts that served well into the nineteenth century. However, the classical and theological underpinnings of stewardship became threatened as 'unmistakable evidences that undesirable changes in nature were made by man began to accumulate in great volume' and as these reached dramatic proportions in the eighteenth and nineteenth centuries. 'For if man cleared forests too rapidly, if he relentlessly killed off wildlife, if torrents and soil erosion followed his clearings, it seems as if the lord of creation was failing in his appointed task, that he was going a way of his own, capriciously and selfishly defiant of the will of God and of Nature's plan.' The philosophical and theological underpinnings of stewardship – a synthesis of classical thought, Christian theology, science, and the practice of stewardship as 'one of the key ideas in the religious and philosophical thought of Western civilization regarding man's place in nature' – were seriously shaken.

William Blake observed and addressed this degradation in the early nineteenth century. Some time between 1808 and 1818 he described this transition from harmony to disharmony using the image of two wheels: a larger wheel representing Creation's economy and a smaller wheel representing the human economy. When the human economy operates *within* the greater economy of Creation, the wheels move harmoniously, in the same direction. However, when the human economy operates *outside of* the greater economy of Creation, disharmony results from one grinding against the other as they move in opposite directions (Fig. 1).

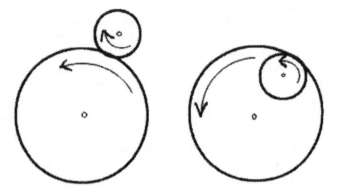

Fig. 1. Visual representation of William Blake's image of two wheels. The left illustration shows the human economy (the smaller wheel) operating outside of Creation's economy (the larger wheel) and the right illustration shows the human economy operating within the larger economy of Creation.

Blake writes:

> I turn my eyes to the schools and universities of Europe.
> And there behold the Loom of Locke, whose Woof rages dire,
> Wash'd by the Water-wheels of Newton: black the cloth
> In heavy wreaths folds over every nation: cruel works
> Of many Wheels I view, wheel without wheel, with cogs tyrannic
> Moving by compulsion each other, not as those in Eden, which,
> Wheel within wheel, in freedom revolve in harmony and peace.

With the industrial revolution, the human economy seemingly had escaped from Creation's economy and ran contrary to it. Conversely, Creation – once the model of order and harmony – had been conceptually transformed into a bundle of 'rude resources' and 'crude resources' stored in a mechanical earth awaiting refinement. The new economy, articulated by John Locke, Adam Smith and others, became the new model for ordering society and God's Creation. Creation's status was transformed from exemplary teacher and book of learning to a vast store of natural and human resources waiting to be extracted. The great variety, texture and abundance of Creation's creatures were reduced conceptually into land, labour and capital. People were transformed from Creation-stewards to human resources; human beings as images of God (*imago Dei*) were re-envisioned as *consumers*, *producers* and *taxpayers*. And *Homo sapiens* – the *Homo* with wisdom – was reconceptualized as *Homo economicus*.

No longer was the former view given credence. No longer would people acknowledge and respect, with the distinguished Swedish taxonomist, Carolus Linnaeus, that we operate within the 'Oeconomy of nature', which we understand as: 'the all-wise disposition of the Creator in relation to natural things, by which they are fitted to produce general ends, and reciprocal uses'.

This was our perspective on the world in 1749, and according to environmental historian Donald Worster, at the conclusion of the seventeenth century the word 'oeconomy' was often applied to divine government of Creation: 'God's economy was His extraordinary talent for matching means to ends, for so managing the cosmos that each constituent part performed its work with stunning efficiency' (Worster 1979: 37).

While the third edition of Webster's Unabridged Dictionary still defines 'economy' as 'God's plan or system for the government of the world', this meaning has largely been supplanted by its more recent definitions: 'the structure of economic life in a country or area: an economic system' and 'a particular type of economic system or stage of economic development'. Over the past two centuries there has been a conceptual transfer of the little wheel of Figure 1 from its position *within* Creation's economy to a position *without* Creation's economy.

With this conceptual relocation, stewardship – particularly in its corrective and directing role in governing human action in Creation – was made obsolete. Stewardship evaporated in the heat of the industrial revolution.

Developing the concept of stewardship for our time

A world-view that perceives human life and endeavour within the wide embrace of Creation's economy is a necessary component of every successful culture. If any culture or civilization is to survive, it must assess the effects of human actions on its biosphere – not just a much-reduced human economy that has been conceptually excised from the biospheric economy. If it fails in this assessment or in its response to its assessment, it collapses. What UCLA geographer and biologist, Jared Diamond, describes for the collapse of Easter Islanders can become a metaphor for our earth. 'When the Easter Islanders got into difficulties, there was nowhere to which they could flee, nor to which they could turn for help; nor shall we modern Earthlings have recourse elsewhere if our troubles increase. Those are the reasons why people see the collapse of Easter Island society as a metaphor ... for what may lie ahead of us in our own future' (Diamond 2005: 119). That is the problem we now confront.

In our day, when Creation largely remains transformed conceptually from teacher to resourceful earth, we are becoming reluctantly aware of large-scale and pervasive alteration and degradation of the biosphere and its life-sustaining processes. Our response has ranged from acceptance and concern to denial of both empirical data and the increasingly reliable

148

biospheric, atmospheric and climate models that became available toward the end of the twentieth century. The reality of biospheric transformation, of biogeographic restructuring of terrestrial ecosystems, and of the trophic restructuring and microbialization of the oceans is beginning to register, not only in our models but also in our experience. The time has come to take appropriate action. To take action that is appropriately sufficient and robust to engage the immensity of our problem, we need to look at how people relate and have related to the earth.

From personal experience and from history, we know that we human beings continuously engage in an interactive process with the world around us. We observe the world, we work and act in the world and act upon the world, we see the consequences of our actions, and we respond in various ways to the consequences of these actions. Because we have vital interests in sustaining ourselves, we often respond in ways that make positive or at least benign contributions to our own sustainability. At a very local scale we often correct actions that have degraded our lawns and gardens so that they might persist and flourish. At the community level we might interact with fellow citizens to shape and reshape our behaviour in the direction of maintaining and improving individual and community health. At the global level we might pursue actions that counter unanticipated detrimental effects of human actions on the biosphere. Our responsive and corrective actions may be done as matters of immediate self-interest, or in behalf of the garden, community, biosphere or God. They may range from selfish to altruistic. They may also be extensions of self-interest extended to our children and grandchildren. In human responsiveness to human actions in the world there is concern for 'right living' – living that sustains our own persons, our gardens, our community, the biosphere and much more. And since such right living, if practised only by a few, is often ineffective on family, community and global scales, it is also accompanied by a commitment to spread such right living among members of our family, community, and around the world.

The relationship we have with our world therefore is necessarily an interactive and dynamic one, with this being true for every human being. Every person on earth derives service from the world, every person does things that have consequences for the world, and every person relates to the consequences of their and others' behaviour with various degrees of action and inaction. The interactive relationship every person has with the world has its effects, large and small, with some of these relationships doing more than others to sustain or degrade things. The collective results of all of these human actions join with changes of day and night, the seasons, currents of wind and water, and geological developments to guarantee a dynamic world. The dynamic world in turn produces dynamic human beings and a dynamic human society. What makes for stewardship and right living, therefore, is also necessarily dynamic.

What all of this means is that what is appropriate for maintaining individuals, communities, and things such as the biosphere, is not a constant. Instead it necessarily is ever changing, ever responding to new and changing environments and to our continuously developing knowledge and understanding of these changing environments. This means, for example, that cutting a tree when forests are abundant might make a positive contribution to human comfort and security but doing so when trees have been made scarce might make a negative contribution to local or regional microclimate and climate. In this example, people might come to learn to provide for natural forest regeneration or engage in tree-planting. Similarly, growth in human numbers may make positive contributions when people are rare and land is abundant but may bring degradation when population densities exceed the capacity of environments to sustain them. Human beings and cultures, therefore, find that behaviours and practices continued from the past into the present – while once appropriate and necessary – no longer are conducive to sustainable life and sustainable environment. This in turn requires changes in human actions in the world – not just any changes, but changes of the right kind. What makes for right living, therefore, is dynamic.

The dynamic nature of human relationship to the world means that individuals and communities must continually or periodically review and re-evaluate human action in the world for the purpose of correcting actions that have ceased from being appropriate and implementing refreshed or new actions that stay the course toward sustainability. Their stewardship must be highly interactive and dynamic.

The essence of stewardship

Successful cultures and civilizations must shape and reshape human behaviour in the direction of maintaining individual, community and environmental sustainability. This has always been necessary, whether or not they sought to improve their human lives and habitations or more simply sought to engage in corrective actions directed toward sustainability. They had to understand their world and its workings by direct experience and accumulated knowledge (scientia), had to gain from their experience and culture an understanding of what constituted right living in the world (ethics), and had to put an interactive and coherent understanding of the world, and how rightly to live, into practice (praxis). Their behaviour had to flow from the interactive and coherent engagement of scientia, ethics and praxis, whether by authority and striving of the leadership or by individuals and communities learning to live with the way things are ordered in the natural world. Such striving for accord with the biosphere and the biospheric economy shaped and reshaped their behaviour in the direction of maintaining individual, community and biospheric sustainability. Such interactive and coherent engagement leads to respect for the worth of the world in providing the conditions and processes whereby cultures and the full array of life on earth survive and flourish; and to respect what or whom creates, preserves and governs the universe. This respect for the service of the biosphere to all life brings a human response that reciprocates with human actions directed toward assuring its continued service. In a dynamic world these actions necessarily have a concordant dynamic. In a biospheric world these actions necessarily affect and respond to the entire biosphere. The result is reciprocating service – the biosphere to its component people and cultures, and people and cultures to the biosphere, all in accord with the way things are ordered in a coherent biosphere and universe. This is the essence of stewardship. *Stewardship dynamically shapes and reshapes human behaviour in the direction of maintaining individual, community, and biospheric sustainability in accord with the way the biosphere works.*

Framework for stewardship: scientia, ethics and praxis

The interactive engagement of scientia, ethics and praxis that is basic for shaping and reshaping human behaviour in the direction of maintaining individual, community and environmental sustainability can be depicted thus:

SCIENTIA
How does the world work?

ETHICS
What ought to be?

PRAXIS
Then what must we do?

The questions at each corner of this triad framework must be addressed interactively and coherently, directed at understanding what sustains a system, what degrades a system and what restores a system, and from this comes a growing understanding of what ought to be, and deriving from this a dynamic understanding of what ought to be done. These questions are identified with the words scientia, ethics, and praxis.

Scientia. Knowledge and understanding of how the world works, from antiquity to the present, require a kind of 'reading' of the 'text' of the biosphere or reading and reciting texts that are written or spoken about the biosphere. Scientia includes what we have come to call *natural science* but goes beyond this to include what we learn in social sciences and humanities, and beyond this to whatever other things human beings learn from living in the biosphere. Scientia is the body of knowledge whose elements we strive to make *coherent* within this body and strive to make *coherent* with the ways things are in the operations of the biosphere.

Ethics. Knowledge and understanding of what ought to be with respect to human actions in the biosphere require reading the 'text' of the biosphere together, and coherently with the written and oral ethical texts transferred to us as long-standing ethical systems that have stood the test of history. From this we may come to realize, for example, that human activity that poisons food supplies ought not to be. So too we may come to realize that human actions that render homes uninhabitable or destroy the regenerative capacity of forests ought not to be. The culture that incorporates into itself a system of beliefs about what ought to be and what ought not to be – its *ethos* – develops a corresponding body of ethical knowledge – its *ethic*. This ethical knowledge is passed from generation to generation through oral traditions and written texts and is the gift derived from long-standing beholders and intentional and unintentional experimenters and participants in stewardship. The body of this knowledge is *ethics*.

Praxis. The actions of human beings in the world, or *practice*, derive from a body of knowledge of how things can be accomplished and are being accomplished in the world. *Praxis* incorporates both this practice and the body of practical knowledge and understanding upon which it depends. Praxis is informed by tradition, scientia and ethics. In turn, praxis informs science on what more we need to know about the world, and ethics on what more we need to consider on what ought to be.

Stewardship does not allow scientia, ethics or praxis to be considered individually, but requires that all three interact, each informing the others. Neglecting any one of these can generate serious problems. For example, bypassing ethics to move quickly from scientific knowledge of rivers and electrical power generation to building hydroelectric dams may severely reduce soil fertility due to exclusion of riverine sedimentary deposits from river flood plains. Bypassing scientia to move directly from ethical concerns for inadequate water supplies for nomads to the drilling of tube wells may result in converting nomadic practices into sedentary ones, thereby resulting in depletion of grazing resources and firewood supplies for large distances out from the well head.

The contribution of two-books theology

Before the advent of modern science people and cultures had developed ways of knowing and understanding the world. The principal way of knowing and understanding in the Western world was through use of the metaphor of Creation as a book – the book of nature. 'By the Middle Ages we find that the book of nature has become adopted universally as the image through which the environment is to be understood' (Mills 1982: 239).

The metaphor of Creation as a book whose author is the Creator had significant power and consequences for the practice of stewardship. This was the case not only for its eliciting the belief in the coherence of Creation, but also its coherence with God's other book, the Bible. The authority of the two books and their internal and inter-related coherence provided the basis for living rightly on earth. Right living was enabled through a coherent understanding of these two books read together and interactively thereby providing the foundation for coherent interacting scientia, ethics, and praxis. This book metaphor is expressed across Christendom through the ages with a particularly descriptive one being given in the Confession of Faith of 1561 from the Low Countries on the European continent:

We know him by two means:

First, by the creation, preservation, and government of the universe, since that universe is before our eyes like a beautiful book in which all creatures, great and small, are as letters to make us ponder the invisible things of God: his eternal power and his divinity, as the apostle Paul says in Romans 1.20. All these things are enough to convince men and leave them without excuse.

Second, he makes himself known to us more openly by his holy and divine Word, as much as we need in this life, for his glory and for the salvation of his own.

In Christendom, stewardship is informed and shaped by a 'two-books theology'. This theology recognizes God as the author of both books, the book of Creation and the book of the Scriptures. This contributes to a robust stewardship derived from reading the text of Creation alongside of the text of the Bible and applying this to right living.

Both books are authoritative and, if their texts are to be preserved, are read non-consumptively. Tearing out pages or degrading the text of either is unthinkable; their texts must be preserved on the printed page and on the landscape. They are read together and interactively and they have concordance by virtue of their having the same author who is characterized by coherence, consistency and rightness.

This is the rich base from which the stewardship of Creation has been based. The two-books theology of this rich tradition is a gift of the Judeo-Christian heritage to all cultures and civilizations.

Reading the book of nature and the book of scripture coherently

Does one have to adopt the kind of description of the two books as given in the Confession of Faith or similar description? Philosopher of science, Peter Kosso, believes not. In his textbook, *Reading the Book of Nature: An Introduction to the Philosophy of Science*, he writes, 'The hermeneutic method of interpretation [of a book] is very similar to the scientific method of understanding the world . . .' (Kosso 1992: 150) and he builds a strong case for building a coherent understanding of the world by reading it as a text. He shows how, in translating a text, one must first speculate on the meanings of its letters, words and sentences. From first speculations come hypotheses about the message of the text, and these are tested against other texts in the book. 'The process of translation advances by a back-and-forth exchange of information between the developing understanding of the plot and the translation of individual passages. The global understanding, the message of the whole work, guides the local understanding of the parts' (Kosso 1992: 150).

Surprisingly, however – at least it would be for a mediaeval Christian – he writes that 'there is no hint that nature must have an author as does a text'. Which means, of course, that for Kosso and perhaps other secular students of the natural world, there is no need to believe in God or a Creator. This conclusion is helpful for building a robust stewardship for our time because it allows for reading Creation as a book in a secular manner, without having to acknowledge an author. People of faith, on the other hand, can read this book, concluding with William J. Mills that 'Viewing the earth as a book entails certain consequences' one of which is that 'A book must have an author' and that therefore it 'is necessary to view it theocentrically' (Mills 1982: 239). Reading the book of nature is advocated either way.

From Kosso we discover that the reading of a book and reading the book of Creation is constrained by the principle of coherence. 'The passages must be consistent and should hold together in a cogent message, at least in sizable sections of the text. As the reading continues, new passages are encountered and must be accommodated within the network of beliefs about the book and its message. Each new passage is like a new observation, of which the reader must make sense and which must be fitted coherently within the theoretical system' (Kosso 1992: 151).

Of particular relevance and importance here is that the reading of the book of scripture – the Bible – is also constrained by the principle of coherence. One of the creeds of Christendom, the Westminster Confession of Faith, presents the widely accepted principle across Christendom in 1646: 'The infallible rule of interpretation of Scripture, is the Scripture itself; and therefore, when there is a question about the true and full sense of any scripture (which is not manifold, but one), it may be searched and known by other places that speak more clearly.'

Both books – the book of Creation and the book of the Bible – share the same author and must be read together and interactively, with this reading constrained by the principle of coherence. While this is implicit by both books having the same author, making this explicit provides a remarkably powerful basis for a robust stewardship.

Context for stewardship in our day

Our civilization is coming out from a lapse or diminution of some two centuries of neglect of the stewardship tradition. This long lapse means that we cannot simply pick up the tradition where we left it at the beginning of the industrial revolution and put it into practice. Instead we need to size up where we are in the stream of time and identify the major happenings in our world which will help to inform and shape our understanding and substance of stewardship for our time.

Among the most significant developments during these past two hundred years have been those of (a) understanding the biosphere, (b) understanding human impacts on the earth, and (c) understanding worldwide transitions in human communities.

Understanding the biosphere

Developments here include (1) our becoming able to view our planet from outer space, with the ability to measure and model major global processes; (2) our gaining knowledge and understanding of the biosphere as an integrated complex life-support system; (3) the shift from conceiving our

155

planet as a relatively fixed and static system to a remarkably vibrant and dynamic biophysical system we call the biosphere; (4) discovery of the remarkably high degree of fitness of the biosphere for sustaining life; (5) discovery of the intimate relationship and total biophysical dependency of human beings and other living things on the operation and health of the biosphere; and (6) coming to know the variety, size, beliefs and extent of the world's major religions.

This understanding informs our stewardship by compelling us to read the text of Creation, to read the book of nature as a coherent text in order to gain a coherent understanding of the biosphere and our biotic and economic place in it.

Understanding human impacts on the earth

Developments here include (1) realization that the human species has become a major geological force on earth, including its acquired capacity to destroy its own species; (2) the human capacity to develop and deploy weapons of mass destruction, with a capacity to destroy the biosphere; and (3) discovery of the universality of human arrogance, ignorance, greed and aggression that form much of the root of social and biospheric degradation.

This understanding informs our stewardship by compelling us to read the religious and ethical books we have available to us – like the Bible – whose text can be and are read as internally coherent and simultaneously coherent with the book of nature in order to gain a coherent understanding of the biosphere and our ethical place in it.

Understanding worldwide transitions in human communities

Developments here include (1) a misplaced and lessened economy; (2) fragmentation of knowledge about ourselves and the world; (3) institution of global transport and communications; and (4) creation of the conditions for global distribution of pollution and disease.

This understanding informs our stewardship by compelling us to evaluate the consequences for us and Creation's economy of simultaneous globalization, fragmentation and breaking barriers to the flows of information, pollution and disease.

Elements of a refurbished stewardship

Core elements of a refurbished stewardship

A refurbished and robust stewardship regains our place in Creation's economy; re-connects science, ethics and praxis; re-equips stewardship with dynamic responsiveness for a dynamic world; re-forms human incentives toward the integrity of community and away from arrogance, ignorance, greed and aggression; reaffirms and expresses in words and actions the passion for right living; re-educates people and communities for the spreading of right living; restores and recreates ecosystems in accord with Creation's economy; reshapes human behaviour in the direction of biospheric sustainability; and recognizes that stewardship is accomplished on behalf of the biosphere and its component systems, on behalf of the processes and persons that sustain the biosphere, and on behalf of its Creator.

The many ways to envision stewardship

There are many other ways to envision stewardship for our day, and any one of these can be added to stewardship's core of shaping and reshaping human behaviour toward sustainability of ourselves, our communities and the biosphere. It can be envisioned as a relationship that responds to needs of the system with a deep interest and compassion. It can incorporate trust and oversight of people and processes that sustain and restore a community or ecosystem. It can be expressed as art, music and literature concordant with Creation and yet developing value that was not there previously. It can include guarding, keeping and defending to prevent damage, degradation or destruction. It can be expressed as an alternative to being motivated by arrogance, ignorance, greed and aggression. It can be expressed as giving to a future generation compensation for gifts received from earlier generations.

Stewardship exemplifies 'true religion'

And in religious terms, stewardship can exemplify what some would call true religion:

> Religion is the passion or desire both to live right and to spread right living as desires conceived as responses to some sort of cosmic demand made to us by the way things are, by the nature of Nature, or

by God who orders Creation and holds all things together with integrity.

Living rightly in response to the way things are is to live in harmony with Creation's economy (DeWitt 2002).

What a refurbished stewardship does in our day

Stewardship dynamically shapes and reshapes human behaviour in the direction of maintaining individual, community and biospheric sustainability in accord with the way the biosphere works.

Chapter 13

Environmental Ethics, Ecological Theology and Natural Selection

Lisa Sideris

Lisa Sideris is an assistant professor in the Department of Religious Studies at Indiana University. Previously she taught at McGill University, Montreal. This article is part of Chapter 1 of her book Environmental Ethics, Ecological Theology and Natural Selection *(2003), in which she seeks to replace the evolutionary and ecological simplicism of many theological writers with a more robust treatment grounded in a firm understanding of science. Although there have been a number of recent examinations of the theological implications of evolution (e.g. Edwards 1999; Haught 2000, 2005; Bowler 2001; Ruse 2001; Berry 2005), there are many questions still outstanding about the scientific understanding of evolutionary ecology (e.g. Berry 1989; Berry, Crawford and Hewitt 1992). Sideris' book is the first major attempt to integrate modern advances in evolution and ecology with the Christian faith. See p. xi.*

'Environmental ethics' suggests a more coherent and systematic set of issues than is actually the case. In reality, the term covers a wide range of issues that may or may not deserve to be treated as a whole, depending on whom you ask. Environmental ethics usually includes such topics as wildlife management, concerns over deforestation, global warming, loss of biodiversity, overpopulation, and in some cases the treatment of farm and laboratory animals (i.e. 'non-wild' animals). Humans are often depicted as both perpetrators and the victims of environmental degradation. Many environmental ethicists believe that certain sectors of the human population – especially minorities and women – suffer, along with nature, at the hands of traditionally powerful and privileged classes of people. Thus calls for social justice and environmental healing are issued in tandem by eco-feminists and others who seek to eradicate deeply entrenched structures of oppression and environmental discrimination.

Moreover, many authors address environmental problems from the standpoint of religion; indeed, the environmental crisis is to some essentially a religious issue. Many ecological theologians fall within this category. Others, most notably Lynn White (1967), have placed the blame for environmental destruction squarely on the shoulders of religion. Whether or not White's characterization of Christianity as the most anthropocentric and environmentally destructive religion in the world is accurate, it is true that his criticisms forced many Christians to take a closer look at their assumptions about nature.

Amid the diversity of opinions surrounding the definition of environmental ethics, we encounter a set of recurring themes and perennial debates. Chief among these are: To what extent are humans really part of nature? Should environmental ethics be eco-centric or anthropocentric (or both at once)? Does an environmental ethic that elevates the moral status of animals dislodge traditional morality, and if so, does it threaten to devalue human life? Or are there already resources within inherited theological and ethical perspectives from which we can fashion an environmental ethic? Many of the fundamental challenges posed by the enterprise of environmental ethics – questions about the role of humans in nature and the limitations of traditional religion and morality – intersect those raised by an evolutionary perspective.

Evolution and ecology

Contemporary ecotheologians are particularly fond of what they call the ecological model of nature. But what is the relationship between this model and an evolutionary account? When an environmental writer such as Sallie McFague sets out explicitly to adopt an 'evolutionary, ecological' perspective on nature, is it legitimate to use *evolution* and *ecology* in conjunction and interchangeably, or do these terms signal distinct models for understanding the natural world? The term *ecology* did not appear until 1866, when it was coined by biologist Ernst Haeckel. Today ecology conjures up for many people a model of nature as an interconnected and fairly stable system of complex relationships. Often the ecosystem concept plays a central role in discussions of ecology. I will use this term guardedly, acknowledging that certain features of the definition, as well as concepts associated with ecosystems such as 'community', remain problematic.

Frequently embedded in the concept of an ecosystem is the assumption of an intricate and often precarious community of living things, a balance of nature that is increasingly threatened by human encroachment and disregard for the environment. Serious disturbances to this system, typically brought on by humans, can upset this balance; if disturbance is serious enough, the entire structure may collapse, perhaps taking us along with it. Environmentalists, both religious and secular, exhort us to live within the limits set by nature, to help restore nature to its proper, ecological conditions. Unlike many other sciences, ecology has enjoyed a great deal of popular enthusiasm, especially since the 1960s. The ecologist is the most beloved of scientists, the scientist whose noble task it is to protect nature and its inhabitants (Worster 1994). For many people today, Donald Worster (p. 10) argues, 'ecology has come to represent the arcadian mood that would return man to a garden of natural peace and piety'. The ecological vision, at least in the popular imagination, is often one in which nature's 'most fearsome aspects have been shut out'.

Evolution, in contrast, may suggest precisely those fearsome aspects: a fierce, competitive struggle for food, shelter and mates. The processes of evolution are described with such words as blind, random and purposeless. Natural selection, we are told, operates according to 'chance'; in fact, some recent evolutionists have begun to highlight the aspects of evolution that reveal its deeper connections to chaos theory. This picture of nature is one that is already as disturbed as it is disturbing: perhaps there is no 'balance' in nature, no homeostasis to be disrupted. The processes of evolution appear unpredictable and wasteful; if organisms 'relate' to one another at all, they do so primarily in terms of eating and being eaten. On this interpretation nature appears to be a system that is not especially conducive to sustaining harmonious relationships with humans or any other creature.

Pre-Darwinian ecological perspectives

The term *ecology* is closely related to the term *economy*. Both words are derived from the Greek *oikos* meaning 'household'; in the eighteenth century, the arrangement of nature was understood to be something very much akin to an orderly household. Eighteenth-century views of nature frequently revolved around the concept of an economy of nature, a benevolent arrangement in which, in Linnaeus' words, all living things are 'so connected, so chained together, that they all aim at the same end and to this end a vast number of intermediate ends are subservient'. Myriad examples of the fitness that exists between an organism and its environment were taken as proof of God's design, expressed in the organization of nature. Before concepts of evolutionary ancestry, organisms were classified according to structural similarities to one another, 'elements of a divine plan' reflected throughout the natural world (Bowler 1984: 60). Linnaeus' great contribution to biology, the well-known system of binomial nomenclature of each plant and animal, embodied the notion of nature's economy. His work assumed without question that nature was 'designed by Providence to maximize production and efficiency'. The entire structure was held together by relationships of benevolent interdependence and mutual assistance. Organisms at or near the top of the economy were thought to be dependent on those beneath in order to survive, and each creature was believed to occupy a precise place with its own resources, within the larger economy. The interdependent structure of the system ensured that no creature would suffer from a scarcity of food or the effects of overpopulation. Nature's beneficent arrangement, revealed in the Linnaean system of classification, was a testimony to God himself, who 'ensured the permanent stability of the system by designing a series of checks and balances that would maintain the population of each species at an appropriate level'. (Bowler 1984: 60)

The economy of nature is one important strand within eighteenth-century science. Another related current of thought sprang from the Romantic tradition. Romantic naturalism is often portrayed as a reaction to the Enlightenment utilitarianism of the economy of nature, yet the two perspectives are similar in some respects. The Linnaean economy had definite mechanistic overtones – nature was portrayed as a 'well-oiled machine' (Worster 1994: 39). This account of nature conveniently resembled the factory system that would soon dominate English urban existence. In contrast to this perception of nature as a fairly static machine, the Romantics drew inspiration from a world that was very much alive and changeable, a natural world envisioned as a single living organism. Both models, however, relied heavily on notions of the interdependence and relationality of all beings in nature.

In Romantic ecology each part of the system was thought to be crucial to the survival of the whole, as in the Linnaean model, but the analogy with a machine composed of interchangeable parts was consciously rejected in favour of a communal, organismic metaphor. The Romantics viewed nature as constituted by 'inviolable interdependence ... a system of necessary relationships that cannot be disturbed in even the most inconspicuous way without changing, perhaps destroying, the equilibrium of the whole' (Worster 1994: 82). This view suggests that our illusion of separation and independence from nature is sustained with great cost to ourselves and other organisms. Humans, as inherently part of this system and yet alienated from it, should seek a new, more intimate relationship to nature as the only cure for spiritual and physical wounds. Nature was understood as the macrocosm mirroring the human microcosm, a place that both nurtured and reflected human relationships, values and states of mind. 'The key word in the Romantic vocabulary was "community"', Worster (p. 84) argues, and especially a community of love, an 'extended net of natural relationships'. In short, the Romantic view amounted to what many environmentalists now regard as an ecological perspective.

Recent ecological models, including those depicting ecosystems as holistic, integrated, interdependent communities, clearly owe much to Romantic thinking. Contemporary environmental ethics rooted in this model of an ecological community often exhorts us, as the Romantics also did, to repair and restore our severed connection to the natural world as a way of healing both ourselves and the environment. For example, in a work entitled *Nature's Web*, Peter Marshall (1992: 334–38) depicts modern

162

ecology as centred on the idea of nature as a 'unified and balanced organism'. Ecology, he argues, has firmly established that 'all life is interdependent, and that the earth itself is a self regulating organism'. Marshall understands the Romantic movement to have 'paved the way for an evolutionary and ecological appreciation of nature', despite the fact that evolution plays little or no role in this account.

Concepts of nature as a self-regulating organism, or a community of benevolent arrangements revolving around some principle of interdependence, have obvious appeal, vague though they may be. As ecologist Frank Golley (1993: 3) observes, such concepts have long provided humans with a sense that 'somewhere out there, there was ultimate order, balance, equilibrium, and a rational and logical system of relations'. Many writers in the field of environmental ethics, both religious and secular, have upheld an image of nature as a community founded on interdependence as the key insight of ecology and have consequently interpreted nature's interdependence and unity normatively (e.g. Fowler 1995). The community ethic implied by the ecological model is one we should all live by. McFague (1997: 151) argues: 'The ethic that emerges from the ecological model is care for all those in the Community'. Like the Romantics, she calls for an ethic of 'loving nature'. McFague tempers this optimistic assertion somewhat with the qualification that 'an ethic of community is not all love and harmony', but she concludes that an ethic rooted in the ecological model demands, at the very least, respecting the 'otherness' of all living things within the community. Committing ourselves to the good of the community (understood in its broadest, ecological sense) repairs the damage we have done to nature and enriches our lives by bringing us back into the relationship: 'The ecological [model] . . . suggests the renewal of a subject-subjects relation' (p. 45). McFague, like Marshall and many other environmentalists, believes that such an ethic is rooted in 'evolutionary, ecological' understanding of nature. Yet in this account, as in Marshall's, little attempt is made to distinguish the terms evolution and ecology; rather evolution is subsumed under a normative, community definition of ecology.

Ecosystem concepts

But are such interpretations of nature and ethics consistent with modern evolutionary and ecological science? Romanticized notions of natural communities as self-regulating, goal-seeking super-organisms persist in much of environmental ethics, but they are regarded as 'anathema to most ecologists' (Hagen 1992: 13).

The super-organism and community metaphors for nature pre-date the term *ecosystem*, yet they are frequently and mistakenly conflated. The ecosystem idea was first proposed by British ecologist Arthur George Tansley (1871–1955) in 1935 in criticism of the claims of the American ecologist Frederic Clements (1874–1945), a chief proponent of the 'super-organism' view of nature (although the concept of nature as a single, living organism has much older roots). Clements recognized that the super-organism changed over time, but he 'abhorred chaos in ecological thought', arguing that the super-organism showed steady movement (referred to as ecological succession) toward a relatively permanent, har-monious, and stable 'climax community' (Hagen 1992: 21). The climax community could persist indefinitely, barring significant disruption from natural disasters, such as forest fires, or anthropogenic sources of damage to nature. Clements' concept of nature as a single, organic whole lends itself to an ethic of preservation – an ethic that typically blames human interference for disruptions and imbalances in nature. As such, it has great appeal for environmentalists to this day.

For Tansley, Clements' ecology took the organism and succession metaphors too far and exaggerated the holistic, collective action of natural systems. Tansley attempted to analyse natural systems as wholes, without resorting to organism or community metaphors that were potentially misleading in their neglect of the relationship between organisms and the surrounding physical and chemical environment. His ecosystem concept was offered as a means of incorporating the organic and the inorganic factors, a bridge between biotic organisms and components of the envir-onment that were typically not included as living 'members' of the com-munity. Organismic and community metaphors, in other words, paid insufficient attention to crucial but 'nonliving' aspects of nature.

Tansley's ecosystem comprised a number of 'subordinate parts', which included 'energy flows, biogeochemical cycles, communities, and popula-tions of species'. This means that a 'community' is not the same thing as an ecosystem but generally refers to one level within the system: groups of species populations living in a specific region. Yet ever since Tansley's formulation, many people (including ecologists) have continued to associate ecosystems with the older concepts that Tansley sought to sup-plement or correct: 'Ecologists tended to misuse the term ecosystem as a more modern expression for the community concept or Clementsian complex organism and thus maintained the confusion that Tansley was trying to overcome' (Golley 1993: 34); indeed, some modern ecologists have thrown out the ecosystem idea owing to a mistaken interpretation of ecosystems as a 'continuation' of the super-organism and other ecological concepts whose time has passed.

There is an ongoing debate among ecologists regarding the definition and usefulness of concepts such as the ecosystem. Whereas Golley defends the concept – shorn of certain associations such as the self-regulating super-organism idea – others, such as Joel Hagen, point to tensions, even incompatibilities, between the ecosystem idea and the field of evolutionary ecology. For now, the key points are that:

1. Models of nature that pervade much of ecotheology and environmental ethics gloss over evolutionary processes and interactions among organisms, focusing almost exclusively on broader ecological themes.

2. Those ecological themes – particularly superorganismic, mutualistic, community themes – are themselves considered outdated, inadequate, perhaps entirely obsolete, by many scientists.

My disagreement is not with the fact that some environmentalists are guilty of deriving normative guidelines from nature – an 'ought' from an 'is' – but rather that the *ought* they are deriving represents only a part of nature's *is*, as science understands it.[1] Darwinism, properly understood and incorporated, offers a corrective to this particular type of myopia in environmental ethics.

Post-Darwinian ecology: discord or harmony?

Obviously, the history of evolutionary theory and its relationship with ecology does not end with the publication of Darwin's works. Subsequent history tells of a continuing debate revolving around ecological and evolutionary paradigms. The development of the ecosystem idea that emerged from a critique of Clements' super-organism concept is an important example. But in the years since Tansley's use of the term, the ecosystem idea has been the target of much criticism, sometimes from those proposing a more 'Darwinian' model.

Early ecosystem models focused attention on the collective level (such as trophic levels or the behaviour of aggregates of organisms); natural selection, on the other hand, was understood to operate at the level of the individual organism engaged in competition (assumptions still questioned by some biologists). Ecosystem studies were at their height of popularity in the 1950s and 60s, owing largely to Eugene Odum's classic textbook, *Fundamentals of Ecology* (with editions in 1953, 1959 and 1971), but the field developed with little reference to evolutionary theory. Odum's concept of the ecosystem stressed the communal benefits of cooperative interaction between the ecosystem's members. Like Clements before him, he believed that ecosystems brought 'order and harmony out of the chaotic materials of existence'. (Worster 1994: 367) Competition between individuals also occurred in Odum's system, but he maintained that the survival and homeostasis of the unified ecosystem depended upon counterbalancing competition with cooperation. Group selection and coevolution provided a crucial offset to competition and contributed to the overall stability of ecosystems. Ultimately, Odum's ecosystem concept (which became the ecosystem idea, as it is popularly understood today) embraced an overt form of holism that Tansley had set out to critique 20 years earlier. In its emphasis on cooperation and organism-like self- regulation, Odum's ecosystem concept bears traces of the much older Romantic perspective. Also, like the Romantics, some ecologists in the 1950s and 60s saw their mission as 'ecologizing' society as a whole, since nature was perceived as a model for human communities, a corrective to our disruptive tendencies. Ecotheologians have carried on this tradition of adopting nature's ideal community as a blueprint for human society.

By the 1970s the case for group selection had been largely discredited, leaving ecosystem ecologists with the difficult task of explaining the relationship between individual competition and overall communal stability. In other words, the assumed counterbalances to competition – such as co-evolution, altruism, and group selection – no longer appeared entirely defensible. Without these, how could *de*stabilizing processes such as individual selection and competition produce and maintain homeostasis and balance in the ecosystem? Perhaps the belief in balance was itself suspect.

Meanwhile, evolutionary science had undergone radical changes of its own, owing to the synthesis of the 1940s that united genetics with palaeontology, biogeography and comparative studies. But these changes were perceived as largely irrelevant to ecosystem biology. By the 1960s, there was a growing belief among many younger ecologists that evolutionary theory had been ignored or misunderstood by their elders. Evolution and ecology were developing in relatively separate spheres, and their separation eventually led to a clash between ecosystem studies and evolutionary studies (Hagen 1992: 148). The divergence of ecosystem and evolutionary studies, moreover, was occurring at a time of heightened interest in environmental problems, and the public was turning to ecologists for answers. Ecological and evolutionary scientists were unable to present a unified front. Finally, the centennial in 1959 of Darwin's publication of *The Origin of Species* brought with it a renewed interest in evolutionary theory and forced ecosystem scientists to re-examine the impact of evolution on 'the development of behaviour and life history, the regulation of populations, and the organisation of communities' (Golley 1993: 5). A new field of evolutionary ecology had emerged, but it was not entirely clear that ecosystem studies could be integrated with the new discipline.

Challenges to ecology from evolutionary science did not stop there. The late twentieth century saw the rise of 'nonequilibrium ecology', as some ecologists began to argue that computer and mathematical analyses (analyses of gene frequencies over time, for instance) revealed a fundamental unpredictability in the natural world; ecological changes appeared to occur at random. In the 1990s one leading ecology textbook devoted only a single paragraph out of 600 pages to the ecosystem concept – a dramatic change from the ecosystem-centred ecology of the fifties and sixties, as exemplified by Odum's classic text. Ecology was 'perceptibly, moving away from that unified theory that had sought to bring the living and nonliving together into a single, coherent, balanced, and orderly, system' (Worster 1994: 390). The extreme randomness of nature, some ecologists have suggested, is consistent with Darwinism; in fact, some have begun to understand the processes of nature as an illustration of chaos theory.

If the chaos challenge proves to be correct, ecologists may be forced to conclude that they can never accurately describe a biotic system's state at any point in time, nor can they predict future events, such as the likelihood of survival of its species. From an environmentalist's perspective, this trend in ecology is an alarming one. As Daniel Botkin (1990) observes, modern ecology has opened up a Pandora's box of resource management issues. When applied to real environmental cases – to marine fisheries, wildlife, and endangered species, for instance – concepts of nature's balance or stability have proven to be deficient and it seems ecology has been forced to jettison its once central tenets. What then becomes of resource management and environmental conservation? The discovery of disorder, of continual fluctuation, as something intrinsic to nature makes resource management difficult to defend, much less implement. Once we concede that some changes in nature are 'natural', 'good' or valuable, how can we then 'argue against any alteration of the environment'?[2] If nature is so fundamentally erratic, how can we know what our impact on the environment is? Which disturbances in nature are caused by us and which are inherent in the system? How can we even judge that 'disturbance' is a bad thing in the first place? Furthermore, how can we know that our efforts to cultivate environmental responsibility, to preserve biodiversity, have any positive results without any background stability against which to compare our efforts? This vision of nature provides no norm whatsoever. As a basis for environmental ethics, this brand of 'Darwinian' ecology seems to counsel doing nothing.

Would a thorough incorporation of a modern evolutionary perspective lead, ironically, to a complete split between evolutionary science and the goals of environmentalists? Are proponents of chaos ecology right to see Darwin as their champion? I do not find this argument wholly plausible. Darwin himself certainly did not understand nature to be completely devoid of order, and, though he stopped well short of Romantic appeals to the harmony of nature, he often envisioned the competitive struggle as leading to some more favourable outcome.[3] Those who equate Darwinism with chaos are overstating the case as much as those who interpret it as perfect adaptation and order. Yet one effect of the contest between the ecosystem paradigm and that of Darwinian science has been a reconsideration of the role of competitive struggle in biology. In the 1950s and 60s the rediscovery of Darwin in modern ecology meant that ecosystem scientists could no longer discount the role of natural selection within ecosystems. As it stands today, the science of ecology is endeavouring to incorporate elements of order and disorder in nature, competition and cooperation, parts and wholes. Even proponents of disequilibrium ecology often perceive a certain regularity to the chaotic shifts in natural systems. It may also be that fluctuations at one level of an ecosystem can prevent fluctuations at higher levels, creating a buffer for the ecosystem as a whole. Likewise, those who defend the ecosystem as a meaningful (and, to some extent, orderly) model of nature acknowledge that concepts such as homeostasis, self-regulation and equilibrium must be qualified in light of scientific developments. Take the concept of equilibrium, for example: Golley argues that equilibrium in ecosystems is not so much a condition of 'balance' or 'stasis' to which a system naturally returns as a 'response system in a dynamic relation with its environment' (Golley 1993: 195). According to this 'relativistic theory of ecosystem behaviour', equilibrium is better understood as a statement regarding the history of a system, an account of its 'past performance' rather than a 'prediction about its future state'. Though ecologists may never predict the behaviour of an ecosystem with complete accuracy, Golley believes that they can 'describe broad limits of possibility'.

Where does this leave us? Many ecologists have begun to regard order and chaos as part of the same picture, 'two distinct manifestations of an underlying determinism' (Worster 1994: 411). Nature is more correctly understood as complex rather than thoroughly chaotic. What this sketch of the Darwinian *versus* ecological (or ecosystem) paradigms should caution environmentalists to remember is that the ecological themes of the balance of nature, the harmoniously interdependent nature of life, are not only too vague but too one-dimensional as well. They continue to capture only one aspect of nature. As Botkin observes, the 'true idea of harmony of nature' as understood in modern ecology 'is by its very essence discordant, created from simultaneous movements of many tones, the combination of many processes flowing at the same time along various scales, leading not to a simple melody but to a symphony at some times harsh and at some times pleasing' (Botkin 1990: 25). While they may disagree on the extent to which older views of ecology emphasized balance and the extent to which recent models truly point to chaos, ecologists and historians of ecology generally agree that there has been a movement away from cooperation, co-evolution, harmony and balance as the predominant ecological themes. Yet, many environmentalists, particularly ecotheologians, still invoke an allegedly naturalistic, scientific norm rooted in these ideas. It may not be an overstatement to say that Christian interpretations of nature have never completely come to terms with the evolutionary perspective. But why is this? Is Darwinism such a dismal outlook that its incorporation into environmental ethics has proved too depressing and onerous a task? Part of the explanation may lie in the complex history of evolution and ecology. Given that ecosystem ecology is not consistently well-grounded in evolutionary science, it is not surprising that ecological theologians neglect evolution as well. Or does the omission of Darwinism reflect a suspicion that the theory of natural selection threatens to destroy traditional tenets of theology and theodicy?

Why the gap?

The gap between environmental ethics and evolution may have more to do with the methods of scientists than with the fears of theologians. The notion that moral implications, good or bad, can be derived from nature has been forcefully discredited by some of the staunchest proponents of evolutionary theory. Rachels (1990) points out that 'friends' of Darwin may hesitate to promote the idea that Darwinism poses a threat to religion and values, even if they believe this to be true. After all, the perception of such a threat is what has often kept Darwinism out of US public schools, thanks to right-wing 'enemies' of Darwinism. Admitting that Darwinism constitutes a distinct set of values, a sort of world-view in and of itself, plays directly into the hands of opponents of evolution who charge that the theory is really a form of quasi-religious dogma-secular humanism – masquerading as objective science in biology textbooks.

Hoping to sidestep charges of dogmatism, evolutionary scientists themselves have lent credibility to the notion that Darwinism, as a set of 'facts', can have no moral implications. Stephen Jay Gould insists that facts of nature can pose no threat to 'moral values'. Science, he argues, 'can no more answer the questions of how we ought to live than religion can decree the age of the earth'. (Gould 1987: 70) Science and religion exist in separate spheres, what Gould (1995) calls nonoverlapping magisteria (NOMA): 'Science gets the age of rocks, and religion the rock of ages; science studies how the heavens go, religion how to go to heaven'. Since, according to this view, no conflict can exist between science and religion, why should theologians trouble themselves with learning the finer points (or even the broad contours) of scientific theories? If ethics and theology lack a firm grasp of science, scientists themselves may be partly responsible for perpetuating the gap between theology and science. Whether or not evolutionary scientists truly believe that there are no moral implications of Darwinism, they may adopt that position, if only to protect the theory from assaults from without.

It is difficult to banish the spectre raised by Darwin himself that evolutionary theory does in fact pose a threat to traditional theology, theodicy and morality, and that Christianity cannot truly absorb the shock of evolution and keep traditional theism intact. Rachels, for example, argues unequivocally that the theory of evolution 'undermines theism ... In particular, it undermines the traditional idea that human life has a special, unique worth'. He maintains that evolution has forced a gradual 'retreat' of traditional theism, persistently edging it out until finally we (like Darwin) must ask ourselves: 'if religious belief is reduced to this, is it worth having? What remains is a "God" so abstract, so unconnected with the world, that there is little left in which to believe'. The best we can hold on to, he argues, is some fragile strand of deism. Even if Darwinism does not 'make theism impossible', he concludes, it 'still makes it far less attractive than ever before' (Rachels 1990: 125–27).

Rachels' argument involves questionable assumptions, however: his contention would seem to be that once we jettison the belief that humans were specially created by God, with a unique and privileged status (he refers to this tenet as the 'image of God thesis'), traditional theology collapses altogether. He (mistakenly) rejects the possibility that anything like traditional theistic belief can endure without an essential core of anthropocentrism. His belief is that Darwinism discredits the 'image of God thesis'; in other words, traditional theism minus the image of God equals deism – the belief that everything was created by a being who can in no way be assumed to have an ongoing personal relationship to what has been created. If we agree with Rachels, then a true 'ecological theology' is an impossibility, an oxymoron.

The brighter side of Darwinism: positive contributions to environmental ethics

Although Darwinism has often been portrayed as a Cartesian perspective, in one very important respect Darwin's work is quite explicitly anti-Cartesian. Darwin's study of animal emotions and states of mind in *The Expression of the Emotions in Man and Animals* reads as a direct rebuttal to Descartes' claim that animals are mere machines, automata possessing no rational faculties. It is striking that in their persistent efforts to dislodge a Cartesian framework ecotheologians rarely if ever make use of Darwin's animal studies (though secular animal advocates such as Regan and Singer have done more with this). Darwin argued repeatedly that animals exhibit a wide range of complex emotions and rational faculties. Descartes had admitted that animals possessed something like emotions, but he likened these responses to mechanical reactions, devoid of any reflective element. A tortured animal's cries of pain were akin to the ringing of a bell – involuntary, automatic responses involving no thought processes.

Darwin's extensive writing on animals paints a very different picture of them as our kin who share many of our most basic emotions and social behaviours. *The Expression of the Emotions in Man and Animals* is filled with sketches of animals displaying a wide range of facial expressions – smiling, frowning, gestures of disappointment, sulking, terror and wonder. Most notably, Darwin also attributed to them what he called 'intellectual emotions', behaviours combining complex mental and emotional responses that differed from humans' only in degree, if at all. He recounts experiments, both his own and those of other researchers, that seem to prove beyond any doubt that animals employ reason and reflection, that they are able to recall past events and deliberately plan future actions.

If a greater concern for our animal relations was one of the contributions of Darwinism to environmental ethics, a second, more indirect, effect was the extension of moral consideration to all nature, including, ultimately, the land itself. Just as Darwin's account of physical evolution underscored the biological continuity of humans and animals, his theory of moral evolution identified a concern for all living things as the pinnacle of ethical development. Roderick Nash (1988) has observed that environmental awareness can be traced largely to Victorian thinkers and especially to the ethical implications of Darwin's work in *The Origin of Species* (1859) and *The Descent of Man* (1871). Darwin's theory influenced American environmentalists as well. Nash points out that Aldo Leopold's formulation of land ethics in the 1940s relied heavily on Darwin's account of the evolution of ethics in *The Descent of Man*; Leopold's treatment of ethics in his much celebrated *Sand County Almanac* (1949) 'nearly plagiarized Darwin' (1988: 68).

Darwin envisioned an evolutionary process involving an ever-expanding circle of moral concern for others that would eventually embrace all creatures on earth. Moral consideration for animals, Darwin argued, was the highest attainment of ethical evolution, the human species' 'latest moral acquisition'. Darwin and Leopold agree that a lack of concern for other living things reveals a deficient, primitive moral development. The sportsman who never learns to regard animals as anything other than 'trophies' or 'certificates' to capture and display is 'caveman reborn' (Leopold 1949: 176). Taking his cue from Darwin, Leopold extended consideration beyond concern for animals to the land itself, maintaining that such an extension of ethics 'is actually a process in ecological evolution .... There is as yet no ethic dealing with man's relation to land and to the animals and plants which grow upon it'. Yet he believed that an ecological conscience would evolve: 'The extension of ethics ... is, if I read the evidence correctly, an evolutionary possibility and an ecological necessity' (p. 203). Current proponents of the land ethic such as J. Baird Callicott and Holmes Rolston continue to make Darwinism and natural selection central to their work. Callicott (1992), for instance, has presented Darwin's account of the evolution of moral sympathies as a foundation for environmental ethics. For the most part, however, most environmentalists – especially Christian environmentalists – have paid little attention to Darwin's theory of natural selection and even less to his account of the evolution of ethics.

Clearly, Darwin's work in biology and ethics contributed much to the development of moral concern for nonhuman animals and nature as a whole. Darwin's theory has also done much to undermine cherished anthropocentric notions regarding the status of humans in the natural world. Because environmentalists of all varieties have often identified anthropocentrism as a major contributing factor in our reckless destruction of the environment, the critique of anthropocentrism is a position that environmental ethics would seem to share with a Darwinian view of nature. As philosopher Mary Midgley has tirelessly argued, the critique of anthropocentrism is a *Darwinian* critique, and yet the myths of both science and religion continually marginalize this perspective: 'Groundless fantasies about a dazzling human future, both on this planet and off it, are developed to justify our chronic abuse of nature ... Most of them rest on extrapolating graphs of human development that contain nothing to justify any such extension. Evolution itself is imagined, quite contrary to Darwin, as following such a graph ...' (Midgley 1988: 190). Despite the widely held assumption that natural selection has permanently dislodged humans from the centre of creation, an 'apotheosis of man' has persisted, ironically with evolutionary science as its driving force:

> Evolution, in these prophecies, figures as a single, continuous linear process of improvement. In the more modest form in which some biologists have used it, the process was confined to the development of life-forms on this planet. But it is now increasingly often extended to do something much vaster – to cover the whole development of the universe from the Big Bang onward to the end of time – a change of scale that would be quite unthinkable if serious biological notions of evolution were operating (Midgley 1992: 147).

Darwin's dethronement of humans remains incomplete. Like other environmentalists, Midgley worries about the effect that our myths of human progress and perfection have had, and continue to have, on our natural environment. She is not alone in this critique of the persistence of anthropocentrism (or 'reductive humanism' as she labels it). For example, James Gustafson has argued that the persistence of the anthropocentric perspective in Western ethics is connected to the fact that ethics and theology have remained strangely untouched by developments in the sciences (Gustafson 1981: II, 9). Darwinism sheds light on a vision of nature that is, admittedly, more disturbing than earlier views; but without this vision the ecological perspective as articulated by some ecotheologians is incomplete, inadequate and outdated. Notwithstanding, while evolutionary theory poses difficult challenges to theology and ethics, it has also contributed significantly and constructively to increasing our understanding of natural processes, to improving our ethical relationship with other animals, and to clarifying the place of humans within the natural world. For all its discomfiting implications, there is still, as Darwin himself said, grandeur in this view of life.

Notes

1. In this respect I disagree with Gould (and I think he disagrees with himself) when he asserts the moral neutrality of scientific data. What Gould objects to most, and rightly so, is reductionistic and uncritical inferences from scientific information.

2. It is particularly interesting that ecotheologians associate the idea of nature's balance with an ecological model assumed to have superseded mechanistic models, given that, as Botkin notes, the preoccupation with the idea of balance in early ecology owed much to machine models of nature such as those that inspired the Lotka–Volterra equations for predator–prey interaction: 'With the machine metaphor for the balance of nature expressed in mathematical models, these became the basis for the [failed] management of fisheries, wildlife and endangered species. In the social and political movement known as environmentalism, ideas of stability may have been less formal, but the same underlying beliefs of a balance of nature predominated' (Botkin 1990: 42). And so they do still among ecotheologians.

3. It is less clear, however, that individual members of a biotic system would experience an outcome that is favourable. While a species as a whole may be 'improved' by natural selection, this occurs at the expense of individuals. Improvement itself is also relative – relative to the specific conditions of the environment at a given point in time. These conditions can change very rapidly and thus improvement has little objective meaning outside these specific contexts.

Chapter 14
Symbols to Live By

Larry Rasmussen

Until his recent retirement, Larry Rasmussen was Reinhold Niebuhr Professor of Social Ethics at Union Theological Seminary in New York, and was Moderator of the World Council of Churches Unit on Justice, Peace and the Integrity of Creation (JPIC) from 1990 to 1998. This text is taken from his book Earth Community, Earth Ethics *(1996), which draws heavily on his experience with JPIC and its presentation at the 1991 Canberra Assembly of the World Council of Churches (WCC).*

What are and what might be the ways we imagine ourselves as distinctive earth creatures? What symbols and models do we or might we live by as we answer who we are and what is required of us?

Dominion

The theology of dominion remains the reigning model where it counts most, in practice. Both industrial and informational 'ecologies' hold it as the practical doctrine of their working cosmologies and sell their promises on the basis of it. It surfaces in religious rhetoric and practice. At the hyped 20-year anniversary gathering for Earth Day in Central Park, New York City, in April 1990, Cardinal O'Connor delivered his punch line, following a condescending remark aimed at all who worry about saving whales and snail darters: 'The earth was made for man, not man for the earth'. Pope John Paul II reaffirmed this in *The Gospel of Life* (1995): 'Everything in creation is ordered to man and everything is made subject to him ... We see here a clear affirmation of the primacy of man over things; these are made subject to him and entrusted to his responsible care.'

[Despite this], careful argument for mastery has largely left the scene. Master and control as the model for our place in the world and the kind of moral totalitarianism it implies, found only an occasional echo in [the WCC Assembly at] Canberra and no resonance at all in the official reports and recommendations.

Steward

Many suckled and raised on mastery have stepped over the threshold to the custodial or steward model. The language itself may still echo of 'dominion', but it is not dominion as mastery and control. Rather, human beings are pictured as *oikonomoi*, trustees of the *oikos* and the tillers and keepers of earth as our patch of creation. The particular accent for this revived image takes account of the modern world and its altered relationship of human power to nature, including human nature. Humans, who often feel so powerless, are recognized cumulatively as wielders of power to affect all of life in unprecedented ways. We possess knowledge to save and knowledge to destroy. This knowledge is outstripped only by our ignorance and its dangers. The moral quest is thus clear: a just, sustaining use of unprecedented knowledge and power, an urgent effort to match wisdom and responsibility. Douglas John Hall (1976, 1982, 1993) has given this biblical notion renewed theological currency, not least by defining 'dominion' christologically [see pp. 139–43]. If Jesus is *dominus* (Lord), then the human exercise of power should be patterned on his kind of lordship – a servant stance in which the last are made first, the weak are made strong, and even the sparrow is cherished, so that all might be gathered into covenantal intimacy on equal terms.

Similarly, Jewish writers have revived the biblical legacy and reaffirmed the long trail of Jewish exegesis of Gen. 1.28 ('Be fruitful and multiply, and fill the earth and subdue it; and have dominion . . .'). The exegetical kernel is that while all living things on earth have some human reference and use, the proper human attitude is one of restraint, humility, and even non-interference, except for matters of necessity (such as daily bread). In fact, the modern capacity to image human beings apart from the rest of nature is largely lost to Jewish exegesis because rabbinic Hebrew, like biblical Hebrew, has no word for nature as a realm separate from human being, nor for creation as a finished state. As with Hall's work, there is a human prominence in this exegesis, to be sure. Precisely for this reason, stewardship is a prominent theme. But it is a prominence within a single Community of Life, before, under, in and with God (the biblical angle is not homocentric or biocentric, but theocentric). 'Dominion' is never, therefore, exegeted by the rabbis as licence for exploitative subjugation. It is humble participation with God in ongoing creation as a totally inter-related reality, accompanied with a high sense of moral responsibility for consequences. We are *shomrei 'adamâ* – guardians of earth.

In a nice twist, humans will retain dominion only so long as humankind is relatively 'righteous', or just, according to the rabbis. When humankind is not, the rest of nature reacts, and the ground itself cries out for justice, challenging these stewards to return in humility to the tilling and keeping of the earth proper to their calling. This is the true custodial task (Gen. 2.15).

175

Michael Lerner (1986: 297) comments, 'Noah is said by the Rabbinical tradition to have spent much time on the ark trying to quieten down fighting among the animals – but never to have been involved in throwing any species off the boat for not fitting his ideal.'

Hebrew conveys this stewardly calling better than English. The charge 'to till and keep' of Gen. 2.15 (NRSV) is literally 'to serve and preserve' (*l'ovdah ul'shomrah*). To serve means, literally, to cultivate. The connection to stewards (*shomrei*) as guardians, custodians and preservers of earth is plain (Hillel 1991: 12, 286 n.; Hiebert 1996c).

The steward's intimacy with the soil is also underscored. 'Adam' is derived from *'adamâ* – a Hebrew noun of feminine gender meaning earth, topsoil, or ground. 'Adam' thus encapsulates something of human origin and destiny itself. Adam derives life and livelihood from the 'dust' from which Adam comes and to which Adam returns. Likewise, Adam's companion is *Hava* – Eve in English. *Hava* literally means 'living'. In the Bible's words: 'The man named his wife Eve, because she was the mother of all living' (Gen. 3.20). Together, then, Adam and Eve signify 'Soil and Life'. This is the identity from which emerges the human vocation of *shomrei 'adamâ*.

Michael Lerner (1995: 416), commenting on this exegetical legacy, emphasizes that it underscores 'a real humility in which we see ourselves as part of the totality of Being, understand that nature itself is permeated with the spirit of God, and recognize that the chosenness of the human species, our ability to develop a certain level of self-consciousness, is at the same time an obligation toward compassion, caring, and stewardship'.

Yet in the rabbinical tradition, it is Sabbath and not dominion that symbolizes the proper relationship of humans to the rest of nature and of all creation together to the creator. Indeed, Sabbath, and not the creation of humans, is the crown and climax of the creation story itself, papal exegesis notwithstanding. Thus while stewardship has real tenure over two millennia of Jewish teaching, and dominion denotes real human prominence in all creation accounts, this has lacked the odour of chauvinism and unrestrained utility that it came to hold in Christian practice after the commercial globalization by the West and the industrial revolution (Ehrenfeld and Bentley 1985).[1]

The ambience of stewardship and dominion-talk at [the WCC Assembly in] Canberra was fascinating and instructive. With support from Asian, African, Pacific Islander and Latin American Protestants, Eastern Orthodox delegates were emphatic that the language of the Report should encompass the place of humans as stewards. By contrast, most Europeans and North Americans stood sober before 'dominion' and were fearful that 'steward', too, might easily slide into the imperial mastery they knew well. Indeed, Christians from the Two-Thirds World were quick to join interpretations that rejected Western domination as an expression of Christian 'civilization' and dominion. At the same time they clamoured for the distinction and high office of the human as 'steward' or householder and 'tiller and keeper'. Power relationships and their history are no doubt as crucial as exegetical ones in this instance. But the exegesis probably sided with the Orthodox and their supporters as well. In the terms 'the image of God' and 'dominion' both Jews and early Christians heard the message of affirmation and dignity married to moral agency and responsibility for history. They heard a task, a calling, a vocation, a commission to be the 'responsible representatives' of none less than God.[2] From the perspective of the globally less powerful, to be named by God the custodians of creation and God's appointed is an empowering word.

In Canberra this message swung over to something like this: 'We've been beaten up by others for centuries, in Europe, Asia, Africa, the Americas and the Pacific. We're tired of it now; we've been tired of it for five hundred years. And we are here to say that this is not the reality we live from! The reality we live from is that we are created in the image of God, and we are the subjects, not the objects, of history.' A Korean, Chung Hyun Kyung, commented: 'We are new wine. You will not put us in the old wineskins.' In such a context as this, backed by centuries of subjugation to colonization and neo-colonization and resistance to them, to be dubbed the custodians and guardians of creation by the divine is a gospel word, just as being crowned 'the prince of creation' (Orthodox language) is heady status.

Due sensitivity to historical context and power did not settle certain sticking points of the steward symbol, however. Its affinity for a human-centred cosmology and ethic ('anthropocentrism' or 'homocentrism') is one of them. We met it earlier in John Paul II's dominion theology. Yet his papal message of 1 January 1990, for the celebration of the World Day of Peace, carries a different tone. Interestingly enough for a message on peace, one continual refrain is 'due respect for nature'. 'The ecological crisis as a moral crisis' runs throughout as well. The Pope writes, the 'ultimate guiding moral norm ... for any sound economic, industrial or scientific progress' is nothing less than 'respect for life'. Then comes the key qualification: 'above all for the dignity of the human person'. Pope John Paul II, even in broadening the moral scope to 'respect for life', aligns critical moral discussion with *the* norm of official Catholic social teaching, 'the dignity of the human person'. His message is thus most accurately struck in the sentence, 'The human race is called to explore this order [the "cosmos"], to examine it with due care and to make use of it while safeguarding its integrity'. Because official Roman Catholic social teaching continues to set a rather abstracted human person at the centre of theological and ethical reflection, papal documents and bishops' pastoral letters have come very late to the ecosocial crisis. The larger point, however, is that there is an anthropocentrism about the steward model that is genuinely here, and that anthropocentrism sticks in the craw of many, including many Catholic theologians (Thomas Berry, Rosemary Ruether, Elizabeth Johnson, Leonardo Boff and Sean McDonagh, for example).

The discussion of stewardship as a fitting model for the needed cosmology will no doubt go on a long while before any resolution on anthropocentrism surfaces, in either secular or religious circles.

An episode at Canberra confirms this. The most contentious paragraphs of the penultimate draft of Section I were these:

> 16. What is our place as human beings in the natural order? The earth itself, this little watery speck in space, is about 4.5 billion years old. Life began about 3.4 billion years ago. We ourselves came on the scene some 80,000 years ago, just yesterday in the twinkling of the Creator's eye. It is shocking and frightening for us that the human species has been able to threaten the very foundations of life on our planet in only about 200 years since modern industrialization began. So where do we belong in the Creator's purpose?

> 17. Some say we are one species co-existent with many others. We hold an awesome power – life and death – in the tiny portion of the universe we will inhabit for but a short period in creation's history. As one species among others in a planetary world that is itself one, from an ecological point of view, we are totally dependent upon the rest of creation. We are precious creatures of God living for a season among other precious creatures of God in an awesome universe, and we are creatures with extraordinary power and responsibility.

> 18. But what of our traditional Christian theology? Many Christians contend that human beings, as created in the image of God and the crown of creation, occupy a special place among creatures, that there is no intrinsic value or morality in nature apart from human beings, that it is for us to introduce morality into nature, and that the redemption of creation will come about through God's redemption of humanity.

These paragraphs were deleted after speaker upon speaker said they offended the biblical dignity of human beings and the divine calling to be earth's stewards. While many readers will not find them offensive, there is no question they threaten a homocentrism that lives deep in Christian theology and much popular culture. Neither is about to lie down and die, or even say 'uncle'.[3]

While stewardship as masking a continuing homocentrism may be the sharpest objection, Canberra touched two others. One is reflected in the substance of the deleted paragraphs and their recollections of 'the slow womb' of earth and humanity's late arrival. Delegates attentive to evolutionary sciences were incredulous over the embrace of the biblical theme of humankind as creation's charter creature and a blessing to it. Hearing this prominence in the symbol of steward, they doubted that the symbolization of stewardship had much basis in earth's story.

Indigenous peoples, prominent at the assembly, were another standing criticism of 'steward'. These people knew stewardship as the flipside of its message of empowerment for subjugated peoples. They knew stewardship as the ideology of the 'civilizers' who had promulgated neo-European ways laced with imperialistic and racist notions. This was stewardship as spoken of by those 'subduing the earth', but as now remembered by the subdued.

Amidst the many-sided debate was one matter of shared consensus. Biblically, 'the earth is the Lord's', and humans truly 'own' nothing. The steward is the one entrusted with things precisely not his or her own. He or she is the employee accountable to the owner for proper handling of domestic concerns, keeping the books, collecting rents and generally managing the affairs of the enterprise or estate. Stewardship, then, is accountability not for what humans do own but for what they do not.

Partner

There is a variation on the steward model that attracts those who reject homocentrism and would give humans a humbler place. It is the symbol of partner. St. Francis usually leads the nominees for patron saint. Creation, at least earth, is playfully imaged as a kind of 'holy democracy' of all creatures great and small. There is an interconnectedness and inter-dependence among all things that humans must respect in exercising their considerable power. Other creatures are co-siblings of creation in the drama of a shared life. They must be listened to in order to know what earth is saying and requires. Humankind is partner to otherkind as, in Stephen Jay Gould's phrase, 'the stewards of life's continuity on earth' (Gould 1985: 431).

Humans are decentred in this cosmology. They are not the only subjects of the moral universe, nor does 'quality of life' pertain to their lives alone. The value of otherkind goes beyond what W. Godfrey-Smith (cited by Birch and Cobb 1981: 150) calls 'silo' value (a stock of resources), 'laboratory' value (the object of learning), 'gymnasium' value (value for human leisure and recreation) and 'cathedral' value (aesthetic pleasure and religious emotion). All these still regard humans as 'the measure of all things' in a way the partner model, with its moral universe of inherent value for all creation's 'agents', rejects. Humans do have a distinctive moral calling and unique moral responsibility. But they are not the only creatures due moral consideration (McDaniel 1989: 51ff.). They are decentred both as the goal of creation and as its moral measure.

Yet in another sense humans are recentred in 'partner' cosmology and ethics, and not least in the stewardly tradition of planetary caretaker. With the human species, the argument goes, life itself has become self-conscious and capable of transformations no other species can effect. To fail to recognize this one species' power in the midst of all things is to court illusion. Humans do exercise dominion. Yes, the rest of nature may well hold the final trump card. But short of an endgame, the fact of human power in so much of nature means we are responsible. The question, then, is: How do we exercise this power? And the answer, reflecting the sober realism carried over from the steward model, is to recentre the powerful partner.

The recentred human partner recognizes that, whatever power we wield as a species, we do not legislate the laws of an encompassing nature. Indeed, we violate them to our own and otherkind's peril, even demise. In WCC language, the 'integrity of creation' is utterly basic, with 'justice' and 'peace' pursued as means to creation's flourishing and fulfilment. Justice and peace are not human goals and states only, but all creation's; and they can be attained only on creation's terms. Creation's integrity sets the terms and requires 'moral considerability' of otherkind in human decisions.[4] The preservation of ecosystem communities is of necessity a first value.

The partnership way could offer an element that stewardship often fails to teach: namely, the revival of a creation-loving asceticism. An asceticism that loves earth fiercely in a simple way of life is desperately needed, above all among the wealthy of the world and others habituated to unsustainable consumption as a lifestyle. There are long-standing traditions here (the Franciscans and other religious orders live on) and some seeds sown more recently. (The movement to simplify lifestyles in the 1960s still has its communities. Some of these may yet be the 'anticipatory communities' of the future.) In the ecumenical movement it may be Asian Christians who give leadership. They have both an unbroken culture of relating voluntary poverty to involuntary and a view of nature as comprehensive of all things, including us. Not by coincidence it was a Korean, Chung Hyun Kyung, whose electric plenary address in Canberra advocated the shift 'from anthropocentrism to life-centrism' within an all-inclusive notion of nature in which humans are wondrous microcosms of the macrocosmos. In any case, this newly emphasized asceticism would be an earth-sensuous asceticism, undertaken not in the pursuit of self-denial as such nor obsessed with sex, but in pursuit of a joyous participation in earth community in nondestructive ways.

Sacrament/priest

For the Orthodox, the key is not a stewardship cosmology and ethic, nor even its variant of partnership. It is a sacramentalist one. Sacramentalism as a model has gained new popularity in recent years. It is rooted in diverse and archaic cosmologies from pre-Augustinian Christianity around the Mediterranean to Celtic Christianity in more northerly climes. Orthodox communions from early centuries onward have consistently understood the sacraments as dramatizations of nature's transfiguration. Humans' high calling is as 'priests of creation', referring the creation back to the creator in acts of liturgical doxology. In such praise humans act as representatives for the whole creation, setting loose, in Jürgen Moltmann's words, 'the dumb tongue of nature' through human thanksgiving. 'So when in the "creation" psalms thanks are offered *for* the sun and the light, *for* the heavens and the fertility of the earth, the human being is thanking God, not merely on his own behalf, but also in the name of heaven and earth and all created beings in them.' This is not meant homocentrically, Moltmann explains, because 'everything that has breath' praises God, and 'the heavens declare the glory of God' in their own way, even without human beings and apart from them (Moltmann 1985a: 71). Nature's tongue isn't wholly dumb. Yet human beings are the singers of the cosmic song and the tellers of its tale in a special way; we can represent creation and give voice to it in a cosmic liturgy of praise and transfiguration. We are mediators, then, but not the centre. We intercede for the Community of Life and speak on its behalf before God. We are the *imago mundi* (image of the world) who, as also *imago dei* (image of God), voice God to creation and creation to God. Such is the Orthodox notion (and the Hasidic Jewish notion as well).

Sometimes called 'panentheism', sacramentalism recognizes and celebrates the divine in, with and under all nature, ourselves included. The creaturely is not identified as God, however. (That is pantheism, not panentheism.) Nature and the world are not of themselves divine and are not worshipped. Rather, the infinite is a dimension of the finite; the transcendent is immanent; the sacred is the ordinary in another, numinous light – without any one of these terms exhausting the other. Sacraments themselves are symbols and signs that participate in the very Reality to which they point, but they are not themselves worshipped. To identify something earthly as holy and sacred is not to say it is God. Rather, it is of God; God is present in its presence.

The natural response to the sacramental in our midst is wonder, awe, amazement, fascination, astonishment, curiosity and surprise. It is also a sense of being very small amidst a grand Reality. At times it is a sense of being unworthy in the face of holy wonder and the awareness that the pulse of God's energy flows through me as it does through all life. In any event, the moral posture is certainly not mastery, control and abstracted distance. Rather, it is presence, relationship, and the care and respect due the sacred. The sacramental 'emphasizes the tender elements of the world', biologist Charles Birch says, and 'the spiritual unity that gives the physical its meaning'. This in turn nurtures 'a humbling sense that all creatures are fellow creatures and that human responsibility extends infinitely to the whole of creation' (Birch 1976: 77, 79). Species humility and responsibility are the proper foci of earth ethics.

At Canberra, sacramentalism was endorsed not only by the Orthodox but even more powerfully by indigenous peoples. They burst forth upon the assembly's stage, often literally dancing, and demonstrated once again in their words and actions that the primal vision of peoples of the land is invariably sacramentalist. The entire cosmos is the sacred community, and life should be lived with the respect and treatment due the sacred – it's that simple and profound. For native peoples generally everything in nature represents transcendent power and order, and all the activities of culture – farming, hunting, cooking, eating, householding – are sacramental. They are visible signs of divine power and presence amidst daily practices.

As with the steward model, sacramentalism is not without its distortions and moral corruption. These are rooted in the picture of society present in many sacramentalist cosmologies. The age-old sacramentalist assumption is that a harmony of social and natural interests exists somewhere just below the surface and that a soft, nurturing process will bring this precious flower to bloom. Sacramentalism's metaphors for society as well as church are thus typically 'organic'. (Feudalism lives on!) Or, in the Orthodox version, 'symphonic'. But metaphors of organisms and symphonies don't expose the unequal and corrupted power relations of life among human beings, nor between humans and other creatures. They mask the fact that struggle and conflict so often *are* the status quo. 'Healing', rather than fundamentally reordered eco-social relationships, thus becomes the 'cure' for 'sin' in much sacramentalist theology, whether of established religious traditions or quasi-religious movements (New Age rituals, for example). It is as though earth's basic problem were illness or bad tuning, not injustice or unequal and corrupted power.

John Haught (1993: 110–14) says it differently. Nature, ourselves included, is not yet what it could be, nor fully revelatory of God. Its beauty is only partial, and its fulfilment remains in the form of promise. Any orientation that is only a mystical affirmation of what is, no matter how deep the experience, falls short; and with that it fails to recognize the long and painful distance between the present state of affairs and a better earth. The sacramentalist stance, lost in wonder at what is, can easily incline to such mystical affirmation and its resident shortcomings. It can glory in what is, to the neglect of what ought to be. When it does, it sacrifices its inherent moral and ethical power.

Both indigenous peoples and feminists marry sacramental and liberation postures. They insist that our striving is amidst and about ordinary, daily activities and that the preciousness of life is found here or it is found nowhere. Either the good and the holy are at the centre of what we do in our lives, or else we must change the ways of living that segregate the good and holy from the everyday. Part of this involves our very way of thinking and imagining, since what people define and imagine as real is real in its consequences. The conclusion is that the symbols of religious traditions must be scrutinized to see whether in fact they are lodged firmly on the side of life and its fulfilment, work against such liberation and fulfilment, or are blandly oblivious to daily affairs.

To conclude: in my judgment, an evolutionary sacramentalist cosmology offers the richest conceptual resources for addressing earth's distress, if infused with a profound earth asceticism and married to prophetic efforts aimed at the 'liberation of life from the cell to the community' (the title of the book by Charles Birch and John Cobb, 1981). But personal choices and commitments aside, the far more important question is that the question in the Garden is still being asked, again and anew. The question is God's: 'Adam, where are you?' (Gen. 3.9); the answer is ours.

Notes

1. 'For Jews and Christians together the institutions of the Sabbath, the sabbatical year and the jubilee year provide a clear vision on economic and ecological reconciliation, social restoration and personal renewal. Sabbath reminds us that time, the realm of being, is not just a commodity, but has a quality of holiness, which resists our impulse to control, command and oppress. In the concepts of the sabbatical and jubilee year, economic effectiveness in the use of scarce resources is joined to environmental stewardship, law to mercy, economic order to social justice. It is not production and consumption that sustains our earth but rather the ecological systems that have to support human life' (Report of WCC Assembly in Canberra, 1991, Section I).

2. James Nash (1991: 102) notes that 'image of God' and 'dominion' have exercised disproportionate influence, despite their virtual absence in the Bible. Both *imago dei* and 'dominion' are associated exclusively with the 'royal theology' (P, or 'priestly' theology) segments of Genesis and are never mentioned again in the Hebrew Bible, with one exception for 'dominion' (in Ps. 8.5–8). In the New Testament the concept of divine image is attached to Jesus Christ only, but without an 'ecological' reference, and dominion in the sense of Genesis 1 is not mentioned at all. Notwithstanding, these images have a lively and important lineage in postbiblical religious ethics, where 'image of God' especially has been a grounding for movements of social justice. The cry for basic human rights by racial-ethnic minorities, women, and religious minorities has often taken its cue from *imago dei*. Energy for the same movements has also come from

the sense of moral agency and responsibility for the world that 'dominion' carries.

3. It was precisely stewardship ethics that were enunciated by seventeenth-century scientists and theologians in keeping with early commercial and industrial advances, and on the basis of mechanistic science and homocentric philosophy and theology. In the religious versions, God has assigned human caretaking and supervisory tasks. Nature was to be managed responsibly for the benefit of human welfare (see Merchant 1992: 72). Stewardship ethics were also the explicit theme of development as the scientific management of resources for the benefit of society in the philosophy and practice of Gifford Pinchot and others early in the twentieth century. And in fact much sustainable development discussion at the UN and among NGOs today moves in this orbit. It focuses on good planetary management, with or without explicit reference to a divine mandate entrusted to a distinctive species. Furthermore, the homocentricity of most past stewardship ethics is retained. Principle I of the Rio Declaration of the 1992 Earth Summit begins, 'Human beings are at the centre of concerns for sustainable development'.

4. One example of moral consideration is being worked out in discussion of animal rights. Birch and Cobb (1981: 155–56) list tenets of the Humane Society of the United States with which they, in discussing the intrinsic value of nonhuman creatures, agree: 'It is wrong to kill animals needlessly or for entertainment or to cause animals pain or torment. It is wrong to fail to provide adequate food, shelter and care for animals for which man has accepted the responsibility. It is wrong to use animals for medical, educational or commercial experimentation or research, unless absolute necessity can be demonstrated and unless such is done without causing the animals pain or torment. It is wrong to maintain animals that are used for food in a manner that causes them discomfort or denies them an opportunity to develop and live in conditions that are reasonably natural for them. It is wrong for those who eat animals to kill them in a manner that does not result in instantaneous unconsciousness. Methods employed should cause no more than minimum apprehension. It is wrong to confine animals for display, impoundment, or as pets in conditions that are not comfortable and appropriate. It is wrong to permit domestic animals to propagate to an extent that leads to overpopulation and misery.'

Chapter 15

Stewardship and its Competitors: A Spectrum of Relationships between Humans and the Non-Human Creation

Christopher Southgate

Christopher Southgate obtained his doctorate in biochemistry, but went on to write poetry and lecture in theology at the University of Exeter. He was the chief editor of God, Humanity and the Cosmos *(1999). His concern in this essay is to put stewardship firmly in the context of humanity with evolutionary, social and theological relationships with other creatures. He has written it especially for this volume.*

That human beings are called to be stewards of creation tends to be the default position within ordinary Christian groups. The concept of stewardship is affirmed in recent major documents in both the evangelical and the catholic traditions (for references to these see McGrath 2002, R.J. Berry 2003). Yet it has been subject to some vigorous attacks, such as Clare Palmer's denunciation of stewardship as being (in the sense in which it is popularly used) unbiblical (Palmer 1992, reprinted in this volume). Richard Bauckham confirms that the explicit understanding within the Christian tradition that humans are stewards of nature dates only from the seventeenth century (Bauckham 2000). Anne Primavesi condemns the concept of stewardship as exploitative and unecological (Primavesi 1991: 106–107). Sean McDonagh is concerned that 'within the context of this analogy the earth is reified and becomes either inert property to be cared for or financial resources to be managed in a way that gives a good return on the investment' (McDonagh 1994: 130). Edward Echlin claims that stewardship 'easily lends itself to a detached and manipulative view of creation' and that it 'has not moved hearts' (Echlin 2004: 16). Bill McKibben regards it as 'so lacking in content as to give us very little guidance about how to behave in any given situation' (McKibben 1994: 51).

My approach here is to set stewardship on a spectrum of options for humans' relationship to the non-human creation, and to propose a model in which the concept can play a part in a matrix of understandings of that relationship.

Any attempt to characterize our relationship to the non-human world should recognize that we are part of the animal world through our shared genetic, metabolic and anatomical make-up, and deeply and obligatorily coupled to that world, depending on it for both food and oxygen. And that we have the capacity both to exercise choices, and potentially alter a whole range of environments in a systematic way. This capacity for systematic alteration of a whole range of environments far transcends that of any other species. It is one aspect of the distinctiveness of human beings. It is recognized in the Christian tradition as in some way God-given, and reflected in such texts as Gen. 1, Gen. 2 and Ps. 8.

Each one of the approaches explored below must be seen in the light of our kinship with and dependence on non-human species; we are not merely detached agents, directing the play from a safe distance of power and control, we are also actors within it. That does not mean (of course) that our role as fellow-actors gives us an understanding of what it is like to experience the world as another creature. As John Habgood properly points out, appropriate consideration of the non-human creation must recognize its otherness (Habgood 2002: 70). Despite humans' long relationship with cats, we have no idea, this side of heaven, what it is like to be a cat.[1]

A spectrum of possible human relationships to non-human creation

At one extreme can be seen models of human being which involve a very 'high', God-given calling to be 'co-creators', or even 'co-redeemers' with God of the unfolding creation. Philip Hefner proposed the term 'created co-creator' as an exploratory model of humans' role (Hefner 1993) and this has since been taken up in the work of Ted Peters (e.g. Peters 1997, 2003). Hefner defines the concept of the created co-creator as: 'Human beings are God's created co-creators whose purpose is to be the agency, acting in freedom, to birth the future that is most wholesome for the nature that has birthed us' (Hefner 1993: 264). This is a strikingly future-oriented proposal – as Peters comments, there is a hope here for 'a future that should be better than the past or present' (Peters 2003: 213).

Even more strikingly, Ronald Cole-Turner proposes that humans, as co-creators, are involved in God's work of redemption as the species with the ingenuity to detect and ultimately to eliminate heritable disease (Cole-Turner 1993: 96–97). At once he nuances this – in a way which is important for all those exploring this understanding of the human vocation

– by adding 'Not only are we created co-creators; we are creatures who constantly stand in need of redemption'. Drawing on the conviction of Jürgen Moltmann that evolution stands in need of redemption (Moltmann 1990: 296–97), I have argued elsewhere for a rather different nuance of co-redemption. I suggest there that humans' part in the healing of the world could involve reducing, and ultimately eliminating, the phenomenon of extinction, which is such a familiar part of the evolutionary process as we know it (Southgate 2002: 818–20 – see below).

Co-creator and co-redeemer approaches share a conviction that human ingenuity, with the power it gives us to modify plant species and domesticate animals, to reshape environments, to make cities and parks and farms, is a God-given part of our nature. They accept the great harm to which anthropocentric approaches have led in the past, and nevertheless suppose that part of humanity's transformation will be the discovery of the right use of humans' gifts in respect of the non-human world. They are, as indicated above, essentially future-oriented – they believe human activity can have a role in engendering a future more positive than the present.

An important understanding of humans' role in relation to the non-human world, still emphasizing humans' God-given specialness, is that of humans as priests of creation, the species that offers up creation's praise to God, the species that combines 'the fruit of the earth and the work of human hands' in sacramental action. This attracts a number of authors, and is usefully set in the context of the science–religion debate by Peacocke (1979: 295–97). It is an idea strong in Eastern Orthodox theology, as expressed by Vladimir Lossky: 'In his way to union with God, man in no way leaves creatures aside, but gathers together in his love the whole cosmos disordered by sin, that it may at last be transfigured by grace' (1957: 111). The idea is beautifully expressed by Wendell Berry:

> To live we must daily break the body and shed the blood of creation. When we do this knowingly, lovingly, skillfully and reverently it is a sacrament. When we do it ignorantly, greedily and destructively it is a desecration. In such a desecration, we condemn ourselves to spiritual and moral loneliness and others to want (W. Berry 1981: 281).

That is a very important passage, but in a sense talk of priesthood does not tell us what or how much we may do, only how we should do it. Stewardship does seem to generate a more definite ethic – we should do what a steward would do (the same may be said of the co-creator and co-redeemer models above). Priesthood, in other words, would seem to be compatible with a wide variety of ethical approaches (if not with the notorious thought of James Watt, Ronald Reagan's Secretary of the Interior, that the impending return of Jesus made conservation of US forests an irrelevance).

Priesthood may also be criticized for failing to take adequate account of the wildness and otherness of the non-human world, and of its enormous age – modern humans have, after all, only existed for a tiny fraction of the age of the biosphere, and the Bible contains numerous references to God's relation to other creatures without reference to a human mediating role (Ps. 104; Job 38–39; Mt. 6.26, etc.). The notion of humans as priestly mediators between God and the non-human creation may also deflect attention from our evolutionary kinship with animals, and our own moment to moment dependence on other components in the biosphere, be it the bacteria in our digestion systems or the photosynthetic activities of plants. However, properly nuanced, human priesthood of creation can be a most helpful over-arching concept (see below).

At the other end of the spectrum from co-creation and co-redemption come the various radically biocentric approaches to the relation of humans to the non-human creation. The advocacy of Arne Naess and followers of his proposal for a 'deep ecology', a movement much influenced by Buddhist spirituality, reflects a strong emphasis on the interdependence just mentioned, on 'dependent co-arising'. With a sense of our dependence on other creatures goes a sense of our radical equality with other species (Naess 1972). Another source of thinking pointing in much the same direction is the writing of Aldo Leopold – in particular his 'land ethic' – 'An action is right where it tends to preserve the integrity, stability and beauty of a biotic community. It is wrong when it tends otherwise' (1949: 224–25).

In contrast to co-creation or co-redemption, this type of proposal seeks to preserve a harmonious present. More often it also hankers for a return to a somewhat romantically conceived past, when there were many fewer human beings, imposing less of a load on the carrying capacity of the planet, and more in touch with our early life as hunter-gatherers. As Thomas Sieger Derr notes, there is a fatalism in this view, which places little premium on continued human existence (see Derr 1995). The past life of indigenous peoples is often celebrated, without any realistic assessment of what that life might have been like (cf. R.J. Berry 2003: 249–50).

Tempting though talk of equality and plain membership is, it runs into problems in practice. As Wendell Berry noted in the passage quoted above, human interests are constantly in tension with those of other species; can it be that there are no circumstances in which humans' survival should be preferred to the overall well-being of the biosystem within which they live? Questions arise too as to whether ecosystems constitute 'communities'. There are powerful reservations, deriving from current scientific thinking, as to whether 'stability' and 'harmony' are characteristics of natural systems. There is, moreover, a paradox inherent in biocentrism – unless we 'lift ourselves up' out of the ecosystem, experiment on it, use our distinctive rationality and ingenuity on it, and gain the perspective on it that science gives us, we cannot know what would promote the health (leaving aside talk of stability and harmony) of a system of non-human organisms. Derr (1995: 100) asserts that:

> The movement as a whole [biocentrism] can offer us very little real guidance about our permissible impact on the natural world. While it would allow us to feed and clothe and house ourselves, it would require of us some degree of self-limitation because of our exceptional talents, including particularly our talent for reproducing ourselves. But it is very difficult to tell what this directive might mean beyond the generalized complaint that we are too clever and thus exceed our space too readily. We have to pretend we are less, in effect, so that other creatures may be more, but how and how much are quite unspecifiable.

So also Sallie McFague (1993: 125) when she asserts that deep ecology will remain important 'for its poetic power more than for its conceptual adequacy'.

Stewardship itself sits between these two extremes – less convinced of its prerogative to alter nature than co-creation or co-redemption, less passively inclined and more convinced of human distinctiveness than biocentrism. A number of problems with the concept have already been identified. One key one is the implicit presumption that there is some state or character of the non-human creation, knowable by humans, that we are in a position to steward. I comment also that the usual connotations of the word 'stewardship' are in terms of caution about the future – 'stewardship' of 'resources' seeks to provide a future no worse than the present.

I leave detailed discussion of this concept to others in this volume. I note only that stewardship may cover a wide variety of approaches. Just as it is helpful to distinguish between weak and strong approaches to sustainability (cf. Daly and Cobb 1989), it may be helpful to make a distinction in the middle of our spectrum between 'weak' stewardship, which would be of a merely conserving kind, 'stewardship as preservation' in Lawrence Osborn's terms (Osborn 1993: 143) and which would incline towards the biocentric end of the spectrum described above (cf. Nash 1991), and 'strong' stewardship, 'stewardship as nurture' (Osborn 1993: 143–44), which would involve change as well as conservation of non-human environments, and would incline towards co-creation (so R.J. Berry 2003).

This distinction reveals two important elements which complicate our discussion and any effort to locate the appropriate position for Christians to adopt on the spectrum outlined above. The first element is the limited nature of our knowledge and understanding of biotic systems. Such systems are known to be very complex; it is estimated that there are millions of species not yet even described. Biological systems' sensitivity to change is also very difficult to predict, given that mathematically they tend to manifest chaotic behaviour.

The second element is a disagreement, not often articulated, as to what systems of non-human organisms ought to be like. We have noted the longing to find 'stability, beauty and harmony' within natural systems, and posed the question as to whether claims for stability and harmony can be substantiated scientifically. In a recent study Lisa Sideris has criticized sharply the work of ecofeminists such as McFague and Rosemary Radford Ruether for their assumption that harmony and cooperation are fundamental characteristics of natural systems (Sideris 2003: ch. 2). Rather, she commends the work of Holmes Rolston III. Rolston has made an eloquent and careful analysis of instrumental, intrinsic and systemic values in the natural world (e.g. Rolston 1988, 1994). He is resolute in asserting that humans should not interfere with the workings of wild nature in wilderness areas. Even where these workings lead to great sufferings within individuals or species, humans should not intervene. This represents a strong conviction that the way that creation has evolved, under the influence of natural selection, is the way it should be. Creation is, for Rolston, 'cruciform', a place of tragedy (2003: 84), but he might have added (paraphrasing Darwin) that 'there is grandeur as well as tragedy in this view of life'. The non-human world possesses its beauty because of the processes that also involve the sufferings associated with predation and parasitism and which engender extinction.

This is a powerful and compelling argument. But the step from scientific description to what-nature-should-be is not a strict logical step. It involves a metaphysical judgment – indeed, for a theist like Rolston, a theological judgment. The Darwinian description of the world involves no prescription as to what-nature-should-be. The impoverishment of a natural system in response to altered environmental conditions – as in the desertification of a previously forested region, the flooding of low-lying coastal systems, or come to that, the onset of a new Ice Age – is as compatible with the processes and descriptions of Darwinism as our present extraordinarily rich and fruitful biosphere. The changes merely lead to the selection of different populations of organisms: thorns and cacti rather than trees and ferns, saltwater fish and plankton rather than the biological communities of wetlands. Humans form judgments about what overall planetary conditions should be promoted, and what striven against, judgments to which Darwinian descriptions cannot themselves give rise. And the notion of a future hope for the organisms of the planet is likewise one on which Darwinism can make no comment – it is a description of processes and phenomena, not of values or hopes.

In considering humans' relation to God and to the non-human creation, the Christian must give an account of values and hopes. Confronted with the possibility of human-induced runaway global warming, which might ultimately render the Earth as uninhabitable as Venus, humans clearly have a duty to avoid such a huge impoverishment of the creation. (Even if we were capable of saving our own species we would still have that duty in respect of the Earth.) Likewise, a nuclear catastrophe might not eliminate absolutely every organism on the planet, but it would be a disastrous depletion of the biosphere. Every effort must be made, surely, to prevent human activity giving rise to either eventuality.

However, our stewardly, precautionary role in seeking to ensure that the future is not radically worse than the present also applies to non-anthropogenic situations. If it were discovered that the next Ice Age was imminent (and in the natural macrocycles of our climate we are heading in that direction) then it would surely be humans' responsibility to seek not merely to sustain human civilization (which might be done in a series of microenvironments) but to seek – if it were possible – to ward off the massive extinctions that would be associated with a major icing-over of the surface of the planet. (Our best plan would be, presumably, to pump as much greenhouse gas into the atmosphere as possible.) So even in respect of wild nature humans have responsibilities. These arise, not out of our Darwinian understanding but out of our sense of the value of God's creatures. We should exert ourselves to hold the boundaries of the Earth's surface environment, the settings, as James Lovelock would put it, of 'Gaia' (cf. Lovelock 1988) within bounds which provide for a rich and fruitful biosphere. God's action to preserve God's lovely and 'good' biosphere would presumably be through humans as agents. It is in this limited sense that I consider it is entirely valid to speak of human stewardship of the planet.

I also share with McKibben, Rolston, and many deep-ecological writers (for a conspectus of these, see Sessions 1995) a sense of the importance to us, scientifically and spiritually, of the continuing existence of wilderness. Our stewardship, as conceived above in terms of seeking to protect some fruitful limits within which the Earth-system as a whole might unfold, would necessarily involve the protection of wilderness as a place con-secrated to our respect for God's creation. It is in wilderness that we can recognize our fellow-citizenship of the biotic community (to pick up on the language of Aldo Leopold). It is in wilderness that we learn most imme-diately from other creatures (as out in a Dartmoor storm I learn the grain of the hill-folds from the shelter-patterns of the sheep). It is through the existence of wilderness that we can reassess our sense of scale, recognizing the immensity of God and of God's work of creation, so movingly por-trayed in passages such as Job 38 and Isa. 40.

I noted above that the notion of human priesthood of creation does not actually offer a clear ethical prescription. Co-creatorly activity is much associated with priesthood, and indeed is central to eucharistic practice – what we offer is both 'the fruit of the earth' and the fruit of the blessing of human ingenuity, 'the work of human hands'. But it might also be argued that humans exercise their priesthood just as truly as contemplatives – though we cannot hear the language of the song of all creaturely praise to which the Psalms refer (cf. Ps. 19.1–4), we can stand with the song in wild places, celebrate it and offer it whole up to God. R.J. Berry helpfully quotes the New Testament commentator Charles Cranfield:

> The Jungfrau and the Matterhorn and the planet Venus and all living things too, man alone excepted, do indeed glorify God in their own ways; but since their praise is destined to be not a collection of independent offerings, but part of a magnificent whole, the united praise of the whole creation, they are prevented from being fully what they were created to be, so long as man's part is missing (Cranfield 1974: 227).

We cannot put human priesthood neatly on our spectrum at any defined point. But a lack of ethical precision does not render the idea of priesthood any less important. The tenor of the great passages on creation in the Hebrew Bible is that we have been placed in a special place by God – as created last (Gen. 1) or first (Gen. 2), as namer before God of the animals, as a little lower than the angels in the song of cosmic praise (Ps. 8). This specialness enables us to see the created world whole, and to offer it up in praise. The creation of humans in the image and likeness of God (Gen. 1.26), and to praise and glorify God for ever, must lie behind every description of our calling in relation to the rest of creation.

There are three broad contexts in which humans might have care for the creation, exerted either actively or passively. One is that of the whole surface of the biosphere; another is the context of what is presently wilderness; the third is that in which humans live alongside the non-human creation and cultivate or actively manage it. I have identified a spectrum of possible roles for humans. The theme of our creation in the image of God both gives weight to our claim to be priests of creation, and also gives us a clue as to how we might use our spectrum.

We are in a sense stewards of the whole surface biosphere,[2] in that we know of certain scenarios which would eliminate all or most of that richness of life, and we have a responsibility to ward off those scenarios, to conserve at the most general level what God's loving activity over 4.5 billion years has made possible on Earth, to make sure indeed that the future is no worse than the present. And part of our status in God's image is our capacity to see Earth as the fragile and beautiful whole that it is, and to guard it with wisdom. In this sense we are in the image of the God who looked upon the creation and found it very good, and held it safe within his rest (Gen. 1.31–2.3).

We are (within that wider perspective) fellow-citizens of wild nature – to hear other creatures' praise of their God, to recognize that they are loved for their own sake, we must quiet the thunder of our own ambitions, our own worship both of God and of idols; we must protect places where that praise can be itself without our distorting it. We should long to hear that praise as Adam heard it, and make space in our lives and our world to ensure that we do. Again, the language of stewardship may be used of this overall protecting role, but does not do justice to the role of contemplative, or praise-giver, which the wilderness can engender in us. In making space for other creatures' praise we are in the image of God who in creation made space for otherness (for recent explorations of this theme of divine kenosis within creation, see Polkinghorne 2001).

We are already the ingenious innovators and managers of new ways of living in and with the non-human creation on a high proportion of the Earth's land surface. Our calling is to bring this ingenuity, and the necessity of breaking the body of creation for our own needs and the needs of the future, humbly into our priesthood (cf. Wendell Berry, quoted above). We are in the image of God the maker and innovator. We should believe, as Hefner proposes, that our future with the non-human creation can be better than the past or the present. But we need not see our co-creative calling solely in terms of technological innovation or biotechnological tweaking – we can create not only new strains of drought-resistant crops for use in the Sahel, but also the loving interspecies communities which are domesticated nature at its best. Our creativity can – must, if it is to be in partnership with God's – express our hope for the growth of love in the world. Our lordship and management can be expressed in service – even within the community of domesticated nature we can exert our creativity and imagination to recognize the value and dignity of the other and to serve its needs with humility and joy. This would mean radical transformation of much current agricultural practice, but only thus could our role come to be in the image of the God who in Jesus expressed lordship – dominion – in terms of servanthood (Mk 10.43; cf. also the ideas of Douglas Hall 1986, 1990).

What God alone could do and has done, once and for all, was to suffer death for the transformation of the world, to bear in Christ the pain of the creation and of human sin. But our lives can side with that sacrifice in ways both ingenious and costly. If we were to grow into the fullness of our life under God we might be able to realize a further call – a call to participate more actively in the healing of a wild nature that may be seen both as 'very good' (Gen. 1.31) and as (through the will of the same God who made it) 'groaning in travail' (Rom. 8.22). In doing so we would be acting in the image of the God that we see, in the life of the earthly Jesus, as being always moved to compassion by the need for healing.

I am not wholly in agreement with Rolston that our interaction with wilderness should be confined to its protection from anthropogenic damage. I do not follow his naturalistic inference that what is in a wild system is what ought to be (cf. Derr 1995). It is very hard to make use of the eschatological visions we find in Isaiah (e.g. 11.6, the leopard lying down with the kid). They are, as Derr puts it, 'hope without details' (1995: 97). It is very hard to see how the leopardness of a leopard could be fulfilled in eschatological co-existence with a kid.[3] Sideris abandons all hope of making any use of these passages (2003: 119). However, from the earliest known Christian writings there has been a strong eschatological emphasis to the faith, and a sense that the Cross is the hinge-point not merely of human but also of cosmic history. In this eschatological– redemptive perspective it is not enough to settle for the equation of what- the-non-human-world-is with what it should or will be. Eschatological hope should be a stronger influence on the Christian understanding than that. Creation is both 'very good' (Gen 1.31) in its fruitfulness, in all the myriad possibility for 'selves' and interactions that it makes possible, and also 'groaning' awaiting 'the freedom and the glory of the children of God' (Rom. 8.21–22), the growing up of humans into the kingdom of fellowship and self-giving that is the life of the divine. That I see as being the most helpful theological analysis of what naturalistically can be described in Darwinian terms. A mark of humans' growing into the life of divine fellowship would be a participation in the divine transformation of the biosphere, the relief of nature's groaning.

Although the reconciliation of predator–prey relationships in a way which does justice to the natures of both would clearly be a work of God, far beyond even human imaginings, it is not too much to suppose that a reduction of extinction, within the current order of the biosphere, would be part of this healing of nature. Extinction is an intrinsic part of the Dar- winian scheme, of the operation of wild nature. For Rolston there is no case for preventing it, if it is not human induced. But extinction of a species means the loss of a whole way of being alive on the planet, a whole aspect of the goodness of creation, a whole way of praising God. It also means particularly acute suffering for the last members of a species (imagine as a thought-experiment the experience of the last members of the newly dis- covered *Homo floresiensis* as they perceive that they are and will be the last of their kind). Part of fulfilled human calling might be, by dint of our knowledge and ingenuity, to have a share in eliminating that experience from the biosphere. That would mean a co-redeemerly 'stewarding' (informed by our experience as priests and fellow-praisers) even of wild- erness, but one which would take a great deal more wisdom as well as a great deal more knowledge than we currently possess. So one great human priority at present must be to gather (non-invasively) as much knowledge and wisdom as we can about the non-human world, and to reduce the very high rate of human-induced extinction to which the biosphere is currently subject (see Leakey and Lewin 1996).

In summary, I have indicated the importance of humans understanding themselves both as part of and distinct from creation. I have explored a spectrum of possible human roles in respect of the non-human creation, and their differing valuations of the future against the past and the present. I have suggested that a range of different understandings of our human role (including that of stewardship) is needed in different contexts. Stewardship finds a strictly limited role in this scheme – a place to do with the holding of limits within which the biosphere can continue to flourish. Such a view is 'detached' (*sensu* Echlin) – it will need to be if we are to fulfil our calling to see nature as a whole, but not manipulative or exploitative (*pace* Echlin, Primavesi). It would contain no sense that the Earth is our property (*pace* McDonagh). I hope (*pace* McKibben) that this very restricted sense of our stewardship preserves a meaningful and helpful level of content. The overarching concept of human priesthood of creation binds our various roles together. I also reject the naturalistic extrapolation of how the non-human world is to how it ought to be, and posit that humans might eventually grow into a co-redeemerly role expressed in particular in the reduction of species extinction.

Notes

1. I thank my wife Sandy for the suggestion that this is the sort of insight we might gain in heaven. That makes heaven, for me, a much more appealing place than some Christian descriptions suggest.
2. I exclude Thomas Gold's proposed 'deep hot biosphere' (Gold 1999), and perhaps the remotest parts of the oceanic biosphere as being effectively beyond the limit of our care.
3. However, there is a poem by James Dickey called 'The Heaven of Animals' which offers a fine image of the unimaginable. It is reproduced in *Staying Alive* (Astley 2002, 221–22).

Part IV
Applications

Chapter 16

Ethics and Stewardship

Chris Patten

Chris Patten, CH (Lord Patten of Barnes) was a leading British politician in the 1980s;
he was Secretary of State for the Environment at the time national contributions to the
'Earth Summit' at Rio were being prepared. The British Government Paper This
Common Inheritance *(1990) was prepared while he was the responsible Minister. It*
stated as a First Principle that 'The starting point for this Government is the ethical
imperative of stewardship, which must underlie all environmental policies'. Lord Patten
went on to be Governor of Hong Kong and then a European Commissioner. He is
Chancellor of the Universities of Newcastle and Oxford. This essay is part of the 1990
Wilson Lecture delivered at Godolphin and Latymer School in March 1990.

One issue on which head and heart can certainly agree is the central, ethical
principle, which underlies the whole of our concern for the environment.
This is the principle of stewardship. We do not have freeholders' rights to
the land we live in, which allow us to do whatever we want with it. We are
trustees, obliged to pass on what we inherited from the last generation to
the next. Ruskin put this particularly well. He said:

> God has lent us the earth for our life; it is a great entail. It belongs as
> much to those who are to come after us, and whose names are already
> written in the book of creation, as to us; and we have no right, by any
> thing that we do or neglect, to involve them in unnecessary penalties,
> or deprive them of benefits which it was in our power to bequeath ...
> Men cannot benefit those that are with them as they can benefit those
> who come after them; and of all the pulpits from which human voice
> is ever sent forth, there is none from which it reaches so far as from
> the grave.

I personally also find in the idea of stewardship a strong and constructive
element of human self-respect, as well as respect for posterity. What we do
to our world says a lot about us collectively, in just the same way as the
choices we make about our lives and surroundings say a lot about us
individually.

In Britain particularly, the feeling that we have some special human responsibility for civilizing the aftermath of the industrial revolution is almost as old as the industrial revolution itself. We all remember William Blake's reference in 'Jerusalem' to 'dark, satanic mills' and the fact that he was apparently referring to churches cannot detract from the industrial power of the metaphor. Later in the nineteenth century, we have Wordsworth and his powerful affirmations, against the background of the industrial age, of regard for nature as the real touchstone of the human spirit. We have William Morris, whose primitive socialism was based on rejection of the shoddy products of the machine age in favour of an ideal in which each working man could be an artisan, relying on his respect for the products of his own hands to maintain his spiritual, as well as his material, place in the world.

Dickens gives us the pulse of that particular industrial age:

> The earth was made for Dombey and Son to trade in, and the sun and moon were made to give him light. Rivers and seas were formed to float their ships; rainbows gave them promise of fair weather; winds blew for or against their enterprises; stars and planets circled in their orbits to preserve inviolate a system of which they were the centre. Common abbreviations took new meanings in his eyes, and had sole reference to them. A.D. had no concern with anno Domini, but stood for anno Dombei – and son.

What Dickens describes here shows why the world was in need of protection from man's industrial excesses. The way in which he describes it shows insight and humanity of the kind that produced the Alkali Act of 1863, the first great legislative monument of environmental stewardship.

Going too far

But today I think that there are many people who feel a genuine ethical concern for stewardship who allow the heart to take them too far in certain directions. The kind of attitudes I mean tend to imply some or all of three loosely connected propositions:

First, that the world can sustain its growing population at a tolerable standard of living only if the developed world drops the idea of economic growth and accepts a decline in living standards towards those of the less-developed world.

Secondly, that the world's natural state is the only truly 'right' state for it, and that human activities should not be allowed to have any effects on nature, which can possibly be avoided.

Thirdly, that any environmental risk is unacceptable and must be avoided.

I should like to look at each of these propositions more closely.

First, the idea of zero or negative growth is a counsel of despair, which we must reject utterly.

Poverty is perhaps the greatest pollutant of the lot, as we can see by looking, not only at the developing world, but also at the magnitude of the ecological disasters, which, as is becoming clear in the new era of *glasnost*, have accompanied economic stagnation in parts of Eastern Europe since the war. The economy and industry are simply not something that we can do without or put into reverse. Nor are they wicked in themselves. They create the wealth and the goods, which are necessary for feeding, clothing, transporting, warming, lighting, curing and educating you and me. Part of the ethical challenge of stewardship is for governments to create conditions which will allow our children, and their children, to live as good or better material lives than ourselves.

The other part of this ethical challenge is of course to create those conditions without fouling the global nest and without growing at the expense of our poorer developing neighbours. Part of the key to this is sound science. But sound economics is just as important. On a global scale this means that we have to grow and develop our economies in sustainable ways – which, in other words, conserve natural resources, rather than depleting them at rates which even renewable resources cannot always recover. The tropical forests are – all too literally – the burning example of this.

For us in the developed world, this means looking afresh at methods of agriculture that do not impoverish the land, at industrial processes that minimize waste and pollution and maximize recycling; and at the development of more efficient ways of using energy. For the poorer countries it means following the same principles while avoiding the mistakes of the first world's industrialization process. And part of the duty of the first world is to ensure that developing countries get the benefit of our environmental know-how on fair and affordable terms.

With the second of the three propositions – the sacrosanctity of the natural order – I quote from no less an authority than Monsieur Jacques Delors, President of the Commission of the European Communities. Opening a G8 Conference on Environmental Ethics, he said (Delors 1990: 23): 'the natural world can no longer bear unbridled pillaging . . . this is the first lesson we must learn: to respect nature for itself and not simply as a means for satisfying our needs. Nature has a logic of its own which may differ from ours.'

No one, least of all me, would deny that there is sound sense in this. And of course, we have seen all too clearly the truth of the proposition that nature will have her revenge if we muck her about. But the flavour of

Monsieur Delors' comments, and of those who take the same line of thought to much more radical extremes – 'leave things alone unless absolutely necessary' – I believe is wrong.

I can perhaps illustrate this point in quoting from the great sixteenth and seventeenth century statesman and scholar, Francis Bacon: 'naturae enim non imperatur, nisi parendo' – it is not possible to direct nature, except by obeying it.

This is quite true. But in fact, Bacon is not saying, 'leave things alone'. He is surely giving an early definition of sustainable development. Another thing to remember is that Bacon's purpose was to set up a new system of natural philosophy on what are now regarded as modern principles. The Aristotelian scheme, which he was reacting against, had held sway for 2000 years, broadly based on the proposition that the secrets of nature could be established by the exercise in the abstract of the intellect alone. Bacon's revolutionary insight was to modify this with an approach based on the 'right understanding of nature' – bringing in the notion that empirical facts are of overriding importance in scientific progress.

So it is likely that what he meant by the Latin tag was that, to manage the world – and he certainly thought that the world existed for man – you must understand and accept how it really works. So it is possible to claim Bacon as the first champion of sound science as a basis for policies for managing the environment – and manage it we clearly must, as he would have been the first to agree. The trick for humankind is to get the management of nature right, not to avoid it altogether.

Finally, there is the proposition that any environmental risk is too much to take. Certainly it is true that prevention is much better than cure, in environmental protection as elsewhere. Policies must continue to aim at preventing damage, rather than clearing up the consequences. Again, sound science is important, and where scientific knowledge is not complete, lack of certainty is no justification for doing nothing.

For example, the Vienna Convention on protection of the ozone layer was negotiated before we had conclusive evidence of ozone damage. Also, the Intergovernmental Panel on Climate Change (IPCC), set up jointly by the United Nations Environment Programme and the World Meteorological Organization, will be reporting later this year [1990] on its work on the greenhouse effect. An important element of that work is scientific assessment. I do not expect the IPCC to provide absolute proof of climate change and its causes, but I do expect a solid scientific consensus which will provide us with the basis we need to start work on a global convention and associated binding protocols.

This precautionary approach is surely the right one. But it obviously can't eliminate all risks altogether. And in some cases, environmental risks have simply not been foreseen or perhaps even been foreseeable: CFCs are a good example of this. They were invented – incidentally by the same man who first thought of putting lead in petrol – as a cleaner and safer means of refrigeration and of blowing foams. It was only after they had been in use for many years that evidence emerged that they were doing real harm to the ozone layer. When new problems come to light in future, no doubt they will continue to come from unexpected quarters.

When this happens, the right approach is to react quickly at the political level, while trusting to science and human ingenuity to tell us what action to take. But again, the ethics of the government's stewardship of the economy means that the costs of the precautions must be proportionate to the risk, and indeed that the costs of compliance with environmental controls of all kinds must be proportionate to the environmental benefits that they produce.

Methods and constraints

The ethical challenge to manage the natural world responsibly and sustainably is to provide a good quality of life for humankind. The need for this kind of balance is as evident internationally as on the national scale. We conclude international agreements like that on climate change partly because of the consideration that we owe to our neighbours and to their posterity. But our neighbours are also our trading and industrial competitors. We need to cooperate with them, and they with us, not just for environmental reasons, but also to safeguard the basis of our prosperity.

International discussion and cooperation can do this by ensuring that their industries and ours work to common standards, and hence have the chance to maintain their competitiveness in a fair and equal market place. Some might criticize this as self-interest. But there is nothing whatsoever ethically wrong with concern for the foundation of our national prosperity, least of all when our best interests and those of our neighbours and competitors coincide.

Deciding what we need to do to protect the environment is one question. How we do it is another, and this, too, has ethical implications.

One school of thought, to which Monsieur Delors firmly belongs, is that we should impose solutions by regulation:

> After all, one of the primary functions of ethics is to illuminate and facilitate decision-making. In other words to pave the way for legislation. Consequently, as soon as possible, a legal framework must be established to convert the responsibilities and duties which I mentioned into full-fledged obligations (Delors 1990: 24).

For myself, I am not by any means so sure that 'facilitating decision-making' and 'paving the way for legislation' are necessarily the same thing.

In the past, governments have relied on direct regulation as their main means of controlling activities which affect the environment. Typical approaches have been to specify quality standards which the air, water and land to which waste is discharged must not exceed; or to permit particular compositions, concentrations and values of effluents or emissions; or to prescribe the processes and techniques which are to be used to reduce pollutants at source; or a combination of all three.

This regulatory approach will always remain an important element in any effective approach to environmental controls. Historically in the UK, it has worked well – largely because it has been operated through close cooperation between the regulators and the regulated, working with the grain of current technologies and practices. But new thinking, particularly in economics, is stimulating discussion of some relative shortcomings and limitations of the classical approach to regulation, and of new means of control that it might be possible to devise to remedy them. The regulatory approach has limitations:

First of all, the strictest controls over discharges and receiving media are of little use if they are not properly obeyed. This has been a problem in some places, though thankfully not in the UK.

Secondly, regulation can provide close, local controls over processes and products, but cannot directly reflect broader political and environmental concerns that may arise when products are used or traded later on. For example, regulation is relatively good at controlling how much lead goes into petrol, but relatively poor at influencing people's decisions about whether to use the leaded or unleaded kind.

Thirdly, the complexity of the standards involved means that they can be expensive to monitor and enforce and that they are not always easy to update quickly to keep pace with scientific and technical advances.

Finally, and perhaps most importantly of all, regulation cannot guarantee always to pitch controls at the level which gives the best and most cost-effective balance between environmental benefits and the cost of compliance, as I would argue the truly ethical approach to the environment requires.

In future, a number of possible economic and market-based control instruments may have an important part to play, alongside traditional regulatory measures, in protecting the environment. There are several possible approaches, but what they have in common is that they operate by introducing a price signal into the market, which better reflects the true environmental costs of the product concerned. A good example of this is the differential between the price of leaded and unleaded petrol introduced by means of a change in taxation, following which the UK market share of unleaded petrol has risen from 4% to 30%.

My special adviser, Professor David Pearce's recent report 'Blueprint for a Green Economy' for my Department offers a conceptual basis for a systematic market-based approach to supplement direct regulation and make it more efficient and effective (Pearce, Markandya and Barbier 1989). One of the key principles is the valuation of environmental costs in order to take them into account in cost/benefit judgments.

The point here is that it is perverse and wrong to treat environmental goods as though they were a 'free lunch'. The more we can reflect in the market the true economic costs of environmental goods, the less we are likely to reach false economic judgments of the kind that have led, for example, to the exploitation of rainforest resources in ways which destroy them totally within the space of a few years.

Economics is about allocating resources according to people's preferences. Hence, on David Pearce's view, preferences for the existence and well-being of whales, elephants and snail darters are as much to do with economics as the price of shares or other materials.

Of course there will always be some limits on what can be valued in concrete, quantified terms – some intangibles will remain intangible. No one believes that everything that should affect our judgment can have a single, accurate cash value attached to it, which can then be juggled with other hard cost-benefit data to produce a 'correct' answer by pure arithmetic. No one believes that any kind of economics can tell us in pounds and pence the true, intrinsic value of a butterfly, or a landscape, or a heronry. But the development of comprehensive approaches to environmental economics, which take account of the relative strength of our preferences about such things, is a real step forward. Approaches like this, by bringing incentives and disincentives into the market, rather than relying entirely on a rigid legal system of control, can provide the means not only of bringing economic considerations into environmental policy, but also of bringing environmental considerations into economic policy.

An important element in this kind of market approach is the 'polluter pays' principle. In other words, polluters must not normally be subsidized to enable them to meet pollution control standards. Nor – although there may need to be some exceptions – are the costs of dealing with pollution from known sources always to be borne by the public purse. The costs involved are very large – about 1.5 to 2% of gross domestic product, in the UK perhaps £7 billion in 1990.

In the end, what this means is that we are the ones who pay these costs through the prices that we pay as consumers for energy, goods and services. This is entirely as it should be: we should remember that it is we as consumers, and not some disembodied 'they', who give rise to environmental damage and the economic and ethical problems that arise from it.

Another powerful argument for caring about elephants and snail darters is that the very diversity of the natural world is itself a huge economic resource. This was brought home to me forcefully in a remarkable talk given by an American called Jessica Tuchman Mathews.

She pointed out that the planet's genetic diversity is heavily concentrated in the rain forests and is therefore disappearing today on a scale not seen since the age of the dinosaurs. She quotes estimates that species are being lost in the tropical forests 1,000 to 10,000 times faster than the natural rate of extinction, and that as many as 20% of all the species now living may be gone by the year 2000. The loss will be felt aesthetically, scientifically, and, above all, economically. Genetic resources provide new sources of food, materials for energy and construction, chemicals for pharmaceuticals and industry, means of health and safety testing, natural pest controls, the basis for adapting crops and livestock to climatic change and dozens of other uses.

As Ms Mathews says, the costs of the losses that are occurring daily are impossible even to estimate. She gives the example of a Mexican graduate student who, a few years ago, stumbled upon a primitive form of perennial corn which appears to exist nowhere else in the world and which would have been quickly wiped out but for his alertness. If this primitive strain can be developed into commercial perennial corn, its eventual value is estimated to be in the tens of billions.

Ms Mathews powerfully makes the point that genetic diversity is a virtually untapped resource. Man makes use of less than 1% of what is available. Among the vast numbers of unused types of edible plants are a great many with more potential than those now in use. It is perhaps a bitter irony that genetic diversity is being lost on a grand scale at the very moment when biotechnology makes it possible to exploit the resource fully for the first time. It is not impossible that part of the solution may be the new science of genetic modification.

Conclusion

Where does all this bring me?

First, that sound science is an absolutely basic necessity for any ethical, or even purely rational, decisions. Part of the government's job is to monitor and reseach the environment. This is essential to allow us to keep right up with the game as new issues arise, and to get on top of their scientific, technical and human implications as fast as we can.

Secondly, if sound science is essential to our understanding of environmental problems, sound economics is just as essential when we come to decide on strategies for dealing with them without wasting resources and without putting our national and international prosperity at avoidable risk.

But, in the end, sound science and economics on their own can never be quite enough. The politicians' job is to build on them to find practical solutions which work in human and political as well as in purely rational and scientific terms. This includes taking decisions about just where we draw the line between precautionary action and scientific uncertainty, and searching for international agreement on common environmental measures which work, and which are fair as regards both the more and the less developed world.

It is increasingly widely recognized that big changes are going to be needed in the way we live and set our priorities if the world is going to be worth living in for our grandchildren and our neighbours' grandchildren. We all need to encourage the growth of a sense of corporate and individual responsibility for the environment. I believe that this sense is growing in Britain.

Chapter 17

Sea Sabbaths for Sea Stewards: Rest and Restoration for Marine Ecosystems

Susan Power Bratton

*Susan Bratton has written widely on environmental theology, e.g. an examination of the importance of wilderness (*Christianity, Wilderness and Wildlife: The Original Desert Solitaire, *1993) and a critical examination of environmental ecofeminism (1994). She has PhDs in ecology from Cornell University and theology from the University of Texas; she currently teaches at Baylor University in Waco. Her essay here was written especially for this volume and puts forward the intriguing idea that we should extend ideas of Sabbath and Jubilee beyond the terrestrial realm into marine systems.*

In the opening chapter of Genesis, the ancient authors award aquatic and marine environments priority in the narrative of creation. God's Spirit 'moves over the face of the waters' (Gen. 1.2). God separates and gathers the waters and fills them with the fish, creeping things and great sea monsters. The waters still occupy two-thirds of the planet, yet Christian environmental ethics is often termed '*Earth* ethics'. Commentaries on stewardship frequently portray environmental care and protection as maintaining a terrestrial garden, based on Genesis 2. Today the seas are in crisis, suffering from 'fisheries collapse' and ubiquitous pollution. One of the challenges for sea stewards is converting the numerous biblical teachings, which in their immediate sense concern agriculture or land-locked humanity, into Christian principles for ocean care.

For example, why should we not apply both the concept of rest for all creation in Gen. 2.1–3 (and in the Levitical laws requiring a seventh year rest for agricultural fields: Exodus 23.10–11) to marine ecosystems and harvests? Most environmental commentaries on the Sabbath adopt human scales, locales and priorities. Norman Wirzba (2004) credits Jewish rabbis for pointing out that at the end of the sixth day, God had one thing left to create – 'the *menuha*, the peace, tranquility, delight, and repose of creation'. The *menuha*, although its human celebration is on the seventh day, is far more pervasive in the biosphere and the great web of living organisms than the flicker of a few candles marking a sacred interval. Environment-ally, we might learn something from creation itself in studying the function of 'rest'. Anyone investigating the natural history of peace and repose in regard to 'the fish of the seas', however, must consider the oceans' (and God's) own scales and purposes.

We humans perceive tranquil and resting states as aesthetic, even won-drous. How many of us might be inclined, in the midst of a slow walk down a beach to stop and sit on a dune to admire a setting sun? Likewise, we inherently distrust excessive restlessness, although we may not recognize that other species, and even entire ecosystems, can be driven to an 'unnatural' exhaustion. Norman Wirzba (2001: 9–12) laments the billion tons of soil lost from farm fields each year, and recognizes that our historic predisposition to give the land no rest has undermined entire civilizations.

We humans are so entranced with 'doing' that we view 'not doing' as a non-state, and we fail to recognize rest has specific 'creative' purposes. A period of reduced metabolism for marine organisms can be an adaptation to avoid harsh conditions or to enhance reproduction. Parrot fish sleep in reef crevices at night in protective slime. Corals are nocturnal and spawn simultaneously, after a period of rest, so fertilization between individual organisms is more likely to occur. Physical inactivity is associated with the processing or storage of energy, tissue repair and cell division. Many pre-dators remain stationary while digesting a large meal. Marine species may rest following migration or breeding. Seals and sea lions haul out on rocks or beaches to conserve energy that would be lost in maintaining body temperature in cold water. Hauling out also permits mothers to nurse their young in relative safety. Periodic alternations of behaviour are frequently associated with nutritional necessity or healing. A grouper relaxing with its mouth open at a fish cleaning station is taking advantage of piscine grooming.

The Creation never attains a state of absolute rest. Life in the open seas is particularly animated as many pelagic species swim continuously. All living tissue is utilizing energy, even if at very low rates. *Menuha* is, how-ever, necessary to the development of higher or more complex forms of life. The mammalian nervous system would deteriorate into dysfunction without the simple escape of sleep. Even schools of fish have periods when they do not feed, or reduce activity levels. *Menuha* is not an alternative to normal biological processes, but an imbedded or interwoven thread of the *ruach* or spirit of God, necessary to the growth and diversification of living cells and tissue. *Menuha* is not, therefore, confined to the Seventh Day, but is always working to renew the Creation. The Sabbath celebrates its value and its origin as a divine gift, and epitomizes its function. Environmentally, we think of *menuha* as applying to systems like wheat fields, and not to ones like cod fisheries. *Menuha* is pervasive, a characteristic of the Earth's biota from the Pacific trenches to the arctic tundra. *Menuha* is a universal thread in the warp and woof of the cosmos.

The great Jewish scholar, Abraham Joshua Heschel, has captured the importance of sacred time to the essence of Creation in several of his works. For him, the Jewish calendar includes fish among the other creatures: 'In the month of Elul during the penitential season, the fish in the streams trembled; on *Lag ba-Omer*, the scholars' festival in the spring, all the trees rejoiced. When a holiday came, even the horses and the dogs felt it' (Heschel 1978: 19). Heschel believes, however, that 'the essence of the Sabbath is completely detached from the world of space' (Heschel 1951: 10). I will argue in a similar way: that the Sabbath, since it links creatures to time, reflects the internal rhythms of the living. The entire biblical system of Sabbaths, holy days and festivals recognizes a range of scales. From a natural or biological perspective, the weekly Sabbath is on the scale of tissue and cell repair (for vertebrates). Norman Wirzba (2001: 39) notes '. . . animals are to be exempted from work on the seventh day. They too need the opportunity to rest.' We humans can avoid injury by resting our muscles from exercise periodically – one day in seven is, in fact, a reasonable average for healing small injuries and allowing regeneration. We also need to refresh our cluttered central nervous systems and process the events of the past few days.

Seasonal celebrations give humans an interval for sharing resources, linking with the natural processes that support us, and renewing ties with our families. The Jewish Passover and the Feast of Booths capture patterns of natural regeneration, flowering and fruiting. For other creatures, the seasons mark periods of dormancy or migration, as well as the renewal of species through new generations. The mole crabs, so busy burrowing in the Atlantic surf zone in summer, scuttle off to deeper water and a less athletic lifestyle for the winter.

The seventh year is on the ecosystemic time-scale, and specifically allows agricultural systems, regeneration of soils, and reproduction to avoid competition with the annual harvest. The 50-year Jubilee is on the scale of longer-lived organisms, and recognizes the need for resource sustainability between successive generations.

Many of our ecological sins consist of denying creation the necessary periods of *menuha*. Both Norman Wirzba (2001) and Walter Brueggemann (1977) identify the significance that the sabbatical for the land has for contemporary ecological care. Heschel (1951: 29) has pointed out the relational nature of the Sabbath: 'Man's royal privilege to conquer nature is suspended on the seventh day'. The Sabbath is a day for 'peace with all things' since 'On the seventh day man has no right to tamper with God's world, to change the state of physical things. It is a day of rest for man and animal alike . . .' We can respect *menuha* by extending our land-based honouring of the Sabbath to 'celebrations' on the seas' myriad of scales and cycles.

210

Too often we ignore the concept of *menuha* until harvested populations are so badly degraded, they have difficulty recovering. This has led to an oft-repeated catastrophe termed 'fisheries collapse'. Fisheries management is usually based on breeding or migration patterns, and measurable declines of population, not on any intrinsic need of fisheries for rest. What we need are sea stewards to point out that all harvested ecosystems and species deserve a Sabbath, whether or not their populations are at risk. We should develop harvest schemes to allow periods of relief from human take so they recover and regain their blessing of fertility.

Sabbaths and a 'sabbatical year' might, for example, help preserve the unique salmon genotypes of colder coasts and rivers. An insidious problem for salmon is the inadequate escape of fertile mature fish from each seasonal breeding cohort or run (Lee 1993; Lichatowich 1999; Scarce 2000). If humans avoided fishing on Sunday then a few adult fish would have a greater chance to make their way upstream (even if bears do not co-operate). Salmon runs fluctuate naturally from year to year. An effective conservation strategy, therefore, might be to deploy the equivalent of the agricultural sabbatical year. Rotating sabbaticals for each individual run would stimulate restoration of populations depressed by over-fishing by allowing one season of exceptional reproduction. The runs are on two, three and four year cycles so 'the seventh year' may not be the optimal interval for all salmon species, but the principle could also be applied by using a double Sabbath on a three or four year rotation.

Native American religions in the US Pacific Northwest had a 'First Fish' ceremony which allowed the first arrivals of every run to proceed safely to their spawning grounds, while the native fishers held a feast and celebrated the gift of the salmon (Taylor 1999).

Sabbaths and sabbatical years might be more effective, because they would have the advantage of allowing fish from a run – and their genes – to stay in the breeding pool, rather than advantaging just 'the first fish' (genetic selection favouring the early portion of the run would slowly change the timing of the migrations, perhaps to less optimal river or ocean conditions). Timed to avoid skewing the salmon's genetics and honoured in sequence through a watershed, it could provide similar advantages to the 'First Fish' ceremonies. A sabbatical period could also serve as a festival honouring God's salmon and their ecosystems.

Sea stewards could also set the fiftieth and hundredth year of each millennium as a year of natural Jubilee. This could be a year for negotiating space for the endangered and a time for celebrating those environmental problems we have actually solved. Many of our conservation models for individual populations and ecosystems look forward fifty or a hundred years in any case: we could proclaim a restoration project preserving an endangered species to fulfil the commandment of Jubilee, especially if it returned species to their original habitats – thus restoring sea creatures to the spaces God crafted for them. Worthy candidates include the queen conch, blue-fin tuna, sharks, and even humble oysters in our bays and estuaries.

God intends us simultaneously to celebrate and care for a Creation which includes fish, creeping things and the great monsters of the mysterious depths. Honouring the Sabbath could deepen our understanding of rest for ocean ecosystems and inspire better strategies for conservation of the seas.

Chapter 18

Soil, Stewardship and Spirit in the Era of Chemical Agriculture

Michael Northcott

Michael Northcott is Reader in Christian Ethics in the University of Edinburgh School of Divinity and a priest in the Anglican Church. He is concerned with justice in society generally, but particularly in how humanity treats the natural world. His book The Environment and Christian Ethics *(1996) is a masterly survey of many of the issues that arise from this. His most recent book is* An Angel Directs the Storm: Apocalyptic Religion and American Empire *(2004). This essay was written especially for this volume.*

The metaphor of stewardship has become very popular amongst agricultural companies and regulators. It was first used by the Dow Chemical Company in 1970 in relation to its efforts to educate users of its products about their safe usage and disposal. The agrochemical company Zeneca, formerly part of Imperial Chemical Industries, gathered together a range of managerial functions including health and safety and quality control under the heading of a 'Stewardship Department' in the early 1990s. Stewardship managers at Zeneca define stewardship as 'the responsible and ethical management of all activities, from innovation to ultimate use of products and beyond', and the first principle of stewardship for Zeneca is that its employees are good at what they do, which is to develop and sell crop protection products and services (Johnen *et al.* 2000). The application of this metaphor is illustrated by Zeneca's product Paraquat, which is widely associated with illness among plantation workers in palm oil and rubber estates in Indonesia. Kurniawan (1998) argues that if the product is used properly it represents no health hazard: stewardship, wise use and good product management will turn a potentially lethal product into a harmless agricultural tool.

    J. R. R. Tolkien wrote his extraordinarily powerful mythic novel *Lord of the Rings* in the earlier days of the chemical industry when many of its scientists were dedicating their skills to the development of nerve agents and other synthesized compounds which could be used in the conduct of war, though they were later to become key ingredients of the 'crop protection' strategies of the modern chemical farmer. Tolkien's imagined world is one in which there is a deep and fundamental struggle between two modes of dwelling on the earth. The first is characterized by an attempt to turn nature itself into service as instruments of warfare which Sauron and his evil forces marshall in their struggle for supreme power over Middle Earth. Tolkien clearly had in mind the burgeoning of industrial technology, and the technologies of warfare developed in the context of two World Wars between which he wrote his great saga. The other mode is that of the gentle people of Middle Earth who include fairies and trees, hobbits and wizards and who dwelt in the 'shires'. The greatest wizard of all is Gandalf and yet he eschews lordship over Middle Earth:

> The rule of no realm is mine, neither of Gondor nor any other, great or small. But all worthy things that are in peril as the world now stands, those are my care. And for my part, I shall not wholly fail of my task, though Gondor should perish, if anything passes through this night that can still grow fair or bear fruit and flower again in days to come. For I also am a steward. Did you not know? (Tolkien 1954–55: Book V, ch. 1).

The heroic wizard who is Lord of the Rings speaks about stewardship in a way which is far distant from the concept of product management. For Gandalf, stewardship is not the claim of the manager to order a domain; his quest is to care for fruit and flower, for life itself, against the rising horde that threatens extinction. There is a double edge to Tolkien's narration of this struggle between technological mastery and the survival of fruit and flower, for it was precisely the turning of chemical weapons developed during the First and Second World Wars into agrochemicals after the war which Tolkien's friend and colleague C. S. Lewis saw in 1946 as the dark portent which threatened the moral order which humans and nonhumans once knew that they shared in their dwelling on the earth and which Lewis called 'the Tao' (Lewis 1946).

The 'stewardship' of crops and soil in the domain of chemical agriculture in the last fifty years has had lasting impacts on planet Earth. In Western Europe many birds which were once common are threatened with extinction because of these chemicals, though the organically farmed fields of Poland and other former Soviet bloc countries still sustain a rich flora and fauna. Agrochemicals and the monocrop fields and plantations that their efficient use favours are a major cause of the mass extinction of species which the earth is experiencing at the present time and of which modern humans are the sole agents. Agrochemical use makes possible a kind of farming in which the quality of the soil is no longer a key ingredient (Thompson 1995: 74, note 5). The modern farmer can extinguish not only weeds but insects, birds and small mammals because he no longer needs to rely on the ecology of the field to reproduce the rich biota and micro-nutrients which make up traditional topsoil. Consequently the organic matter present in a field that has been chemically farmed for a generation is vastly reduced compared to that of a traditionally farmed field because with chemical inputs and mechanical tillage the farmer no longer has to nurture the soil to get a good crop (Northcott 2003).

The concept of stewardship is critiqued by modern theologians such as Palmer, Page, Fern and Scott because they associate it, as do the managers of Dow and Zeneca, with the managerial arrangements of private property regimes (Palmer 1992; Page 1996; Fern 2002: 212–13 ; Scott 2003: 213–18). But this use of stewardship is unfaithful to the origins of the term in the common property arrangements of hunter-gatherer and premodern agrarian and nomadic societies such as those of ancient Israel. Tim Ingold identifies the origins of the notion of stewardship – or custodianship, his preferred term – with the earliest forms of nomadic and semi-nomadic agriculture in which individual family units agreed to share land according to common property arrangements which nonetheless gave to each family the right of use of a particular area of land. This right of use did not, however, mean that they could deny others access to the land, hence the Old Testament tolerance for the practice of gleaning, but only that the primary benefit of its use went to them. As Ingold puts it, 'possession in traditional cultures was not about ownership in the Roman and Western sense but rather about looking after the country, or tending the creative powers that reside there' (Ingold 1986: 227). So-called 'owners' are in reality no more than the custodians of parts of a world that belongs to all, and they exercise their rights on behalf of the collectivity. In other words, what an owner possesses, to the exclusion of others, is the privilege of custodianship, not that which is held in custody.

This is why in traditional societies the privilege of ownership is associated not with garnering and guarding a 'personal' resource but rather with gift exchange, distribution and sharing either of hunted animal, fruits or crops with the community (Ingold 1986). It is in this sense that we can understand the parable of Jesus about the farmer who had amassed so much land that he needed to build bigger barns to store the surplus (Lk. 12.16–21). It is in this vein also that we can understand Old Testament laws which proscribe excessive landholdings by some, gained at the expense of the poor management or poor luck of others. The Jubilee law as described in Leviticus 25 was designed quite explicitly to prevent debt slavery and landlessness, and hence maldistribution of the gifts of the creation, among the people of Israel.

Garret Hardin's account of the 'tragedy of the commons' indicates precisely what happens when such common property arrangements for using and distributing the goods of the earth fall into disuse or are ruptured by colonial and postcolonial private property regimes (Hardin 1968).

Under such regimes, right of use and ownership are coterminous, and consequently common resources such as earth, air and water, because they 'belong' to no one, tend to be exploited unsustainably. Modern farmers, whether they work for a corporation or own their own farm, are trained by the property regimes and by the new conventions of chemical farming to see the soil no longer as a shared resource which they are responsible for nurturing and passing on to future generations in a better state than they find it. The key resources of the chemical farm are the inputs of agro-chemicals, knowledge, machinery and seeds.

By contrast, the ancient conception of stewardship was centrally concerned with the condition of the soil. The names of the first inhabitants of the earth, Adam and Eve, are associated in the book of Genesis with the soil and with life: Adam, *adama* in the Hebrew meaning earth or topsoil, is the son of the soil because he is formed from the dust of the earth. Eve is the 'mother of all living' according to Gen. 3.20 and so, as Theodore Hiebert suggests, Adam and Eve are literally 'soil and life' (Hiebert 1996c). Their responsibility to steward the soil, and towards its living inhabitants, emerges from their identification with the soil, and with the living things to which they have given names. As Larry Rasmussen points out, ancient Hebrew had no word for nature apart from human beings, and so stewardship neither implied that humans were responsible for something we now call 'nature', nor that they were separate from it by virtue of their rule over it (Rasmussen 1996: 231). The word *radah*, usually translated 'dominion' in Gen. 1.28, is better understood as referring to the role of the human as custodian of the soil rather than as dominion, with its associated implication of 'reigning over', and hence the sometime translation of *radah* as vice-regent by Islamic and Jewish exegetes. The concept of vice-regency implies relation both to Yahweh the Creator, and to the earth, the realm of creatures. It further implies right relations, for only when humans order their distribution and use of the earth justly and righteously – so as to maintain right relations among the people of God and to give space to the other animals – will their tenure of the earth be rewarded with its fertility and with divine blessing. When humans abandon right relations, with each other and with all creatures, the earth itself will lose its fertility and the ground will cry out for justice, according to the traditions of ancient Israel (Rasmussen 1996: 231; Northcott 1996: 188).

When modern conservative American Christians resist the modern idea of environmental stewardship, the first ground of their objection is that it is used to enhance the regulatory power of the state over the individual property owner and this, they argue, is contrary to the will of God as declared in the Old Testament, that each owner of property should retain the inalienated right to the enjoyment of the fruits of his (and they mean his) land and labour upon it (e.g. Alvarado 1986–87). When more ecologically sensitive theologians critique stewardship it is, ironically, for the

216

same reason: they associate stewardship with the hubristic claims of states or supranational environmental bodies to manage the Earth's environment. Both critiques are misguided for they fail to see the complex interaction in the original texts, and the culture which generated them, between divine ownership of creation, the divine intent for the just sharing of its goods between humans and non-humans, and the privileges and responsibilities of those who temporarily use the Earth in their lifetime. The Old Testament has no conception of absolute ownership such as moderns, including many evangelical Christians, claim to find within it. By analogy, stewardship is not about the human governance or management of the Earth on behalf of an absent landlord so much as human partnership with the creator Spirit, and with all other creatures, in sustaining the Earth's fertility and goodness.

The presence of the Spirit in creation is acknowledged by the agrarian Hebrews in the association with the word *nephesh* between Spirit, breath and blood which lies at the heart of their animal husbandry, butchery and sacrificial practices. For the ancient Hebrew, as for the modern hunter-gatherer, the act of killing a living breathing mammal, even for sustenance, was dangerous and threatening to the natural and social order. The Garden of Eden was a paradise in which there was no killing. Stewarding creation involved keeping it alive, but the way out of Eden, and the making of human society, involved killing. As Klaus Eder suggests, the sacrificial system of the Hebrews was their way of dealing with the taboo of killing. By sanctifying their butchers as priests, and by setting aside the precious life blood of the animal to be eaten and sacrificed, the sanctity of life, and the safety of the community, are both preserved (Eder 1996: 58, note 96). Modern animal husbandry and butchery, like modern chemical crop husbandry, are organized in such a way that non-butchers, and non-farmers, are not affected by their activities:

> De-publicizing the relationship to nature is the complement to the instrumental rationalization of the relationship to nature ... 'the myth of creation is destroyed. Nature is subjugated to society'. At the same time however the state of nature catches up with society, objectively in the sense that society reaches the limits of nature ... nature rebels against the instrumentalization of nature in an irrational act of resistance (Eder 1996: 99).

Christian conceptions of earth healing and restitution do not rely on sacrifices because the sacrifice of Christ's life blood on the cross put an end to the need for all sacrifices. But inasmuch as modern civilization relies on the cruel incarceration of millions of animals in factory breeding systems, on the sacrificial extinction of species as the instrument of economic efficiency, and on the instrumental degradation of topsoil, it continues to sustain a sacrificial system, albeit largely out of the sight and mind of most modern city dwellers. It may not seem to the modern city dweller to matter that their meat is intensively reared in vast sheds, the wastage from which no longer fertilizes farmers' fields but instead generates harmful new bacteria – such as *E. coli 451* – and pollutes rivers and groundwater. It may not seem to matter that their cheap bread has been provided by a form of farming which involves systematic degradation of the topsoil and the extinction of species. But when the privatized city dweller visits the countryside she may wonder at the silence in the fields. And when virulent new strains of *E. coli* infect the food chain, she may develop an interest in food hygiene while still having no conception of the taboos which butchers and farmers alike now systematically break.

The metaphor of stewardship, apart from the truth of divine creation and the grace of redemption, and apart from common property arrangements and the associated privileges and responsibilities of ownership with which it was originally associated, may not be able to evoke a new and more responsive mode of dwelling on the Earth and turn moderns away from their new sacrificial systems. Christians who claim to know the Bible, but are trained by the rituals of capitalism and private property, misconstrue stewardship as indicating the rights of ownership rather than the responsibilities of shared creaturehood. However Wendell Berry, a Kentucky small-holder and a lyrical and profound essayist, suggests that stewardship can be recovered, but only when food and farming are rescued from the corporation, the state and the university. For Berry, the farmer who pays attention to the condition of the soil is a farmer who expresses in his working practices something of what Aristotle and St Paul meant by good character and the virtues. The university-trained expert who advises the farmer, regulates or subsidizes the market for his products, and sells him his inputs, has advised him for fifty years to ignore this traditional indicator of the quality of his farm and instead to seek for greater efficiency, higher output, and so become complicit in the now widely shared illusions that food is cheap, and that topsoil, earth, the 'gift of good land', is not precious (W. Berry 1978). Farming which conserves the soil, which respects the landscape and seeks the good of all its inhabitants and not just the monocrop, is farming which involves justice, prudence, fidelity and patience. Such virtues are not valued by the narrow cost-benefit calculus of the productionist farming metaphor that drives chemical agriculture. Berry does not suggest that we can escape cost-benefit calculations altogether but he argues that the true costs of producing quality food should be recognized and shouldered by the consumer and the producer community, instead of being visited on the community of species which already suffers under the assault of modern agricultural technology.

For Christians the ultimate cost to redeem the creation has already been paid on the cross of Christ in exchange for the ultimate benefit – the enlivening gift of the indwelling Spirit of God who is the guarantee of salvation. Christians are trained by their membership of the body of Christ to associate this ultimate gift with a prior divine claim not only on the body of the earth but on their own bodies and desires. St Paul tells the Christians at Corinth who had been engaging in the licentious sexual practices of their pagan neighbours that their bodies were not their own but instead belonged to God: 'Do you not know that your body is a temple of the Holy Spirit, who is in you, whom you have received from God? You are not your own' (1 Cor. 6.19). For Christians the idea of absolute ownership has no place, because even the body of the Christian is not her own to dispose with at will: mutual service is the mark of the Christian disposition. If Christians are not owners but stewards of their own bodies, they can hardly adopt the language of stewardship as a device for hallowing the privatized practices of modern agrochemical farming and the global food economy with which they interact. Berry is right to suggest that a biblical understanding of divine ownership, 'the earth is the Lord's', involves a critique of the vast accumulations of land and wealth that characterize the modern corporately controlled and managed global economy, for human ownership of land 'quickly becomes abusive when used to justify large accumulations of real estate' (W. Berry 1992: 97). The Incarnation of God in Christ involves the affirmation that 'God made the world and made it to be good and for his pleasure and that he continues to love it and to find it worthy, despite its reduction and corruption by us' (W. Berry 1992: 97). There is no deism here, no distant landlord who has left the property in charge of a hireling manager. The Incarnate redeemer is also the creator God who gifted the original blessing and abundance of the earth to our primaeval ancestors, and so we will discover that for these reasons our destruction of nature is not just bad stewardship, or stupid economics, or a betrayal of family responsibility; it is the most horrid blasphemy. It is flinging God's gifts into his face, as if they were of no worth beyond that assigned to them by our destruction of them (W. Berry 1992: 98).

If we are to stop flinging God's gifts in his face we must find ways of paying more for our food, and of requiring our farmers to make fewer sacrifices for its production. Organically produced food, food grown without large doses of agrochemicals, costs more because it visits fewer of its costs on other creatures, whether in the form of groundwater pollution, soil erosion or species extinction. The household that seeks out local supplies of traditionally produced food may need to expend more energy, time and money in so doing. But this would be an example of good stewardship and of spiritual service, for why else does God give us these things than to treasure God's creation.

Chapter 19

Religion and the Environment

Crispin Tickell

Sir Crispin Tickell, GCMG, KCVO was a career diplomat whose final posting was as UK representative at the United Nations (1987–90) where he was one of the initiators of the UN Conference on Environment and Development (the 'Earth Summit'). He was Warden of Green College, Oxford University, 1990–97. During a sabbatical period in his diplomatic service he studied the potential impact of climate change and has subsequently campaigned both nationally and internationally for the dangers to be recognized and responded to. This paper is previously unpublished. It was originally given as a lecture at Harvard University in October 2003.

Environment is the stuff of religion, and religion is the stuff of the environment. Their relationship once went without saying. Yet we live at a time when they are being prised apart. This is the slow-acting result of two main factors: our vastly increased knowledge of the natural world and the place of the human species within it; and our vastly increased knowledge of the human mind, and how and why we believe and act as we do.

But there are limits on all human understanding, and the way such understanding changes from generation to generation. For example, in the twinkle of time which is the last hundred years, we have had our notions of time and space stretched to a hitherto unimaginable degree. For our ancestors time was measured in thousands of years; for us we count in billions to measure the time light has taken to reach us from the visible ends of the universe when it was still young. As for space, it was not until the 1920s that we realized that the galaxy, in which our own solar system is an extremely small and suburban member, was not the universe, and that billions of other galaxies stretched in all directions. The immensity of time and space is a constant reminder of our own insignificance. Yet for us all this is relatively new.

As for our own little planet, that too has a history which has only recently been understood. Over its 4.6 billion years there have been changes of unimaginable magnitude. Life itself may have begun around 3.4 billion years ago but that too has been changing all the time. Life has also had many shocks in its long history. Perhaps the most devastating was 250 million years ago when over 90% of marine species perished. Then there was the likely impact of the bolide which hit the earth 65 million years ago, and ended the long dominance of the dinosaur family. So far life has always recovered, and assumed new forms. The degree to which there is some constraint on such forms, particularly among multi-celled organisms, is a matter of continuing scholarly debate. Evolution of new forms will not continue indefinitely. The life expectancy of life on earth is limited. Eventually our sun will become a red giant, and expand to near the orbit of the earth around it. Long before then life on earth will be extinct.

Where in all this are humans? Physicists point out that our bodies, which look so solid to the eye and touch, are mostly empty space at the atomic level, and the atoms themselves are mostly space as well. Then look at our prized source of selfhood. Are we each of us one person or many? Our individual decision-making process has been described as a boardroom of quarrelsome directors, some apparently rational but others pushing deeper agendas. Is awareness of self a convenient illusion, changing as often as the cells which make up our bodies?

Seen from space we are no more than mites on the skin of the Earth, and inside as well as outside us are countless billions of mites, all profoundly connected in mutual dependencies. Without them, or their ancestors now embedded within us, we could neither move, nor breathe, nor eat. The dry weight of a human body is 10% bacteria. Charles Darwin put the point very well when he wrote: 'We cannot fathom the marvellous complexity of an organic being, but ... each living creature must be looked at as a microcosm, a little universe, formed of a host of self propagating organisms, inconceivably minute, as numerous as the stars in heaven.'

The particular assemblage of chemicals and micro-organisms which is ourselves is recent in the history of life. Humans evolved from bipedal, tree-living apes living in Africa some two to three million years ago. This is not the place to attempt to trace our complicated genealogy since those times. There are continuing uncertainties about the variant hominid species which emerged in response to changing environmental conditions, in particular the cooling, and eventual ice ages, of the last two million years. Only two such species seem to have been around one hundred thousand years ago: these were *Homo neanderthalensis*, with a specific adaptation to ice age conditions, and the archaic ancestors of *Homo sapiens*. By less than thirty thousand years ago, the Neanderthalers were gone, probably destroyed or absorbed by our own ancestors, who henceforth were the only humans. Until around ten thousand years ago, they were hunters, gatherers and scavengers of no fixed address. Since the latest recession of the glaciers and warming of the earth, they have developed agriculture, cities, industrial exploitation of resources, and now information technology.

Most of us will agree that religion is one of the elements that holds us together, and indeed the society of which we are all part. Even among the most sceptical, religions and ethical beliefs have a profound hold. It is worth asking why. In my view there are five main reasons. All relate to the natural environment.

First, humans are social animals and their welfare depends on the communities to which they belong, whether families, villages, tribes or nations. From the early days humans were under constant threat from other predators, and their survival depended on the strength of their groups and communities. Belief in gods or God helped establish identity and acted as powerful social glue. Many peoples have believed themselves to be chosen, and drawn strength from it. As a unifying force, it has had profound effects throughout human history, sometimes for good in bringing out the best in people, both as individuals and as communities, and sometimes for evil as a cause of intolerance, oppression of others, violence, cannibalism and thought-policing of society.

The second reason flows from the first. If religion has been of social value in the widest sense, then over thousands of years there may have been a measure of natural selection in favour of those with genes with a religious predisposition. An evolutionary understanding of our genetic development suggests a strong disposition towards those qualities – altruism, cooperation and morality – which underlie religion. Of course environmental circumstances in the form of social pressures in the same sense may have been of as great if not greater importance. As Richard Dawkins (1976) has well shown, memes – or units of information and ideas – pass far more quickly, moving laterally from one person to another, than genes ever could, moving vertically down the generations. Notions about gods or God have received powerful reinforcement from both sources.

The third reason arises from one of the qualities which most clearly distinguishes humans from other animals. We have an abiding curiosity about the world around us. The personification of natural forces and phenomena, whether organic or inorganic, whether as large as the sky or as small as a tree or spring of fresh water, whether a human emotion like love or power or wisdom – all represent a search for an explanation for what otherwise seems arbitrary and unaccountable. An extension of this search is the old theological argument for design made famous by Archdeacon Paley in the late eighteenth century. Here the explanation lies in the way that everything fits together so that God is seen as the designer of each component and of the functioning of the natural order as a whole.

The fourth reason follows on. If God constitutes the explanation, then God helps humans gain some measure of control over their environment, or at least reduce the element of arbitrariness. We are not the only animals which seek to control their surroundings: beavers build dams, ants create centrally heated or air-conditioned structures, some flowers even heat their sexual organs to attract visitors. But humans change their environments on an incomparably vaster scale. We still talk about conquering or taming nature; and when some point out the less agreeable consequences, the reply comes that we are in some sense stewards of the earth, and that the role of steward is divinely ordained.

My fifth reason is less flattering. We are afraid of death, that 'undiscovered country from whose bourn no traveller returns'. We are afflicted by misfortune. We see the wicked flourish and the virtuous come to grief. Here God gives us consolation, expurgates guilt, promises justice in another life, and thereby makes past and present more tolerable. Prospects of heaven and hell are the great equalizer. They also help give motivation beyond simple human needs and ambitions. God is justification as well as consolation. Nietzsche may have said that God was dead; but he also remarked that it was better to have the void as purpose than to be void of purpose.

So religion has an integral role in human evolution. Beliefs have of course evolved as societies have evolved. Whether God made man in his own image seems to me a proposition of little or no meaning; but man certainly made God in his image. Over time God has served as many varieties of human writ large: creator, destroyer, liberator, terrorist, king, conqueror, law giver, judge, arbiter, engineer, friend, father, son, victim and lover. It is in the literature of many cultures. But because God constitutes a social as well as individual experience, a huge apparatus has grown up to regulate and interpret human access to the divine.

Oracles, ritual, sacraments and holy texts are vital in this respect. Fundamentalists of all religions interpret almost everything, including science, in their light. Thus the creationists in Christianity who rely on literal reading of the Bible. Thus also some bizarre science in Islam. Recently a physicist in Islamabad calculated that Heaven was receding from the Earth at one centimetre per second less than the speed of light. This was based on a verse in the Qur'an which said that worship on the night on which the book was revealed was worth a thousand nights of ordinary worship. This amounted to a time dilution factor of 1,000, which the physicist put into a formula of Einstein's theory of special relativity.

Of the five main reasons for religious belief that I have suggested, some may be of declining importance. But for many, God remains the ultimate guarantor of ethics, those broad rules by which humans regulate relations with each other, and to a lesser extent with other forms of life as well. They continue, in some countries more than others, to survive as part of traditional culture. Even if some find belief implausible they prefer not to challenge it.

They also continue to offer something of an explanation. Science has enormously enlarged human knowledge of the universe and of the human mind, but there are still frontiers beyond which it cannot penetrate. What was there before the Big Bang? What is the universe expanding into? Why are things as they are? Why did life begin? Have humans a role beyond that of animals? Is consciousness significant? There has been new interest in the so-called Anthropic Principle which in a nutshell means that our ability to observe the universe has implications for what it is and the laws by which it works. From this flows the idea that the laws must be such as to permit observers to exist. We are not now far from Archdeacon's Paley's arguments for design. Some astronomers believe our universe to be 'special', thereby opening the possibility of other universes with different physical constants and other paths of evolution. Others reject the notion, notably Heinz Pagels, who described the Anthropic Principle as 'needless clutter in the conceptual repertoire of science'. The debate continues.

But, however many arguments we can adduce – moral, social, genetic, scientific or other – for religion, we still have to ask ourselves the awkward, inescapable, fundamental question. Is it true? Here I think there is only one answer. We simply do not know. This may be enough for some people. It was not enough for others, who have embarked on a search for religion without revelation, or developed the evolutionary epic as substitutes for religion. Others have made similar efforts in the same direction. But none has reached anywhere near the human core. Some people may not believe in God, but most people want to believe in something.

The present collectivity of life on earth cannot be distinguished from the present collectivity of its physical surroundings. The animate and the inanimate shade into each other. This is the environment. As I have suggested, it was – and in some cases still is – the stuff of religion. But it has also been the stuff of science. James Hutton, the geologist, recognized it as long ago as 1785. T.H. Huxley did likewise in 1877. Almost a century later James Lovelock developed ideas on the same subject which, on the advice of the novelist William Golding, he called Gaia.

There are, I suppose, two main approaches. One is the familiar product of the age of specialists in which we live. Many inhabit little boxes, and rarely like to lift the lid. They are better at reducing problems to their constituent elements than in seeing the connections between them and how the resulting mechanism works. Research assessment has a marked aversion to interdisciplinarity. In this view Gaia seems almost impossibly difficult, and should be relegated to poets or philosophers.

The other approach is to give life a teleological character, and through it trace evidence of God's design in the creation of humankind and a nature subservient to it. They thereby give Gaia an implied capacity for conscious manipulation.

It is not easy to find a middle way. In one sense the living world is a combination of individuals who respond to and make their physical environment. In another they do constitute something which can be compared to a superorganism. It can be seen most clearly with bacteria which, through their direct cell division and promiscuous exchange of DNA, can indeed be seen as one. The same cannot be said for multicellular organisms which are ephemeral combinations of individuals. But as we know from recent advances in genetic engineering, genes can and do transfer laterally, and in any case have a high degree of mutual dependence.

This is a long way from seeing any superorganism as conscious and purposeful. But if the animate and inanimate worlds do shade into each other, then feelings about religion are bound to enter in. It is hard to imagine any system of belief which is not grounded in nature and in different ways expresses reverence for life.

There is a wide spectrum. At one end are those for whom nature is self-sufficient and self-regulatory. Life is a constant flux and humans should put themselves in harmony with it. One of the favourite symbols of Taoism is water: humans should 'be the stream of the universe'. Buddhists likewise look for harmony. All life is one and indivisible. The overriding moral value is compassion for all beings. Neither Taoists nor Buddhists find it necessary to invoke God as a manipulator of his creation. Hindus have many gods but associate them with a nature vibrating with life. Such life allows animals, including humans, to move in and out of each other through reincarnation.

At the other end of the spectrum are the religions with a God, sometimes supported by a hierarchy of beings – ranging from angels to saints – who often serve as personifications of this or that place or activity. Such religions are usually characterized by sharp distinctions between God, humans, and other living creatures. To some extent Judaism, Christianity and Islam share this tradition. The notion that nature is made for human delectation, that humans are a creation separate from the rest, and that only humans have souls, also has roots in later Greek philosophy. Thus Aristotle wrote that as nature made nothing without purpose, it must have made animals for the sake of man. No wonder that after Darwin published *The Origin of Species* in 1859, a Victorian lady observed that she hoped that his ideas about evolution were not true, but that if they were, they would not become generally known.

Somewhere in the middle of the spectrum, and evident to some degree in almost all religious traditions, is the idea of divine immanence in nature. This immanence can show itself through natural objects, or as a kind of electric charge, which in the words of the Jesuit poet Gerard Manley Hopkins 'will flame out, like shining from shook foil'.

I doubt if the long-term effects of science, and in particular Darwinism, have yet worked themselves through the way we think, and in particular through systems of religious belief. Recently many religious leaders have sought to align themselves with green issues. Here the idea of humans enjoying special God-given status as stewards of the earth has proved attractive. In my view it is a considerable presumption. As James Lovelock once said: 'we should no more expect humans to be stewards of the earth than goats to be gardeners'. This is not to say that humans would not do better to regard themselves as stewards rather than goats.

225

Lectures usually end with conclusions. After this prolonged excursion around ideas of religion and the environment, some of you may expect no less from me. If so I will disappoint. It is the nature of this debate that we cannot draw conclusions. But there are still certain things that can be said. Let me express them in a series of propositions.

- There are limits to human knowledge and understanding. This does not mean that we should not try to know and to understand, but it does mean that we should recognize the relativity of all intellectual models and paradigms. Looking back at those of the past, we can foresee that future generations will look sceptically at ours. Life itself in its unity, diversity and complexity is in our direct experience. We are an integral, not always modest, part of it. Once we see it as a whole, we realize it is the most precious thing that we know or can know.

- Life has no particular tenderness for humans. Darwin once described the evolutionary process as 'clumsy, wasteful, blundering, low, and horribly cruel'. Organisms compose and decompose. Death is the counterpart of sex. It is the process over millions of years which survives.

- Most current attitudes towards the natural world are profoundly destructive. Human society faces five main threats: overpopulation of one animal species, our own; degradation of soils; pollution of water both salt and fresh; human-made changes in the chemistry of the atmosphere; and impoverishment of the other forms of life on which we depend. These threats are interconnected, and none can be seen in isolation from the others.

- The ideology of industrial society, driven by notions about economic growth, ever rising standards of living, and faith in the technological fix, is in the long run unworkable. In changing our ideas, we have to look towards the eventual target of a human society in which population, use of resources, disposal of waste, and environment generally are in healthy balance.

- Above all we have to look at life with respect and wonder. We need an ethical system in which the natural world has value not just for human welfare but for and in itself. The universe is something internal as well as external.

I give the last word to the twelfth-century abbess Hildegard of Bingen who wrote of God

> ... I ignite the beauty of the plains,
> I sparkle the waters,
> I burn in the sun, and the moon and the stars ...
> I adorn all the earth,

I am the breeze that nurtures all things green ...
I am the rain coming from the dew that causes the grasses to laugh
with joy of life.

Let us likewise rejoice.

Chapter 20

Environmental Stewardship Needed for the Core Mission of Public Bodies

Derek Osborn

F.A. (Derek) Osborn, CB was Director-General of Environmental Protection in the Department of the Environment in the 1990s. He was subsequently Chairman of the European Environment Agency and co-chaired the United Nations negotiations in 1997 for the five-year review of progress on the Rio Earth Summit. He was a Visiting Fellow of Green College, Oxford, and is currently a visiting Professor at University College London. This essay was written especially for this volume.

The concept of environmental stewardship powerfully illuminates and inspires humankind's individual responsibilities towards the environment. It ought also to inspire our collective responsibilities as exercised through public and private bodies. But a variety of institutional barriers and prejudices stand in the way.

The essence of the steward is that he or she willingly accepts the obligations of stewardship. (S)he is glad to be part of the master's great enterprise, and proud to take on the privileges and responsibilities of looking after the estate on the master's behalf. (S)he is left in charge but remains vividly conscious of the absent master's wishes. Even without external laws and regulations (s)he internalizes those wishes as rules of personal behaviour. The still small voice of conscience pricks if (s)he goes astray.

In the modern world the concept of the master is perhaps more problematic. Who is the Master? Does there have to be a Master? For whom or what can we regard ourselves as being stewards? For some people the strongest answer is that God is the Master and source of all moral obligation and duty. Looking after the natural riches of the world he has given is part of our duty towards him. For others unable (or unwilling) to believe in a personal God as the definer of all moral duties, the source of environmental commitment may lie in their sense of responsibility to hand on to their children and future generations a better world – or at least not a fundamentally damaged one. For others again the pristine and wonderful qualities of the natural world inspire their commitment and loyalty; while some may go further and describe this as a commitment to maintaining the integrity and proper functioning of the whole global ecosystem or Gaia.

It is not necessary to insist on the primacy of one view rather than another. Our sense of stewardship obligations can be created or reinforced by whatever it may be outside ourselves that inspires devotion and commitment. This may be God, the needs of present and future generations, the natural world itself, or any or all of these.

There is potent biblical imagery concerning rewards and penalties for good and bad stewardship. The essence of the steward is that (s)he is given considerable authority and scope. (S)he is put in a position of trust. While the master is away, the steward has full powers to act or not to act. But when the master returns, any sins of commission or omission catch up with the steward and (s)he is judged. The good steward is amply rewarded; but the bad steward who fails to discharge his or her responsibilities adequately is punished or cast into some form of outer darkness.

The problem for the Christian and the environmental life is the same: many of the rewards and punishments are long delayed. In Christianity, the ultimate rewards and punishments belong to the afterlife; at the day of judgment the blessed are separated from the damned. In a similar way many of the worst impacts of environmental misbehaviour or carelessness are likely to be felt more by future generations than our own. In both cases we are blessed – or cursed – with the opportunity to fall short of ideal behaviour for our own short-term reasons or for selfish gratification, without immediate retribution. In both cases it is necessary to bolster good behaviour by a mixture of externally imposed laws and internally inculcated belief and self-discipline. This is necessary for the Christian and the environmentalist alike.

Failures to look after the environment are of course legion in the world, and wherever possible we would all like the perpetrators to be penalized in accordance with the polluter pays principle. But environmental crimes are difficult to define and even harder to enforce. We need to complement and reinforce the effect of environmental laws by nourishing as widely as possible the sense of personal obligation to good behaviour.

What are the obligations of environmental stewardship? The good environmental steward takes the trouble to understand the environment, and how human actions affect it. (S)he takes part in appropriate collective actions to safeguard the environment. And (s)he tries to apply good environmental principles in his or her own behaviour, even when there may be no legal obligation to do so. (S)he is conscience driven as well as rule driven. (S)he metaphorically hears the still small voice of the absent master (God, unborn children, Gaia) as (s)he stoops to gather a piece of litter, or takes an energy-saving measure, or recycles waste, or joins some communal activity to improve or protect the environment.

The tasks of stewardship are becoming ever more difficult and urgent as the scale and potential impact of the environmental threats facing us become greater and more global. Environmental stewardship is no longer simply a matter of promoting good neighbourly behaviour. It must increasingly involve more far-reaching transformations of the way we produce and consume. Popular knowledge and concern about these issues is growing. But increasingly the tasks are getting beyond the scope of individuals to manage by themselves.

Stewardship ought to be as important as a collective activity as it is an individual one. We want our political leaders, legislators and bureaucrats, and our captains of industry and other leaders of society to take seriously the metaphor of themselves as stewards for the whole of society and of future generations, to ensure that our common environment is maintained and passed on in good order. We speak of good politicians and bureaucrats as those who 'own' problems and feel a personal responsibility for moving their organization or society to act on them appropriately. Here we may think of these leaders as being the stewards to the rest of society to achieve the necessary results.

But at this level of collective action difficulties arise. Businessmen are extremely reluctant to accept any responsibility beyond compliance with the law and maximizing their bottom-line profits. However seriously they may take their personal or private stewardship obligations, they tend to leave these thoughts at the office door, and insist that it is for governments and others to worry about externalities and to impose any necessary restraints by regulation or taxation if they must – and the less the better. For all the talk of enlightened self-interest impelling businesses to adopt a more steward-like approach, the reality is that most voluntary action by businesses is modest in the extreme, and impelled mainly by anticipation of new regulations to come (or the hope of warding them off), or by fear of reputational damage.

Even in the public sector the task of embedding an environmental stewardship approach securely within the central goals of the sector is far from complete and has suffered many setbacks. The concept of environmental stewardship clearly has many similarities or congruences with the concept or ethos of public service. At its best, public service conveys the idea of service undertaken voluntarily or for comparatively modest reward in the interests of the public at large. The concept also involves a sense of looking to the longer-term good rather than concentrating solely on immediately pressing needs or short-term political priorities. Other virtuous themes associated with the public service ethic are the transcendent importance of integrity and honesty in the management of public business, of basing policy on facts and evidence, of transparency and openness, of respect for the law and due process, and of high regard for equity and fairness. We want the leaders of our public life to regard themselves as guardians – or stewards – for the public good.

In Britain this ethos gradually became the dominant model of public life and service during the nineteenth century. It was classically inculcated and reinforced in the civil service with the introduction of rigorous methods for recruiting and training the top echelons of the service (the Northcote Trevelyan reforms) and instilling a strong collective sense of the public service ethos and its duties and responsibilities. In spite of efforts to introduce a more business-inspired approach to public life, elements of that public service ethic remain strong even today.

Environmental stewardship ought naturally to form part of this broad concept of public service duties and obligations. It has the same concerns with the longer term, and the same needs for integrity and due process. The environment can of course only be one part of the overall concerns of the public service. But adding together environmental and social concerns we find the concept of sustainable development which certainly ought to be at the core of the mission of public service and indeed of society as a whole.

The core values of sustainable development have been well elaborated in a number of canonical statements. Mrs Brundtland's classic formulation in 1987 of meeting the needs of the present without prejudicing the needs of future generations is still central. The Rio Principles elaborated in 1992 a fuller statement of values and principles to guide international and national action in the field of sustainable development. The more recent Earth Charter developed a set of principles for care of the Earth and of humanity in a way that speaks more eloquently to the individual and represents one of the best modern statements of the values and goals of sustainable development and the obligations of environmental stewardship.

At this broad level of principle many Governments and organizations have endorsed and adopted some or all of these formulations. The problem arises when it comes to putting them into practice. This is difficult enough conceptually; but it is made more difficult because there are powerful forces at work to counter the effective integration of environmental stewardship into the central public sector mission and public sector ethos.

There are four great giants to slay:

Growth comes first. Economic growth is the central goal; anything that contributes to economic growth as conventionally measured must be good regardless of whether it damages well-being or the environment, particularly if those adverse impacts are distant in time or place.

Efficiency comes first. Efficiency is a central goal; any goods or services that can be procured more cheaply must be better regardless of the social or environmental impacts of the method of procurement.

Money comes first. Anything that cannot be bought and sold or valued in

231

economic terms is essentially a second order consideration not to be taken too seriously in reaching decisions and taking action.

The present comes first. The future is uncertain and short-term effects of actions are the only ones worth taking seriously.

These giants are ferocious and wily. Overcome them in one place and like dragons' teeth they spring up again to bite you in another. Their chief lair in Britain is in the Treasury and other places where hard-nosed business-oriented economists gather together. Like Oscar Wilde's cynic they know the price of everything and the value of nothing. They are eloquent about such challenges as climate change when addressing audiences of environmentalists, but much more sceptical privately when contemplating the kind of measures that would be needed to make big changes in behaviour.

What pebbles can the Davids of sustainable development cast against these giants? How can the citadel be taken? Essentially they must be tackled head-on. The giants are everywhere but they are not omnipotent. They represent imperfect economics. They fail to take seriously the visible signs of strain and danger in the world's environment. And increasingly they are out of touch with what many people now want. More and more people want governments, public bodies and businesses that will devote themselves to environmental stewardship as whole-heartedly as many individuals would like to do themselves.

Growth of GDP should NOT be the be-all and end-all of economic policy. We want growth in welfare (including good environments as part of welfare) with the kind of economic growth that can support that end. The UK Sustainable Development Commission's path-breaking tract on *Redefining Prosperity* (2003) has recently elaborated the implications of this, and proposed a more rounded version of the central goals of society.

Purchasing the cheapest goods and services with no regard to their impacts on society and the environment is NOT the best policy. To take just one example: procurement policies that insist on much greater energy efficiency in the goods and services they purchase have an immense potential for reducing energy consumption and hence the impact of energy consumption on greenhouse gases and climate change. They may cost a little more at the outset but are much more efficient in a broader sense when all externalities are taken into account.

There are many important goals for society that are NOT measurable in money terms. Proper assessment of environmental sustainability is an essential part of good decision-making. Lip service is often paid to this goal and the tools are available. But they are not yet used widely enough or seriously enough. At the moment of decision, short-term cost minimization in the narrowest sense still too frequently prevails as the decisive consideration.

The needs and wishes of the present should NOT be allowed to prevail over the needs of future generations. Discounting the future in deciding on present action is very risky and reckless, particularly since we are now dealing with threats to the functioning of the ecosystems of the whole planet through greenhouse gas emissions, pollution and over-exploitation of resources. The precautionary principle must prevail in such cases, and much lower discount rates applied.

Slay the four giants of unsustainability and embody these more sustainable approaches at the heart of the public sector approach and values, and we shall be well on the way to bringing our environmental stewardship past the office door, and reintegrating our public and private values. Environmental sauce for the individual goose must be good for the public sector gander as well.

Chapter 21

Conservation Grows a Human Face

Martin Holdgate

Sir Martin Holdgate, CB is a zoologist who has worked extensively in the Antarctic, but who spent much of his career as an administrator, at first in the British Civil Service, rising to be Chief Scientist in the Department of the Environment, then as Director General of the World Conservation Union. He is a former Chairman of the Governing Council of the United Nations Environmental Programme. His publications include A Perspective of Environmental Pollution *(1979) and* From Care to Action: Making a Sustainable World *(1996). This essay was written especially for this book.*

In 1980 the International Union for Conservation of Nature and Natural Resources, the United Nations Environment Programme and the World Wide Fund for Nature joined together to produce a World Conservation Strategy (WCS). It had a long gestation and traumatic birth, but along the way something happened that was to transform the nature conservation movement. For decades that movement had been protectionist in character – seeking to shield wild nature from rampant humanity. The WCS was likewise conceived as a habitat-by-habitat assessment of how the main ecosystems of the Earth could be safeguarded from destructive development. But as the authors prepared draft after draft and sent them out for criticism, it became more and more evident that the 'protectionist' approach was no longer acceptable, especially to the United Nations Environment Programme that was one of the co-sponsors of the document. The final text of the Strategy put people at the heart of conservation. To quote its second paragraph:

> Humanity's relationship with the biosphere (the thin covering of the planet that contains and sustains life) will continue to deteriorate until a new international economic order is achieved, a new environmental ethic adopted, human populations stabilize, and sustainable modes of development become the rule rather than the exception. Among the prerequisites for sustainable development is the conservation of living resources.

234

And in paragraph 5 the new philosophy of conservation was articulated:

> Conservation, like development, is for people: while development aims to achieve human goals largely through use of the biosphere, conservation aims to achieve them by ensuring that such use can continue. Conservation's concern for maintenance and sustainability is a rational response to the nature of living resources (renewability + destructibility) and also an ethical imperative, expressed in the belief that 'we have not inherited the earth from our parents, we have borrowed it from our children' (World Conservation Strategy 1980).

The goal of the Strategy was stated as 'the integration of conservation and development to ensure that modifications to the planet do indeed secure the survival and well-being of all people'. If it is not explicitly a blueprint for global stewardship, it comes close to being one, and in its 20 double-page spreads it sets out practical guidelines for husbanding the resources of the Earth. Many governments grasped the concept and prepared their own National Conservation Strategies. But there was a sense that the Strategy was still too much rooted in environmental science, and too dismissive of the massive human social problems that impeded achievement of its goals. Some condemned it as echoing what they called 'the North Atlantic brand of anti-human environmentalism'. Six years later, in 1986, a conference in Ottawa called for a new Strategy, with humanity at its heart (Jacobs and Munro 1987).

The concluding message of Ottawa was that

> in seeking sustainable development we do not turn our backs on the natural world. Rather, we stress that humanity can only enjoy life to the full in harmony with nature; in harmony with other species and with the great systems of the creation of which we are part and on which we utterly depend. This emphasis on harmony, on caring for the earth and all its peoples, on sustainable development as an expression of conservation, is the new spirit and ethic of Ottawa and represents a forward leap as great as that provided by the World Conservation Strategy itself.

The debate at Ottawa inspired the three sponsors of the World Conservation Strategy to go away and develop a new version – one with a 'human face'. That new document was entitled *Caring for the Earth: A Strategy for Sustainable Living*, and it was launched simultaneously in 65 countries around the world on 21 October 1991.

Caring for the Earth

The central message of *Caring for the Earth* is stated in the first three paragraphs of its Summary, under the heading 'A Message to the World'.

Humanity must live within the carrying capacity of the Earth. There is no other rational option in the longer term. Unless we use the resources of the Earth sustainably and prudently, we deny people their future. We must adopt life styles and development paths that respect, and work within, nature's limits. We can do that without rejecting the many benefits that modern technology has brought, provided that technology itself works within those limits.

Because of the way we live today, our civilisations are at risk. The 5.3 billion people alive now, especially the one billion in the best-off countries, are mis-using natural resources and seriously over-stressing the Earth's ecosystems. World population may double in 60 years, but the Earth will be unable to support everyone unless there is less waste and extravagance and a more open and equitable alliance between rich and poor. Even then the likelihood of a satisfactory life for all is remote unless present rates of population increase are drastically reduced.

Our new approach must meet two fundamental requirements. One is to secure a widespread and deeply held commitment to a new ethic, the ethic for sustainable living, and to translate its principles into practice. The other is to integrate conservation and development: conservation to keep our actions within the Earth's capacity, and development to enable people everywhere to enjoy long, healthy and fulfilling lives.

The nine principles for sustainable living

Caring for the Earth sets out nine principles as a guide to sustainable living. The following paragraphs are summaries, using words drawn from the document itself.

1. *Respect and care for the community of life*

An ethic based on respect for each other and the Earth is the foundation for sustainable living. Development ought not to be at the expense of other groups or later generations, nor threaten the survival of other species. The ethic should be developed by a dialogue between religious leaders,

236

thinkers, leaders of society, citizens' groups and all caring people. States should adopt a universal declaration and covenant on sustainability that commits them to the world ethic of care, and should incorporate its principles into their national constitutions and legislation. Peoples in all walks of life should incorporate the ethic into codes of personal behaviour and professional conduct. A new world organization should be established to watch over the implementation of the world ethic and draw public attention to major breaches of it.

2. *Improve the quality of human life*

The aim of development is to improve the quality of human life. It should enable people to realize their potential and lead lives of dignity and fulfilment. Economic growth is part of development, but it cannot be a goal in itself; it cannot go on indefinitely. Although people differ in the goals they would set for development, some are virtually universal. These include a long and healthy life, education, access to the resources needed for a decent standard of living, political freedom, guaranteed human rights and freedom from violence. Development is real only if it makes our lives better in all these respects.

3. *Conserve the Earth's vitality and diversity*

Development must be conservation-based: it must protect the structure, functions and diversity of the world's natural systems, on which our species depends. To this end we need to:

> *Conserve life-support systems.* These are the ecological processes that keep the planet fit for life. They shape climate, cleanse air and water, regulate water flow, recycle essential elements, create and regenerate soil and enable ecosystems to renew themselves.

> *Conserve biodiversity.* This includes all species of plants, animals and other organisms; the range of genetic stocks within each species; and the variety of ecosystems.

> *Ensure that the use of renewable resources is sustainable.* These resources include soil, wild and domesticated organisms, forests, rangelands, cultivated land and the marine and freshwater ecosystems that support fisheries. A use is sustainable if it is within the resource's capacity for regeneration.

Four kinds of action need to be taken to implement this principle. First, pollution must be prevented. Second, the integrity of the Earth's ecosystems must be maintained. This means adopting an integrated approach to

237

their management, and making sure that natural ecosystems are used in a sustainable way. Third, biological diversity – the world's total pool of genes, species and ecosystems – must be conserved. Fourth, any harvests of biological resources must be based on the capacity of the stocks; monitoring must allow any over-use to be swiftly corrected.

4. *Keep within Earth's carrying capacity*

There are finite limits to the 'carrying capacity' of the Earth's ecosystems: to the impacts that they and the biosphere can withstand without dangerous deterioration. The limits vary from region to region, and the impacts depend on how many people there are, and how much food, water, energy and raw materials each person uses and wastes. Policies that bring human numbers and lifestyles into balance with the Earth's carrying capacity must be complemented by technologies that enhance that capacity by careful management.

5. *Minimize the depletion of non-renewable resources*

The depletion of non-renewable resources such as minerals, oil, gas and coal must be minimized. While these cannot be used sustainably, their 'life' can be extended, for example by recycling, by using less of a resource to make a particular product, or by switching to renewable substitutes where possible.

6. *Change personal attitudes and practices*

To adopt the ethic for living sustainably, people must re-examine their values and alter their behaviour. Society must promote values that support the ethic and discourage those that are incompatible with a sustainable way of life. Information must be disseminated through formal and informal education so that needed actions are widely understood. It is important that these changes are promoted with due sensitivity, and in a non-patronizing way.

7. *Enable communities to care for their own environments*

Communities and local groups provide the easiest channels for people to express their concerns and take action to create securely based sustainable societies. However, such communities need the authority, power and knowledge to act. People who organize themselves to work for sustainability in their own communities can be an effective force whether their community is rich, poor, urban, suburban or rural. Communities need effective control over their own affairs, including secure access to resources and an equitable stake in managing them. They also need the right to participate in decisions, and appropriate education and training. Finally, communities must be able to meet their essential needs sustainably, while conserving their environment.

8. *Provide a national framework for integrating development and conservation*

All societies need a foundation of information and knowledge, a framework of law and institutions, and consistent economic and social policies if they are to advance in a rational way. A national programme for achieving sustainability should involve all interests and seek to identify and prevent problems before they arise. It must be adaptive, continually redirecting its course in response to experience and to new needs.

Four kinds of national action are needed. First, governments should establish a cross-sectoral institution, capable of an integrated and forward-looking approach to decisions. Second, all countries should have comprehensive systems of environmental law that safeguard human rights, the interests of future generations, and the productivity and diversity of the Earth. Third, economic policies and improved technology should be developed so as to increase the benefit from available resources and maintain natural wealth. The fourth requirement is for knowledge, based on research and monitoring. Without it, policies for sustainability will lack foundation and credibility.

9. *Forge a global alliance*

Global sustainability will depend on a firm alliance among all countries. But levels of development in the world are unequal, and the lower-income countries must be helped to develop sustainably and to protect their environments. Global and shared resources, especially the atmosphere, oceans and shared ecosystems, can be managed only on the basis of common purpose and resolve. The ethic of care applies at the international as well as the national and individual levels. No nation is self-sufficient. All stand to gain from worldwide sustainability – and all are threatened if we fail to attain it.

A major need is to strengthen international law. A second area of action is to help lower-income countries address environmental priorities. Official debt should be written off, non-environmental trade barriers to exports should be removed, and investment encouraged. Third, financial flows from the poorer to the richer countries need to be turned around. Fourth, international commitment and capacity needs to be strengthened, for example by strengthening and streamlining the capacity of the United Nations system.

Sustainability by sectors

The nine principles apply across all sectors of the environment and the economy. But the traditional approach to managing the environment has been sectoral, treating agriculture, forestry, fisheries, nature conservation, pollution prevention, energy, industry, the planning of human settlements and other activities as if they were unconnected. Often they have been the preserve of different, and jealously independent, ministries or agencies. Recognizing this fact, *Caring for the Earth* follows the original World Conservation Strategy in developing guidelines for sustainability with sectors. The following paragraphs summarize the proposals, again largely using words culled from the document itself.

Energy

Action needs to be taken to prepare long-term energy strategies for all countries. There must be increased efficiency in energy generation from fossil fuels, and increased use of alternative, particularly renewable, energy sources. The distribution of energy must also be made more efficient, and there must be reduced energy use per person in all sectors, particularly in developed countries.

Business, industry and commerce

The lower-income countries must develop their industry to escape from acute poverty and to achieve sustainability. But this development must not be the kind that blighted the environment and imposed heavy social costs in many areas of high-income countries.

We must adopt practices that build concern for the Earth into the structure of business, industry and commerce. We need to introduce processes that minimize the use of raw materials and energy, reduce waste and prevent pollution. And we need products that do not damage people or the planet.

These needs will be met only if we bring governments, business and the environmental movement into new dialogue. Business should commit itself to sustainability and environmental excellence, expressed in high performance standards and encouraged by economic incentives.

Human settlements

In all countries, changes in city design, transport systems and resource use will be essential if sustainability is to be assured. The poverty suffered by

240

the minority of urban dwellers in richer nations and the majority in the poorer ones can be drastically reduced without a large expansion in consumption. In both kinds of country, more effective and representative local governments and more far-sighted national governments are required. An ecological approach to human settlement planning needs to incorporate an efficient and sustainable urban transport policy.

Farm and range lands

If agriculture is to be sustainable, countries must develop strategies and plans to use agricultural land optimally. They should control the use of fertilizers and pesticides, and promote the conservation of genetic resources. National strategies should protect the best farmland against conversion to non-agricultural use. The impact of agriculture on marginal land should be reduced. Good husbandry will need encouragement. Integrated pest management should be favoured, and regulations and economic incentives adopted so that the use of agricultural chemicals is less wasteful and hazardous. International and national action should ensure the conservation of crop and livestock breeds and their wild relatives, as essential genetic resources for the future.

Forests

The world's forests are a part of our life support system and a priceless natural resource. Each country needs to prepare an inventory of its forest resources and a strategy for their management. They should protect areas of natural forest including 'old growth', ensure that any use is sustainable, and establish plantations for intensive production. Local communities should be involved in forest management. International action should create markets for the products of sustainably managed forests, ensuring that the low-income countries derive maximum benefit from sound resource use.

Fresh waters

Life on Earth depends on water, and it may prove the key limiting resource in the twenty-first century.

Four kinds of action are needed. First, the information base must be strengthened and public awareness of the water cycle promoted. Second, integrated management of water and land should be developed. Third, aquatic species and ecosystems should be conserved, and fourth,

241

international action should be strengthened because 40% of the world's people live in river basins that are shared between several countries.

Oceans and coastal seas

The oceans cover more than two thirds of the planet. The coastal seas are the most productive ecosystems on Earth, supporting 80% of the world's fisheries and yielding mangrove and other important products. Natural barriers such as coral reefs, mangroves and salt marshes protect densely populated coastal lands from storms. Yet the seas, and especially the coastal zones, are increasingly polluted from the adjacent land, on a scale that threatens to impair ecological function and reduce yield.

Action should be taken to make people more aware of the importance of oceans and seas. Integrated approaches to coastal and ocean management should be promoted. Local communities should be involved in the management of marine resources. Coastal and oceanic ecological systems should be conserved and global cooperation strengthened.

Targets and progress

Caring for the Earth proposed 130 specific actions as the foundation for a sustainable society. It set targets, to focus that action and as a basis for evaluating the results. Six months after the launch of the Strategy an unprecedented gathering of Heads of State and Government assembled in Rio de Janeiro and adopted a plan for the twenty-first century known as 'Agenda 21', which in many ways paralleled *Caring for the Earth* but went into much greater detail (Robinson 1993).

Ten years afterwards, it is clear that progress has been uneven. About a third of the world's nations have adopted national plans for conservation and sustainable development – plans for the stewardship of national resources. On the ground, a vast array of projects has moved particular communities forward. Health and quality of life have advanced in much of the developing world, except where the tragedy of HIV/AIDS has shortened life expectancy and reversed decades of painstaking medical progress. Education continues to advance. But inequity, avoidable death, acute poverty and illiteracy still stalk large areas of the world and hamper the care for the Earth's vitality, diversity and productivity which are foundations of the human future. Extinctions of wild species continue to accelerate, and it is not clear that humanity is on course to live within the Earth's optimal carrying capacity. Personal attitudes and practices, in rich and poor countries alike, are not changing fast enough. There are some inspiring examples of communities that have taken care of their own environments, and grown in prosperity in consequence, and all too many examples of environmental degradation. War, disease and civil strife still pervade the world. Poor nations and people have got poorer, while the rich have got wealthier. The United Nations and the other components of the much-needed global alliance have not made much progress since 1991.

Strategies can only do so much: the test is whether they really galvanize action. Since the WCS was published, and even since *Caring for the Earth* appeared, actions have lagged behind need in many sectors. Human-induced climate change, resulting from the unconstrained burning of fossil fuels, threatens to displace vegetation zones, imperil ecosystems, change agricultural patterns, raise sea levels and – especially if the use of coal, oil and gas reserves continues to be unconstrained – displace millions of people as 'environmental refugees'. The infuriating irony is that there is ample knowledge in the world to allow the prescriptions of the 1990s to be implemented. Stewardship is not being impeded by lack of understanding. Nor is there any shortage of machinery for national action and international cooperation. The obstacles are deeply engrained in the fabric of society, and are, in essence, a failure to value nature and natural resources adequately, a failure to take the long-term view, a naïve assumption that future technology will put everything right, and a blindness to the interdependence of all human communities and all species on the planet. The need for the ethic of care and the responsible stewardship that springs from it remain undiminished (Holdgate 1996).

Part V
Relevance/Ways Forward

Chapter 22

From Ecological Lament to a Sustainable *Oikos*

Anne M. Clifford

Anne Clifford is Associate Professor of Theology at Duquesne University in Pittsburgh and a member of the Sisters of St Joseph. She served as a consultant in the US Catholic Conference's Environmental Justice programme and contributed an essay to the volume of essays And God Saw That It Was Good *(Christiansen and Grazer 1996) that came from the programme. The article printed here is reproduced with permission from a symposium* God's Stewards *(Brandt 2002), produced by World Vision at the time of the World Summit on Sustainable Development in Johannesburg. Dr Clifford links creation care firmly to the need for sustainable development.*

Over the mountains, break out in cries of lamentation,
over the pasture lands, intone a dirge:
They are scorched, and no one crosses them,
unheard is the bleat of the flock;
birds of the air as well as beasts,
all have fled, and are gone (Jer. 9.10).[1]

Throughout the Hebrew Scriptures lament rises from the depths of the human spirit in times of great distress. The lament of ancient Israelis usually focused on the people's suffering due to their infidelity to the sacred covenant that God initiated. What sets Jeremiah's lament apart from many is its focus on the effects of sinful human choices on the land and the suffering of all creatures dependent on it for existence. The land is ravaged; the people are the cause. The words of Jeremiah herald a 'contrast experience'. Things ought not to be this way. Something is radically wrong. Human sinfulness has created a serious imbalance in the creation that God has made with his 'outstretched arm' (Jer. 27.5).

The lament of Jeremiah, likely proclaimed *circa* 597 BCE, is limited to a relatively small territory and population. Although the majority of the world's six billion people no longer live in a pastoral society that resembles the Judah of Jeremiah's era, the call to 'break out in cries of lamentation' poignantly illustrates the exhortatory power of sacred Scripture to reach beyond the limitation of the time and place of its first articulation to us today. As in the case of Jeremiah's situation, we humans have brought devastation upon ourselves and the rest of creation. The difference today is that the devastation is of global proportions. *Oikos*, our earthly home, is imperiled.

Our present situation and the question of sustainability

Due largely to the indiscriminate application of science and technology, we now inhabit a planet that is under a more dangerous sun, with less arable land, and with a far greater burden of the legacy of poisonous wastes than Jeremiah did. This is part of Earth's lamentable story. In 1992 the 'Earth Summit' addressed these and related problems. Economics played a key role in the conversations. Rooted in the Greek word *oikos*, 'economics' points to the laws and organization of our planetary household. Those gathered seemed to recognize that economic progress, benefiting a segment of the human population, was not necessarily compatible with the health of Earth. This was not a new idea. During the previous quarter of a century, a growing chorus of voices drew attention to the ways in which the human-created economy was unsustainable because it was not compatible with the 'great economy' of Earth's complex ecosystems (W. Berry 1987).

At the Earth Summit, sustainability emerged as a central focus. Ten years later a 'World Summit on Sustainable Development' was held in Johannesburg, South Africa. Definitions of 'sustainable development' abound. The UN uses a definition proposed by the Brundtland Report, *Our Common Future* (1987):

> Sustainable development is development that meets the needs of the present without compromising the ability of future generations to meet their own needs.

It contains two key concepts: the concept of 'needs', in particular the essential needs of the world's poor, to which overriding priority should be given; and the idea of limitations imposed by the state of technology and social organizations on the environment's ability to meet present and future needs (*Our Common Future* 1987: 43).

Preparing for the Johannesburg Summit, Nitin Desai (2001), Under-Secretary General for Economic and Social Affairs at the UN, treated the 'two key concepts' in a manner that sounds very much like a lamentation, however. He bemoaned the fact that poverty and under-nourishment had not been reduced since the Earth Summit, and no significant progress had been made in improving the conditions of the environment.

The majority of the most influential decisions that impact sustainability are being made in Western countries where Christianity is at least nominally the majority religion. The importance of the sustainability question has been recognized by some Christian churches. Both the US Catholic Bishops' statement, *Renewing the Earth* (in Christiansen and Grazer 1996)[2] and the Presbyterian Church (USA) document *Hope for a Global Future* (1996) address the issue of sustainability. It is an issue ripe for ecumenical dialogue and effort. Indeed 'ecumenism' is another term that finds its roots in the word *oikos*. In its broadest sense, ecumenism affirms the belief that the Earth is not only one household; it is the household of God. This is usually conceived by Christians in terms of a grand edifice comprised of many churches. But as Christine Burke (2001) points out, ecumenism also captures 'the sense of the whole inhabited earth as one household of God'. Mindfulness that the household of God is also the household of life can provide Christians with a common starting point for a theology that realistically acknowledges that there is much to lament about where the health of the Earth is concerned. And the mournful dirge of lament can be replaced if we engage our own spiritual traditions in developing a theological grounding for a sustainable *oikos*.

A Christian theology of *oikos* and its formidable challenges

Sustainability and related environmental and ecological concerns are still novel for most Christian churches, but they must respond to these issues if they are to be faithful to the justice teachings of Jesus Christ and the prophets, never mind their own traditions.

The articulation of Christian foundations for a theology of sustainable *oikos* requires that some serious critiques put before Christian doctrines by environmentalists and ecologists need to be addressed. These critiques have challenged the most basic beliefs that Christians share about creation and its relationship to redemption. By facing these challenges, components for an ecological theology responsive to the question of sustainability can be articulated.

Only two of these critiques will be considered here. The first challenge was poignantly raised in a widely cited article written by Lynn White (1967). [See Harrison (pp. 17–31) and Bauckham (pp. 32–50)]. The second is broader, arguing that Christianity is more interested in having its adherents achieve the goal of 'an after-life' than concern for the earthly household of life.

Does biblical faith in redemption put *oikos* in the background?

In response to the second challenge, it is true that Christianity places great emphasis on the redemption offered through Jesus Christ and human salvation. Beginning in the Enlightenment period, this emphasis contributed to the neglect of non-human nature and to ecological disasters. However, a careful look at the biblical sources shows that the neglect of *oikos* overlooks the ways in which God's work of creation provides the cosmic purpose behind God's redemptive activity. This is true for the Old Testament (e.g. Fretheim 1991: 12–14, etc.) as well as for the New. In Psalm 146, for example, we find a hymn composed by someone who has learned that there is no other source of salvation (v. 3), than God the Creator, 'the maker of heaven and earth, the seas and all that is in them' (v. 6).

It is this same God who

> secures justice for the oppressed,
> gives food to the hungry … sets prisoners free …
> gives sight to the blind …
> raises up those who are bowed down …
> protects the stranger …
> [and] sustains the orphan and the widow,
> but thwarts the way of the wicked (vv. 7–9)
> [see also Ps. 19].

In each activity, God responds to the creatures most in need, offering them the liberation of a redeemed life.

In the New Testament, creation and redemption are treated as two related aspects of God's one engagement with the world in and through Jesus Christ. Through the Incarnation, God comes into relation with the world of creatures in a personal and intimate way. In a manner that resonates with Psalm 146, Jesus brings glad tidings to the poor, proclaims liberty to prisoners, gives sight to the blind, and secures justice for the oppressed (Luke 4.18). While it is true that these activities are directed towards people, this passage ends with a proclamation of a Sabbath year. This is a year of favour in which not only are slaves to be freed and debts cancelled, but also, planting, pruning and harvesting for storage are forbidden. The earth itself is to be given Sabbath rest in honor of the Creator (Lev. 25.2–7; Deut. 15.7–11).

Further, through Jesus' life, death and resurrection, God's creative activity continues as a work of redemption. This is clearly affirmed in an early Christian hymn in Colossians that proclaims that God, through Christ, the first born of all creation, reconciled to himself all things (human

250

and non-human creatures), whether on earth or in heaven (Col. 1.1–20). The saving work of Jesus Christ, therefore, cannot be simplistically limited to 'an after-life' for human beings. Redemption in Jesus Christ is not reductively anthropocentric. It extends to the entire household of life with God embracing all creatures in and through Jesus Christ; in Jesus Christ, the transcendent and the immanent, the 'other-worldly' and the 'this-wordly' meet.

Conclusions

This limited treatment of creation and redemption provides a theological basis for approaching sustainability in an explicitly ecological way. The definition of sustainable development adopted by the United Nations places emphasis almost exclusively on human economic development. It is laudable for its concern for the poor whose very existence is threatened daily, as the gap between the economically poor and the affluent continues to widen. Yet the definition is myopically anthropocentric in its emphasis. It supports concern for the environment in so far as it must be sufficiently healthy to meet present and future human needs. It contains a very important emphasis, but it does not bring a holistic ecological conscious-ness to bear on the world situation. It fails to acknowledge that humans are but participants in a highly complex network of life comprised of delicate ecosystems.

An arguably more adequate definition of sustainability is that given by Larry Rasmussen, who speaks of sustainability as 'the capacity of natural and social systems to survive and thrive together indefinitely. It is also a vision with an implicit earth ethic ... and a picture of earth as *oikos*' (Rasmussen 1996: 127). This definition is preferred because it takes into account the inherent capacity of earth systems to strive to maintain their own balance and replenishment. It also places humanity within the eco-sphere as a participant, rather than as the sole referent in determining global policies. It further recognizes that an earth ethic must be oriented to *oikos* as a whole, and therefore be thoroughly ecological.

A Christian theology of sustainability must recognize the close link between both human poverty and affluence, and the degradation of the health of *oikos* (Rasmussen 1996: 103). Socioeconomic injustice among humans is evident in statistics that indicate that 1.2 billion of the 6.1 billion people on the planet are overweight, while another 1.2 billion are seriously malnourished (Gardner and Halweil 2000). The affluent of the Northern hemisphere, where most of the 1.2 billion obese reside, consume the majority of the Earth's resources and create most of its non-biodegradable and toxic wastes, resulting in species extinction that is wiping out forms of life that took millions of years to evolve. *Oikos* can no longer afford the minority affluent who define well-being in terms of their own accumulation of wealth and resources.

Kinship solidarity, foundational for a Christian ecological theology of sustainability, provides us with a 'world vision' that extends the realm of justice to the whole of creation. It takes seriously that *oikos* is not only the household of life, but also the household of God. As the household of God, *oikos* has an inherent sacrality, even a sacramentality. To paraphrase John Calvin, every creature is engraved with the unmistakable marks of God's glory. For Jeremiah's lament to be replaced by an *oikos* rejoicing with cries of gladness (Ps. 100.1–2), a program for a sustainable eco-justice – one which affirms the intrinsic value of all creatures – must be adopted.

Notes

1. This verse is from a longer section, Jeremiah 8.4–10.25, in which the dominant theme is disaster and the need for repentance. Lamentation is also the central theme of Jeremiah 14.1–15.9 where drought and war, famine and sword are interwoven. See also Hosea 4.3 ('Therefore the lands mourns, and everything that dwells in it languishes: The beasts of the field, the birds of the air, and even the fish of the sea perish' [NAB] and Isaiah 24.4–5 ('The earth mourns and fades, the world languishes and fades; both heaven and earth languish. The earth is polluted because of its inhabitants, who have transgressed laws, violated statutes, broken the ancient covenant').

2. Sustainability appears 16 times in the chapter 'Renewing the Earth, an Invitation to Reflection and Action on Environment in the Light of Catholic Social Teaching' in *And God Saw That It Was Good: Catholic Theology and the Environment* (Christiansen and Grazer 1996: 223–43), the response to the US Roman Catholic Bishops' call for creation care.

Chapter 23

Partnership with Nature according to the Scriptures: Beyond the Theology of Stewardship

Paul Santmire

H. Paul Santmire is one of the pioneering prophets of Christian understanding of the environment; his Brother Earth *(1970) was among the first theological works of its kind. His highly regarded historical study of Christian theologies of nature,* The Travail of Nature *(1985), is still widely used by students of religion and the environment. A teaching theologian of the Evangelical Lutheran Church in America, now retired and living in the Boston area, Dr Santmire has served in both academic and pastoral settings. The article reproduced here is a shortened version of one published in the* Christian Scholar's Review *in 2003; more complete references and documentation will be found in the original. It won the Charles Miller Award for the best essay of the year in that journal. In this article, he argues that the first phase of stewardship theology in the Christian community has run its course and that we must therefore enter a new and more complex phase, which he calls partnership, predicated on a fresh reading of the biblical theology of nature. He identifies three emphases of a full, biblically informed approach toward nature: creative intervention, sensitive care and awestruck contemplation.*

No one can legitimately fault the National Religious Partnership for the Environment, the Advertising Council, and the Environmental Defence Fund for working together to encourage religious communities and their members to respect the earth, to 'reduce, reuse, recycle', to buy recycled goods, and to use energy efficiently, all for the sake of environmental justice. The rationale for this campaign is fundamentally sound, both biblically and theologically. As a church poster in rural Maine put it: 'The earth is the Lord's. We are its stewards.'

'Stewardship' has been promoted in response to the environmental crisis more than any other theological theme. In support of that commitment, an enormous amount of biblical and theological work has been invested in defining and defending the theology of stewardship, some of it very sophisticated. Of particular importance is the prophetic emphasis on 'eco-justice' espoused by some of the most outspoken advocates of the stewardship theme (see Fretheim 1984; Simkins 1994; Knierim 1995; Hiebert 1996a, b; W.P. Brown 1999). With these kinds of theological and ethical commitments, ecumenical and denominational agencies and local congregations have joined with various public interest groups in the name of better stewardship of the Earth's resources to influence the policies of timber companies, agricultural conglomerates, and other corporate interests, sometimes with tangible, positive results. This can be called the first wave of theological responses to the global environmental crisis.

Stewardship has had its theological critics. But given the fact that, until very recently, Christians in the modern West generally have shown little sustained interest in the theology of nature and in related environmental concerns, and given the fact that churches around the world are now being mobilized by the imperatives of the stewardship of nature, it would seem imprudent, to say the least, to do anything to block or even to divert this theological trend.

Yet what if the Scriptures in fact teach us something richer and more complex? If this is the case, is not the time at hand for the Church's preachers and teachers to work energetically to launch a second theological wave of responses to the global environmental crisis? This is even more urgent because of the revolution in scholarly studies of the biblical theology of nature in the last two decades. Hence, this essay. I will not use the term 'stewardship' in the discussion that follows, because of what in my judgment is its problematic character.[1] Of primary importance at this point in the Church's life is this challenge: in light of recent scholarly research, to set forth as concisely and as accessibly as possible, a more complete statement of the biblical theology of nature, as it depicts the human relationship with nature as God has intended it to be. My contention is that in order to reflect the complexities and the richness of the biblical witness, it is best for us to develop a theology of partnership with nature, which will hopefully begin to take the place of what appears to be the more limited theology of stewardship of nature which now is being widely preached and taught.[2]

The biblical theology of partnership with nature is by no means a one-dimensional construct. We encounter its complexity and richness in three fundamental expressions or emphases: creative intervention in nature, sensitive care for nature, and awestruck contemplation of nature. The first of these emphases validates and in some fundamental ways corrects standard theological expositions of the stewardship doctrine. I consciously join those within the believing community who position themselves to listen to the witness of the whole Bible as the Word of God to us, and do so with a 'critically engaged reading' (Green 2002: 19), reading the Scriptures as the Church has traditionally read them, as telling the Great Story of the God of grace and God of glory. This is the story 'that runs from creation to new creation, with the Christ-event as its interpretive middle' (Green 2002: 20).

In the midst of that macro-narrative, there are several historical micro-narratives which enrich and help define the whole, some of which we can identify here – the priestly, the Yahwist, the Deuteronomic, the Prophetic, the Sapiential, the Jobean, and the Messianic trajectories.[3] For the purposes of this essay, I concentrate on the priestly, the Yahwistic, and the Jobean micro-narratives, without for a moment denying the importance of the others. This approach allows us to identify the biblical 'baseline,' important in itself, but also as a witness to the redeemed life. The witness of the priestly writers, the Yahwist, and Job helps to identify that new place, which as believers in Jesus Christ is where we should have been living had we not become captives of the powers of sin. This is our divinely mandated relationship with the good creation-history of God to which God's redeeming act in Jesus Christ has restored us; it is the focus of the three micro-narratives, identifying how we as humans are intended by God to be in partnership with nature.

The priestly story

The biblical story commences with an account of the beginning of all created things and, implicitly, the continuation and the fulfilment of all things. We have this micro-narrative in Genesis 1.1–2.3(4a) from the hands of tradents, usually called 'the priestly writers'.

> This cosmic overture to the entire canon is the literary and theological point of departure for all that follows, from creation to consummation. By virtue of its placement at the Bible's threshold, this quintessential creation story not only relativizes the other biblical cosmogonies interspersed through the Old Testament, but also imbues all other historical material, from historical narrative to law, with cosmic background (W.P. Brown 1999: 36).

The very first verse speaks the most important word – God. Genesis 1.1 begins a story, which, however circuitous, interrupted or obscured, is a story of a God 'whose giving knows no ending'. And this self-giving of God is always understood not as some impersonal force, however serendipitous that force might be envisioned to be, but as an amazing and mysterious personal giving and sharing, indicated in Genesis 1 by the repeated witness to God speaking. A 'force' does not speak. We will encounter this motif more than once in the witness of the Yahwist and of Job.

The divine speaking always signifies the divine commitment to personal sharing, to be the I of an I–Thou relationship, the giving of oneself to the other. This relationship will differ with different kinds of creatures. Perhaps the best way to express the distinction between God in relationship with a variety of creatures and God in relationship with the human creature is to see all God's *ad extra* relationships as His gracious *communication* of Himself to others, and the particular relationship of God with the human creature as a form of *communion*. In other words, His communication with the human creature is internal and tangible, known more by insight than by sight.[4] That general kind of communication also presupposes a kind of partnering with all creatures on God's part, entailing God's working with the other creatures and even, on occasion, depending on them to respond by their own canons of creaturely spontaneity and praise.

Genesis 1 does not begin with a *locus de Deo* as a dogmatic treatise might, but with God bringing that history into being and partnering with the many creatures He called into existence. The Lord takes a long time to arrive at the human creation, for a reason: He is launching a history of the whole world, with many creatures, not just the human creature. This is why we hear the repetition of the phrase 'and God saw that it was good'. Each stage of God's creative activity has its own integrity and its own meaning. God chooses to share His life with all these creaturely domains. Humans are created to 'rule' over the earth (Gen. 1.28), but in the same language, the sun and the moon are made to 'rule' over the day and the night (Gen. 1.16–18). We see here a vision of a wonderfully interrelated whole of many different creatures, all of which are created by God to have a history with Him. It is indeed the whole point of the project. When God finally 'gets around' to creating the human creature, He does not rejoice over the emergence of the human creature as if that were the whole point of His creativity (as some later Christian interpreters have imagined): God saw 'everything that he had made, and indeed it was very good' (Gen. 1.31). The whole point of God's creativity is the prospering – and implicitly, the fulfilment – of the whole in all its diversity.

In keeping with the motif of the goodness of every creature, God does not rush on through the first five days. All creatures are partners with God's creativity, not merely objects of His creative will posited for the sake of His relationship with humans.

On the other hand, humans alone are created according to the image of God (Gen. 1.27). This surely suggests a special relationship between God and humans. The creation of humans is introduced as a unique product of divine intervention: whereas the land-based creatures are products of the land (Gen. 1.24), human beings are not. 'The opening command is "Let us make human beings in our image," not "Let the earth bring forth human beings". Unlike the Yahwist's anthropogeny in the next chapter of Genesis, the writer makes clear that the land is not the source of human identity but only humankind's natural habitat' (W.P. Brown 1999: 43f.). This relationship is reciprocally personal; here for the first time in the story of God's creative acts, God speaks in the first person (Gen. 1.26): the divine 'I' calls the human thou not just into being and becoming in partnership with Him, but into communion, the intimacy of personal communication.

In this respect, the priestly writers, given their cultic interests, must have presupposed that the divine–human relationship is one of self-conscious praise on the part of humans. The seventh day as the appointed setting for the humans to glorify the Creator for all His good works, cannot have been far from the priestly writers' minds as they shaped the construct of humans created according to the image of God. From this priestly perspective, the relationship between God and the human creatures is teleological, in a way that God's relationship with the other animals is not: the Creator brings the human beings into existence so that they may in some sense 'image forth' His purposes on the earth, both by working to establish human community ('making history' as Jürgen Moltmann likes to say) and by actively worshipping the Creator.

This radically theocentric project envisioned by the priestly writers is also thoroughly cosmocentric and anthropocentric. For the priestly tradents, God is profoundly with all His creatures, related to them and interacting with them as they respond to His creative initiatives. Terence Fretheim's summary of the Old Testament's view of God's creative presence with His creation surely reflects overall the witness of the priestly writers in Genesis 1:

> God is graciously present, in, with, and under all the particulars of his creation, with which God is in a relationship of reciprocity. The immanent and transcendent God of Israel is immersed in the space and time of this world; this God is available to all, is effective along with them at every occasion, and moves with them into an uncertain future. Such a perspective reveals a divine vulnerability, as God takes on all the risks that authentic relatedness entails (Fretheim 1984: 78).

In this sense, the theology of the priestly writers in Genesis 1 is subversive. It has often been observed that the priestly accounts of the creation may have received their final editing in the setting of the Exile – and the Babylonian society of the Exile was a hierarchical, command society. Soberingly, historic Israel from the era of David and Solomon until at least the Exile often took that kind of command royal ideology for granted and, with it, images of God as the chief monarch of the cosmos. The relational, ecological vision of the priestly tradents *contradicts* that ideology.

Walter Brueggemann (1982: 32) has suggested that this is due to an inner-theological dynamic. The vision of God of the priestly writers is very like that presupposed by the prophet Ezekiel (chapter 34), who wrote in the same kind of socio-political context; for Ezekiel, God is the 'shepherd

King' who cares for His flock. An anti-monarchical polemic seems to emerge in this priestly setting and is taken for granted by the priestly writers, insofar as humans are said to be created according to the 'image of God' (Gen. 1.27); in the ancient Near East, typically only kings were thought of as bearing the image of a god or gods (Brett 2000: 77). Thus, while the monarchical imagery in Genesis 1 is evident, even essential for the priestly tradents in light of their faith in the power of the God of wisdom and mercy who creates by speaking, that imagery is indeed profoundly qualified by other theological assumptions. These keep this text well within the overall Old Testament and, indeed, the general canonical view of God as the God of self-giving love, a faith rooted in experience of the earliest of Israelite communities.[5] It is in this exegetical context that the much-discussed theme of human dominion over the earth should be heard (Gen. 1.28).

The priestly writers in Babylon lived in a hierarchical and highly organized urban society, presupposing massive human intervention to sustain its economy, above all through irrigation projects; if there was going to be urban life of any scope, such large-scale interventions in nature were a *sine qua non* of social existence, contrasting with the simple agrarian life of small communities in regions like the hill country of Palestine. One would expect economic realities such as these to be reflected in biblical texts that were shaped in such a socio-political world. And indeed they contrast to the simple, agrarian assumptions of the Yahwist in Genesis 2 (to which we will turn presently): 'The Priestly account acknowledges that human life in the land cannot exist in effortless harmony with creation; it can flourish only by establishing some measure of control over the earth. The Yahwist's notion of forcefully and painfully working the soil as a consequence of the curse is regarded by the priestly narrator as a noble exercise' (W.P. Brown 1999: 44). Such human intervention in the earth is theologically noble for the priestly writer, since it represents carrying out the particular partnership with God that is part of God's creative purposes; it makes the land 'fillable' with human life: 'As God is no divine warrior who slays the forces of chaos to construct a viable domain for life, so human beings are not ruthless tyrants, wreaking violence upon the land that is their home. By dint of command rather than brute force, the elements of creation are enlisted to fulfil the Deity's creative purposes' (W.P. Brown 1999: 45).

To underline this, Brown points beyond Genesis 1 to Noah, a later figure in the unfolding priestly narrative. He observes that Noah 'models primordial stewardship' (I would prefer to speak here of 'partnership') by sustaining 'all of life in its representative forms. His "subduing" of the earth entails bringing together the animals of the earth into his zoological reserve, a floating speck of land, as it were. By fulfilling humankind's role as royal steward over creation (1.28), Noah is a beacon of righteousness in an ocean of anarchy. Noah exercises human dominion over creation by preserving the integrity and diversity of life' (W.P. Brown 1999: 60).

Strikingly, Noah takes both the clean and the unclean animals with him in the ark. Had his assignment been to 'make this a better world', he might have seized upon the opportunity to leave the unclean behind – or the mosquitoes, for that matter. Human intervention in nature is envisioned by the priestly writers as within limits, both theocentric and cosmocentric. In this sense, God might expect humans to establish their own unique communities, but always in cooperation with and respect for all the other divinely mandated domains of creation; each creaturely domain is created with its own goodness in the eyes of God. This, then, is the consummately beautiful mosaic of God's creativity at the very beginning; it is why all things, taken as a beautiful whole, with each creature or creaturely domain with its own purpose in the greater scheme of things, all working together in majestic harmony, are seen by God, in the priestly vision, as 'very good' (Gen. 1.31). Brueggemann (1982: 37) comments that "good" in this sense refers to an aesthetic rather than a moral quality; it might be better translate "lovely, pleasing, or beautiful" (cf. Eccl. 3.11)'.

That ordered, cosmic goodness is celebrated in many ways throughout the Bible. Psalm 104 is particularly worth recalling here, both because it stands in a close relationship to Genesis 1 and also – in contrast to the measured cadence of Genesis 1 – because it expresses a vision of God's beautifully diverse and lavish creation. It can be read as a kind of poetic commentary on Genesis 1. We see God wrapping Himself in light, as with a garment (v. 2), riding on the wings of the wind (v. 3), establishing the earth on its foundations (v. 5), speaking powerfully to rebuke the waters with His thunder (v. 7), and making springs gush forth in the valleys (v. 10). We see the human community established by God in the midst of all this natural splendour and riches and beauty, blessed with a life of joy, with plenteous food and 'wine to gladden the human heart' (v. 14).

Then we meet a theme that is implicit in Genesis 1 and which recurs again, dramatically, in the poetry of the book of Job. The Psalmist takes it for granted that, given the magnificence and mystery of God's universal history with all creatures, there are times when humans' active engagement with nature will cease and become one of awestruck contemplation. God has purposes with all creatures that are often wondrous to behold in themselves, even if they are on occasion repulsive to humans. God makes the high mountains for the wild goats (v. 18), and the night when a whole variety of animals can come creeping out, when the young lions, in particular, 'roar for their prey, seeking their food from God' (vv. 20–21). The note of violence here – lions seeking their prey – represents a view of primordial goodness that differs, in this respect, from the non-violent vision of the priestly tradents. This theme of nature red in tooth and claw recurs in an even more vivid form in the narratives of Job. The witness of

259

the Psalmist and the priestly writers stand in tension with each other at this point, in a way that may not even be complementary.[6]

Even more removed from the human world, and more wondrous and fearful to behold, according to the Psalmist, is the sea 'great and wide', with 'creeping things innumerable' (v. 25). Strikingly, God has His own mysterious purposes with what for the Psalmist was the greatest and most awesome of creatures of the deep, the Leviathan. God 'rejoices' in this creature, or 'plays' with it (v. 26: both translations are possible). It is as if a poet in our time were to say that God rejoices in the billions of galaxies in our universe – and plays with them! The Psalm then celebrates, one more time, the immediacy of God's interaction with all of His creatures, possibly with an allusion to the 'Spirit of God' hovering creatively over the primaeval waters (Gen. 1.1): 'When you send forth your Spirit they are created; and you renew the face of the ground' (v. 30).

After the Psalmist rejoices in all this created glory and calls upon God Himself to rejoice in all His works (v. 31), an ominous note is introduced at the very end (v. 35), alluding to the rampant human sinfulness described by the priestly writer in Genesis 6.7: 'Let sinners be consumed from the earth, and let the wicked be no more'. We are left with the vision of the great and wonderful world of God's creation, in which God is immediately engaged, the whole of which is indeed very good, but with a sobering hint of human malfeasance introduced at the very end.

Genesis 1 itself goes further at this point: to a seventh day for God's creative project, which, although it stands in continuity with the others, is quite different. This is the day when God rested from all his creative activity (Gen. 2.2). Here the accent shifts from goodness to holiness. 'As all creation is directed toward completion, completion sets the stage for consecration. Goodness and holiness, bounded and separate as they are, are also bound up in teleological correspondence, an integrity of temporal coherence. The primordial week, in turns out, is also a holy week' (W.P. Brown 1999: 52). While the whole creation in the first six days is very good, with the Sabbath and the mystery of the divine rest drawing the whole creation to it, all things are in some sense to be sanctified, made holy, or perfected. That seems to be the priestly vision. Gerhard von Rad (1961: 60f.) goes further, suggesting that there is an awareness here of 'the Fall' and its aftermath, that the Sabbath as the eternal day of divine rest is a day yet to dawn fully in this world. Hence the Sabbath can be interpreted as an eschatological day. Note that, in contrast to the other six days of creation, the Sabbath is never said to end. We do not read: 'And there was evening and there was morning, the seventh day.' In this sense, the Sabbath is ongoing.

So it is possible to hear this text about primordial beginnings suggesting also the promise of ultimate endings, pointing toward the time when perfect peace, *shalom*, will finally be established once and for all, when the

universal history of God will one day be consummated beyond the sinfulness and the finitude of this world. Later, for sure, an explicit eschatological confession emerges: in the day of the promised 'new heavens and
the new earth', all flesh will come to worship before the Lord, 'from sabbath to sabbath' (Isa. 66.22f.).

Whether or not we understand the Sabbath in such eschatological terms,
the second creation story in Genesis 2 may be read as a fleshing out of the
human story. From the perspective of the final editors of Genesis, the
events of Genesis 2 could only have unfolded on the sixth day. This is the
Yahwist story of Eden and its aftermath.

The Yahwist story

The Yahwist story complements the narrative of Genesis 1. The setting
here is small-scale agrarian, rather than urban and institutional (Schmid
1984). This is not to suggest that social settings necessarily determine
theological meanings but to underline that certain theological affirmations
emerge with much greater fluidity in some historical settings than in others.
To highlight the rather subtle complementarity of Genesis 1 and 2, we
need to step back and to focus on the first two dimensions of the scriptural
witness to God's intentions for humans' relationships with nature: partnership with God and nature as creative intervention in the earth, and
partnership with God and nature as sensitive care for the earth.

Genesis 1 projects a normative vision of the human relationship with
nature in terms of intervention for the sake of building human community:
to fill the earth with justice and peace, as the human family expands to all
lands. René Dubos has described this as 'the Benedictine' in contrast with
'the Franciscan' which is more contemplative, predicated on respect and
filial love (Dubos 1970: 126).

The Yahwist creation story in Genesis 2 exemplifies what sensitive care
for the earth can mean.[7] As Theodore Hiebert (1996b: 28f.) has emphasized, for the Yahwist 'arable land is the primary datum in his theology of
divine blessing and curse'. In response to human sinfulness, the divine
curse diminishes the land's productivity. God's blessing of Abraham is
chiefly the gift of arable land. For the Yahwist, the three great harvest
festivals of Israel shape the cultic calendar, their primary activity being the
presentation to God of the first fruits of the land and the flock. So it comes
as no surprise to hear in the Yahwist's creation story that Adam is made
from the earth – *adamah*. This observation is frequently made, but Hiebert
(1996b: 28) wants to extend it: Adam is not just created from the earth; he
is created from the 'arable soil'. 'It is the claim that humanity's archetypal
agricultural vocation is implanted within humans by the very stuff out of
which they are made, the arable soil itself'. Humans, made from farmland,

are destined to farm it in life and to return to it in death (Gen 3.19, 23) (Hiebert 1996c: 28). After forming the human creature from the arable soil, Yahweh Himself 'planted a garden in Eden', where He placed the human creature. The strong implication seems to be that Yahweh Himself is involved in the care and the protection of this garden, setting the stage for the human creature to do likewise; 'wherever humans touch the soil, God's footmarks and fingerprints are already there' (Kahl 2001: 55).

For the Yahwist, the land is a character in its own right in this theological drama. The land has its own essential place in the greater scheme of things; it is not just a platform to support human life. The reason why the human is created is that there was no one to serve the land (Gen. 2.5). So we see Yahweh forming the human from the arable soil – a theme that is missing from the priestly account – and then taking the human and placing him in the Garden of Eden in order to serve (*abad*) the land and protect (*samar*) it. The familiar English translations of these words, 'to till and to keep', are misleading. *Abad* has the same Hebrew root as the word used by Isaiah to refer to 'the servant of the Lord'; *samar* has the same root as the word used in the Aaronic blessing, 'May the Lord bless you and keep you'. With only the received translation before them, general readers of this text might well understand it as a kind of capitalist manifesto: to develop the productivity of the land and keep the profits. They would have no reason to think that the words refer in fact to identifying and responding to needs of the land itself and protecting the land from abuse or destruction.

The image here is of an experienced family farmer communing with the land, gently transplanting a seedling, seeking a source of water for the plant, and then finding ways to protect the plant from predators. Or we see the same farmer pruning a fruit tree, so that it can blossom to its fullest, and then fertilizing it with carefully gathered manure. The sensitive care of nature that the Yahwist champions comes into view, complementing but also contrasting with the priestly writer's vision of creative intervention in nature.

In much the same manner, the Yahwist depicts the human's relationship to the animals in terms of tangible solidarity rather than intervention, certainly not any kind of domination. Both the human and the animals are made from the same arable soil (Gen. 2.7, 19), a motif that is missing from the priestly narrative. Further, there is no apparent theological reason, as there was for the priestly writers, to define sharply the differentiation between the two families of creatures, no 'image of God' construct. Instead, the Yahwist is apparently quite comfortable with the thought that God makes both the human and the animal a 'living soul' (*nephesh hayya*) (Gen. 2.7, 19).

The account of Adam naming the animals reflects the same Yahwist assumptions, although the text has often been interpreted otherwise (e.g. Ramsey 1988). Many nineteenth-century commentators regarded naming as an act of power – Adam's naming of the animals was to be interpreted in terms of dominance. In its context, the text actually tells a radically different story. The Creator is depicted as withdrawing from the scene, when He brings the animals to Adam (Gen. 2.19). But this can be read as a thoughtful withdrawal to encourage creaturely bonding, rather than a disinterested deistic act whose purpose would be to hand over power to the human. The naming itself can be understood as an act of affection on the part of the human, akin to the notion that Yahweh gives Israel, his beloved, a name (for example, Isa. 56.5) or when Adam gives the woman who is to be his personal partner, a name (Gen. 1.23). Comradeship on the part of Adam with the animals seems to be implied here in this naming scene, perhaps even with nuances of friendship and self-giving.[8]

Notwithstanding, the Yahwist leaves us in little doubt that the human is distinct from the animals and destined for personal fellowship with God and other humans in a way that animals are not. Adam finds no one with whom to commune among the animals; he only – and exuberantly – finds such a partner in the woman, who Yahweh fashioned not from the arable land directly, as Adam and the animals were, but from Adam's own flesh. The idea of intense personal intimacy is sealed by the notion that the two are to be 'one flesh' (Gen. 2.24). Likewise the idea of the humans' intimacy with Yahweh is sealed by the story of Yahweh conversing with them (for example, Gen. 2.16), as He does not do with the animals.

Moreover, while Adam and then Eve are placed in the Garden to serve it and to protect it, there is no sense that their daily work was in any sense burdensome for them. The Garden was a place of delights where they communed intimately with their Creator, who walked with them, where they found bountiful and beautiful blessings in the creatures all around them, and where they lived at peace in a kind of fellowship with all the animals.

What was intended by God went awry in the human domain. This, of course, is the story of what traditionally has been called 'the Fall', recorded in Genesis 3 (Fretheim 1994). This story is of critical importance for our explorations, first, because it is a grievous chapter in what we are thinking of as the Great Story of the Bible, but second and more particularly, because it portrays destructive ramifications for the humans' relationships with nature, that are only healed by the death and resurrection of the Redeemer, Jesus Christ.

What is the the meaning of the divine curse on nature? Specifically, what does it mean that the woman's pain in child-bearing is increased and she falls into a relationship of subservience to the man (Gen. 3.16); and 'the ground is cursed' because of the man, and he is consigned to a life of painful toil (Gen. 3.17–19)? The woman's pain means at least this much: the pattern of domination of one person by another has emerged. Likewise, the arable soil, once the congenial source of his life, now becomes a taskmaster for the man, a crushing burden. Brown's instructive summary of the meaning of the divine curse for the Yahwist is that

> The couple's disobedience has introduced not just the element of alienation, but also an ontology of bondage. Relationships between human beings and their environment are now based on power and control, as a matter of survival. As the man has been thrust into the harsh environment of the highlands of Canaan to eke out his existence, the woman is transported into the painful world of familial hierarchy and childbearing (W.P. Brown 1999: 150).

The divine curse is further intensified in the life of Cain, who killed his brother, Abel. Here the 'arable soil' itself takes on the role of juridical witness as it swallows up Abel's blood and then demands redress. In response, God drives Cain from the 'arable soil', to exile in 'a social domain devoid of refuge and rife with violence, a realm of a social anarchy infinitely remote from the harmonious order of the garden' (W.P. Brown 1999: 169).

It is important to note here that there is no doctrine anywhere in the Bible of any kind of 'cosmic fall'.[9] Sin comes into this primaeval world by Adam and Eve's 'grab for wisdom', which was 'an outright betrayal of trust' in God. Sin results in God's expulsion of the couple from their intended home of blessing to a world of alienation from God; from each other; and from the land, exemplified all the more dramatically by Cain's further expulsion into a world not just of alienation but of violence and chaos. The soil, in contrast, remains innocent; it remains the soil, outside the Garden. It does not change. The divine curse rests on it, because of the disobedience of humans and because of the fruits of violence that grow from that disobedience.[10] The priestly writers take much the same approach to cosmic goodness and order; sin, for them, is clearly a social, not a cosmic reality.[11] This allows us with the eyes of astronauts to contemplate this beautiful, fragile blue and green island of Planet Earth in the midst of the darkness of 'outer space': metaphorically, we humans are living in Eden, yet behaving as if we were living outside it. It is no fault of the Earth that the sinful violence of our lives, individually and collectively, sometimes pounds the earth and then rebounds back upon us with even greater destructive power – as in the case of global warming driven mainly by consumer greed. The fault is ours. And the rebound effect is a veritable divine curse upon our sin.

Sadly the rebounding curse typically affects some more than others, above all the poor. Thus the impoverished masses of Bangladesh will in all likelihood be among the first to experience the mass devastations of global warming. That is why *both* the priestly and the Yahwist micro-narratives must be heard, especially by the prosperous, so that the complementary priestly vision of a world full of justice and peace and the Yahwist vision of a world where humans serve and protect nature will all the more powerfully enlighten our world of poverty and violence and looming ecological chaos.

The promise is that, in Christ, with that deep human fault healed and the curse therefore removed, we humans can begin to live as if in Eden again. Both the priestly writers and the Yahwist give us glimpses of the kind of life that is possible in that very good world of God's own making, which is the life our faith in Christ makes possible for us today, even as we dwell in a world dominated by the powers of sin, violence, and gross injustice.

The Book of Job

The book of Job gives us glimpses of human life in the very good world of God's creation. Yet with this micro-narrative, we encounter an almost entirely different way of seeing things. Call this a world at the edges of Eden. Job's personal story of suffering and loss, a life of forced labour and no hope of liberation is well known. Job angrily takes his case to God and is berated by sages for doing so. But all this is but a prelude to the place to which the Jobean narrator wishes to take us.

The narrator leads us into the experience of wildness explicit in the creation theology of Psalm 104, but barely hinted at by the priestly writers and largely outside the imaginative purview of the Yahwist. This is the world of nature beyond the creative intervention and sensitive caring of human engagement and, for that reason, untouched by the divine curse. This is the world of nature as God sees it and partners with it in His own ways.

This is also a world where nature remains innocent, as it is for both the priestly writers and the Yahwist. But it is an innocence that astounds and overwhelms, and even, at times, repels – especially when, with the eyes of Job, we contemplate the pervasiveness of death in nature.[12] Here the creative intervention in nature and the sensitive care for nature in the priestly writers and the Yahwist respectively, give way to a theme of awe-struck contemplation of nature. Partnership with God in the midst of nature and with nature itself, means stepping back, letting nature be and seeing it apart from the interventions and the caring of humans. This kind of partnership is, *mutatis mutandis*, akin to the partnership of a loving parent with an adult child: when the parent 'lets go' and perhaps fearfully steps back from the life of their adult child in times of challenge or trial, it is always with rapt attention.

In recent years a number of scholars have opened up the book of Job in fresh ways, sometimes with compelling clarity. Brown is perhaps the most insightful of these interpreters. Although cosmology in the book of Job is all-encompassing, beginning as it does with the earth's foundation and the sea's fluidity, Brown helps us to see that the voice that we hear speaking mainly addresses what might be called the alien goodness of wildness. Brown's summary of that Jobean vision is:

> There, mostly wild animals, from lions to Leviathan, freely traverse the wasteland's expanse, sustained by Yahweh's gratuitous care and praise. The wilderness is where the wild things are, playing and feasting, giving birth and roaming, liberated from civilization and ever defiant of culture, even in death. Undomesticated and unbounded, these denizens of the margins revel in their heedless vitality and wanton abandonment, unashamed and unrepentant of their unbounded freedom, which rests on a providence of grace (W.P. Brown 1999: 394).

Experiencing a whirlwind of torment of his own, instructed unhelpfully by the counsel of sages, Job is driven into that world of wildness, and there he discovers who he is and who God is. The alien goodness of nature is expressed above all by the theophanous speech of God from the whirlwind to Job. This speech has a twofold pedagogical purpose: to broaden Job's moral horizon and to demonstrate Job's own innocence. It appears that there is something of Adam before the Fall in Job, given Job's announced innocence. God's speech never suggests any hint of punishment against Job. Be that as it may, Job encounters a world of innocence in nature, wild as it is. In His speech, God shows the care and precision with which the earth is established (38.4–7). 'God is the architect and the earth is God's temple, not unlike the way in which the cosmos is patterned in Gen. 1.2–2.3' (W.P. Brown 1999: 341). While the earth is thus a safe place, the sea is something else, in keeping with dominant apperceptions of the ancient Near East. It is depicted as flailing like an angry infant, needing restraint. God, however, is up to the task. He fastens the doors to keep the sea from overwhelming the earth (38.10–11). Indeed, God Himself appears as a midwife and caretaker of the sea, not unlike the role God assumed in Job's own birth (10.18). With the cosmos thus established, God leads Job into the wilderness.

This is indeed a wild place. In the Jobean discourse, we meet none of the images of cordial (albeit fecund) transformation of the wilderness that we find in prophets like Isaiah – the levelling of mountains or the raising up of the valleys (cf. Isa. 40.4). This is nature as it is in itself, apart from human culture, raw and bloody, yet teeming with life, populated with exotic creatures with their own domains. The animals appear two by two, lion and raven (38.39–41), mountain goat and deer (39.1–4), onager and auroch (39.5–12), ostrich and warhorse (39.13–25), and hawk and vulture (39.26–30). 'The animals highlighted in Yahweh's answer to Job were by and large viewed as inimical forces to be eliminated or controlled, an expression of cultural hegemony over nature within the symbolic world-view of the ancient Orient' (W.P. Brown 1999: 350). Kings, indeed, went forth to 'conquer' such animals in ritualized royal hunts, in an effort to demonstrate their own ontic triumph over the forces of chaos by their triumph over these wild creatures, thereby establishing themselves for all to see as lords of both nature and culture, of the entire cosmos.

Seen in this context, the Jobean discourse is radically counter-cultural. The great beasts of the wild are indeed great and glorious and noble: 'flagrantly at odds with their stereotypical portrayals attested elsewhere in ancient Near Eastern tradition' (W.P. Brown 1999: 360). The lion and raven are used as illustrations. They are beautiful creatures in their own right, fed by God: 'Can you hunt the prey for the lion, or satisfy the appetite of the young lions, when they crouch in their dens or lie in wait in their covert? Who provides for the raven its prey, when its young ones cry to God, and wander about for lack of food?' (38.39–41). The lion and the raven are here transformed to objects of divine compassion from objects of contempt in the established culture of the time (1999: 361).

The Jobean discourse penetrates deeply in its celebration of the wild. We see noble, wild creatures nurtured by God, but also celebrated, precisely because they resist human domestication. The wild ox, for example, was profoundly feared. It used its horns for goring. Job is taunted by God about the noble alienness of the wild ox: 'Can you tie it in the furrow with ropes, or will it harrow the valleys after you?' (39.10). The ostrich is likewise paraded: 'It deals cruelly with its young, as if they were not its own; though its labor should be in vain, yet it has no fear . . . When it spreads its plumes aloft, it laughs at the horse and its rider' (39.16–18). This creature 'connotes joy unbounded; its wild flapping and penetrating laughter exhibit the throws of ecstasy, confounding Job's preconceived notions about the somber ostrich'.[13] In all this, it is significant that the animals are not brought to Job for their naming, as they were to Adam in the Yahwistic creation story. Rather, 'he is catapulted into their domains. Instead of being presented with a parade of exotic animals, Job has come to see what they see, to prance with their hooves, to roam their expansive ranges, and to fly with their wings to scout out prey' (W.P. Brown 1999: 365). Finally, the most alien creatures of all, the behemoth and the leviathan, emerge before Job and are described in great and vivid detail. These are God's creatures par excellence, profoundly dwarfing Job, untouchable by any human reckoning.

Brown concludes: 'No longer is conquering and controlling nature part of the equation for discerning human dignity.' Human dignity is precisely to be one of God's many creatures, never forsaken by God, appearances to the contrary notwithstanding. Job is therefore able to claim new meaning for his life, *coram Deo*, as one among many creatures, all of whom are God's children, all of whom have been nurtured and set free by God (W.P. Brown

1999: 375f.). At the end, Job returns to his own, divinely created domain, the human community, with a self-understanding and new awareness of the needs of others, especially the needs of those whom his society typically scorned or rejected.

> While Job does not forsake the wilderness, neither does he take up permanent residence there ... Having become kin to these animals, Job retracts his patriarchy, both his honorable right to receive redress from the Lord of the whirlwind and his royal right to cultivate the non-arable landscape, and returns to his home and community, gratuitous of heart and humbled in spirit. Although restored with a new family, Job is no longer willing to see the despised and the disparaged as objects of contempt. Like the animals, they are his siblings in the wild; they have become partners in a kinship of altruism (W.P. Brown 1999: 395).

Having once been a stereotypical patriarch, then a social pariah, Job has now become 'a vulnerable partner' (W.P. Brown 1999: 380). One can even think here of Job as a kind of 'suffering servant' figure, paralleling or foreshadowing some of the proclamations of Isaiah. In Gerald Jantzen's words,

> The mystery of God's royalty is imaged in dust-and-ashes Job, suffering inexplicably, unshakably loyal to a God whom he does not yet understand, and invited finally to share with God in the celebration of a world where the accepted risk of freedom is the creative ground of cosmic fellowship. It is not far from this to the astounding portrayal of Yahweh's 'arm' in Isaiah 53 – the servant whose spoils of victory are won, not at the expense of enemy peoples, but on their behalf through unmerited suffering (Jantzen 1987: 53).

This is the legacy of the Jobean vision of awestruck contemplation of nature.

In today's context, the Jobean vision can be read not only in terms of God's purposes with the wilderness areas of this planet – the fecund mountain ranges, the majestic oceans with their fragile coral reefs, the great whales and grand polar caps, the Siberian tigers, wildebeests, humming birds, and snail darters – but also in terms of God's purposes with the 'great things' of the whole cosmos, purposes that we can only barely begin to imagine – purposes with the billions and billions of galaxies, the supernovas, the black holes, and the nearly infinite reaches of dark matter. Even more, it can be read in terms of the final fulfilment of all things.

Nature, too, as it groans in travail, has its divinely promised future, its final cosmic fullness and rest. Nature, including all the wild things and indeed all the galaxies and their mysterious cosmic milieu, writhes in anguished vitality, awaiting the day when, with human redemption finally completed, it will be able to reciprocate without bounds in its partnership with God, in the day when all things will be made new, when God will be all in all, when even the Leviathans of the cosmos will find perfect peace (cf. Rom. 8.19–22).

A biblical theology of partnership

We have, then, a complex and rich biblical theology of partnership between God and humans, between God and all creatures, and between humans and every other creature. That God has a partnership with us humans, and we with one another, is a thought that most students of the Bible take for granted. That God has a partnership with nature, and humans with nature likewise, are thoughts that may well need to be introduced to our churches and to at least a few of our preachers and teachers. These thoughts, as it were, do not come naturally (Santmire 1985: chs. 7, 8). But this is what the Bible shows us. God has a history with nature and values nature in itself, independent of his relationship with the human creature. God creates a grand and beautiful world of nature for His own purposes. It is harmonious. It is very good. But at its edges, it is also mysterious and even threatening to us.

But that is God's business and His infinite joy (cf. Ps. 104.31). God fashions us and invites us into partnership, not only with Him and with one another, but also with the beautiful and harmonious world of nature with its deep mysteries and its occasionally horrendous ambiguities. The partnership with nature to which God calls us is expressed in the three major ways described above: by the priestly writers, the Yahwist, and the narrator of Job.

There is indeed a time for everything; a time to build, a time to care, and a time to contemplate. The witness of the Scriptures is so complex and rich that it is all the more challenging for the faithful to take that witness to heart and for the Church to embody it in its public testimony and corporate practice. Thankfully, as Jesus Christ restores us to the place in God's history with His creation that God intended for us from the very beginning, Jesus also empowers us. He breathes on us His Spirit. And that Spirit will inspire us to discern which time is which: to read the signs of the times as well as to hear the voice of the Scriptures for these times. This is where the biblical theology of partnership challenges our churches and our preachers and teachers, as we seek to be God's faithful servants in this era of global ecological crisis, rampant poverty, and mounting cosmic alienation (Santmire 2000: ch. 1): inspired by the Spirit, so that we will then be able to foster creative intervention in nature, sensitive care for nature, and awestruck contemplation of nature whenever appropriate and in every complementary way, in partnership with God, with one another, and with nature. It is a daunting challenge. But good, biblically conversant guidebooks are available to help us to discern the signs of the times and to find ways to appropriate and enact, individually and corporately, the kind of exegetical findings that have emerged from this essay. (Among the best such guidebooks are Nash 1991; Bouma-Prediger 2001; Hessel and Rasmussen 2001).

Notes

1. A major problem is that the term 'stewardship' itself has such a widely established usage in the general culture and in the life of grassroots Christian congregations, especially in North America, that it resists normative theological definition. ExxonMobil, for example, regularly uses the language of stewardship in its promotional materials, which seek to explain how that corporation is wisely using and protecting the planet's resources. This kind of public relations material helps to define how the language of stewardship is heard in grassroots Christian communities and perhaps even in some scholarly circles. True, theologians and biblical scholars and preachers point to texts like 1 Cor. 4.1, 'stewards of the mysteries of God', and 1 Peter 4.10, 'Like good stewards of the manifold gifts of grace', with the intent to shape the construct by the theocentric theology of grace, but sociological forces – like the ExxonMobil materials – keep dragging the stewardship theme back to anthropocentric and secular default meanings in general cultural usage. The public discussion in church circles often comes down to whether church members should support 'wise use' of the environment for the sake of sustaining the current economic system and perhaps improving its functioning (the preference of the theological right) or 'wise use' of the environment for the sake of addressing the needs of the poor around the world (the preference of the theological left). In both cases, the assumptions are anthropocentric and managerial in character. The chief concern on both sides is how best to manipulate or exploit nature for the sake of human well-being.
2. In this sense, founders of the National Religious Partnership for the Environment were pointing the way to what I am identifying as a second wave of theological responses to the environmental crisis when they chose to think of themselves in the language of *partnership*. But they were very much being carried along by the first wave of responses, insofar as they opted to explain their purposes in the language of stewardship.

3. This approach to Scripture in terms of universal history takes the place of what biblical and systematic theologians in the twentieth century, such as G. Ernest Wright, Gerhard von Rad, Oscar Cullmann, Rudolf Bultmann (in existentialist terms) and Karl Barth used to refer to as the history of salvation (*Heilsgeschichte*) as the fundamental biblical interpretive category. Exegetically, the history of salvation approach set salvation over against creation in general and nature in particular. Nature was viewed as the stage for the history of salvation. That view still finds advocates.

4. I find the phenomenology of Teilhard de Chardin helpful. Teilhard held that all creatures have a 'within' as well as a 'without'. This is a subjectivity which becomes increasingly definitive of creatures' identities as they become more complex. Teilhard held that it is only in the human creature that the 'within' comprehends the 'without'. Accordingly, the divine personal communication with the human creature is, in terms I am using here, a *communion*, a personal *ad extra* relationship of God with a creature who is created according to the image of the personal God. This Teilhardian phenomenology meshes well with Martin Buber's phenomenology of I and Thou.

5. 'God is thus portrayed not as a king dealing with an issue at some distance, nor even as one who sends a subordinate to cope with the problem, nor as one who issues an edict designed to alleviate suffering. God sees the suffering from the inside; God does not look at it from the outside, as through a window. God is internally related to the suffering of the people. God enters fully into the hurtful situation and makes it his own. Yet, while God suffers with the people, God is not powerless to do anything about it; God moves in to deliver, working in and through leaders, even Pharaoh, and elements of the natural order' (Fretheim 1984: 128).

6. In a sense the Psalmist and Job collapse the two-stage thinking of the priestly writers into one stage. That is to say, humans are vegetarians before the Fall for the priestly writers; they are only permitted to eat meat after the covenant with Noah. The priestly writers, in that sense, allow that violence in nature is divinely ordained and also assume that after Noah, violence among the animals is the divinely permitted rule. For the Psalmist and Job – and for the Yahwist, according to Hiebert – the food chain, with some animals killing others, is given right from the start, with the goodness of the creation.

7. 'God creates not by brute force but with great care. The human task of subduing the earth does not pit humanity against nature, but reflects a working with nature through cultivation and occupation, through promoting and harnessing creation's integrity' (W.P. Brown 1999: 126). This is similar to what I am here calling 'creative intervention' as it takes shape in the priestly vision.

8. Note that Adam names only the living things, not all things. On the meaning of 'naming' more generally in the Old Testament, Fretheim (1984: 100) comments: 'Giving the name opens up the possibility of, indeed admits a desire for, a certain intimacy in relationship. A relationship without a name inevitably means some distance. Naming the name is necessary for closeness.'

9. 'History appears to have fallen out of the rhythm of cosmic order, whereas the cosmic order itself reflects the ongoing presence of creation. It remains loyal to its origin ... And it knows about it ... Ps. 19:1–6, 103:19–22, and 148:1–6 are examples of how the cosmic space proclaims daily and without end the glory of God, and itself as his handiwork' (Fretheim 1984: 39).

10. This is akin to the witness of some of the prophets, for example, Isaiah 1.2 and Jeremiah 8.7, where 'we find animals conforming to the will of God for their existence in ways not true of human beings' (Fretheim 1987: 29).

11. 'In the hands of the priestly cosmologist, chaos is banished from the created order with the mere stroke of a stylus, put to rest, as it were. Rather than reifying, much less deifying, chaos as a necessary evil of cosmogony, Priestly tradition embeds chaos within the matrix of life itself, particularly human life, not as a necessity but as an ever present possibility. Chaos is violence run amok. It denotes the human violation of prescribed boundaries that foster the stability of community, a social contravention based on fear of and contempt for Yahweh's created order, in short, a desecration of creation and community' (W.P. Brown 1999: 129).

12. I take it that death in the sense of mortality, along with its anguish and pain, belongs to nature as created good. Note that nature is created very good, but not perfect, according to Genesis 1. That perfection must await the coming new heavens and new earth, when death will be no more. On the other hand, in the wake of human sin, death does become 'the enemy' par excellence, in human history (Wilkinson 1976; Fretheim 1994: 52).

13. 'Over against ... attempts to order and secure oneself and one's own in a dangerous world, the ostrich that lays its eggs on the unguarded ground constitutes Yahweh's description of birdly wisdom, a wisdom that appears as folly to the mentality of the Enuma Elish, the Baal myths, and, indeed, aspects of the royal Jerusalem theology at least as popularly understood' (Jantzen 1987: 53).

Chapter 24

Priest of Creation

John Zizioulas

John Zizioulas is a Professor Emeritus at Salonica University, a Fellow of the Academy of Sciences in Athens, and Metropolitan Bishop of Pergamon in the Orthodox Patriarchate of Constantinople; he previously held the Chair of Systematic Theology at Glasgow University where he taught for 14 years; and he has taught at a number of other universities. He has also served as Secretary of the Faith and Order Division of the World Council of Churches. His article reproduced here is taken from three lectures given at King's College London in 1989 which were published under the title 'Preserving God's Creation' in King's Theological Review *12: 1–5, 41–45; 13: 1–5. They were reprinted in* Sourozh, *and then in* Theology in Green *(now* Eco-Theology*), nos 5: 15–26; 6: 16–25; and 7: 20–31. I am grateful to Professor Zizioulas for allowing me to use them again here.*

It is becoming increasingly evident that 'the ecological crisis' is perhaps the number one problem facing the worldwide human community. Unlike other problems it is a global problem concerning all human beings regardless of the part of the world or the social class to which they belong, and has to do not simply with the wellbeing but with the very being of humanity and perhaps of creation as a whole. It is, indeed, difficult to find any aspect of what we call 'evil' or 'sin' that would bear such an all-embracing and devastating power as the ecological evil. If we follow the present course of events, the prediction of the apocalyptic end of life on our planet at least is not a matter of prophecy but of sheer inevitability.

In view of this situation what does theology have to offer to humanity? Christian theology and the Church can hardly be excused on this matter, particularly since they have both been accused of having something to do with the roots of the ecological problem. If they have nothing constructive to say, they risk being irrelevant and unable to live up to their own claim to the Truth.

Solutions to the ecological problem in our western societies tend to be based on *ethics*. Whether enforced by state legislation or taught and instructed by churches, academic institutions, and so on, it is ethics that seems to contain the hopes of humankind. If only we could behave better! If only we could use less energy! If only we could agree to lower slightly our standards of living If, if ... But ethics, whether enforced or free,

273

presupposes other, more deeply existential motivations in order to function. People do not give up their standards of living because such a thing is 'rational' or 'moral'. By appealing to human reason we do not necessarily make people better, while moral rules, especially after their dissociation from religious beliefs, prove to be more meaningless and unpleasant to modern man.

The experience of two world wars and their destructive consequences came as a blow to the optimism of the eighteenth- and nineteenth-century prophets of the Enlightenment who thought that with the cultivation of reason and the spread of knowledge, the twentieth century would be the era of human paradise. Humanity does not always behave rationally and cannot be made to behave so either by force or by persuasion.

Fear of paganism and all that it implies can justify a great deal of the attitude that led to sheer rationalism. But Church and theology ought to have found better ways to respond to such a fear than the way of separating the rational from the mythical, the sacred from the secular. For they, after all, claim that faith in Christ implies a unity between the transcendent and the immanent, and an *anakephalaiosis*, a summing up of all in the Person of Christ. Appealing, therefore, only to the ethical solution, as so many Christians seem to do today, would only reinforce the reasons that led to the ecological crisis in the first place.

I shall try to show why I think we stand in need of a new culture in which the liturgical dimension would occupy the central place, and perhaps determine the ethical principle. If I were to give an overall title to this effort, it would be that of man as the Priest of Creation, with the notion of 'priesthood' freed from its pejorative connotations and seen as carrying with it the characteristic of 'offering', in the sense of opening up particular beings to a transcending relatedness with the 'other' – an idea more or less corresponding to that of *love* in its deepest sense. The underlying assumption is that there exists an interdependence between man and nature, and that the human being is not fulfilled until it becomes the *anakephalaiosis*. Thus, man and nature do not stand in opposition to each other, in antagonism, but in positive relatedness.

The nature of creation

Lynn White was quite categorical in attributing the ecological problem to the western intellectual tradition with its rationalistic view of man, and in assigning to theology and the Church an important role in this development (White 1967). Furthermore, it can hardly be disputed by anyone that history must have something to teach us about the roots of the present crisis and that religion, and Christianity in particular, being a dominant force in the shaping of our culture throughout the centuries – at least up to the Enlightenment – must have had some role to play in its background. It will be necessary, therefore, to go back to the earliest stages of Christian history and to try to identify the forces that may have led to the subsequent developments up to our time.

Classical Christianity took shape under the influence of two cultures, the Hebrew or Semitic and the Hellenic. Historians on the whole agree that the Hebrew mind tended to attach decisive importance to history (in particular of the elect people of God) and to see God as revealing himself mainly in and through his acts in history. Nature played a secondary role in this revelation, and very often such a role was totally denied to it under the influence of an obsession with the fear of paganism that threatened the specific identity of the people of Israel.

This preoccupation with history rather than nature resulted in the development of prophetism at the expense of cosmology in Hebrew culture. God was expected to reveal himself in future events that would supersede and at the same time give meaning to the previous ones, and the final event – the *eschaton* as it came to be called in the Greek-speaking Jewish communities of the New Testament period – would be all that mattered to the Hebrew mind.

Greek culture, on the other hand, attached little significance to history. In fact history was looked upon with distrust and suspicion as the realm of change, flux and disorder. Nature offered to the Greek the sense of security he needed, through the regular movement of the stars, the cyclical repetition of the seasons, and the beauty and harmony which the balanced and moderate climate of Attica offered. Cosmology was a major concern of the Greek philosophers who saw God present and operating in and through its laws of cyclical movement and natural reproduction. Aristotle could not avoid worshipping the stars, while Plato, the theologian *par excellence* of classical Greece, could reach no further than a creator God who would be an artist creating a universe in accordance with pre-existing matter, space and ideas.

Hebrew and Greek attitudes to nature imply two points relevant here:

(1) The Hebrew mind seems to lack cosmological interest, while the Greek lacks prophetism. If Christianity were to make use of both Hebrew and Greek cultures it ought somehow to arrive at what may be called 'cosmological prophecy'. We find this for the first time in the book of Revelation in which a Christian prophet following the best Hebrew tradition rises above history and views the fate not of Israel alone but of creation, i.e. of the natural world, from the angle of eschatology, of God's final act in history. Cosmological prophecy marks the beginning of a new approach to man's relationship with nature, which the Church would pick up and develop further later on.

(2) In contrast, the world for the Greek was a reality which contained in

itself sufficient energy to live for ever – hence the understanding of the universe as eternal – while for the Hebrew it was an event, a gift, to be constantly referred back to its Creator in order to live. The early Church therefore had to combine a worldview that believed in its rationality of nature, in its *logos* or *logoi* with one that regarded it as a *gift* and an *event*, dependent upon its Creator and Giver. Out of this combination early Christianity developed its 'Eucharistic cosmology', which, like cosmological prophecy, took a view of the world as *finite* and subject to its limitations in its nature, but capable of survival in and through being referred back to its Creator. The earliest eucharistic prayers of the Church, being composed in the best Hebrew liturgical tradition, involved a blessing over the fruits of the earth, but in such a way as to involve also an affirmation of faith in the survival of creation and nature. It is at this point that the responsibility of man as the one who refers the world back to the Creator arises and forms the basis of what we have called here his capacity to be the Priest of Creation.

Whereas in paganism faith in the survival of the world emerges from faith in the world's eternal and inevitable self-perpetuation, in Christian cosmology the world contains in itself no guarantee of survival except in so far as it is in communion with *what is not world by nature*, namely God as understood in the Bible. The crucial point, therefore, in the survival of the world lies in the act or the event of its communion with God as totally other than the world. Man's responsibility becomes in this way crucial for the survival of nature.

This was the situation in the first centuries of the Christian era, but the Church was led to a seriously modified consciousness with regard to the relationship between man and Nature.

1. Platonic and Gnostic dualism in the second and third centuries undermined the importance of the material world. Origen in particular, who was widely read by the monks of Egypt, influenced a considerable part of eastern monasticism. The Church had to face and dissociate itself from both the *Gnostic* interpretation of creation, and what we may call the *Platonic* or classical Greek philosophical view.

Gnosticism took the view that the world in which we live is so penetrated with evil, pain, suffering, and so on, that it could not have been created by God the Father whose goodness would never have allowed him to create such a world. Thus, in order to keep God the Father free from any responsibility for the evil that permeates the world, Gnosticism attributed creation to the lowest of the intermediaries between the ineffable Father and the world. This it called *Demiourgos* (literally 'Creator'), and made him responsible for creation. Gnosticism believed that creation is bad by definition and had no interest in saving it, particularly in its material form. Man was created (according to certain Gnostic myths) before the material world was made, and his present material state of existence constitutes his fall. Salvation is achieved through knowledge (*gnosis*), a secret knowledge of the truth taught by the teachers of the Gnostic schools. It is through an escape from time and space that man can be saved. Caring for this material world is the most absurd and in fact sinful thing there is. The sooner you get away from the material world the better.

The Church took a very negative attitude towards Gnosticism. Great theologians, in particular St Irenaeus, Bishop of Lyons at the end of the second century, wrote treatises against the Gnostics. The result of this anti-Gnostic polemic was to have a statement included in the early baptismal creeds of the local churches, which finally became part of the Creed ('I believe in God the Father, maker of heaven and earth'). Consequently the material world ('all things visible and invisible') is good, since it was made by God the Father himself. Evil is of course a problem. But this should not lead us to the conclusion that the world is bad by nature and not God's creation. The Church had to find other ways of explaining the presence of evil without attributing it either to God or to the material world.

2. In the West a dichotomy developed, regarding man as superior to nature, and as the centre of everything. St Augustine and Boethius, for example, defined consciousness and introspectiveness as the supreme aspects of human and indeed divine existence. The human being was singled out from nature as the sole being that mattered eternally – apart, of course, from the angels who, owing to their spiritual and immaterial existence, were of an even higher value than the human souls. In St Augustine's vision of the last things there is no place for nature; it consists of the survival of the eternal souls. The Church gradually lost consciousness of the importance of the material creation, evident in the way it treated the sacraments: instead of being a reference to the blessing of the material world with gratitude and dedication to the creator, the eucharist became a memorial service of the sacrifice of Christ and a means of grace for the nourishment of the *soul*. The dimension of the cosmos disappeared from sacramental theology in the West.

3. Scholasticism in the Middle Ages and the Reformation reinforced the idea that the *imago Dei* consists in human *reason*. The sacraments remained to a large extent irrelevant to the material world, and the gap between man and nature widened even further. The Enlightenment strengthened further the view that the thinking rational being is all that matters. Romanticism reinforced the dichotomy between the thinking, conscious subject and non-thinking, non-conscious nature, clearly giving superiority to the former and allowing the latter to be of value only in so far as it contained in itself the presence of the former. Pietism, mysticism and other religious and theological movements operated without any reference to nature, while Puritanism and mainstream Calvinism exploited the Genesis verse urging

man to 'multiply and to dominate the earth', thus giving rise to capitalism and eventually to technology and to our present-day Western civilization.

To this man-centred and reason-dominated worldview, our modern Western world produced two intellectual antibodies, both of them outside the area of theology and the Church.

1. The first was *Darwinism*, which relegated humans from their status as the only intelligent beings in creation. And by defending its reason-centred culture, the Church failed to respond constructively to the challenge of Darwinism and preferred either to enter into antagonistic battle with it, or to succumb to it by accepting its downward-looking anthropology.

2. The second came through *Einstein* and modern quantum physics. Here the effect was of a different and perhaps deeper kind: it signified the end of the dichotomy between *nature* or substance and *event*; space and time coincide with each other. Quantum mechanics indicated that observer and observed form an unbreakable unity, the one influencing the other. The universe in its remotest parts is present in every single part of it.

Creation and liturgy

1. All ancient liturgies, especially in the East, involve a sanctification of matter and of time. There is no introspective and self-conscious attitude towards the human soul; everything is aimed at the involvement of the praying individual in an event of communion with the other members of the worshipping community and with the material context. Apart from the bread and wine, themselves parts of the material world, the ancient liturgies involved all of man's senses: the eyes through the icons and the liturgical vestments; the ears through hymns and psalmody; the nose through the smell of incense, and so on. In addition, prayer for 'seasonable weather, for an abundance of the fruits of the earth', and so on, places the liturgy right in the middle of creation.

2. All ancient liturgies centred not so much on the consecration of the elements, even less on a psychological anamnesis of the cross of Christ, as on the *lifting up of the gifts of bread and wine to the Creator Father*, what is called in all the ancient Greek liturgies the *Anaphora* (literally, the 'lifting up'). Liturgiologists today tend to stress this forgotten detail, which can be of particular significance for a theology of creation. For it attaches at least equal centrality – if not more – to man's act as the priest of creation as it does to God's act of sending down the Holy Spirit to transform the offered gifts into the body and blood of Christ. This forgotten aspect was so central in the consciousness of the early Church as to lend itself for identifying and

naming the entire eucharist service: the service was called, not without significance, purely and simply *Anaphora* or *Eucharistia*, both terms having to do with man's priestly action as representative of creation.

3. All ancient eucharistic liturgies began their eucharistic prayer or canon with thanksgiving for creation in the first place, and only afterwards for redemption through Christ. The priestly aspect of the eucharist – and this is worth underlining – did not consist in the notion of sacrifice, as it came to be understood in the Middle Ages, but in that of offering back to God his own creation. It is a great pity, indeed, that sacrificial notions came to occupy the meaning of priesthood for centuries. It is a pity not so much because this gave rise to endless controversy between Roman Catholics and Protestants, preventing them from reaching a common mind on the eucharist, but mainly because it has meant the loss of the dimension of creation from the notion of priesthood. It is important, therefore, to recover and restore this dimension for the purpose of facing the ecological problem.

A second area in which the ancient church can help us recreate our theology today is that of *Asceticism*. Here things need some explanation, for asceticism has been normally associated with hostility or, in the best of cases, with contempt towards the material world. With the exception of certain trends in ancient monasticism that were under the direct influence of Origenism, asceticism was by no means associated with neglect or contempt of the material creation. In the earlier *Gerontikon* (collections of stories about monks and their sayings) we encounter stories of ascetics who wept over the death of birds or who lived in peace with wild animals.

Besides this respect for nature, it must be noted that it was in the circles of the desert theologians especially that the idea developed that the 'image of God' in man is to be found in his body as well as in his mind. Indeed, asceticism was accompanied in the early Church by the breaking of one's own selfish will so that the individual with his or her desires to dominate the external world and use it for their own satisfaction might learn not to make the individual the centre of creation. This is a spirit which is needed in order to teach modern man how to solve the ecological problem. But it can only be meaningful if, combined with the liturgical experience, it creates an *ethos* rather than a prescribed rule of behaviour. It is in this sense that it can be useful to theology, which in turn can be helpful in facing the problem of our time.

One could add to the list of elements borrowed from tradition many others, such as the use of space and matter in architecture, the use of colour and shape in painting, of sound in music, and so on. In general, it is a matter of *culture* which theology must aim at. Nostalgic voices of a return to Byzantine forms of art are abundant today among the Orthodox. We do not intend to offer any support to such voices: our modern world has passed through changes that make a return to the past impossible, and therefore undesirable. Theology today must use the past with respect, for it has indeed managed to overcome paganism without falling into gnosticism, and it must try to learn from that. But it must try to adjust it to the present by creatively combining it with whatever our contemporary world has achieved or is trying to achieve in all areas of thought – science, art, philosophy, and the rest.

How then does Christian theology view creation and man's place in it? If Christian theology has somehow led the world to its present crisis, by what ideas can it now help the world to deal with it?

Doctrines of creation

The Church did not react to Platonism in the same polemical way as it did in the case of Gnosticism. She seemed to like the idea that the world was attributed to a 'creator' (even called the Father-God by Plato) and some of her greatest theologians, such as Justin Martyr in the second century, came out strongly in favour of Plato on almost all counts, including creation. Yet it would be a mistake to regard the Church of the first centuries as having accepted the Platonic or the ancient Greek view of the world. For the differences were very deep. Let us consider them briefly.

It we look carefully into the issues that divided the Church from ancient Greek philosophy, the crucial difference lay in the question of whether the world has had a *beginning* or not. This question has such far-reaching implications, that it can be said to constitute one of the most important aspects of the relation between Christian theology and the ecological problem.

That the world should have a beginning in any absolute sense seemed utter nonsense and absurdity to all ancient Greek thinkers. Indeed, 'the view that the universe has had a beginning was denied by everybody in European antiquity outside of the Judaeo-Christian tradition' (Sorabji 1983: 194). For ancient Greeks the world was eternal. One may argue that Plato in his *Timaeus* (the famous work that deals with creation) accepts the idea of a beginning in creation, but the fact is that this beginning, as indeed all notions of beginning in ancient Greek thought, presupposed something from which the world (or anything for that matter) was created. In the case of the *Timaeus*, this presupposed 'something' which the creator used in order to create the world was *matter, ideas* and even *space (chora)*, all of which acted as conditions limiting the creator's freedom. Creation was therefore beginning-less, and the world, though particular beings in it could be said to have beginnings, has had no beginning when taken as a whole.

The Church and the Fathers felt that this view limited God's freedom in creating, since He had to work with pre-existent matter and other conditions, and it made God and the world eternally somehow 'coexistent'. They modified Platonism by rejecting the idea that matter was not created by God. This modification removed to a large extent the crudest and, to the Christian mind, most provocative aspects of Plato's doctrine of creation.

The idea that the world has an absolute beginning could only be expressed through the formula that the world was created 'out of nothing', *ex nihilo*. But what does 'nothing' mean in this case? Can there ever be something out of nothing? The ancient Greeks replied categorically in the negative. Christians had to find ways of making sense out of this statement. Thomas Aquinas in the Middle Ages gave a meaning to 'nothing' which amounted to more or less a source out of which creation came, while Karl Barth in our time, if studied carefully, seems to understand 'nothing' as a sort of void which God *rejected* in opting for Christ pre-eternally as the one in whom and through whom he created the world.

One could say that the nothingness out of which the world came into being affects every single being within the universe. Death is experienced as a return to nothingness, in spite of the fact that new entities may emerge out of old ones that have died. The message of Christian theology is that the world and every part of it exists under the threat of nothingness because it was created out of nothing in the absolute sense of the word. The world possesses no natural power in itself which would enable it to overcome this situation, for if it did it would be immortal and eternal by nature; it would have had no beginning in the absolute sense, as the ancient Greeks rightly observed. A Christian who wishes to have both his or her doctrine of *creatio ex nihilo* and a faith that the world possesses in its nature some kind of means for eternal survival is bound to be logically inconsistent. For what such a combination implies is that the eternal God created an eternal world, that is, another God by nature, which amounts to the total denial of the doctrine of creation out of nothing and at the same time to the abolition of the distinction between created and uncreated being – a distinction on which the entire Patristic tradition insisted.

But if we exclude the assumption that the world possesses in its nature some factor securing its survival and still want to secure this survival, we are left only with one solution: we must find a way of uniting the world with God, the only eternal and immortal being, other than by *natural* affinity. We must find a link between the two, which will secure the communication of life between them without abolishing the natural 'otherness' of God and creation. Can such a link be found? And can such a link make any sense?

Christian faith goes hand in hand with hope and love. If God created the world out of love – for what other motive can we attribute to him, knowing what he has done for the world? – there must be hope for the world's survival. But how? A simple, perhaps simplistic, answer to this might be that since God is almighty He can simply order things to happen so that the world may survive in spite of its contingency. In other words, miracle working could save the world. But Christian faith does not believe in *deus ex machina* solutions. We cannot, like the ancient Greeks, introduce divine intervention at the end of a tragedy in which everything moves with mathematical accuracy to destruction. In creating the world, God did not leave it without the means for survival. In creating it he provided for its survival as well. What does this mean?

Christian doctrine offers as a solution to this problem the place of man in creation. It is in the human being that we must seek the link between God and the world and it is precisely this that makes man responsible, the only being, in a sense, responsible for the fate of creation. What an awful responsibility and what a glorious mission at the same time!

What is man?

Darwinism was in many ways a healthy and helpful reaction against the view that human beings are superior to the rest of creation because of the intellect they possess. It implied that it is in and through man's reason that the world can be joined to God and thus survive. Even today the idea of man as the 'priest of creation' is understood by some in terms of rationality.

Rationality has contributed a great deal to producing the ecological problem. For rationality can be used in both directons: as a means of referring creation to the Creator in a doxological attitude, but also as an argument for turning creation towards man, which is the source of the ecological problem.

Before we discuss what the Christian tradition has to say on this matter let us have a quick look at what the non-theological world is saying. There seems to be something in man's creativity that we can hardly attribute to rationality, since in fact it is its opposite. Man, and only man, in creating his own world very often goes against the inherent rationality of nature, of the world given to him: he can even destroy the given world. In wishing to create his own world or simply to assert his own will, he is disturbed by the already existing world. All great artists have experienced this. Michelangelo used to exclaim: 'When shall I finish with this marble to start doing my own work?' Picasso is reported to have said similar things about forms, shapes and colours. Plato's creator, too, being conceived by the philosopher as an artist in the *Timaeus*, suffers because he has to create out of pre-existing matter and space, which impose on him their conditions. No creator can be content with the given. If he succumbs to it, he is frustrated and uneasy; if he does not succumb to it, he has to destroy it and create out of nothing. But as creating *ex nihilo* can only be the privilege of the uncreated Creator, all attempts by man to create his own world, whether in art, history or other areas of civilization, are bound to lead to frustration. There have, of course, been forms of human 'creativity' in history which have involved a copying of the world as it is. However, hardly anyone would call such things true art. Whatever involves a succumbing to the given, this man has in common with the animals. Whatever is *free* from it constitutes a sign of the presence of the human. This can lead as far as the *destruction* of the given by man. At this point the human phenomenon emerges even more clearly. For no animal would go against the inherent rationality of nature. Man can do this, and in so doing he shows that his specific characteristic is not rationality but something else: it is *freedom*.

What is freedom? We normally use this word in order to indicate the capacity to choose between two or more possibilities. We are free to read or not to read this book; we are free to vote for this or that party, and so on. But this is a relative, not an absolute freedom. It is limited by the possibilities given to us. And it is this givenness that constitutes the greatest provocation to freedom. Why choose between what is given to me and not be free to create my own possibilities? You can see how the question of freedom and that of the creation out of nothing are interdependent: if one creates out of nothing, one is presented by something given; if one creates out of nothing, one is free in the absolute sense of the word.

It is at this point that the idea of the *imago Dei* emerges. Christian anthropology since its earliest days has insisted that man was created 'in the image and likeness of God'. This expression appears for the first time in the Genesis account of the creation. Various meanings have been given to it, including the one mentioned earlier which identifies the image of God in man with his reason. Whatever the case may be, one thing is certain: if we speak of an 'image and likeness of God', we must refer inevitably to something which characterizes God in an exclusive way. If the 'imago Dei' consists in something to be found outside God, then it is not an image of God. We are talking, therefore, about a quality pertaining to God and not to creation.

This forces us to seek the *imago Dei* in freedom. Gregory of Nyssa in the fourth century had already defined this idea as the *autoexousion* (man's freedom to be master of himself). And if this freedom is taken in the way in which it is applied to God – which is what it ought to be if we are talking about an image of God – then we are talking about absolute freedom in the sense of not being confronted with anything given. But this would be absurd. For man is a creature, and cannot but be confronted with a given.

It is at this point that another category, pertaining exclusively to the definition of the human, emerges: it is *tragedy* – the impasse created by a freedom driving towards its fulfilment and being unable to reach it. The tragic applies only to the human condition; it is not applicable either to God or to the rest of creation. It is impossible to have a complete definition of man without reference to the tragic element. And this is related directly to the subject of freedom.

Dostoevsky put his finger on this crucial issue when he placed the following words in the mouth of Kirilov, a character in Dostoevsky's *The Possessed:*

> Every one who wants to attain complete freedom must be daring enough to kill himself . . . This is the final limit of freedom, that is all, there is nothing beyond it. Who dares to kill himself becomes God. Everyone can do this and thus cause God to cease to exist, and then nothing will exist at all.

If man wishes to be God, he has to cope with the givenness of his being. As long as he is faced with the fact that he is 'created', which means that his being is given to him, he cannot be said to be free in the absolute sense.

And yet man in so many ways manifests his desire to attain to such an absolute freedom; it is in fact precisely this that distinguishes him from the animals. Why did God give him such an unfulfillable drive? In fact many people would have wished for themselves – as well as for others – that they were not free in this absolute sense. The Christian Church herself has produced throughout the centuries devices by the help of which man, particularly the Christian, would be so tamed and so domesticated that he would give up all claims to absolute freedom, leaving such claims only to God. But certainly, if God gave such a drive to man, if he made him in his own image, he must have had a purpose. We suggest that this purpose has to do precisely with the survival of creation, with man's call to be the 'priest of creation'. But before we come to see how this could be envisaged let us see how in fact man has applied this drive and how creation has been affected by that.

Man's failure

Christian anthropology speaks of Adam as having been placed in Paradise with the order to exercise dominion over creation. That he was supposed to do this in and through his freedom is implied in the fact that he was presented with the opportunity to obey or disobey a certain commandment by God (not to eat from a certain tree). This commandment involved the invitation to exercise the freedom implied in the *imago Dei*, that is, to act as if man were God. This Adam did, and the result is well-known. We call it in theological language the *Fall* of man.

At this point questions arise: why did man fall by exercising what God himself had given him, namely freedom? Would it have been better for him and for creation had he not exercised, but rather sacrificed and abolished this absolute kind of freedom? Would it not perhaps have been better for all of us if Adam had been content with relative freedom as befits a creature? Did the tragedy of the Fall consist in exceeding the limits of human freedom?

The answer commonly given to these questions is a positive one: Yes, Adam exceeded the limits of his freedom, and this is why he fell. It is for this reason that Adam's Fall is commonly associated with Adam's *fault*, a fault understood therefore forensically: man should not exceed his limits if he wishes to avoid punishment.

Now, this sort of attitude to the Fall of man provokes two reactions. The first is that it reminds one immediately of ancient Greek thought. We all know the Greek word *hybris*, by which the ancient Greeks indicated that the human being 'falls', that is, sins and is punished every time he exceeds his limits and tries to be God. This of course does not prove in itself that the Christian view of things ought to be different from that of the ancient Greeks. The real difficulty comes with another question: if Adam ought not to exercise an absolute freedom, why did God give him the drive towards it?

We must seek ways of interpreting the Fall other than by placing the blame on Adam for having exceeded the limits of his freedom. We shall have, perhaps, to abandon forensic categories of guilt. It may be more logical, more consistent with our view of the *imago Dei*, if we followed not St Augustine but St Irenaeus in this respect.

St Irenaeus took a very 'philanthropic' and compassionate view of Adam's Fall. He thought of him as a child placed in Paradise in order to grow to adulthood by exercising his freedom. But he was deceived and did the wrong thing. What does this mean? It means that it was not a question of exceeding the limits of his freedom. It was rather a question of applying absolute freedom in the wrong way. Now this is very different from saying that Adam should have adjusted his drive for freedom to his creaturely limitations. For had he adjusted his freedom this way, he would have lost the drive to absolute freedom, whereas now he can still possess it, though he needs to re-adjust and re-orient his freedom.

The implications of what we are saying here are far-reaching. They include all sorts of consequences for legalistic views of sin, which, not by accident, go hand in hand with cries for relativized freedom. But we shall limit ourselves to the implications that have to do directly with our subject, which is the survival of creation through man. Man was given the drive to absolute freedom, the *imago Dei*, not just for himself but for creation. How are we to understand this?

Man, the hope of *all* creation

We have already noted that creation does not possess any natural means of survival; if left to itself, it would die. The only way to avoid this would be communion with the eternal God. This, however, would require a movement of *transcendence* beyond the boundaries of creation – in other words, freedom in the absolute sense. If creation were to attempt to achieve its survival only by obedience to God, in the sense of its realizing its own limitations and not attempting to transcend them, its survival would require a miracle or *Deus ex machina* intervention. This would result in a claim which would bear no logical relation to the rest of Christian doctrine, as is the case with all *Deus ex machina* solutions. If we accept the view that the world needs to transcend itself in order to survive (which is the logical consequence of accepting that the world has had a beginning), we need to find a way of achieving this transcendence. And this is what the *imago Dei* was given for.

The transcendence of the limits of creation requires on the part of creation a drive to absolute freedom. The fact that this drive was given to man made the whole of creation rejoice. In the words of St Paul, 'creation awaits with eager expectation the revelation of the glory of the children of God', i.e. of man (Rom. 8.19–21). Because man, unlike the angels (who are also regarded as endowed with freedom), forms an organic part of the material world, being the highest point in its evolution, he is able to carry with him the whole of creation to its transcendence. The fact that the human being is also an *animal*, far from being an insult to the human race, constitutes the *sine qua non* for his glorious mission in creation. If man gave up his claim to absolute freedom, the whole creation would automatically lose its hope for survival. And this allows us to say that it is better that Adam fell because of his claim to absolute freedom, than that he should give up this claim, for this would reduce him to an animal. In this understanding of the Fall it is not right to speak of a 'total depravity' of the image of God in man. Man in his negative attitude to God still possesses and exercises his claim to absolute freedom, albeit going against his own good and against that of creation. For only his claim to absolute freedom can lead to a revolt against God.

But how can man liberate creation from its boundaries and lead it to survival through his freedom?

Man's priesthood

We have already referred to man's tendency to create a new world. This tendency is what distinguishes him from the animals and in this sense is an essential expression of the image of God in him. If analysed deeply this means that man wishes to pass through his own hands everything that exists and 'make it his own'. This can result in one of the following possibilities:

1. 'Making it his own' means that man uses creation for his own benefit, in which case creation is not truly lifted to the level of the human, but

subjected to it. This is one of the ways in which man can understand God's commandment to have dominion over the earth; it could be called the *utilitarian* way. It has two implications: theologically speaking man would become the ultimate point of reference in existence, i.e. become God; and anthropologically speaking man would cut himself off from nature as if he did not belong to it himself. The utilitarian attitude to creation goes hand in hand with the view that man differs from the rest of creation through his capacity to *dissociate* himself from it; and also with the possibility of denying God and divinizing man. In other words, atheism and man's dissociation from nature are interconnected.

The 'ecological problem' is rooted deeply in this kind of anthropology. Understanding the world as man's possession, as a means of self-satisfaction and pleasure, is what taking the world into man's hands means. Science and technology would in this case signify the use of man's intellectual superiority for the purpose of discovering ways by which man can draw the biggest possible profit from creation for his own purposes. A theology based on the assumption that the essence of man lies in his intellect would be co-responsible with science and technology for the ecological problem.

2. Making the world *pass through* the hands of man, on the other hand, means something entirely different. Of course man would still use creation as a source from which to draw the basic elements necessary for his life, such as food, clothing, building materials, etc. But to all this he would give a dimension which we could call *personal*. What would this personal dimension involve?

    (a) A person cannot be understood in isolation, but only in relation to something or someone else. This could be both or either God and/or creation. It is not in juxtaposition to nature but in association with it that man would find his specific identity. Man would be other than nature not by separating himself from it but by relating himself to it.

    (b) The personal as distinct from the individual dimension would involve what we may call *hypostasization* and *catholicity*. These terms are technical in theology but they can be easily transferred to non-theological language. A *hypostasis* is an identity which embodies and expresses in itself the totality of a nature. For example, killing someone could be regarded as a crime against the totality of human nature, whereas in fact it is only a crime against a particular individual. It could be argued that murder would be more 'rationally' and perhaps more effectively prevented in a society which does not appeal to the rationality of the 'rights of the individual', but has a view of each human being as the hypostasis of the totality of human nature. (Trinitarian doctrine can be particularly

287

helpful in such a case). The personal approach makes every being unique and irreplaceable, whereas the individual approach makes it merely a statistic (cf. the casualties in a war). If man acts as a person rather than as an individual in treating creation, he not only lifts it up to the level of the human, but sees it as a totality, a catholicity of interrelated entities. Creation is thus able to fulfil the unity which is inherent in its very structure.

All this the human being can do without any reference to God. Certainly in the utilitarian approach, God is not needed except, in the best of cases, in order to be thanked for what he has given us to have dominion over and enjoy – a rationalistic or sentimental thanksgiving, like the one we find in so much of Christian tradition. But in the personal approach things cannot stop with man; they cry loud for a reference to God. Why?

The most serious consequence of Adam's Fall was death. This has normally – ever since St Augustine influenced our thinking – been taken to mean that death came to creation as a punishment for Adam's disobedience. This, however, implies a great deal of unacceptable things. It would mean that God Himself introduced this horrible evil which he then tried through his Son to remove. It would also seem to imply that before the arrival of man in creation, there was no death at all. This would contradict the entire theory of evolution, and would also make it cruel and absurd on the part of the creator to punish all creatures for what one of them did.

These difficulties lead us to the conclusion that the view of Irenaeus, Maximus, *et al.* is more reasonable on all counts, including the theory of evolution. Their view sees creation as being from the beginning in a state of mortality – owing to its having a beginning. Adam's Fall brought about death not as something new in creation, but as an inability to overcome its inherent mortality.

If we take Adam's Fall to consist in his making man the ultimate point of reference in creation, we can easily see why death entered creation through his Fall: it was simply because Adam himself was a creature and creation could not overcome its limitations, including that of mortality. This could have been avoided, had man acted as the Priest of Creation.

Personhood in man demands that he should at all times embody in himself the totality of creation. The drive towards freedom implies that in everything man does, the whole world should be involved. But if all that he seeks to embody in himself is to survive, to truly be, then it must also be related to what is not creation. Otherwise man's personhood will remain tragic and unfulfilled, and ultimately creation will be subject to its natural mortality.

I have deliberately avoided doctrinal language as much as I could. Perhaps it is time that I translate some of what I have said into such a language.

We Christians believe that what Adam failed to do Christ did. We regard Christ as the embodiment of the *anakephalaiosis* of all creation and, therefore as the Man *par excellence* and the Saviour of the whole world. We regard Him, because of this, as the true 'image of God' and we associate him with the final fate of the world. And consequently we believe that in spite of everything the world will survive, for the true Man is now a reality. In Christ he exists.

On the basis of this belief we form a community which in a symbolic way takes from this creation certain elements – bread and wine – which we offer to God with the solemn declaration 'Thine own do we offer Thee', thus recognizing that creation does not belong to us, but to God, who is its only 'owner'. By so doing we believe that creation is brought into relation with God and not only is it treated with the reverence which befits what belongs to God, but it is also liberated from its natural limitations and transformed into a bearer of life. We believe that in doing this 'in Christ', we act as priests of creation. When we receive these elements back after having referred them to God we believe that because of this reference to God we can take them back and consume them no longer as death but as life. In this way, creation acquires for us a sacredness which is not inherent in its nature but 'acquired' in and through our free exercise of our *imago Dei*, that is, our personhood. This distinguishes our attitude from all forms of paganism, and attaches to the human being an awesome responsibility for the survival of God's creation.

All this is a belief and a practice which cannot be imposed, and may easily be mistaken for sheer ritualism. Nevertheless we believe that it involves an *ethos* that the world needs badly in our time. Not an ethic, but an *ethos*. Not a programme, but an attitude and a mentality. Not a legislation, but a culture.

Conclusion

The ecological crisis is a crisis of culture. It is a crisis that has to do with the loss of the *sacrality* of nature in our culture. There are only two ways of overcoming this. One is *paganism*. The pagan regards the world as sacred because it is penetrated by divine presence; he therefore respects it to the point of worshipping it and does no damage to it. But he never worries about its fate because he believes in its eternity. He is also unaware of any need for transformation of nature or transcendence of its limitations; the world is good as it stands and possesses in its nature all that is necessary for its survival.

The other way is that which we have described as being the Christian way. The Christian regards the world as sacred because it stands in dialectical relationship with God; thus he respects it (without worshipping it, since it has no divine presence *in its nature*), but he regards the human being as the only possible link between God and creation, a link that can either bring nature in communion with God and thus sanctify it; or condemn it to the state of a 'thing', the meaning and purpose of which are exhausted with the satisfaction of man.

Paganism sees man as *part* of the world; the Christian way sees him as the crucial link between the world and God, as the only person in creation that can lead it to survival. It is the second one that attaches to man responsibility for the fate of creation. Unless we decide to return to paganism, this second way would appear to be the only way to respect again the sacrality of nature and grapple with the ecological crisis.

Chapter 25

To Render Praise: Humanity in God's World

Murray Rae

Murray Rae is Senior Lecturer in Theology at the University of Otago in Dunedin, New Zealand. Previously he taught at King's College London, where he took his PhD. This paper is one given at the St George's House consultation in 2000 (see p. xi).[1]

In summing up a consultation on 'A Christian Approach to the Environment', a number of themes were identified for further discussion. Houghton (1999) wrote:

> Some thought that the word 'stewardship' tended to be too anthropocentric and to create a misleading impression regarding our relationship to the environment – although most seemed to agree that it was the best word available. More specific questions relating to stewardship are: what human activity is carried out for the sake of Creation; what did God intend when he instructed humans to care for Creation; is it not possible to argue that the rest of Creation would be better off without humans? Further, how is the 'image of God' apparent in the relationship of humans to Creation? Can we formulate God's purposes for Creation which are at the basis of our stewardship?

In seeking to explore these themes, I make some preliminary remarks about the concept of stewardship; second, offer a necessarily brief outline of the Christian doctrine of Creation; third, elaborate in a little more detail the particular purposes of God in Creation and redemption; and finally, attempt to consider how we may conceive the relation between humankind and the created order of which we are a part. In this final section, I revisit the concept of stewardship and consider some of the other models for that relation which have sometimes been put forward.

The notion of stewardship

Although the concept of stewardship has been subjected to quite harsh criticism in some quarters (for example, Palmer 1992), recognition ought to be given to the worthy intentions which have sought expression through this concept. In the first place, we should have no hesitation in approving as a model for humanity's relation to the created order the preference for stewardship over exploitation and domination. While Lynn White's influential allegation (1967) that Christian theology must bear the primary responsibility for the modern ecological crisis has been shown to be superficial in several important respects, his claim is nevertheless salutary insofar as it draws attention to Christian collusion at least in the domination and exploitation of our environment. By way of correction, contemporary usage of the term stewardship clearly suggests that humanity has a duty of care for the environment and is not to regard it as a mere commodity at its disposal. Clare Palmer's contrary suggestion that because the idea of stewardship originated in a society based on slavery or serfdom it represents a despotic and autocratic form of government seems to neglect the fact that the meanings of words do evolve over time, both shedding old connotations in the process and taking on new ones. Palmer further argues that 'the political message encoded in stewardship is one of power and oppression; of server and served', but I would judge that in contemporary usage the ideas of care and responsibility are much more readily associated with the concept of stewardship than the negative associations proposed by Palmer.

A second positive aspect of the notion of stewardship is the implication contained within it that the environment is not to be cared for by human beings simply out of self-interest. Stewardship is usually exercised on behalf of some other party. When asked, therefore, on whose behalf we are to be regarded as stewards of the Creation, Christians may give the answer first, that it is on behalf of God who has entrusted Creation to our care, and second that it is on behalf of the Creation itself. Humanity has the capacity, frequently indulged, to destroy that which is the good Creation of God. The notion of stewardship on behalf of the Creation may hint therefore at a responsibility to let the Creation be itself (Gunton 1992, 1998). Conversely, and this is a criticism of the notion that has been made by some, stewardship may suggest far too paternalistic a relation to the environment as though it somehow needs our intervention and management in order to be what it is.[2]

The third party on whose behalf we may act as stewards is our neighbour, most especially our impoverished neighbours who have often been the victims of first world exploitation of the environment, but also our neighbours of future generations to whom we must hand on, still as blessing, that which has been provided as blessing in God's good Creation (Guroian 1994).

Notwithstanding, in both the emphasis upon the duty of care and the suggestion that such duty is held in trust from God for the sake of Creation itself and on behalf of others, stewardship serves as a suggestive if not completely unequivocal model. A more problematic use is a fondness for the secular serviceability of the term as a model for humanity's involvement in Creation, expressed in much Christian literature advocating the use of stewardship. The term has proved useful in broader discussions involving people outside of biblical faith. This perceived strength, however, may also be a weakness, for what the term especially lacks is any explicit theological reference. That may be useful in not immediately alienating those who share a concern for the environment but do not share the biblical faith, but that supposed advantage may very well tempt us, unwittingly perhaps, to portray the theological content of our concern, no longer as foundational but as an optional extra to the basic stewardship model. That, I think, is a very grave danger.

Let me explore this weakness a little further before seeking to redress it. I have mentioned that the notion of stewardship carries no explicit theological reference. In particular it gives no indication that, whatever responsibility humanity might carry for the Creation, it does not bear this responsibility alone, but rather as the covenant partner of God. The notion of stewardship, on its own, however, gives no indication that God is involved with his Creation. It offers no safeguards against the faults, too often evident in Christian tradition, of divorcing Creation from redemption, of conceiving God's relation to the world in merely deistic terms, and, what amounts to the same thing, of failing to conceive of the relation between God and the world in Trinitarian terms. It is possible in elaborating the model of stewardship that God may be referred to as the Creator and as the one who has set humanity in its place as steward of Creation, but the term itself does not make it apparent that God and not humanity is the one who sustains and preserves Creation and directs it toward its fulfilment. It will no doubt be the case that Christian advocates of the model of stewardship will want to thank God for what he has given us to be steward over and enjoy,[3] but what reason is there to believe that even this reference to God is any more than an optional extra for the pious?

None of these faults, to be sure, are *entailed* by the use of stewardship in the context of environmental ethics, but they are potential and perhaps even probable faults if our understanding of stewardship is allowed to float free of a proper theology of Creation and redemption. It is to the task of outlining the rudiments of such a theology then, that we now turn.

Creator and creation: God's relation to the world

In the account of God's Creation of the world provided to us in Genesis chapter 1, it is repeated several times that the Creation is good. It is important to note, however, that this is not humanity's verdict but God's. In the world as it now is, the goodness of Creation does not yield itself unambiguously to human inquiry. The notion of the goodness of Creation is, therefore, an article of faith. It is affirmed theologically as an act of trust in God's word. That this must be so is apparent when it is understood that goodness is a teleological concept; it is necessary to ask the question of anything good, 'good for what?' Some notion of purpose is essential to understanding in what this goodness consists. The biblical view is that Creation is good by virtue of its being suited to God's purpose. Creation is the suitable means for bringing about God's intention of a particular form of relationality between himself and the world, expressed in its divine–human dimension as covenant love. Creation is thus a project in progress under the blessing and promise of God. That it is God's project and not humanity's is thus the first theological principle that distinguishes a biblical conception of humanity's relation to the environment from other accounts of that relation.

This distinctiveness is of course of the utmost importance. It will both provide a very particular motivation for the care of Creation and dissuade us from the temptation to believe that everything depends on us. Ironically, it is just that belief that is often urged upon us by those who are otherwise adamant that anthropocentricity is the first evil to be overcome in the present ecological crisis. Christianly conceived, however, the ecological crisis does not call, in the first instance, for more concerted human activity, albeit that it is our activity by and large that has created the problem in the first place. The overcoming of the disorder which now mars the Creation is not simply a matter of human invention and determination. A patient and prayerful waiting upon the Lord is equally part of the human responsibility in relation to the created order – alongside various forms of activity. There is a theological reason for this warning against the human presumption that we can fix the problem. It is that stated by Christoph Schwöbel (1997: 150):

> ...the preservation or restoration of creation cannot be a human task if this creation is continuously created and preserved by God who brought it into being in the first place. Theologically, creation, including the sustaining and preserving of creation, is a divine and not a human work.

However we shall develop it therefore, a Christian ecological ethic will not presume that the preservation and sustenance of Creation is a feat of human prowess, but will rather understand human care for the environment as an obedient cooperation in the purposes and work of God. Conservation, meaning a cooperative service, is thus the proper human responsibility, while Creation and preservation are the undertakings of God alone.

Here we may bring to bear another principle of the biblical under-standing of Creation, namely that the divine act of Creation takes place *ex nihilo*. The Creation is brought into being by God 'out of nothing'. This means, in contrast with Greek conceptions of the matter, that the material world is neither eternal nor has any necessary existence. It is a contingent reality and, as John Zizioulas (1989: 3) has pointed out, 'it contains in itself no guarantee of survival'. It has, in other words, no capacity to sustain and preserve itself. Its survival, Zizioulas further explains, depends on its being in communion with what is not world by nature '... namely God.' That communion is precisely what has been disrupted by humanity's fateful decision, constantly renewed, to go its way in defiance of the Creator. The ecological crisis is but one of many symptoms of this breakdown in rela-tionality between Creation and Creator. Just as human beings are the primary cause of Creation's having been brought in this way into bondage to decay, so their redemption and reorientation to God are an essential pre-requisite of the whole Creation's being restored to its true relation to God and set again upon its divinely given trajectory of fulfilment. The ecological aspect of this redemption is that humanity is enabled again to enjoy and use the Creation in the ways that God has given it to be used and enjoyed.

While referring to the 'created order', we have also had cause to refer to the disorder which now mars the Creation. Here there *is* a self-evidence attending the claim that is being made, although its root cause is again not discernible apart from the disclosure of God's purpose. This is, of course, the reality of evil, and in particular in the present context, that evil which strips Creation of its blessedness, rendering it inhospitable to the living creatures of God's fashioning and scarring its beauty with the imprint of human greed and exploitation. Deriving from the fact that human beings are set in the Creation, not as already perfected beings but as enabled to grow up in love for the Creator and in harmony with his Creation, it is possible that we may not grow up in that loving and harmonious relation but turn away from it. The point has been ably expressed by Douglas Farrow (1995: 348) in regard to Irenaeus' contention that Adam as first created by God was imperfect:

> The 'imperfection' is this: the love for God which is the life of man cannot emerge *ex nihilo* in full bloom; it requires to grow with experience. But that in turn is what makes the fall, however unsur-prising, such a devastating affair. In the fall, man is 'turned back-wards.' He does not grow up in love of God as he is intended to. The course of his time, his so-called progress, is set in the wrong direction.

We have to do here with the thwarting of the purpose of Creation, with the erection of barriers in the way of the realization of God's purpose. What is commonly called the ecological crisis is a theological problem at root because it is the disruption of God's ordering of things. It betrays a lack of attention to, and wilful disregard of, the divinely bestowed goodness of Creation. The result, of course, is not good, but evil. That the problem is theological at root means also that there must be a theological basis for its overcoming. About this too, we shall have more to say in due course.

The second point following from the recognition that Creation is God's project is that we are concerned here not only with what is, but also with what will be. Creation is not simply something given to sustain humanity in the present. It is not to be regarded as a transient home for the temporarily embodied human soul, ultimately to be left behind when the disembodied soul returns or progresses to some spiritual realm after death. This is the Gnostic error which has been repeated all too frequently in the Christian tradition (May 1994; Gunton 1998: 47–50). The biblical view, in contrast, consistently held throughout Old and New Testaments, is that not merely the human soul but also the material Creation itself has a future. The vision of the book of Revelation of a new heaven and a new earth summarizes the hope articulated throughout the Bible that, far from treating the material world as a cast-off in the process of the human soul's redemption, God's purpose is to redeem the world as a whole, to establish within it and in relation to himself that harmonious co-existence of all that he has made. The prevalence in the Bible of images incorporating the non-human Creation is a striking feature of this eschatological vision. In Isaiah's vision of the peaceful kingdom, for example, it is proclaimed that 'the wolf shall live with the lamb, the leopard shall lie down with the kid, the calf and the lion and the fatling together and a little child shall lead them' (Isa. 11.6). What is the reason for this harmony? Isaiah explains in verse 9 that 'they will not hurt or destroy on all my holy mountain; for the earth will be full of the knowledge of the Lord as the waters cover the sea'. If we ask further how this knowledge of the Lord has arisen, then the answer is supplied in the opening verses of the chapter. 'A shoot shall come out from the stump of Jesse, and a branch shall grow out of his roots. The spirit of the Lord shall rest upon him, the spirit of wisdom and understanding ...' (vv. 1–2). Isaiah's vision of the kingdom of God is set within the context of his hope for the coming Messiah.

The remarkable consistency of this vision across the vast variety of the biblical witness is evident again when in the prologue to John's Gospel it is proclaimed that the Word became flesh. In the incarnate life of Jesus Christ, the Word of God and second person of the Trinity graces material reality with his own presence thus confirming its goodness, and showing it to be an object of God's loving purpose. In Jesus Christ, God's relation to the world takes the form of his becoming a subject within it. The one through whom and for whom all things were created and hold together (Col. 1.16–17) renews through his presence that which human sinfulness had subjected to disorder and decay and 'reconstitutes it in its relation to

God'. The pneumatological dimension is crucial here. Just as it is through the Spirit's agency that a body is shaped for Christ in Mary's womb, thus enabling, as Colin Gunton (1992: 52) has put it, 'this part of earth to be fully itself, to move to perfection rather than to dissolution', so too the Pentecostal pouring out of the Spirit upon the world completes Christ's action in redirecting the world to its destiny in communion with God. The Irenaean metaphor of the Son and Spirit active in Creation as the two hands of the Father is appropriate here as the divine creativity is redemptively exercised in redirecting the fallen Creation towards its intended fulfilment.

This makes a Christian concern for the environment an essentially christological and pneumatological matter. It is only in Christ and through the power of the Spirit that the created order is enabled to become what it is purposed to be. It confirms, too, the point already made that so far as humanity's being in the world is concerned we are reliant first of all not upon human prowess, nor even upon a more faithful stewardship, but rather upon the forgiving, redemptive and revitalizing love of God. It is only because God does not abandon his Creation that there is a hope and a goal for which we may strive with all our energy and ingenuity.

This soteriological theme alerted the writers of the New Testament to the fact that Christ and the Spirit are related to the created order, not merely as the agents of a rescue operation when it has suffered the disruptions of human sin, but as those through whom the Creation has come into being and is sustained in being. Thus the author of Colossians writes that 'in [Christ] all things in heaven and on earth were created' (Col. 1.16), the Letter to the Hebrews proclaims that Christ 'sustains all things by his powerful word' (Heb. 1.3), and in Pauline writings particularly the Spirit is identified as the one who 'gives life'. Or again, the Word that became flesh as announced in the opening proclamation of John's Gospel is the 'Logos', 'through whom everything was made and without whom nothing was made that was made' (John 1.3). Though not consciously Trinitarian in their articulation of the matter, the Old Testament writers too wrote that the Creation was brought into being by the utterance of God's Word, and is enlivened and sustained by God's having 'breathed' into it his own *ruach* or spirit. The Creation quite literally owes its life to God, not just in its beginnings but in every moment that it draws breath. Apart from God, therefore, the Creation dies.

The Christian celebrations of Christmas and Pentecost may thus be seen as critical to the doctrine of Creation, for in those feasts it is recognized that God who is other than the world is nevertheless not remote from it. The Creator has not left the world to its own devices but rather manifests his love for it, both by becoming a subject within it for the sake of its redemption, and by filling it anew with his Spirit so that it is preserved and renewed in its capacity to bring forth life. We should understand 'life' here to mean, not mere existence, but that fullness of creaturely being which is realized in communion with the Creator, and which yields as its consequence the restoration of a proper relationality amongst God's creatures. It is of the greatest significance that among the first gifts of Pentecost are speaking in other languages and *koinonia*, both of which abolish the barriers that have divided people from one another. It is the Spirit of God who is responsible for this reconciliation and is responsible too, as the Bible elsewhere affirms, for the renewal and revitalization of the non-human Creation as well. In Ezekiel 36, for example, God's promise to pour out his Spirit upon Israel is accompanied by a renewing of the abundance of the grain and the fruitfulness of the tree. Significantly for our present theme, Ezekiel insists that this renewing of the fruitfulness of the earth should provoke the people of Israel to remember and repent of their evil ways. The passage in Joel (2.21–29) recording God's promise that his Spirit shall be poured out on all flesh is another example of the close relation between the work of the Spirit and the regeneration of the earth. Significant too is God's further admonition that it is not for Israel's own sake that he will do these things. Is it then for the sake of the earth itself that God reverses these consequences of human sin? If this be the case then it is right to resist that form of anthropocentricity which regards the Creation as being nothing other than God's provision for humankind. Theologically we are bound to see that the non-human Creation is brought into being by God, not only as blessing for humankind but also for its own sake.

The passage from Colossians 1, already quoted, which looks to Christ as the one through whom all things were created and hold together, affirms too that 'through him God was pleased to reconcile to himself all things, whether on earth or in heaven, by making peace through the blood of his cross' (Col. 1.20). The redemption wrought here, the reconciliation won and the peace established, does not refer simply to human beings but to 'all things, whether on earth or in heaven'. The distinctiveness of a Christian approach to ecology is nowhere more apparent than in this affirmation. If there is hope for our world, if the promise of a harmonious co-existence of all created things is to be fulfilled, if a peace may be found which gives to each created being the capacity to be fully realized as that which it was purposed to be, then this will be because of Christ, and more particularly, according to Colossians, because of the blood of his cross. How shall this be understood?

Between Christmas and Pentecost, and mediating the transition, lies Holy Week and Easter. Here most especially God's love for his Creation is made apparent. Through the trials of Gethsemane and his death on the cross at Calvary, the son of God, through whom all things were created and hold together, exposes himself to the reality of this world's dissolution, drains once and for all time the cup of bitterness that has been filled to overflowing with human treachery to God and his Creation, and thus ensures that not even the worst that humanity does can thwart God's purpose of communion with all that he has made. If death means the same thing as a life alienated from God, as a life exhausted of the Spirit's breath, then in submitting himself to that death the Son of God, by virtue of the fact that it is he who suffers these things, robs humanity of its power to render the world Godless and saves us thus from the dread consequence of our sin. Or to put it in the language of John's prologue, the term 'Logos', used there of Christ, signifies the reason and order of the universe. He is the world's reason for being and the one who gives it its order and intelligibility. That this Logos, therefore, should confront on the cross humanity's tragic efforts to foist upon the world an order of its own making, and to wrest from God, by crucifying his Son, the prerogative to preserve the world and guide it to its fulfilment – that Christ should confront this evil at the greatest depths to which it may sink, establishes and confirms his sovereignty at the point of humanity's most profound rebellion against it. What this means is that the world is not finally in our hands but in God's. This does not mean that we have not been called to care for it. Indeed we have, and we remain capable of abusing that trust. We remain capable of making a hell out of that which has been created for good. But we are not capable of defeating the steadfastness of God's love for the world, for even where we do our worst, God is to be found there, in the crucified figure of Jesus, gathering together in himself all things in heaven and on earth, and preparing them for that day when all things will be completed and presented to the Father.

Here again the distinctiveness of the Christian understanding of things is readily apparent. The kingdom of God is not yet, and disbelief has evidence upon which it can base its claims. So the faith of which we have been speaking, as also the act of redemption itself, is yet an anticipation of things hoped for. The work of Christ does restore God's project, and does rescue the Creation from its unfaithful stewards, but it requires us still to wait for and work towards something that is not yet. Such hope and work is founded, however, upon that further aspect of Christ's encounter with evil not yet brought to bear, namely his resurrection and ascension. The victory over chaos is not accomplished solely through the presence within it of the Logos himself, but also through God's raising to new life the one whose faithfulness to the world had taken the form of suffering love within it. The chaotic human arraying of things is robbed not only of its Godlessness, but also, and concomitantly so, of its bondage to death. The resurrection of Christ, the first born of a new Creation, is the beginning and condition of the transformation towards fulfilment of the whole of God's Creation. And Christ's ascension to sit at the right hand of the Father in glory, confirms, once and for all, this Logos and not our own as the Word by which the world will be upheld.

The purpose of God

I have suggested that to pronounce the Creation good is to affirm its suitability for the bringing about of God's purpose, and that is to bring about a particular form of relationality between himself and the world. It is an insight of the Trinitarian understanding of God that the form of this relationality is not arbitrary but is connected to and is indeed constituted by God's own being as love – the mutual love of the three persons of the Trinity. The project of Creation, the giving and fulfilling of creaturely life, while not necessary to God, may be understood as an event of God's being for the other.[4] It is the expression and outworking of who he truly is as love, for the sake of that which he is not.

In this way the Creation is an event of God's glory. In creating that which is other than God and in giving to that 'other' the freedom to love him or not, God shows forth his glory as the one who is love, who loves, and who is worthy of love. It is proper to say therefore that the purpose of Creation is to show forth God's glory, but it must immediately be noted that this is not an exercise in self-gratification. The glory of God is shown forth in God's love for the other. There is no more profound statement of this truth than that which is developed through the course of John's Gospel: In the prologue, John writes, 'The word became flesh and dwelt among us, and we have seen his glory' (John 1.14), but as the Gospel unfolds it becomes ever more apparent that the glory is manifest most clearly in Jesus' 'hour' upon the cross. It is here, most especially, that Creation is rescued from its efforts to thwart God's purpose. And it is here, most especially, in giving himself utterly for the other, that the glory of the Lord is revealed.

Christoph Schwöbel (1997: 170) has correctly pointed out that if the glory of God is the proper end of Creation, then 'the utility of Creation for humans may never become the ultimate objective of human interaction with Creation'. The Creation of which they are a part is undoubtedly 'of use' to human beings just as in its complex interrelationality all the parts of Creation are mutually 'of use' to one another, but this mutual inter-dependence enabling the Creation to be what it is, is directed ultimately towards the glory of God; or to put it another way, it is directed towards the realization of that harmonious communion of love which is the reflection of God's own being. 'To the glory of God' then defines a direction for our human action, both in respect of interpersonal relations and in our relation to the environment, which is radically different from the satisfying of our own desires at the expense of the other.

This quest for communion may otherwise be described as the rendering of praise to our Maker. Participation in that form of relationality which we have been describing is an act of grateful agreement with the Creator's purpose. It is a response of love and an offering of the Creation back to the

Father in acknowledgment of the fact that it is precisely by virtue of its relation to God that the Creation can be called good. The Evangelical Declaration on the Care of Creation thus says that it is humanity's task to 'offer creation and civilisation back in praise to the Creator' (Berry 2000: 17–22). Here we find, not a particular environmental ethic or policy, but an ethos and a goal within which and towards which our habitation of the world must be directed.

Although this reconciliation with God is cosmic in its scope, embracing and drawing together the whole Creation, the Bible makes clear, as is reflected in the Declaration, that humanity is called upon to exercise a unique responsibility in the Creation's relatedness to the Creator. It is human beings who are created in God's image and human beings who are called by God to exercise dominion over all the creatures of the earth. It is through humanity too that the relation of love between Creator and creature may come to expression, for it is the human being whom God addresses in the garden and who is expected to be the responsive voice of the Creation to the loving call of God. There is thus an ecological responsibility bestowed upon humanity which is called to act on the Creation's behalf. In confirmation of this, though disastrously so, the first ecological crisis comes when humanity chooses to pursue an alternative plan – when it answers the call of the serpent and evades the call of God (Gen. 3.17). It is characteristic of the biblical world-view that this human disobedience should be seen as a crisis for the cosmos and not just a crisis for the human soul. It is humanity's exploitation of the fruit of the earth for its own ends and against the command of God that instigates the crisis and is the disruption of God's ordering of things. Thus instead of giving glory to God and offering the response of praise to its Maker, the whole Creation groans in travail (Rom. 8.22), awaiting the fulfilment of God's purposes. The question then becomes, does God abandon the Creation to its travail? Has God left the world to its inevitable decline? James B. Torrance (1996: 14) describes well the action of God in response to humanity's failure:

> The good news is that God comes to us in Jesus to stand in for us and bring to fulfilment his purposes of worship and communion. Jesus comes to be the priest of creation to do for us men and women, what we failed to do, to offer to the Father the worship and praise we failed to offer, to glorify God by the life of perfect love and obedience, to be the one true servant of the Lord. In him and through him we are renewed by the Spirit in the image of God and in the worship of God in a life of shared communion.

Here again, the overcoming of the cosmic catastrophe is seen to depend not first of all upon our own action, but rather upon the covenant faithfulness of God. Both communion with God and Creation's response of

301

praise are fulfilled and enabled by the action of God himself through his Son and Spirit. Hovering once more over the chaos, the Spirit redirects the world towards its unity and koinonia in Christ who offers it in turn to be perfected as the loved and loving Creation of God. Drawing from the letter to the Hebrews (Heb. 8.2), Torrance goes on to speak of Christ as our *leitourgos*, the leader of our worship and the one who fulfils on humanity's behalf the role that it was called to exercise on behalf of all Creation.

This does not mean, of course, that the communion is already fully restored or that paradise has been won. The evil of discord and exploitation continues to scar the world, inhibiting its praise and masking the glory of God. But in Christ and through the Spirit the world is set again on its path towards fulfilment, a fulfilment which is anticipated wherever human people meet in worship, and most particularly in the eucharist where the fruits of the earth are offered back to God, and the communion wrought through the death and resurrection of Christ is celebrated in thanksgiving and in hope (see Zizioulas 1989).

We have spoken several times of Creation's being brought to fulfilment, and we have defined this fulfilment in terms of the re-establishment of the communion for which the world was made and the harmonious co-existence of all its parts. It is important to make clear that this communion does not describe some static state but is rather a dynamic relationality in which the world is able to flourish and be fruitful according to God's good design. We learn from Genesis that the earth was appointed to 'bring forth fruit' (Gen. 1.11), and further, that the cultivating of this fruitfulness is a responsibility of humankind (Gen. 1.28, or more plainly, Gen. 2.15). This is not to say that the earth cannot bring forth fruit on its own account – the earth's fruitfulness precedes the Creation of humankind, both in the Genesis account and, obviously, in fact – but cultivation enables the earth's fruitfulness to be directed to a particular purpose, namely the realization of its character as blessing, for animals and for humankind, and that flourishing which is evident in a garden not overcome by weeds but cultivated so as to show forth the beauty of each plant according to its kind. This form of letting the Creation be itself does depend on human care and serves the end of rendering praise to God.[5] An important ecological principle therefore, that ought to guide Christian decision-making, is the safeguarding and enhancement of the earth's fruitfulness, especially as that is understood within the dual scope of God's blessing of Creation and the rendering of praise to the Creator.

There is one final point to be made concerning God's purpose for Creation before we turn to a fuller consideration of the particular role that humanity may play in the working out of that purpose. The disorder brought about by human sinfulness is of such devastating consequence that nothing short of a new Creation is required in order to overcome its tragedy. This means that the world in its fallenness stands in need of a miracle. Its regeneration cannot simply be a natural process and in so many respects the disruptions of sin have wrought a chaos that exceeds humanity's power to put right. What Christianity proclaims as a matter of faith and hope, however, is that the miracle has taken place. With the raising of Jesus from the dead, the Creation has in Jesus' own material humanity been restored to life with the Father. It is for this reason that our hope for the world consists in its being gathered together in him. That communion with the one through whom the world was made and in whom all things hold together is the only basis upon which all things will be made new (Rev. 21.5). In turning now to a consideration of humanity's relation to 'all things' in Creation, our task must be to seek clarification of the ways in which our being in the world and responsibility towards it may serve and celebrate that christocentric purpose.

Humanity and the created order

My primary concern here is whether the relation of humanity to the natural world is helpfully described in terms of the model of stewardship. Two other models, however, also present themselves for consideration: that of dominion and that of priesthood.

Dominion

It would seem useful to begin with the notion of dominion, first, because under the influence of Lynn White, especially, it is this notion that is commonly blamed for our current ecological problems, and second, because dominion is the model suggested in the first account of Creation in Genesis; we cannot simply ignore it or cast it aside. We begin, however, by acknowledging that dominion appears to be the least promising of our three models for the relation between humans and their environment. Many would follow Lynn White in suggesting that humanity's pretensions to dominion over the created order are precisely the problem. It is humanity's exploitation of the environment in service of its own ends, and its destructive carelessness of species and habitats which have led directly to what is now called a crisis in the ecology of Creation. Dominion is read as domination and the command to subdue the earth is taken as an instruction to do with it what we will. But these are simply errors, succumbed to undoubtedly by devout readers of the Bible as well as by those who urge the abandonment of these biblical imperatives. We have as much need to repent of our hermeneutical waywardness as of our ecological sins. For what is ignored most especially in this misreading of 'dominion' is the Christian conviction that dominion or 'Lordship', if we may translate the term, receives its proper definition in the one who is confessed as Lord by the writers of the New Testament. The eternal Logos and second person of the Trinity, through whom all things were created and hold together, exercises his Lordship by becoming a servant in the midst of Creation, by directing his ministry towards the reconciliation of all things to God, and by offering his own life as a sacrifice of atonement for all that mars God's good Creation. This is what dominion means when it is exercised by the Lord himself. In this light the suggestion that dominion means exploitation and domination couldn't be further from the truth. Christianly understood, humanity's own exercise of dominion is not the imposition of our own rule upon the Creation, but a faithful following after the order that is established by Christ. Servanthood, reconciliation and self-sacrifice become the distinctive marks of humanity's dominion exercised in faithfulness to God. Because of its truthful orientation to the pattern of God's own dominion of Creation in Christ, such human action, seen first in Christ himself, may be conceived in this way as an act of worship, a rendering of praise to God in respect for and glad agreement with God's own purposes.

Priesthood

A second model for conceiving humanity's responsibility toward the Creation is priesthood. Favoured especially by theologians of the Eastern Orthodox tradition, this model suggests that humanity is the priest of Creation. The key elements of this model are blessing and offering. Created in the image of God, humanity is called to continue God's blessing of Creation, preserving its beauty and nurturing its fruitfulness. It is called upon also, however, to act as the priest who offers back to God that which has come originally from God's hand. In expounding this notion, Vigen Guroian cites the example of Noah who at the conclusion of the flood story built an altar to the Lord and offered burnt offerings there of every clean animal and of every clean bird. God's response is to preserve the blessing of Creation and never again to destroy the living creatures as he had done in the flood. Noah's priesthood, his offering of the Creation back to God, became the reason why Creation itself was to be preserved (Guroian 1994: 162). It is tragically the case, however, that humanity has generally failed in this task of priesthood. Only in Christ is our human responsibility once and for all fulfilled. And this means that God's covenant commitment to the Creation is secure. He will never again turn against it nor abandon his purpose to bring it one day to the fulfilment of reconciled relationship with himself. What is in doubt, however, is how long humanity will continue to rebel against this purpose, and in its reckless disregard of the Creation's blessedness and order, will impel Creation towards the brink of chaos. The question remains open as regards how much havoc we will wreak before we consent to the offering of Creation back to God made on our behalf by Christ. In the meantime the Christian celebration of the eucharist, the taking of bread and wine, 'fruits of the earth and the work of human hands' as one liturgy puts it, is the memory of a priesthood fulfilled, the celebration of the continuing intercession of Christ on our behalf, and the anticipation of things hoped for in the feast of the kingdom of God. Again this liturgical action suggests a pattern for ecological responsibility. The things of earth are to be handled with thankfulness that they are indeed a blessing, and their use by humanity is to be directed towards the purpose of communion among the creatures of the earth and a worshipful reconciliation with God.[6]

Stewardship

We return finally to the concept of stewardship. How well does it serve as a model for humanity's ecological responsibilities? As we have seen, the key criticism levelled against it is that on its own the model of stewardship provides no check against a deistic conception of God's relation to the world. It offers a conception of humanity's task without explicit reference to the theological context of Christ's creative and redemptive agency. Christianly conceived that is a serious fault but it is certainly not the case that all Christians who employ the concept of stewardship do so in disregard of the christological themes we have been elucidating. The question to be addressed, therefore, is whether under the umbrella of these wider theological considerations, stewardship might serve a useful role. We have noted that writers such as Clare Palmer are sceptical about that. Palmer finds little explicit reference in the Bible to the idea that humanity is the steward of Creation. She also argues that the association of stewardship with the culture of slavery renders it particularly unsuitable for use in a Christian context. I have already suggested, however, that Palmer takes insufficient cognizance of the way words are subject to a degree of semantic transformation over time and I doubt very much that the oppressive associations she evinces for the term are those most readily called to mind today. Be that as it may, I propose that the recovery of an ethos of servanthood and obedience is precisely what we do need in order to make a better fist of our ecological responsibilities.

Let me develop this idea with reference again to John's Gospel, and in particular, to an occurrence of the idea of stewardship that is to be found within it. It is the occasion of the wedding feast in Cana, the first of John's 'signs', in which Jesus transforms water into wine. At face value, Jesus' intervention simply staves off a disastrous social embarrassment for the host; but it is clear that John intends the story to represent a great deal more than this. The narrative is rich with theological overtones. The transformation of water into wine takes place at a wedding feast. Marriage is, of course, a familiar biblical metaphor for the relation between God and his people. We are told too that the water was stored in jars for the Jewish rites of purification. The theme here evoked is atonement and reconciliation – the setting right of humanity's unfaithfulness to God. The question is, how does this miracle take place? Two factors are significant for our present theme.

It is a characteristic of John's Gospel that his whole narrative builds towards and foreshadows Jesus' hour of glory when he is lifted up on the cross. That is the decisive moment of transformation of the whole cosmos. In that lifting up, in sacrifice, in obedience and in offering of the world back to God, Jesus redirects Creation back towards its *telos* in communion with God, and inaugurates through his resurrection the promised new heaven and new earth.

The cosmic scope of this transformation is apparent too from the retrospective allusions in John's story of the wedding feast at Cana. This is not the first biblical story in which wine has dried up. In Isaiah 24 God's judgment upon human sin impacts strikingly upon the whole earth:

The earth dries up and withers,
the world languishes and withers,
the heavens languish together with the earth.
The earth lies polluted under its inhabitants;
for they have transgressed laws, violated the statutes,
broken the everlasting covenant ...

The wine dries up, the vine languishes ...

There is an outcry in the streets for lack of wine ...

Isa. 24.4–5, 7, 11

The turning of water into wine through the ministry of Jesus is the overcoming of this devastation. It is the beginnings of the reversal of the cosmic catastrophe wrought by human sin.[7] It is through Christ's agency and not our own that the new Creation is inaugurated and the new wine poured out in abundance. That is the first point. But the second point, bearing directly upon our concern with stewardship, is the role that is to be played by those around Jesus. When Mary, Jesus' mother, speaks to the servants at the wedding she instructs them to do whatever Jesus tells them. 'Now standing there were six stone water jars for the Jewish rites of purification, each holding twenty or thirty gallons. Jesus said to them, "Fill the jars with water". And they filled them up to the brim. He said to them, "Now draw some out, and take it to the chief steward". So they took it' (John 2.6–8). There is a heavy emphasis on obedience. The miracle takes place as the servants are obedient to the instruction of Jesus. Again this is a reversal; a contrast is being made with the disobedience that, according to Isaiah, had laid the earth to waste in the first place. The stewardship enacted here is not undertaken on behalf of an absent landlord, as may sometimes be suggested in the environmental debate. Rather it is carried out in strict obedience to the Lord who is himself present and whose presence in the midst of the created order is precisely that condition by which the new Creation may begin to emerge.

What will obedience to the Lord mean in practice? The story of the wedding in Cana gives us a clue also to this. We have noted already that the story is rich with theological overtones. As well as recalling the Isaiah passage it also looks forward even more emphatically to the crucifixion and resurrection of Jesus.

In the whole of John's Gospel there are seven miracle stories, or seven signs if we are to use John's own language. By calling them signs, John draws our attention, not just to the miracles themselves but more importantly to what these events point to. He tells us of these events, he says, so that the glory of the Lord might be revealed. Seven is, of course, the biblical number signifying perfection and completion. It is the number drawn from the Creation of the world in seven days. So the story John is unfolding here through the seven miracle stories, the seven acts of transformation, is nothing less than the re-Creation of the world. John's seven signs reveal how the new Creation is to take place and simultaneously disclose the glory of the Lord. The miracle stories, therefore, are not isolated incidents that can be left to stand on their own. Rather, John arranges them in a chiastic structure so that they can be understood in relationship to one another[8]:

(1) The wedding feast at Cana (2.1–12)
  (2) The restoration of the dying son (4.46–54)
    (3) The Sabbath healing at Bethesda (5.1–16)
      (4) The multiplication of loaves (6.1–71)
    (5) The Sabbath healing of the blind man (9.1–41)
  (6) The restoration of Lazarus to life (11.1–44)
(7) The great hour of Jesus: his mother, the cross and the issue of blood and water from Jesus' side (19:25–37)

So, for example, the central sign of the seven, the fourth sign, is the story of Jesus' feeding of the five thousand. Among other themes, we see here the divine overcoming of the inadequacy of human provision and the bountiful replenishment of the fruits of both land and sea. There is also a strong connection with Passover which in turn makes a link with signs one and seven. The six other signs are arranged symmetrically around this central miracle. Thus the third sign, which is the healing of a man on the Sabbath prompting outrage from the scribes and pharisees, is parallel with the fifth sign, the healing of a man born blind. The man's physical blindness draws attention to the spiritual and theological blindness of the religious authorities who would not tolerate a healing taking place on the Sabbath.

Similarly there is a parallelism between the second and the sixth signs. The second sign is the healing of the official's son who was close to death and the sixth sign is the raising of Lazarus. The emphasis here is on the victory of Jesus over death, culminating in the saying of Jesus, 'I am the resurrection and the life'.

But the pair of signs which is of especial interest is the first and the seventh sign. The first is the turning of water into wine and the seventh sign is the crucifixion and, I would add, the resurrection of Jesus. With the careful arrangement of his Gospel, John is suggesting that these two signs be understood together. But why is this? What is the point that John is making here? Let us listen again to the story of the wedding feast and note the parallelism which John constructs. John's story of the wedding begins, 'On the third day there was a wedding in Cana in Galilee.' On the third day. This is a familiar biblical symbol that something momentous is about to happen. On the third day Jesus was raised from the dead. The turning of water into wine foreshadows the day when, because of Jesus' resurrection, Isaiah's catastrophe, with all its destructive implications for the environment, is reversed. It foreshadows the day when all things are made new and the earth once more yields good wine which is made available to all. The earth may be renewed. The world may have wine. John is telling us how we may have it.

When the wine failed the mother of Jesus said to him, 'They have no wine' and Jesus said to her, 'Woman, what have you to do with me?' Only once more in the Gospel does Jesus address his mother. It is at the crucifixion, at the time of the seventh sign. When Jesus saw his mother and the disciple whom he loved standing near, he said to his mother, 'Woman, behold your son.' The words, 'Woman, what have you to do with me?' foreshadow a time when in his loneliest hour she is one of only a very few who will still have anything to do with him. Again John is confronting us with the challenge. Is it transformation and new Creation that we want? Then the question is asked of us too, what have we to do with Jesus?

In response to his mother's inquiry about the wine, Jesus continues, 'My hour has not yet come.' These too are words that foreshadow unmistakably Jesus' agony upon the cross. The parallels between the first and the seventh signs are carefully constructed. The transformation from water to wine is the transformation from old life to new, from a desolate and withered earth to the new Creation envisaged in all the biblical language about the kingdom of God. Water will be turned to wine, the earth will be transformed but John tells us that the transformation takes place because of one who so loved the world that he gave his life for it upon the cross. That is the place of transformation; that is the decisive act through which the earth will be renewed. And that renewal depends crucially, not on human prowess, but on our obedience to the one through whom all things were created and hold together.

As we read John's account of the seventh sign we are told that in order to prevent the bodies remaining on the cross on the Sabbath, the Jews said to Pilate that the legs of the crucified victims should be broken. This would hasten death and the bodies could then be taken away. 'So the soldiers came and broke the legs of the first, and of the other who had been crucified with him; but when they came to Jesus and saw that he was already dead, they did not break his legs. But one of the soldiers pierced his side with a spear and at once there came out blood and water' (John 19.32–34). Blood and water, water and wine. The world may be renewed – it may have new wine. Through his evocative linking of these two signs, John is making clear how that miracle takes place.

It may appear that I have wandered far from our concern for whether stewardship can be a model for our ecological responsibility. But the point of my recalling in such detail this story from John's Gospel is to emphasize the point that if we are to retain the notion of stewardship, then we must be clear that, Christianly understood, stewardship does not entail that humanity is the Lord and master of the world, even if only as deputy while the true Lord of all is absent. Rather it means obedience, to the Lord who is to be found in our midst. Like those who were obedient to his instruction at the turning of water into wine, those who would be stewards now are called upon to follow after the pattern of Jesus' life which led him to the cross. Self-sacrifice rather than selfish indulgence; the offering of all things to God, rather than the accumulation of things for one's own ends; the laying aside of power, rather than the will to dominate; the acceptance of lowliness and even suffering for the sake of the glory of God: none of these amount to rules for ecological action, but they do represent an ethos, or a Christian framework within which our stewardship of Creation may be exercised in faithfulness to the author of Creation himself. The biblical view is that such faithfulness has a direct impact upon the fruitfulness and blessing of the earth itself.

Concluding remarks

I have been attempting to outline here a theological framework within which our human responsibility for the environment may be understood. The primary point of my argument is simply that whatever language we are to use of that responsibility, be it dominion or priesthood or stewardship or anything else, that language will be filled with its proper content only in attentiveness to the action of God through Christ and the Holy Spirit. This means that, while not rejecting it, we cannot make do with a merely secular meaning of the term stewardship. To care for the earth and to accept some responsibility for its well-being are commendable virtues, but these hold no power on their own to reconcile the earth to God, and to offer it in praise to its Maker.

A second point I have been emphasizing is that the world is God's Creation, not ours, and it is God who is finally responsible for bringing the Creation to its fulfilment. We human beings are graciously embraced as partners in that purpose, and our environmental responsibilities, therefore, must be worked out in faithfulness to him.

And my third point is simply that we look forward in Christian hope, not simply to the maintenance of this present order, but to its transformation. Foreshadowed and inaugurated in the resurrection of Christ himself, God's purpose is to make all things new. It is of the utmost importance to recognize that the old is not discarded. It is to be transformed. That is the ultimate basis for nurturing and caring for this present Creation, for it is this world and not some other that is to take its place in the final out-working of God's purpose. It is as stewards of that hope that Christians have a basis also to be stewards of the Creation itself.

Notes

1. This paper has been published previously in Rae 2001.
2. Richard Bauckham is among those who have raised this objection. See Bauckham (2000: 103). Oliver O'Donovan (2000: 91), though not specifically critical of the idea of stewardship in this regard, also warns against imagining that we must manage nature 'as if it was a pathetic dependent upon our kind consideration and foresight'.
3. I owe the point to John Zizioulas. See Zizioulas 1989 (reprinted in pp. 273–290 of this volume). Clare Palmer (1992: 74) similarly claims that some 'perceptions of stewardship have difficulty in accommodating the idea of God's action or presence in the world. God is understood as an absentee landlord, who has put humanity in charge of his possessions'. (Palmer 1992 is reprinted in pp. 63–75 of this volume.) I agree with Palmer's basic point but would prefer not to imply (if Palmer does) that the idea of stewardship entails a deistic theology. It need not! My own view is simply that without careful qualification it fails to guard sufficiently against deism, and that it is this fault that must be addressed.
4. It is the error of various forms of process theology that God needs

Creation in order to realize his own being. Such an error is made conspicuous by the pantheism in which it inevitably results.

5. The point is made similarly by Colin Gunton who writes that humanity has a responsibility to 'be and to act in such a way as to enable the created order to be itself as a response of praise to its maker' (Gunton 1998: 12).

6. Richard Bauckham (1999: 101; 2000: 104) makes a valid point when he argues that we must beware in using the model of priesthood of intruding 'our inveterate sense of superiority exactly where the Bible will not allow it'. The Creation, he says, does not need us to offer praise on its behalf. It praises God just by being itself. He further points out that the Bible offers several instances of the Creation praising God without our aid. The point notwithstanding, a particular role for humanity, vested in it by virtue of its being made in the image of God, is also an idea drawn from the biblical source. The key here, I think, is that humanity alone among the creatures has the capacity to reciprocate the love God has for the Creation – to enter, in other words, into that distinctively personal form of relationality which is mutual love, and it is in this relation that the communion between Creation and Creator obtains its highest goal. Where humanity fails in this, Creation as a whole suffers; where humanity succeeds through the priesthood of Christ, the whole Creation is restored.

7. Raymond Brown (1966: 105) notes that 'one of the consistent OT figures for the joy of the final days is an abundance of wine (Amos 9.13–14; Hos. 14.7; Jer. 31.12)'.

8. This structural analysis of John's signs was drawn to my attention by Alister Rae, unpublished sermon, May 1986. It is supported by Joseph A. Grassi (1986) and before him by M. Girard (1980). Note that this selection of seven signs, including the crucifixion but omitting the walking on the water, is also agreed to by John Marsh (1968: 65f., 141–50) who notes, too, the strong parallelism between the first and the seventh signs.

Part VI
Conclusion

Chapter 26

Stewardship for the Twenty-first Century

John Houghton

Sir John Houghton, CBE, FRS is a former Professor of Atmospheric Physics at Oxford University who became Director-General of the UK Meteorological Office (1983–91). He served as Chairman of the Royal Commission on Environmental Pollution 1992–98 and chaired the Scientific Panel of the Inter-governmental Panel on Climate Change from its inception in 1988 until 2002. He currently chairs the John Ray Initiative (www.jri. org.uk). He has written this paper especially for this volume.

In March of this year, 2005, the United Nations published its Millennium Ecosystem Assessment (MA) (www.millenniumassessment.org) – a very thorough assessment by over 1,000 scientists from all over the world on the state of living systems on the planet and how they are impacted by human activities. It begins with a stark warning that 'human activity is putting such strain on the natural functions of Earth that the ability of the planet's ecosystems to sustain future generations can no longer be taken for granted'. It states clearly that we are using up 'natural capital' at an alarming rate and 'living on borrowed time'. For instance, we are using supplies of fresh groundwater faster than they can be recharged and many of the world's fish stocks are in a 'dire state'. Further, 'human activities have taken the planet to the edge of a massive wave of species extinctions, further threatening our own well-being'. The MA concludes with the simple message that 'pressures on ecosystems will increase globally in coming decades unless human attitudes and actions change'.

The MA is not the only such assessment to be published under UN auspices during the early years of this century. In 2001, the Intergovernmental Panel on Climate Change (IPCC) published its Third Assessment Report (www.ipcc.ch) on the influence of human activities, especially the burning of fossil fuels, on the Earth's climate. Over 2,000 of the world's scientists were involved in the IPCC's very thorough and comprehensive study; it described the increasingly strong evidence that human activities are already causing significant climate change. It further concluded that the rate of climate change during the twenty-first century is likely to be faster than at any time in the last 10,000 years and will cause large problems of adaptation both for humans and for ecosystems. The major impacts will result from significant sea-level rise and increases in the number and intensity of many extreme climate events, such as heat waves, floods and droughts. Since floods and droughts are the worst disasters the world experiences, the fact that there will be more of them and with greater intensity is very bad news, especially for some of the world's poorest countries that are the most vulnerable to such events.

There are other challenges the world faces too – such as the unrelenting growth in world population, poverty and lack of access to clean drinking water. These were addressed at the World Summit on Sustainable Development held in Johannesburg in 2002, where goals were agreed to halve, by the year 2015, the sixth of the world's people (about one billion people) whose income is less than $1 a day and who have no access to safe drinking water. Little progress is as yet being made with these goals. The rich–poor divide is growing wider and the flow of money in the world continues to be increasingly from the poor to the rich.

A common response to these problems is denial about their magnitude or impact. Much misinformation is purveyed by those with vested interests who argue either that the problems are overstated or that they lie too far in the future to be of concern now – they can be tackled and fixed when they become more apparent or closer to home. Even for communities of Christians who understand that a biblical calling to live distinctively in the world applies to all aspects of their lives, there is also often similar denial and disconnection.

The response from policy makers and political leaders has generally been to see the problems as subservient to an overriding requirement for economic growth or to assume that technology aided by the market will provide the necessary solutions. Fortunately, that is beginning to change. In a speech to the Energy and Environmental Ministerial Roundtable on 15 March 2005, Gordon Brown, UK's Chancellor of the Exchequer, said:

> Environmental issues – including climate change – have traditionally been placed in a category separate from the economy and from economic policy. But this is no longer tenable. Across a range of environmental issues – from soil erosion to the depletion of marine stocks, from water scarcity to air pollution – it is clear now not just that economic activity is their cause, but that these problems in themselves threaten future economic activity and growth.

The economy, technology and the market are tools – powerful ones but still only tools – and must not be allowed to be masters. Never has the concept of stewardship been more important, especially in our thinking about how to use the tools at our disposal.

What help can we as Christians offer to the world as it struggles to get to grips with the major problems of our time? We need a theology of stewardship to form a solid foundation for our thinking; that is what this book is particularly concerned with. We also need to repent for our abject failure as stewards in not caring for the Earth or for our neighbours who suffer from lack of basic resources or from environmental degradation. This is disobedience to God – in other words, it is sin (pp. 11, 135, 260, 288). But further, we need a praxis of stewardship that is more thoughtful, honest and holistic than much of what is on offer. I say holistic because environmental action is littered with examples of 'solutions' that have failed to address all the inter-connected issues – scientific, technological, economic, environmental, social and spiritual. And our overall attitude as we address such complex issues must be one of humility, recognizing that we do not have all the answers.

People often say to me that I am wasting my time giving lectures and writing about global warming and climate change. 'The world', they say, 'will never agree to take the necessary action'. I reply that I am optimistic for three reasons. First, I have experienced the commitment of the world scientific community in painstakingly and honestly working together to understand the problems and assessing what needs to be done. Secondly, I believe the necessary technology is available for achieving satisfactory solutions. My third reason is that I believe God is committed to his creation. He demonstrated this most eloquently by sending his son Jesus to be part of creation and by giving to us the responsibility of being good stewards of creation. What is more, I believe that we do not do this on our own but in partnership with him – a partnership that is presented so beautifully in the early chapters of Genesis where we read that God walked with Adam and Eve in the garden in the cool of the day.

In Luke chapter 12, Jesus tells a parable describing his going away and instructing his disciples to be faithful stewards during his absence. 'Unto whomsoever much is given, of him shall be much required' he told them (Lk. 12.48). But elsewhere he also promised to be with them all the time they work for him (Mt. 28.20). The challenge to us individually and corporately, and the opportunities open to us are unmistakeable. Stewardship is not an option; it is integral to God's order in creation. We need to live each day as if we will die tomorrow, but to look after the Earth as if we will be on it for ever.

Bibliography

Alexander, D. 2001 *Rebuilding the Matrix*. Oxford: Lion.

Altmann, A. 1968 ' "Homo Imago Dei" in Jewish and Christian Theology'. *Journal of Religion*, **48**: 235–59.

Alvarado, R.C. 1986–87 'Environmentalism and Christianity's Ethic of Dominion'. *Journal of Christian Reconstruction*, **11**: 201–15.

Anderson, B.W. (ed.) 1988 *Creation in the Old Testament*. Minneapolis, MN: Fortress Press.

Aquinas, T. 1964–76 *Summa theologiae*, trans. T. Gilby. London: Blackfriars.

Astley, N. (ed.) 2002 *Staying Alive*. Tarset: Bloodaxe.

Attfield, R. 1991 [1983] *The Ethics of Environmental Concern*. Athens, GA: University of Georgia Press, 2nd edn.

—— 1994 *Environmental Philosophy: Principles and Prospects*. Aldershot: Avebury.

—— 1999 *The Ethics of the Global Environment*. Edinburgh: Edinburgh University Press.

—— 2001 'Christianity', in *A Companion to Environmental Philosophy*, pp. 96–110. D. Jamieson (ed.). Oxford: Blackwell.

Bacon, F. 1857–74 *The Works of Francis Bacon*. J. Spedding, R.L. Ellis and D.Heath (eds). London: Longman.

Banner, M. *Christian Ethics and Contemporary Moral Problems*. 1999 Cambridge: Cambridge University Press.

Barber, R. 1993 *Bestiary*. Woodbridge: Boydell.

Barbour, I. (ed.) 1973 *Western Man and Environmental Ethics: Attitudes towards Nature and Technology*. Reading, MA: Addison-Wesley.

Barr, J. 1968 'The Image of God in the Book of Genesis: A Study of Terminology'. *Bulletin of the John Rylands Library*, **51**: 11–26.

—— 1972 'The Ecological Controversy and the Old Testament'. *Bulletin of the John Rylands Library*, **55**: 9–32.

Bauckham, R. 1986 'First Steps to a Theology of Nature'. *Evangelical Quarterly*, **58**: 229–31.

—— 1993 'Moltmann, Jürgen', in *Blackwell Encyclopaedia of Modern*

Christian Thought, pp. 385–88. A.E. McGrath (ed.). Oxford: Blackwell.

—— 1994 'Jesus and the Wild Animals (Mark 1:13): A Christological Image for an Ecological Age', in *Jesus of Nazareth: Lord and Christ. Essays on the Historical Jesus and New Testament Christology*, pp. 3–21. J.B. Green and M. Turner (eds.). Grand Rapids, MI: Eerdmans.

—— 1999 'The New Testament Teaching on the Environment. A Reply to Ernest Lucas'. *Transformation*, **16**: 99–101.

—— 2000 'Stewardship and Relationship', in *The Care of Creation*, pp. 99–106. R.J. Berry (ed.). Leicester: InterVarsity Press.

—— 2002a *God and the Crisis of Freedom*. Louisville, KY: Westminster John Knox Press.

—— 2002b 'Joining Creation's Praise of God'. *Ecotheology*, 7: 45–59.

Beckerman, W. 1995 *Small is Stupid: Blowing the Whistle on the Greens*. London: Duckworth.

Bell, D. 1992 *Wholly Animals. A Book of Beastly Tales*. Kalamazoo: Cistercian Publications.

Berry, R.J. 1989 'Ecology: Where Genes and Geography Meet'. *Journal of Animal Ecology*, **58**: 733–59.

—— 1993 *Environmental Dilemmas: Ethics and Decisions*. London: Chapman & Hall.

—— 2003 *God's Book of Works: The Nature and Theology of Nature*. London: T&T Clark.

—— 2004 'Did *Homo sapiens* become *Homo divinus?*' in *Listening to Creation Groaning*, pp. 172–86. L. Vischer (ed.). Geneva: John Knox International Reformed Center.

—— 2005 'The Lions Seek their Prey from God'. *Science & Christian Belief*, **17**: 41–56.

Berry, R.J. (ed.) 2000 *The Care of Creation*. Leicester: InterVarsity Press.

Berry, R.J., T.J. Crawford and G.M. Hewitt (eds.) 1992 *Genes in Ecology*. Oxford: Blackwell Scientific.

Berry, Thomas 1988 *The Dream of the Earth*. San Francisco, CA: Sierra Books.

Berry, Wendell 1978 *The Unsettling of America: Culture and Agriculture*. New York: Avon Books.

—— 1981 *The Gift of Good Land*. San Francisco, CA: North Point Press.

—— 1987 *Home Economics*. San Francisco, CA: North Point.

—— 1992 *Sex, Economy, Freedom and Community*. New York: Pantheon Books.

Birch, L.C. 1976 'Creation, Technology and Human Survival'. *Ecumenical Review* **28**: 66-79.

—— 1986 *Peace, Justice and the Integrity of Creation*. Potsdam Working Group Report; Geneva: WCC.

Birch, L.C. and J.C. Cobb 1981 *The Liberation of Life: From the Cell to the Community*. Cambridge: Cambridge University Press.

Black, J. 1970 *The Dominion of Man*. Edinburgh: Edinburgh University Press.

Blackwell, T. and J. Seabrook. 1993 *The Revolt against Change*. London: Vintage.

Blair, T. 1999 'Foreword', in *A Better Quality of Life*. Cm 4345. Norwich: The Stationery Office.

Bonaventure 978 *The Life of St Francis*, trans. C. Cousins. London: SPCK.

Bookchin, M. 1987 'Thinking Ecologically: A Dialectical Approach'. *Our Generation*, **18**.2: 3–40.

Botkin, D. 1990 *Discordant Harmonies: The New Ecology of the Twenty-first Century*. New York: Oxford University Press.

Boüard, M. de 1930 'Encyclopédes Médiévales. Sur la "Connaissance de la Nature et Dumonde" au Moyen Âge'. *Revues des Questions Historiques*, **16**, series 3: 258–304.

Bouma-Prediger, S. 1997 'Creation as the Home of God: The Doctrine of Creation in the Theology of Jürgen Moltmann'. *Calvin Theological Journal*, **32**: 72–90.

—— 2001 *For the Beauty of the Earth: A Christian Vision for Creation Care*. Grand Rapids, MI: Baker Academic.

Bouma-Prediger, S. and P. Bakken (eds.) 2000 *Evocations of Grace: Writings on Ecology, Theology and Ethics by Joseph Sittler*. Grand Rapids, MI: Eerdmans.

Bowler, P. 1984 *Evolution: The History of an Idea*. Berkeley, CA: University of California Press.

—— 2001 *Reconciling Science and Religion: The Debate in Early Twentieth Century Britain*. Chicago: Chicago University Press.

Boyer, P. 1992 *When Time Shall Be No More*. Cambridge, MA: Belknap Press.

Boyle, R. 1688 *A Disquisition about the Final Causes of Things*. London.

Brandon, S.G.F. 1963 *Creation Legends of the Ancient Near East*. London: Hodder & Stoughton.

Brandt, D. (ed.) 2002 *God's Stewards: The Role of Christians in Creation Care*. Monrovia, CA: World Vision.

Bratton, S.P. 1984 'Christian Ecotheology and the Old Testament'. *Environmental Ethics*, **6**: 195–209.

—— 1988 'The Original Desert Solitaire: Early Christian Monasticism and Wilderness'. *Environmental Ethics*, **10**: 31–53.

—— 1993 *Christianity, Wilderness and Wildlife: The Original Desert Solitaire*. Toronto: Associated University Presses.

—— 1994 'Ecofeminism and the Problem of Divine Immanence/Transcendence in Christian Environmental Ethics'. *Science and Christian Belief*, **6**: 21–40.

Brett, M.G. 2000 'Earthing the Human in Genesis 1-3', in *The Earth Story in Genesis,* pp. 73–86. N.C. Habel and S. Wurst (eds.). Cleveland, OH: Pilgrim.

Brooke, G.J. 1987 'Creation in the Biblical Tradition'. *Zygon,* **22**: 227–48.

Brooke, J.H. 2000 ' "Wise Men Nowadays Think Otherwise". John Ray, Natural Theology, and the Meanings of Anthropocentrism'. *Notes and Records of the Royal Society,* **54**: 199–213.

Brown, P.G. 1994 *Restoring the Public Trust: A Fresh Vision for Progressive Government in America.* Boston: Beacon Press.

—— 1998 'Towards an Economics of Stewardship: the Case of Climate'. *Ecological Economics,* **26**: 11–21.

Brown, R. 1966 *The Gospel According to John I-XII. The Anchor Bible Commentary.* New York: Doubleday.

Brown, W.P. 1999 *The Ethos of the Cosmos: The Genesis of Moral Imagination in the Bible.* Grand Rapids, MI: Eerdmans.

Brueggemann, W. 1977 *The Land.* Minneapolis, MN: Fortress Press.

—— 1982 *Genesis.* Atlanta, GA: John Knox.

Burke, C.E. 2001 'Globalization and Ecology', in *Earth Revealing, Earth Healing,* pp. 21–44. Denis Edwards (ed.). Collegeville, MN: Liturgical Press.

Butler, D.C. 1966 *Western Mysticism: The Teaching of Augustine, Gregory and Bernard on Contemplation and the Contemplative Life.* New York: Harper & Row, 2nd edn.

Callicott, J.B. 1992 'Can a Theory of Moral Sentiments Support a Genuinely Normative Environmental Ethic?' *Inquiry,* **35**: 183–98.

Calvin, J. 1847 *Genesis,* trans. J. King. Edinburgh: Banner of Truth Trust.

Caring for the Earth: A Strategy for Sustainable Living. 1991 Gland, Switzerland: International Union for the Conservation of Nature (IUCN).

Carmody, J. 1983 *Ecology and Religion: Towards a New Christian Theology of Nature.* New York: Paulist Press.

Carson, R. 1962 *Silent Spring.* Boston: Houghton Mifflin.

Chenu, M.-D. 1968 *Nature, Man and Society in the Twelfth Century.* Chicago: University of Chicago Press.

Christian Approach to the Environment, A 1999 Consultation meeting organized by the John Ray Initiative, February 1999. *Transformation,* **16**: 72–113 (reprinted by John Ray Initiative, 2005).

Christians and the Environment 1991 'A Report by the Board for Social Responsibility'. GS Misc. 367. London: General Synod Board for Social Responsibility.

Christiansen, D.S.J. and W. Grazer (eds.) 1996 *And God Saw That It Was Good: Catholic Theology and the Environment* Washington, DC: United States Catholic Conference.

Clifford, R.J. 1988 'Genesis 1-3: Permission to Exploit Nature?' *Bible Today.*

Coats, G. 1975 'God and Death: Power and Obedience in the Primeval History'. *Interpretation,* **29**: 227–39.

Cobb, J.B. 1992 *Is It Too Late?* Beverley Hills, CA: Bruce .

Cohen, J. 1989 *'Be Fertile and Increase. Fill the Earth and Master It'. The Ancient and Medieval Career of a Biblical Text.* Ithaca, NY: Cornell University Press.

Coleman, W. 1976 'Providence, Capitalism and Environmental Degradation: English Apologetics in an Age of Revolution'. *Journal of the History of Ideas,* **37**: 27–44.

Cole-Turner, R. 1993 *The New Genesis: Theology and the Genetic Revolution.* Louisville, KY: John Knox Press.

Cooke, A. 1977 *America.* New York: Knopf.

Copenhaver, B.P. and C.B. Schmidt 1992 *Renaissance Philosophy.* Oxford: Oxford University Press.

Costanza, R., R. d'Arge, R. de Groot, S. Farber, M. Grasso, B. Hannon, K. Limburg, S. Naeem, R.V. O'Neill, J. Paruelo, R.G. Raskin, P. Sutton and M. van den Belt 1997 'The Value of the World's Ecosystem Services and Natural Capital'. *Nature,* **387**: 253–60.

Cox, P. 1983 'The Physiologus: A Poiesis of Nature'. *Church History,* **52**: 433–43.

Cragg, K. 1965 *Counsels in Contemporary Islam.* Edinburgh: Edinburgh University Press.

Cranfield, C.E.B. 1974 'Some Observations on Romans 8: 19-21', in *Reconciliation and Hope,* pp. 224–30. R. Banks (ed.). Grand Rapids, MI: Eerdmans.

Curley, M. (trans.) 1979 *Physiologus.* Austin, TX: University of Texas Press.

Daly, H.E. and J.B. Cobb 1989 *For the Common Good.* Boston, MA: Beacon Press.

Dawkins, R. 1976 *The Selfish Gene.* Oxford: Oxford University Press.

Deane-Drummond, C. 2004 *The Ethics of Nature.* Oxford: Blackwell.

Delors, J. 1990 'Opening Address', in *Environmental Ethics: Man's Relationship with Nature, Interactions with Science,* pp. 19–28. P. Bourdeau, P.M. Fasella and A. Teller (eds.). Luxembourg: Commission of the European Communities.

Derham, W. 1715 *Astro-Theology or a Demonstration of the Being and Attributes of God from a Survey of the Heavens.* London.

Derr, T.S. 1995 'The Challenge of Biocentrism', in *Creation at Risk? Religion, Science and Environmentalism,* pp. 85–104. M. Cromartie (ed.). Grand Rapids, MI: Eerdmans.

Desai, N. 2001 Statement to the Second Committee. Introducing Item 98: Environment and Sustainable Development. http://www.johannesburgsummit.org

Descartes, R. 1950 *Discourse on Method*, trans. L.J. Lafleur. New York: Liberal Arts Press.

DeWitt, C.B. 1994 *Earth-Wise*. Grand Rapids, MI: CRC Publications.

—— 1995 'Ecology and Ethics: Relation of Religious Belief to Ecological Practice in the Biblical Tradition'. *Biodiversity & Conservation*, 4: 838–48.

—— 1998 *Caring for Creation: Responsible Stewardship of God's Handiwork*. Grand Rapids, MI: Baker Book House.

—— 2002 'Complementarities of Scientific Understanding of Nature with Religious Perspectives of Creation', in *Good in Nature and Humanity: Connecting Science, Religion and Spirituality*. S.R. Kellert and T. Farnham (eds.). Washington, DC: Island Press.

—— 2003 'Biogeographic and Trophic Restructuring of the Biosphere: The State of the Earth under Human Domination'. *Christian Scholar's Review*, 32: 347–64.

DeWitt, C.B. (ed.) 1991 *The Environment and the Christian: What Can We Learn from the New Testament?* Grand Rapids, MI: Baker Book House.

—— 1996 *The Just Stewardship of Land and Creation*. Grand Rapids, MI: Reformed Ecumenical Council.

DeWitt, C.B. and G.T. Prance (eds.) 1992 *Missionary Earthkeeping*. Macon, GA: Mercer University Press.

Diamond, J. 2005 *Collapse: How Societies Choose to Fail or Succeed*. New York: Penguin Books.

Dod, B. 1982 'Aristoteles latinus', in *The Cambridge History of Later Mediaeval Philosophy*, pp. 45–79. N. Kretzman, A. Kenny and J. Pinborg (eds.). Cambridge: Cambridge University Press.

Dubos, R. 1968 *So Human an Animal*. London: Rupert Hart-Davis.

—— 1970 *Reason Awake: Science for Man*. New York: Columbia University Press.

—— 1973 *A God Within*. London: Angus & Robertson.

—— 1974 'Franciscan Conservation and Benedictine Stewardship', in *Ecology and Religion as History*, pp. 114–36. D. Spring and E. Spring (eds.). New York: Harper & Row.

Duke of Edinburgh and M. Mann 1989 *Survival or Extinction: A Christian Attitude to the Environment*. Wilton: Michael Russell.

Duncan, J. 1972 *Milton's Earthly Paradise*. Minneapolis, MN: University of Minnesota Press.

Dutton, Y. 1992 'Natural Resources in Islam', in *Islam and Ecology*, pp. 51–67. F. Khalid and J. O'Brien (eds.). London: Cassell.

Echlin, E.P. 2004 *The Cosmic Circle: Jesus and Ecology*. Blackrock, Co. Dublin: Columba Press.

Eckberg, D. and J. Blocker 1989 'Varieties of Religious Involvement and

Environmental Concerns: Testing the Lynn White Thesis'. *Journal for the Scientific Study of Religion*, **28**: 509–17.

Eder, K. 1996 *The Social Construction of Nature.* London: Sage.

Edwards, D. 1999 *The God of Evolution.* Mahwah, NJ: Paulist Press.

Ehrenfeld, D. and P.J. Bentley 1985 'Judaism and the Practice of Stewardship'. *Judaism*, **34**: 301–11.

Farrington, B. 1964 *The Philosophy of Francis Bacon: An Essay on its Development from 1603 to 1609 with new Translations of Fundamental Texts.* Liverpool: Liverpool University Press.

Farrow, D. 1995 'St Irenaeus of Lyons: The Church and the World'. *Pro Ecclesia*, **4**: 333–55.

Fern, R.L. 2002 *God and Humanity: Envisioning an Ethics of Nature.* Cambridge: Cambridge University Press.

Finger, T. 1998 *Evangelicals, Eschatology and the Environment.* Wynnewood, PA: Evangelical Environmental Network.

Flavell, J. 1669 *Husbandry Spiritualized.* London.

Flexner, J.T. 1962 *The Pocket History of American Painting.* New York: Washington Square Press.

Foltz, B.V. 1984 'On Heidegger and the Interpretation of the Environmental Crisis'. *Environmental Ethics*, **6**: 323–38.

Fowler, R.B. 1995 *The Greening of Protestant Thought.* Chapel Hill, NC: University of North Carolina Press.

Fox, M. 1983 *Original Blessing.* Santa Fe, CA: Bear.

—— 1990 'Creation-centred Spirituality: A Vision for the 1990s'. Lecture given at St James's Church, Piccadilly, London, 14 July 1990.

Fraenkel, P. 1961 *Testimonia Patrum: The Function of the Patristic Argument in the Theology of Philip Melanchthon.* Geneva: Droz.

Franck, R. 1687 *A Philosophical Treatise.* London.

Frei, H. 1974 *The Eclipse of Biblical Narrative.* New Haven, CN: Yale University Press.

Fretheim, T. 1984 *The Suffering of God: An Old Testament Perspective.* Minneapolis, MN: Fortress Press.

—— 1987 'Nature's Praise of God in the Psalms'. *Ex Auditu*, **3**: 16–30.

—— 1991 *Exodus: Interpretation: A Bible Commentary for Teaching and Preaching.* Louisville, KY: John Knox Press.

—— 1992 'Creator, Creature, and Co-creation in Genesis 1-2', in *All Things New: Essays in Honor of Roy A. Harrisville*, pp. 11–20. A.J. Hultgren, D.H. Juel and J.D. Kingsbury (eds.). *Word and World Supplement Series*, no. 1. St Paul, MN: Lutheran Seminary.

—— 1994 'Is Genesis 3 a Fall Story?' *Word and Work*, **14**: 144–53.

Gardner, G. and B. Halwei 2000 'Underfed and Overfed: The Global Epidemic of Malnutrition'. *WorldWatch Paper*, **150**: 1–68.

Gilkey, L. 1959, 1965 *Maker of Heaven and Earth.* New York: Anchor Books.

Girard, M. 1980 'La composition structurelle des sept signes dans le quatrième Èvangile'. *Studies in Religion,* **9**: 315–24.

Glacken, C.J. 1967 *Traces on the Rhodian Shore. Nature and Culture in Western Thought from Ancient Times to the End of the Eighteenth Century.* Berkeley, CA: University of California Press.

Glanvill, J. 1665 *Scepsis Scientifica.* London.

—— 1668 *Plus Ultra.* London.

Gold, T. 1999 *The Deep Hot Biosphere.* New York: Springer-Verlag.

Golley, F.B. 1993 *A History of the Ecosystem Concept in Ecology: More than the Sum of the Parts.* New Haven, CT: Yale University Press.

Gould, S.J. 1985 *The Flamingo's Smile.* New York: Norton.

—— 1987 'Darwinism Defined. The Difference Between Fact and Theory'. *Discover,* **8**: 64–70.

—— 1990 'The Golden Rule – a Proper Scale for our Environmental Crisis'. *Natural History Magazine* (reprinted in *Eight Little Piggies,* pp. 41-51. London: Jonathan Cape, 1993).

—— 1995 *Rocks of Ages: Science and Religion in the Fullness of Life.* New York: Ballantine.

Gowan, D., and M. Schumaker 1980 *Subduing the Earth: An Exchange of Views.* Kingston, Ont: United Church of Canada.

Granberg-Michaelson, W. (ed.) 1987 *Tending the Garden: Essays on the Gospel and the Earth.* Grand Rapids, MI: Eerdmans.

Grant, G. 1959 *Philosophy in the Mass Age.* Toronto: Copp Clark Pitman.

Grassi, J.A. 1986 'The Role of Jesus' Mother in John's Gospel'. *Catholic Biblical Quarterly,* **48**: 67–80.

Green, J.B. 2002 'Scripture and Theology: Failed Experiments, Fresh Perspectives'. *Interpretation,* **56**.1: 5–20.

Gregorios, P. 1978 *The Human Presence: An Orthodox View of Nature.* Geneva: World Council of Churches.

Gunton, C. 1992 *Christ and Creation.* Carlisle: Paternoster.

—— 1998 *The Triune Creator: A Historical and Systematic Study.* Edinburgh: Edinburgh University Press.

Guroian, V. 1994 *Ethics After Christendom.* Grand Rapids, MI: Eerdmans.

Gustafson, J. 1981 *Ethics from a Theocentric Perspective,* 2 vols. Oxford: Basil Blackwell.

Habel, N.C. (ed.) 2000 *Readings from the Perspective of the Earth.* Cleveland, OH: Pilgrim.

Habgood, J. 2002 *The Concept of Nature.* London: Darton, Longman & Todd.

Hagen, J. 1992 *An Entangled Bank: The Origins of Ecosystem Ecology.* New Brunswick: Rutgers University Press.

Hall, D.J. 1976 *Lighten Our Darkness: Towards an Indigenous Theology of the Cross.* Philadelphia, PA: Westminster.

—— 1979 'Rethinking Christ: Theological Reflections on Shusaku Endo's Silence' *Interpretation* no.33.

—— 1982 *The Steward: A Biblical Symbol Come of Age*. New York: Friendship Press (Rev. edn 1990).

—— 1986 *Imaging God: Dominion as Stewardship*. Grand Rapids, MI: Eerdmans (reprinted 1996; new edition, Eugene, OR: Wipf & Stock, 2004).

—— 1993 *Professing the Faith: Christian Theology in a North American Context*. Minneapolis, MN: Fortress Press.

Hamilton, W.D. and T.M. Lenton 1998 'Spora and Gaia: How Microbes Fly with their Clouds'. *Ecology, Ethology & Evolution*, **10**: 1–16.

Hardin, G. 1968 'The Tragedy of the Commons', *Science* **162**: 1243–48.

Harrison, P. 1998a 'Reading the Passions: the Fall, the Passions and Dominion over Nature', in *The Soft Underbelly of Reason: The Passion in the Seventeenth Century*, pp. 49–78. S. Gaukrodger (ed.). London: Routledge.

—— 1998b *The Bible, Protestantism and the Rise of Natural Science*. Cambridge: Cambridge University Press.

—— 1999 'Subduing the Earth: Genesis 1, Early Modern Science, and the Exploitation of Nature'. *Journal of Religion*, **79**: 86–109.

—— 2001 'Curiosity, Forbidden Knowledge, and the Reform of Natural Philosophy in Early-Modern England'. *Isis*, **92**: 265–90.

—— 2002 'Original Sin and the Problem of Knowledge in Modern Europe'. *Journal of the History of Ideas*, **63**: 239–59.

—— 2004 'Design', in *Europe 1450-1789: Encyclopedia of the Modern World*, II, pp.132–34. J. Dewald (ed.). New York: Charles Scribner's Sons.

Hart, I. 1995 'The Teaching of Luther and Calvin about Ordinary Work'. *Evangelical Quarterly*, **67**: 35–52, 121–35.

Hartlieb, E. 1996 *Naturs als Schöpfung. Studien zum Verhältnis von Naturbegriff und Schöpfungsverständnis bei Günter Altner, Sigurd M. Daecke, Hermann Dembowski & Christian Link*. Frankfurt am Main: Peter Lang.

Hassan, M.K. [forthcoming] 'World-view Orientation and Ethics: A Muslim Perspective', in *Development, Ethics and Environment*. Kuala Lumpur: Institute for Policy Research.

Haught, J. 1993 *The Promise of Nature*. New York: Paulist.

—— 2000 *God After Darwin: A Theology of Evolution*. Boulder, CO: Westview Press.

—— 2005 'Darwin, Design and the Promise of Nature'. *Science & Christian Belief*, **17**: 5–20.

Hefner, P. 1993 *The Human Factor: Evolution, Culture, Religion*. Minneapolis, MN: Fortress Press.

Heidegger, M. 1971 *Poetry, Language, Thought*. New York: Harper & Row.

Heschel, A. 1951 *The Sabbath: Its Meaning for Modern Man.* New York: Farrar, Straus & Giroux.

—— 1965 *Who is Man?* Stanford, CA: Stanford University Press.

—— 1978 *The Earth is the Lord's: The Inner World of the Jew in Eastern Europe.* New York: Farrar, Straus & Giroux.

Hessel, D. and L. Rasmussen (eds.) 2001 *Earth Habitat: Eco-Justice and the Church's Response.* Minneapolis, MN: Fortress Press.

Hiebert, T. 1996a 'Re-imaging Nature: Shifts in Bible Interpretation'. *Interpretation,* **50.**1: 36–46.

—— 1996b *The Yahwist's Landscape: Nature and Religion in Early Israel.* New York: Oxford University Press.

—— 1996c 'Rethinking Traditional Approaches to Nature in the Bible', in *Theology for Earth Community: A Field Guide,* pp. 23–30. D. Hessell (ed.). Maryknoll, NY: Orbis Books.

Hiers, R.H. 1984 'Ecology, Biblical Theology and Methodology: Biblical Perspectives on the Environment'. *Zygon,* **19**: 43–59.

Hillel, D. 1991 *Out of the Earth: Civilization and the Life of the Soil.* Berkeley, CA: University of California Press.

Holdgate, M.W. 1979 *A Perspective of Environmental Pollution.* Cambridge: Cambridge University Press.

—— 1996 *From Care to Action: Making a Sustainable World.* London: International Union for the Conservation of Nature [IUCN]/ Earthscan.

'Hope for a Global Future: Towards Just and Sustainable Human Development' 1996 Louisville, KY: Office of the General Assembly of the Presbyterian Church.

Houghton, J.T. 1999 'Epilogue'. *Transformation,* **16**: 112–13.

—— 2004 *Global Warming: The Complete Briefing.* Cambridge: Cambridge University Press.

—— 2005 'Climate Change and Sustainable Energy'. The Prince Philip Lecture at the Royal Society of Arts, 11 May 2005. Exeter: The Met Office.

Hughes, G. 1672 *An Analytical Exposition of the First Book of Moses.* London.

Hume, C.W. 1967 'Animals', in *A Dictionary of Christian Ethics,* ed. J. Macquarrie. London: SCM Press).

Ingold, T. 1986 *The Appropriation of Nature: Essays on Human Ecology and Social Relations.* Manchester: Manchester University Press.

Integrity of Creation (see Niles 1992).

Jacobs, P. and D.A. Munro (eds.) 1987 *Conservation with Equity: Strategies for Sustainable Development.* Gland, Switzerland and Cambridge, UK: International Union for the Conservation of Nature (IUCN).

Jantz, H. 1951 *Goethe's Faust as a Renaissance Man: Parallels and Prototypes.* Princeton, NJ: Princeton University Press.

Jantzen, J.G. 1987 'Creation and the Human Predicament in Job'. *Ex Auditu* **3**.

Jeeves, M.A. and R.J. Berry 1998 *Science, Life & Christian Belief*. Leicester: Apollos.

Jegen, M. 1987 'The Church's Role in Healing the Earth', in *Tending the Garden*, pp. 93–113. W. Granberg-Michaelson (ed.). Grand Rapids, MI: Eerdmans.

John Paul II, Pope 1989 *Sollicitudo Rei Socialis* (reprinted in D.J. O'Brien and T.A. Shannon [eds.], *Catholic Social Thought: The Documentary Heritage*. Maryknoll, NY: Orbis Books).

—— 1995 *The Gospel of Life*. New York: Random House.

Johnen, B., L. Foster and M. Thomas 2000 'Stewardship in the Agro-chemical Industry'. *Pesticide Outlook*, **11**: 161–64.

Jones, J. 2003 *Jesus and the Earth*. London: SPCK.

Joseph, L.E. 1990 *Gaia: The Growth of an Idea*. Harmondsworth: Penguin Books.

Kahl, B. 2001 'Fratricide and Ecocide: Rereading Genesis 2–4', in *Earth Habitat: Eco-Justice and the Church's Response*. D. Hesse and L. Rasmussen (eds.). Minneapolis, MN: Fortress Press.

Kasser, T. 2002 *The High Price of Materialism*. Cambridge, MA: MIT Press.

Katz, E. 1993 'Judaism and the Ecological Crisis', in *Worldviews and Ecology: Religion, Philosophy and Environment*, pp. 55–70. M.E. Tucker and J.A. Grim (eds.). Lewis, PA: Bucknell University Press.

Kidner, D. 1967 *Genesis*. London: Tyndale.

King, C.M. 2002 *Habitats of Grace: Biology, Christianity and the Global Environmental Crisis*. Adelaide: Australian Theological Forum.

Knierim, R.P. 1995 'Cosmos and History in Israel's Theology', in *The Task of Old Testament Theology: Substance, Method and Cases*, pp. 171–224. Knierim, R.P. (ed.). Grand Rapids, MI: Eerdmans.

Kosso, P. 1992 *Reading the Book of Nature: An Introduction to the Philosophy of Science*. Cambridge: Cambridge University Press.

Kristeller, P.O. 1985 'The Active and Contemplative Life in Renaissance Humanism', in *Arbeit, Musse, Meditation: Betrachtungen zur Vita Activa und Vita Contemplativa* , pp. 133–52. B. Vickers (ed.). Zurich: Verlag der Fachvereine.

Küng, H. and K.-J. Kuschel (eds.) 1993 *A Global Ethic: The Declaration of the Parliament of the World's Religions*. London: SCM Press.

Kurniawan, A.N. 1998 'Product Stewardship of Paraquat in Indonesia'. *International Archive of Occupational & Environmental Health*, **68**: 516–18.

Leakey, R. and R. Lewin 1996 *The Sixth Extinction: Biodiversity and its Survival*. London: Weidenfeld & Nicolson.

Lee, K.N. 1993 *Compass and Gyroscope: Integrating Science and Politics for the Environment*. Washington, DC: Island Press.

Leiss, W. 1972 *The Domination of Nature*. New York: George Braziller.

Leopold, A. 1949 *A Sand County Almanac*. New York: Oxford University Press.

Lepenies, W. 1982 'Linnaeus's *Nemesis divina* and the Concept of Divine Retaliation'. *Isis*, **73**: 11–27.

Lerner, M. 1986 *Surplus Powerlessness: The Psychodynamics of Everyday Life*. Atlantic Highlands, NJ: Humanities Press International.

—— 1995 *Jewish Renewal: A Path to Healing and Transformation*. New York: Putnam.

Leslie, J. 1982 'The Anthropic Principle'. *American Philosophical Quarterly*, **19**: 141–51.

—— 1993 'Creation Stories, Religious and Atheistic'. *International Journal for Philosophy of Religion*, **34**: 67–77.

Lewis, C.S. 1946 *The Abolition of Man*. London: Geoffrey Bles.

Lewis, L.M. 1992 *The Promethean Politics of Milton, Blake and Shelley*. London: University of Missouri Press.

Lichatowich, J. 1999 *Salmon without Rivers: A History of the Pacific Salmon Crisis*. Washington, DC: Island Press.

Linzey, A. 1994 *Animal Theology*. London: SCM Press.

Little, D. 1970 *Religion, Order and Law: A Study in Pre-Revolutionary England*. Oxford: Blackwell.

Lohfink, N. 1994 'God the Creator and the Stability of Heaven and Earth: The Old Testament on the Connection between Creation and Salvation', in *Theology of the Pentateuch*, pp. 116–35. N. Lohfink (ed.). Edinburgh: T&T Clark.

Lomborg, B. 2001 *The Skeptical Environmentalist*. Cambridge: Cambridge University Press.

Lossky, V. 1957 *The Mystical Theology of the Eastern Church*. London: J. Clarke.

Lovelock, J.E. 1979 *Gaia: A New Look at Life on Earth*. Oxford: Oxford University Press.

—— 1988 *The Ages of Gaia: A Biography of our Living Earth*. Oxford: Oxford University Press.

—— 1991 *Gaia: The Practical Guide to Planetary Medicine*. London: Gaia Books.

McDaniel, J.B. 1989 *Of God and Pelicans: A Theology of Reverence for Life*. Louisville, KY: Westminster/John Knox Press.

McDonagh, S. 1990 *The Greening of the Church*. London: Geoffrey Chapman.

—— 1994 *Passion for the Earth: The Christian Passion to Promote Justice, Peace and the Integrity of Creation*. London: Geoffrey Chapman.

McEvoy, J. 1972–74 *Microcosm and Macrocosm in the Writings of St Bonaventure.* Rome: Padre di Editori Quaracci.

McFague, S. 1987 *Models of God: Theology for an Ecological, Nuclear Age.* Philadelphia, PA: Fortress Press.

—— 1993 *The Body of God: An Ecological Theology.* Minneapolis, MN: Augsburg/Fortress Press.

—— 1997 *Super, Natural Christians.* Philadelphia: Fortress Press.

McGrath, A. 1987 *The Intellectual Origins of the European Reformation.* Oxford: Blackwell.

—— 2002 *The Re-Enchantment of Nature: The Denial of Religion and the Ecological Crisis.* New York: Doubleday.

McKibben, B. 1994 *The Comforting Whirlwind: God, Job and the Scale of Creation.* Grand Rapids, MI: Eerdmans.

Manahan, R. 1991 'Christ as the Second Adam', in *The Environment and the Christian,* pp. 45–56. C.B. DeWitt (ed.). Grand Rapids, MI: Baker Book House.

Marchant, C. 1980 *The Death of Nature: Women, Ecology, and the Scientific Revolution.* San Francisco: Harper & Row.

Margulis, L. and D. Sagan 1986 *Microcosmos: Four Billion Years of Microbial Evolution.* New York: Simon & Schuster.

Marsh, J. 1968 *Saint John.* Harmondsworth: Penguin Books.

Marshall, P. 1992 *Nature's Web: Rethinking Our Place on Earth.* London: Simon & Schuster.

Marx, K. [1967] *Capital.* New York: International Press.

Mason, M.E. 1961 *Active Life and Contemplative Life: A Study of the Concepts from Plato to the Present.* Milwaukee: Marquette University Press.

Masonic Tract on Charity Matters 1979 Addlestone: Lewis Masonic.

Masri, Al-H. 1992 'Islam and Ecology', in *Islam and Ecology,* pp. 1–23. F. Khalid and J. O'Brien (eds.). London: Cassell.

May, G. 1994 *Creatio ex Nihilo: The Doctrine of 'Creation Out of Nothing' in Early Christian Thought.* Edinburgh: T&T Clark.

Merchant, C. 1992 *Radical Ecology: The Search for a Livable World.* New York: Routledge.

Midgley, M. 1988 'The Paradox of Humanism', in *James F. Gustafson's Theocentric Ethics: Interpretations and Meanings.* H.R. Beckley and C.M. Swezey (eds.). Macon: Mercer University Press.

—— 1992 *Science as Salvation: A Modern Myth and its Meaning.* London: Routledge.

Millennium Ecosystem Assessment 2005 *Living Beyond Our Means: Natural Assets and Human Well-being.* Nairobi: United Nations Environmental Programme.

Mills, W.J. 1982 'Metaphorical Vision: Changes in Western Attitudes to the Environment'. *Annals of the Association of American Geographers,* 72: 237–53.

Minns, D. 1991 'The Birds and Their Habitats', in *The Nature of Scotland.* M. Magnusson and G. White (eds). Edinburgh: Canongate.

Mitcham, C. and J. Grote (eds.) 1984 *Theology and Technology: Essays in Christian Analysis and Exegesis.* New York: University Press of America.

Moltmann, J. 1980 *Experiences of God.* London: SCM Press.

—— 1985a *God in Creation.* London: SCM Press.

—— 1985b *The Crucified God.* London: SCM Press.

—— 1990 *The Way of Jesus Christ.* London: SCM Press.

—— 1991 *The Way of Jesus Christ: Christology in Messianic Dimensions.* Minneapolis, MN: Fortress Press.

—— 1999 *God for a Secular Society.* London: SCM Press.

Moncrieff, L. 1970 'The Cultural Basis of our Environmental Crisis'. *Science,* 170: 508–12.

Moore, A. 1889 'The Christian Doctrine of God', in *Lux Mundi ,* pp. 57–109. C. Gore (ed.). London: John Murray.

Mowle, A. 1991 'The Managing of the Land', in *The Nature of Scotland.* M. Magnusson and G. White (eds). Edinburgh: Canongate.

Naess, A. 1972 'The Shallow and the Deep, Long-range Ecology Movement. A Summary'. *Inquiry,* 16: 95–100.

Napier, B.D. 1962 'On Creation-faith in the Old Testament'. *Interpretation,* 16: 21–42.

Nash, J.A. 1991 *Loving Nature: Ecological Integrity and Christian Responsibility.* Nashville, TN: Abingdon.

Nash, R. 1988 *The Rights of Nature.* Madison, WI: University of Wisconsin Press.

Nicholls, D. 1989 *Deity and Domination.* London: Routledge.

Nicholson, E.M. 1970 *The Environmental Revolution. London:* Hodder & Stoughton.

Niles, D.P. (ed.) 1992 *Between the Flood and the Rainbow: Interpreting the Conciliar Process of Mutual Commitment (Covenant) to Justice, Peace and the Integrity of Creation.* Geneva: WCC.

Noble, D.F. 1999 *The Religion of Technology: The Divinity of Man and the Spirit of Invention.* New York: Penguin Books.

Noreña, C. 1970 *Juan Luis Vives.* The Hague: Nijhoff.

North, R.D. 1995 *Life on a Modern Planet.* Manchester: Manchester University Press.

Northcott, M. 1996 *The Environment and Christian Ethics.* Cambridge: University Press.

—— 2003 '"Behold I have set the land before you" (Deut 1:8)', in *Reordering Nature: Theology, Society and the New Genetics,* pp. 85–106. C. Deane-Drummond and B. Szerszynski (eds.). London: T&T Clark.

—— 2004 *An Angel Directs the Storm: Apocalyptic Religion and American Empire.* London: I.B. Taurus.

Nourse, T. 1700 *Campania Foelix.* London.

O'Donovan, O.M.T. 2000 'Where were you...?' in *The Care of Creation*, pp. 90–93. R.J. Berry (ed.). Leicester: InterVarsity Press.

Odum, E. 1953 *Fundamentals of Ecology.* Philadelphia: Saunders.

Oeschlaeger, M. 1994 *Caring for Creation: An Ecumenical Approach to the Environmental Crisis.* New Haven, CN: Yale University Press.

Ophuls, W. 1977 *Politics of Scarcity.* New York: W.H. Freeman.

Origen 1957 *The Song of Songs, Commentaries and Homilies*, trans. R. P. Lawson. London: Longmans, Green.

Osborn, L. 1993 *Guardians of Creation.* Leicester: Apollos.

Our Common Future 1987 The Report of the World Commission on Environment & Development, chaired by Gro Harlem Brundtland. New York: Oxford University Press.

Our Responsibility for the Living Environment 1986 A Report of the General Synod Board for Social Responsibility. London: Church House Publishing.

Page, R. 1991 *The Incarnation of Freedom and Love.* London: SCM Press.

—— 1993 'The Fellowship of All Creation'. *Theology in Green* no.7: 4–12.

—— 1996 *God and the Web of Creation.* London: SCM Press.

Palmer, C. 1992 'Stewardship: A Case Study in Environmental Ethics', in *The Earth Beneath* pp. 67–86. I. Ball, M. Goodall, C. Palmer and J. Reader (eds.). London: SPCK.

Passmore, J. 1980 [1974] *Man's Responsibility for Nature.* London: Duckworth.

Paterson, J.L. 2003 'Conceptualizing Stewardship in Agriculture within the Christian Tradition'. *Environmental Ethics*, 25: 43–58.

Patten, C., T. Lovejoy, J. Browne, G. Brundtland, V. Shiva and the Prince of Wales 2000 *Respect for the Earth: Sustainable Development.* London: Profile Books.

Paul VI, Pope 1967 *Popularum progressio.* Encyclical letter; London: Catholic Truth Society.

Peacocke, A.R. 1975 'A Sacramental View of Nature', in *Man and Nature*, pp. 132–42. H. Montefiore (ed.). London: Collins.

—— 1979 *Creation and the World of Science.* Oxford: Oxford University Press.

Pearce, D., E.B. Barbier, A. Markandya, S. Barrett, R.K. Turner and T. Swanson 1991 *Blueprint 2: Greening the World Economy.* London: Earthscan.

Pearce, D., A. Markandya and E.B. Barbier 1989 *A Blueprint for a Green Economy.* London: Earthscan.

Pelikan, J. 1996 *The Reformation of the Bible, the Bible of the Reformation.* New Haven, CN: Yale University Press.

Peters, T. 1997 *Playing God? Genetic Determinism and Human Freedom.* New York: Routledge.

—— 2003 *Science, Theology and Ethics.* Burlington, VT: Ashgate.

Pettus, J. 1674 *Volatiles from the History of Adam and Eve.* London.

Pimm, S.L. 2001 *The World According to Pimm.* New York: McGraw-Hill.

Polkinghorne, J.C. (ed.) 2001 *The Work of Love: Creation as Kenosis.* London: SPCK.

Porter, R. 2000 *Enlightenment: Britain and the Creation of the Modern World.* London: Allen Lane.

Prance, G.T. 1996 *Earth Under Threat.* Glasgow: Wild Goose.

Preuss, H.D. 1995 *Old Testament Theology.* Louisville, KY: John Knox Press.

Primavesi, A. 1991 *From Apocalypse to Genesis: Ecology, Feminism and Christianity.* Tunbridge Wells: Burns & Oates.

Rachels, J. 1990 *Created from Animals: The Moral Implications of Darwinism.* Oxford: Oxford University Press.

Rae, M. 2001 'To Render Praise: Humanity in God's World', in *Science and Christianity. Festschrift in Honour of Harold Turner and John Morton.* pp. 177–201. L.R.B. Mann (ed.). Auckland: University of Auckland Centre of Continuing Education.

Ramsey, G.W. 1988 'Is Name-giving an Act of Domination in Genesis 2:23 and Elsewhere?' *Catholic Biblical Quarterly,* 50.1: 24–35.

Rasmussen, L. 1996 *Earth Community, Earth Ethics.* Maryknoll, NY: Orbis Books.

Raven, C.E. 1947 *English Naturalists from Neckam to Ray.* Cambridge: Cambridge University Press.

—— 1953 *Natural Religion and Christian Theology: Science and Religion.* Cambridge: Cambridge University Press.

Redefining Prosperity 2003 *Redefining Prosperity: Resource Prosperity, Economic Growth and Sustainable Development.* London: Sustainable Development Commission.

Reichenbach, B. 2003 'Genesis 1 as a Theological-Political Narrative of Kingdom Establishment'. *Bulletin for Biblical Research,* 13: 47–69.

Reichenbach, B. and V.E. Anderson 1995 *On Behalf of God: A Christian Ethic for Biology.* Grand Rapids, MI: Eerdmans.

Reintegrating God's Creation 1987 Church & Society Document no. 3. Geneva: WCC.

Rifkin, J. 1983 *Algeny.* New York: Viking Press.

Robinson, N.A. (ed.) 1993 *Agenda 21: Earth's Action Plan.* New York, London and Rome: Oceana Publications.

Rolston, H. 1988 *Environmental Ethics: Duties to and Values in the Natural World.* Philadelphia, PA: Temple University Press.

—— 1994 *Conserving Natural Value.* New York: Columbia University Press.

—— 1999 *Genes, Genesis and God*. New York: Cambridge University Press.

—— 2003 'Naturalizing and Systematizing Evil', in *Is Nature Ever Wrong, Evil or Ugly? Religion, Science and Value*, pp. 67–86. W.B. Drees (ed). New York: Routledge.

Routley, R. and V. Routley 1980 'Human Chauvinism and Environmental Ethics', in *Environmental Philosophy*, pp. 96–189. D. Mannison, M. McRobbie and R. Routley (eds.). Canberra: Australian National University.

Ruse, M. 2001 *Can a Darwinian Be a Christian?* Cambridge: Cambridge University Press.

Russell, B. 1931 *The Scientific Outlook*. New York: Norton.

Russell, C.A. 1993 *The Earth, Humanity and God*. London: UCL Press.

Salisbury, J. 1994 *The Beast Within: Animals in the Middle Ages*. London: Routledge.

Santmire, P. 1970 *Brother Earth: Nature, God, and Ecology in a Time of Crisis*. New York: Thomas Nelson.

—— 1985 *The Travail of Nature*. Philadelphia, PA: Fortress Press.

—— 2000 *Nature Reborn: The Ecological and Cosmic Promise of Christian Theology*. Minneapolis, MN: Fortress Press.

—— 2003 'Partnership with Nature according to the Scriptures: Beyond the Theology of Stewardship'. *Christian Scholar's Review*, **32**: 381–412.

Scarce, R. 2000 *Fishy Business: Salmon, Biology and the Social Construction of Nature*. Philadelphia, PA: Temple University Press.

Schaeffer, F.A. *Pollution and the Death of Man*. 1970 London: Hodder & Stoughton.

Schmid, H.H. 1984 'Creation, Righteousness and Salvation: "Creation Theology" as the Broad Horizon of Biblical Theology', in *Creation and the Old Testament*, pp. 102–17. B.W. Anderson (ed.). Philadelphia, PA: Fortress Press.

Schwöbel, C. 1997 'God, Creation and the Christian Community', in *The Doctrine of Creation: Essays in Dogmatics, History and Philosophy*, pp. 149–76. C. Gunton (ed.). Edinburgh: T&T Clark.

Scott, P. 2003 *A Political Theology of Nature*. Cambridge: Cambridge University Press.

Senault, J.-F. 1650 *Man Becom Guilty, Or the Corruption of Nature by Sinne, according to St Augustin's Sense*. London.

Serageldin, I. 1991 'A Justly Balanced Society: One Muslim's View', in *Friday Morning Reflections at the World Bank*, pp. 55–73. D. Beckmann, R. Agarwala, S. Burmester and I. Serageldin (eds.). Washington, DC: Seven Locks Press.

Sessions, G. 1995 *Deep Ecology for the Twenty-First Century*. Boston, MA: Shambala.

Sheldon, J.K. 1989 'Twenty-one Years after the "Historical Root of our

Ecologic Crisis": How has the Church Responded?' *Perspectives on Science and the Christian Faith*, **41**: 152–58.

—— 1992 *Rediscovery of Creation: A Bibliographic Study of the Church's Response to the Environmental Crisis*. Metuchen, NJ: Scarecrow Press.

Sherrard, P. 1992 *Human Image: World Image. The Death and Resurrection of Sacred Cosmology*. Ipswich: Gorgonzola Press.

Sider, R. 1977 *Rich Christians in an Age of Hunger*. Downers Grove, IL: InterVarsity Press.

Sideris, L. 2003 *Environmental Ethics, Ecological Theory and Natural Selection*. New York: Columbia University Press.

Simkins, R.A. 1994 *Creator and Creation: Nature in the Worldview of Ancient Israel*. Peabody, MA: Hendrickson)

Singer, P. 1976 *Animal Liberation*. London: Jonathan Cape.

Sittler, J. 1954 'A Theology for Earth'. *The Christian Scholar*, **37**: 367–74.

—— 1970 'Ecological Commitment as Theological Responsibility'. *Zygon*, **5**: 172–81.

Skinner, Q. 1988 'Political Philosophy', in *Cambridge History of Renaissance Philosophy*, pp. 418–21. C. Schmitt and Q. Skinner (eds.). Cambridge: Cambridge University Press.

Sölle, D. 1978 *Beyond Mere Dialogue: On Being Christian and Socialist*. Detroit, MI.

—— 1983 *Life in Its Fulness*. Address to the Vancouver Assembly of the WCC.

Sorabji, R. 1983 *Time, Creation and the Continuum: Theories in Antiquity and the Early Modern Ages*. Ithaca, NY: Cornell University Press.

Southgate, C.C.B. 2002 'God and Evolutionary Evil: Theodicy in the Light of Darwinism'. *Zygon* , **37**: 803–24.

Southgate, C.C.B. (ed.) 1999 *God, Humanity and the Cosmos*. Edinburgh: T&T Clark.

Spedding, J., R.L. Ellis and D.D. Heath 1857–58 *The Works of Francis Bacon* Vol. IV. London: Longman.

Spring, D. and E. Spring (eds.) 1974 *Ecology and Religion in History*. New York: Harper & Row.

Steffen, L.H. 1992 'In Defence of Dominion'. *Environmental Ethics*, **14**: 63–80.

Strawson, P.F. 1964 *Individuals : An Essay in Descriptive Metaphysics*. London: Routledge.

Taylor, J.E. 1999 *Making Salmon: An Environmental History of the Northwest Fisheries Crisis*. Seattle, WA: University of Washington Press.

Taylor, L.H. 1958 *The New Creation*. New York: Pagent.

This Common Inheritance 1990 White Paper on the Environment. Cm 1200. London: HMSO.

Thomas, J.M. (ed.) 1993 'Evangelicals and the Environment: Theological

Foundations for Christian Environmental Stewardship'. *Evangelical Review of Theology,* **17**.2: 117–286.

Thomas, K. 1983 *Man and the Natural World.* London: Allen Lane.

Thomas, W.L. (ed.) 1956 *Man's Role in Changing the World.* Chicago: University of Chicago Press.

Thompson, P.B. 1995 *The Spirit of the Soul: Agricultural and Environmental Ethics.* London: Routledge.

Thompson, P.E.S. 1971 'The Yahwist Creation Story'. *Vetus Testamentum,* **21**: 197–208.

Tolkien, J.R.R. 1954–55 *Lord of the Rings.* London: George Allen & Unwin.

Torrance, J.B. 1996 *Worship, Community and the Triune God of Grace.* Downer's Grove, IL: InterVarsity Press.

Traherne, T. 1675 *Christian Ethicks.* London.

Trevelyan, G.M. 1938 *England Under the Stuarts.* London: Methuen.

Trinkhaus, C. 1970 *In Our Image and Likeness, Humanity and Divinity in Italian Humanist Thought.* London: Constable.

Trousson, R. 1976 *La Thème de Prométhée dans la Litérature Européene.* Geneva: Droz.

Van Bavel, T. 1990 'The Creator and the Integrity of Creation in the Fathers of the Church'. *Augustinian Studies,* **21**: 1–33.

Vickers, B. 1984 'Bacon's So-called "Utilitarianism" Sources and Influences', in *Francis Bacon: Terminologia e Fortuna nel XVII Secolo*), pp. 281–314. Marta Fattori (ed.). Rome: Edizione dell Ateneo.

Vischer, L. (ed.) 2004 *Listening to Creation Groaning.* Geneva: John Knox International Reformed Center.

von Rad, G. 1961 *Genesis.* Philadephia, PA: Westminster.

Waddell, H. 1949 *Beasts and Saints.* London: Constable.

Walker, G. 1641 *The History of the Creation.* London.

Wallace-Hadrill, D.S. 1968 *The Greek Patristic View of Nature.* Manchester: Manchester University Press.

Ward, B. and R. Dubos 1972 *Only One Earth: The Care and Maintenance of a Small Planet.* London: Andre Deutsch.

Watanabe, M. 1992 'Francis Bacon: Philanthropy and the Instauration of Learning'. *Annals of Science,* **49**: 163–73.

Watt, W.M. 1963 *Truth in the Religions.* Edinburgh: Edinburgh University Press.

Webster, C. 1975 *The Great Instauration. Science, Medicine and Reform, 1626-1660.* London: Duckworth.

Weinberger, J. (ed.). 1980 *F. Bacon. The Great Instauration and New Atlantis.* Arlington Heights, IL: AHM Publishing.

Weiser, A. 1962 *The Psalms.* London: SCM Press.

Wersal, L. 1995 'Islam and Environmental Ethics: Tradition Responds to Contemporary Culture'. *Zygon,* **30**: 451–59.

Westerman, C. 1974 *Creation*. London: SPCK.

—— 1984 *Genesis 1-11*. Minneapolis, MN: Fortress Press.

Whale, J.S. 1941 *Christian Doctrine*. Cambridge: Cambridge University Press.

White, J. 1656 *A Commentary upon the First Three Chapters of the First Book of Moses*. London.

White, L. 1964 *Medieval Technology and Social Change*. Oxford: Oxford University Press.

—— 1967 'The Historical Roots of our Ecologic Crisis'. *Science*, **155**: 1203–207.

—— 1968 *Machina ex Deo*. Cambridge, MA: MIT Press.

—— 1973 'Continuing the Conversation', in *Western Man and Environmental Ethics*, pp. 55–64. I.G. Barbour (ed.). Reading, MA: Addison-Wesley.

White, T.H. 1954 *The Book of Beasts*. London: Cape.

Whitney, E. 1993 'Lynn White, Ecotheology and History'. *Environmental Ethics*, **15**: 151–69.

Wilkinson, L. 1976 'A Christian Theology of Death: Biblical Imagery and "the Ecologic Crisis" '. *Christian Scholar's Review*, **5**: 319–39.

—— 1980a *Christian Stewardship of Natural Resources*. Grand Rapids, MI: Eerdmans (revised as Wilkinson, 1991).

—— 1980b 'Global Housekeeping: Lords or Servants?' *Christianity Today*, 27 June.

—— 1981 'Cosmic Christology and the Christian's Role in Creation'. *Christian Scholar's Review*, **11**: 18–40.

Wilkinson, L. (ed.) 1991 *Earthkeeping in the '90s*. Grand Rapids, MI: Eerdmans, rev. edn.

Willey, B. 1953 *The Seventeenth Century Background*. Garden City, NY: Doubleday-Anchor.

Williams, A. 1948 *The Common Expositor: An Account of the Commentaries on Genesis, 1527-1633*. Chapel Hill, NC: University of North Carolina Press.

Wilson, E.O. 1998 *Consilience*. New York: Knopf.

Wirzba, N. 2001 *The Paradise of God*. Oxford: Oxford University Press.

—— 2004 'Sabbath Rest for the Creation', Paper presented at Conference on Christian Faith and the Soul of a University, Baylor University, Waco, Texas.

Wise, D. 1991 'A Review of Environmental Stewardship Literature and the New Testament', in *The Environment and the Christian*, pp. 117–34. C.B. DeWitt (ed.). Grand Rapids, MI: Baker Book House.

Wokomir, M. *et al.* 1997 'Substantive Religious Belief and Environmentalism'. *Social Science Quarterly*, **78**: 96–108.

World Conservation Strategy 1980 Living Resource Conservation for Sustainable Development. Morges, Switzerland: IUCN/UNEP/WWF.

World Council of Churches 1991 *Come Holy Spirit – Renew the Whole Creation*. Report of the Seventh General Assembly, Canberra. Geneva: WCC Publications.

Worster, D. 1979, 1994 *Nature's Economy: A History of Ecological Ideas*. Cambridge: Cambridge University Press.

—— 1993 *The Wealth of Nations*. New York: Oxford University Press.

Wybrow, C. 1991 *The Bible, Baconianism, and the Mastery over Nature: The Old Testament and Its Modern Misreading*. New York: Peter Lang.

Zerbe, G. 1991 'The Kingdom of God and Stewardship of Creation', in *The Environment and the Christian*, pp. 73–92. C.B. DeWitt (ed.) (Grand Rapids, MI: Baker Book House).

Zizioulas, J.D. 1989 'Preserving God's Creation. Three Lectures given at King's College London'. *King's Theological Review* **12** (1989): 1–5, 41–45; **13** (1990): 1–5; and reprinted in *Theology in Green* no 5 (1993): 16–26; no 6 (1993): 15–25; no 7 (1993): 20–31.

Index